Staley

**THE WORKING CLASS
IN AMERICAN HISTORY**

Editorial Advisors
James R. Barrett
Alice Kessler-Harris
Nelson Lichtenstein
David Montgomery

*A list of books in the series appears
at the end of this book.*

Staley

THE FIGHT FOR
A NEW AMERICAN
LABOR MOVEMENT

Steven K. Ashby
and C. J. Hawking

UNIVERSITY OF
ILLINOIS PRESS
Urbana and Chicago

© 2009 by the Board of Trustees
of the University of Illinois
All rights reserved
Manufactured in the United States of America
1 2 3 4 5 C P 5 4 3
∞ This book is printed on acid-free paper.

Library of Congress Cataloging-in-Publication Data
Ashby, Steven K.
Staley : the fight for a new American labor movement /
Steven K. Ashby and C. J. Hawking.
p. cm. — (The working class in American history)
Includes bibliographical references and index.
ISBN 978-0-252-03437-4 (cloth : alk. paper) —
ISBN 978-0-252-07640-4 (pbk. : alk. paper)
1. Labor unions—United States.
2. Labor movement—United States.
3. Working class—United States.
I. Hawking, C. J. II. Title.
HD6508.A758   2009
331.880973—dc22   2008037214

For a new generation of labor activists,
with hope they find inspiration
from the Staley workers' struggle

Contents

Preface

From 1992 through 1995 workers at the A. E. Staley Company waged one of the most hard-fought struggles in recent labor history, perfecting innovative strategies that today are being increasingly debated by a labor movement under siege.

In 1988 Tate & Lyle, the largest sugar conglomerate in the world, bought Staley and launched a full-scale assault on the union workforce at Staley's largest corn-processing plant, in Decatur, Illinois. Allied Industrial Workers (AIW) Local 837 responded by educating and mobilizing its members to win a fair contract. Workers ran an "in-plant" campaign for nine months and then built a national solidarity movement when the company locked them out in June 1993.

When the Staley workers were joined on the picket lines in 1994–95 by striking members of the Auto Workers union at Caterpillar and the Rubber Workers union at Bridgestone/Firestone, the media labeled Decatur "Strike City." Decatur unionists dubbed their town the "War Zone." "Decatur was a turning point," says AFL-CIO staffer Joe Uehlein. "What happened in Decatur during that period is as big a moment as was the Homestead strike of 1892."[1]

Despite their tragic defeat, the Staley workers leave an enduring legacy filled with lessons to strengthen today's labor movement.

This book has three purposes. The first is to tell the workers' story through their own voices. The Staley workers and spouses spoke with great candor in scores of interviews. We sought to write a book that would be true to the Staley workers' fight as the workers and their families lived it.

Our second goal is to appeal to readers who are concerned about the deterioration of workers' rights in American society but do not have extensive knowledge of unions. We hope readers who are looking for a book that will introduce them to the U.S. labor movement, with all its strengths, weaknesses, and challenges, will find this work accessible and compelling. Throughout the book we explain common union terms and describe how unions work; we've included a glossary to further this goal.

The last goal is to write for an audience of trade unionists looking for a how-to manual on standing up to management and winning justice in the workplace. In 1992 the Staley workers were anxious for information that could help them stand up to a multinational corporation that was ravaging their lives. They brought labor educators to their union hall and read voraciously about labor history. Today workers across the country are facing similar assaults, and, as were the Staley workers, they are looking for ways to fight back.

Through the workers' voices, readers will learn how the members transformed themselves from a typically inactive, complacent workforce to an educated, mobilized, and committed local union. We describe how the union organized its successful work-to-rule campaign, its Road Warrior program, and the activities of the Staley Workers Solidarity Committees. We recount how the union garnered the support of the Decatur community.

We also describe the union's corporate campaign and the workers' heated debates over strategy. We analyze the workers' difficult personal struggles over using nonviolent civil disobedience and the many obstacles and risks that unions face when they demonstrate at plant gates. We describe, in frank terms, the deep racial divisions in the union prior to the lockout and show how the African American workers organized to challenge white workers' racism and gain the support of Decatur's black community.

Finally, this work pulls no punches in exposing the weaknesses of the U.S. labor movement. "My idea of a perfect labor movement," says AFL-CIO president John Sweeney, "is one which consistently re-examines itself and corrects its own imperfections."[2] In that spirit, this book looks critically at organized labor. The Staley workers did not simply fight Tate & Lyle's lockout; they also sought to build a new American labor movement. We tell their story in hopes that other workers will find insights to help win their own struggles against corporate greed. Let "Remember Decatur!" be the cry of a new labor movement, say the Staley workers.

We make no claim to impartiality. The authors were both leaders of the Chicago-area Staley Workers Solidarity Committee, Local 837's flagship solidarity group. We were among the coordinators of the union's June 1994 civil disobedience actions and attended a number of strategy sessions with union leaders. C. J. Hawking moved to Decatur as a volunteer organizer, staying there from January to July 1994 to spark outreach efforts aimed at the religious and black communities. Where we appear in these pages, we have chosen to describe our roles in the third person in order to maintain the narrative flow. We did not seek to interview Staley or Tate & Lyle officials. We wrote this book to honor the Staley workers and their families—the most courageous, dedicated, and noble group of people we have ever known.

Acknowledgments

It has been a privilege to write this book. Many of the Staley workers invited us into their homes and shared candidly about their public and private lives during the lockout. We gratefully list the interviewees in the appendix.

We deeply appreciate the unionists who collected precious resources, especially Jerry Fargusson, who videotaped every union meeting, rally, and local television newscast for three years, and his wife, Ethel, who shared the videos with us after Jerry's tragic death. We give special thanks to Mona Williams, who, after three years of diligently clipping and saving every Decatur newspaper article about the union, loaned them to us.

With an eye toward the struggle's legacy, the following dedicated unionists, advisers, and supporters saved and then graciously loaned us their files: Dave Watts, Art Dhermy, Mike Griffin, Nancy Hanna, Bill Winter, Tamra McCartney, Laurie Clements, Mark Crouch, Jerry Tucker, Ray Rogers, and Michael Szpak. We also thank the United Paperworkers International Union in Nashville for access to its files.

We draw on the skillfully crafted videos produced by the St. Louis–based Labor Vision and the Chicago-based Labor Beat. We are very grateful to the People's Law Office of Chicago, which allowed us access to the pretrial depositions of the November 2000 trial against the Decatur police.

We were pleased to have access to the papers of the beloved Decatur labor priest Martin Mangan, now deceased, located at the University of Illinois at Urbana-Champaign. His papers became the first items deposited into the Staley Workers Archives.

We are indebted to the savvy reviews by Jim Barrett, Peter Rachleff, Jerry Tucker, and Steven Pitts. We give special thanks to Jane Slaughter for her editing expertise. We also greatly value the guidance from our editor, Laurie Matheson, and our copyeditor, Bruce Bethell, at the University of Illinois Press.

We are forever indebted to the Staley workers, those mentioned in this book and those unnamed, who allowed us and thousands of others to witness a workers' struggle that made labor history. We gratefully acknowledge the workers for their incredible inspiration and for sharing with us their wisdom, laughter, and tears.

Prologue
Jim Beals

Phyllis Beals walked into her home in the late afternoon on May 15, 1990, after working all day as a sales representative. She punched the play button on the answering machine and heard the cheerful voice of her husband, Jim, asking her to bring his supper to the plant. There was nothing out of the ordinary in Jim's voice or in this routine. Lately the company had often required overtime, so that Phyllis had to drive Jim's supper to him. She looked at her watch: it was 4:30 P.M. She had just enough time to pick up some fast food and get to the plant by 5:00 to meet Jim in the parking lot.

Phyllis and Jim had met at a skating rink when she was twelve years old and Jim was fourteen. The connection they felt was instant and lasting. In January 1990 they had celebrated their twenty-sixth wedding anniversary. They had two sons, Rick, twenty-five, and Dan, twenty-two. "[We were] at the point in our lives where it could start being us," said P. J. (as she was known to her friends), "and we could start thinking about the things we wanted to do and reaping rewards from all the years of working." A year earlier P. J. and Jim had bought a big, beautiful new home, a place where they planned to grow old together and welcome any grandchildren that might come along.[1]

As P. J. pulled into the Staley parking lot, she was surprised to see rescue units with flashing lights. P. J. parked the car and joined a married couple carrying out the same meal-delivery ritual. When the man started walking back into the plant, the woman said to P. J., "This damn place makes me so mad. When are they going to take care of safety?" Their eyes were fixed on the rescue trucks.

P. J. replied with a comment that has haunted her: "Oh, probably when they kill somebody."

The woman's husband reappeared in the parking lot and asked P. J. to come into the plant. She anxiously went inside, where a group of workers told her,

"Jim and some other men were working inside a tank. There was an accident. Jim has been hurt. We're working on getting him out." A cold chill went up her spine. Trying hard to shake off feelings of despair, P. J. called Rick and Dan at her mother-in-law's house, and her boys rushed over to the plant.

News of the accident spread quickly. Day-shift workers, some accompanied by their spouses, began returning to the corn-processing plant after hearing that someone was seriously injured. Gene Sharp, the former president of the local union and Jim's uncle, heard the news and rushed to the plant. Several dozen workers and spouses nervously waited with P. J. and her sons for news of Jim's condition.

After two and one-half hours, Staley CEO Larry Cunningham came into the room and told P. J. that Jim was dead. P. J. looked at him in disbelief. The life of her beloved Jim, only forty-three years old, had been stolen. Tears streamed from her eyes as waves of shock swept over her.

Gene Sharp and other workers tried to console her and urged P. J. and her sons to go home. "My initial thought was, 'I can't just leave him here,'" recalled P. J. "They still didn't have him out of the tank. They had a rescuer down there far enough to make sure that Jim was not alive, but I didn't want to leave until I knew he was out. But I thought it was best for my sons to get away from the situation, and I could tell that they wouldn't leave if I didn't. Later the coroner came. He told me that Jim's body was out and he had been pronounced dead."

Soon she would learn that Jim had filed a complaint that very afternoon about a safety hazard in the tank in which he died.

"Tragedy Is Just around the Corner"

Born and raised in Decatur, Illinois, Jim Beals started at Staley a few months after he graduated from high school in 1963. Working at Staley was a family affair for Jim, as it was for many others: his father, uncle, two cousins, and sister all worked for the company. Jim was always a passionate believer in unions, and as he got older his involvement grew. Over the years he was elected to a variety of union positions, including head of the safety committee and chairperson of the bargaining committee during the 1989 contract negotiations.

Jim Beals filed grievances against the company whenever he saw a violation of the contract or the law that might endanger one of his co-workers. Since 1988, when the London-based multinational sugar conglomerate Tate & Lyle had bought the Staley plant, management's regard for safety had steadily deteriorated. "We've had a large number of near misses where workers almost died," said Staley worker Dan Lane.[2] As supervisors continually forced workers into hazardous circumstances, unionist Henry Kramer commented that management's mind-set was "We're not going to do things the safest way possible. We're going to do them the cheapest way possible."[3]

The Staley workers were growing increasingly anxious and angry about their safety but encountered bullying tactics when they complained to the plant's new management. "There was an atmosphere of intimidating people from filing safety grievances," recalled Bill Strohl, who served as local union president for seven years in the late 1970s and early 1980s. "When they were filed, sometimes they would be found in a foreman's desk weeks later. Sometimes they would just disappear. People were afraid of saying anything for fear of being fired."[4]

"People don't report accidents, because if you do, you're going to lose your job," said mechanic Don Moore. "If you say something to [your supervisor] about an accident, they're ready to throw you out the gate. You've got people out there getting injured every day who are afraid to go to First Aid."[5]

But Jim Beals was the exception. Weeks before, he had filed a grievance challenging the lack of safety procedures when tanks were cleaned. Management had refused to address the grievance, so the union planned to take it to arbitration.

Just two hours before his death, Jim Beals had gone to the union's small office within the plant to talk to union officer Jim Shinall and to file another safety grievance. "Something has to be done about the propylene oxide problem," said Beals, "because tragedy is just around the corner."[6] Several workers later reported that they could sometimes smell the toxic fumes outside the building.[7]

Later that afternoon a supervisor assigned Beals and three co-workers to repair a cornstarch processing tank. Beals and Jerry Sumner would enter the tank to clean it while Larry Shook and Bob McKinney would be stationed outside the tank. All the men were worried. Jerry Sumner tells what happened:

> This was a boilermaker's job. None of us had ever done this job before, and we asked why a boilermaker wasn't doing it. The supervisor said, "This vessel is as safe as can be. Just go in there." . . . I got in the tank first. It was slimy inside. Jim got down in there. You had to worm your way in. The opening was only about twelve by eighteen inches. It was round inside, so it was difficult to walk. . . . We hadn't been in there fifteen minutes when all of a sudden a liquid started pouring in through an opening in the vessel. The first stuff that came through was clear and there were no vapors. . . . But then we started choking and realized it was propylene oxide. It took our breath away and we were suffocating.[8]

"P.O. [propylene oxide] takes the oxygen right out of the air, like that," recalled Shook as he snapped his fingers.[9]

The leak came from a reactor connected to the tank. In the past the reactor had always been shut down during repairs, but the new owners had disregarded the safety rule. "I think it changed because of corporate greed," said Larry Shook. "They wanted to make more money. If both reactors had been down, this accident could never have happened."

Sumner continued:

> Our eyes were burning. I told Beals I was getting the hell out of there. I'm not sure how I got out. I just remember going toward the light. The next thing I knew I was outside the opening. I tried going back in for Jim but my eyes were burning too much. I stuck my head in the opening and yelled to him. He must have been gone by then. We tried to go in with an air pack but the opening was too small. We found out later that there was almost no oxygen in the air pack. We also tried using emergency escape masks, but we tried eight of them and none had any air in the bottles. Finally we tried using an air horn to blow air into the vessel, but you couldn't stay near the opening—the fumes were just too strong. My skin felt like it was on fire. I couldn't wait any longer to get to the shower. But I kept saying to myself, "Jim's dead, Jim's dead."

"I Think It Was Murder"

Jim Beals's death was the fulfillment of a prophecy. Beals had constantly warned that someone would get killed under Tate & Lyle's lax safety enforcement. That it happened to the prophet was almost too much to bear.

"I think it was murder," recounted a twenty-year Staley veteran in July 1993. "The guy who was supposed to be doing the testing, he had the wrong meter. He wasn't properly trained. The guy who isolated the vessel was from a different part of the plant; he didn't know. The supervisor filled out the form from behind his desk. He didn't check it out."[10]

The company's first reaction was to cover up the violations that led to Beals's death. Walter Maus recalled that he was immediately ordered to break open lockers in the maintenance shops: "They were looking for the small five-minute escape masks that you put over your head in an emergency situation. There were none available anywhere. I said, 'What good are they going to do now?' They wanted to place them near the site of the accident and make it appear they had been available."

P. J. Beals and her sons feel an anger toward Staley/Tate & Lyle management that will never leave them: "I don't believe that the company wanted somebody to die, but I believe they closed their eyes to the danger involved and the great possibility that it could happen. Their profit, their time schedule—all that was more important. . . . It's such an atrocity when money becomes more important than a human life."

The union had lost one of its strongest leaders. "Jim Beals was highly involved with the union," reflected Allied Industrial Workers Local 837 president Dave

Watts. "We're upset about this both because it was Jim and because it could have been any one of the workers here." The local draped its union charter in black, and members wore black armbands for a week.[11]

Large numbers of Staley workers attended the visitation to honor their fallen co-worker. The visitation was scheduled to last from six to eight in the evening, but as 8:00 P.M. approached, recalled Jim's wife, "you still couldn't see the end of the line." The funeral director asked people to skip the visitation and attend the funeral; otherwise, the family would be there long into the night.

Years after her husband's death, P. J. Beals's voice still cracks and tears come to her eyes as she talks of her husband: "He was my soul mate. Jim was my lover, my husband, the father of my children, and my very best friend. There is a hole inside of me that will always be there. I will die loving Jim Beals."

Within a year, P. J. moved out of her new home. "I found myself roaming around in this great big house, feeling so alone." Jim's sister, a Staley office worker, took early retirement within a year—she couldn't stand working for a company that had held her brother's life in such low regard.

"Never Received a Penny"

While money was inconsequential to the devastated and grief-stricken P. J., her family and friends urged her to seek compensation for the company's gross negligence. "Everyone said that [Tate & Lyle] knew that they were wrong. They're not going to fight you on this. . . . Everyone thought it would be cut and dried."

But the company fought ruthlessly. After seven years of investigation and litigation, P. J.'s lawyers had exhausted all avenues for compensation from Tate & Lyle. Workers' compensation provides medical expenses and a minimal amount of money for workers injured or killed on the job, but the law prohibits a worker from suing the employer.[12] "We could not directly sue A. E. Staley," said P. J. "That's another thing that made it a hard pill to swallow."

Workers' compensation, explained Charles Jeffress, assistant secretary of labor for the Occupational Safety and Health Administration during the late 1990s, "does not provide you replacement for the wages that you'll not earn the rest of your life. It does not provide any incentive to a company to prevent the next accident from occurring."[13]

The family's only recourse, said P. J., was to sue the three companies that had built and installed the tank. Two of the companies settled out of court for relatively small amounts, but when a suit against the third company went to trial, the Beals family lost. When the jurors were informally polled after the verdict, they said that it was obvious that Staley/Tate & Lyle was at fault. The jurors wrongly assumed that Staley had paid a large settlement. Beals's lawyer was prohibited from explaining the truth to them.

In fact, Staley never paid the Beals family one penny for its negligence in Jim's death.

In May 2001, when Jim would have been fifty-five and eligible for an early pension, the company never informed his wife. Fortunately, a union official and family friend contacted her and helped file the necessary papers. Otherwise, said P. J. Beals, "I might have died and never received a penny of Jim's pension."[14]

The union demanded an investigation of Beals's death. From July through October 1991 the federal Occupational Safety and Health Administration (OSHA) conducted an intensive, wall-to-wall inspection of the plant. In late 1991 OSHA charged the company with 298 violations, most of them serious, and levied a fine of $1.6 million, the twelfth-largest fine in the twenty-one years since Congress had passed the Occupational Safety and Health Act.

While the company made some changes in response to the OSHA investigation, workers noted that conditions very quickly deteriorated once more. Maintenance worker Jerry Sumner recounted that he was ordered to check a seal in one of the reactor rooms. "We go up to the door which says 'check with your foreman for the SOP [standard operating procedure] before you enter this room.' We called the supervisor and he doesn't even know what I'm talking about. . . . It's amazing that after somebody loses their life, they still don't have a standard operating procedure for doing work on something like that."[15]

The Staley workers had been growing increasingly angry over the company's disregard for safety, but with Jim Beals's death their anger turned to rage—and determination to fight back. "The nail in the coffin was when Jim Beals was killed," Bill Strohl reflected. "It was the most tragic thing that ever happened to a member. We've had people killed before, but to knowingly do what they did— put him in a vessel and not have it completely blocked off . . . We had problems under the old Staley company. But compared to Tate & Lyle, they stood out like a saint. Tate & Lyle did not make any bones about telling you that your value to them was really nothing."[16]

Beals's death was a watershed moment and a wake-up call in the life of the Staley workers. "Remember Jim Beals" quickly became the rallying cry for the labor war that was about to begin.

Five thousand supporters march to A. E. Staley's west gate on June 25, 1994; the Staley office is in the background. Photograph by Jerry Fargusson; courtesy of Ethel Fargusson.

Dan Lane (with bullhorn), Local 7837 president Dave Watts, Ron VanScyoc, and Art Dhermy (seated) after being pepper-sprayed by Decatur police on June 25, 1994. Photograph by C. J. Hawking; courtesy of photographer.

Shannon Williams and friend at the "Woman and Children's Rally" at Staley's west gate on March 9, 1994. Photograph by Jerry Fargusson; courtesy of Ethel Fargusson.

Supporters from Champaign-Urbana and St. Louis blocking the Staley plant gate at June 4, 1994, nonviolent civil disobedience action. Three dozen other protesters soon joined them. Photograph by Jerry Fargusson; courtesy of Ethel Fargusson.

Workers and supporters from across the country sitting peacefully with their backs to the police at the Staley plant's west gate as the Decatur police unleash papper spray without warning on June 25, 1994. Photograph by Jim West; courtesy of photographer.

Royal Plankenhorn, Dwayne Carlyle, Jeanette Hawkins, and Ron VanScyoc with fifty other workers and spouses march forty miles from Decatur to the state capitol in Springfield on November 29–30, 1994. Their numbers swelled to four hundred by the end of the march. Photograph by Jerry Fargusson; courtesy of Ethel Fargusson.

AFSCME representative Buddy Maupin (far right) presents a donation to Dan Lane, Lorell Patterson, and Dave Watts at a May 1994 union meeting at the AIW union hall. Photograph by C. J. Hawking; courtesy of photographer.

Seven thousand supporters from across the country coming over the four-lane viaduct that cuts through the Staley plant, October 15, 1994. Photograph by Bill Haenny; courtesy of photographer.

Illegally terminated Caterpillar worker registers his outrage after Decatur police aim pepper spray into a crowd that included children and reporters on June 25, 1994. Photograph by Jim West; courtesy of photographer.

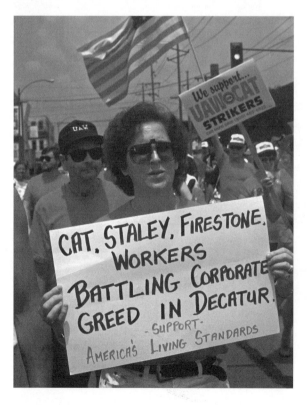

Decatur resident protests corporate greed on June 25, 1995, with a placard signifying that three local unions were walking picket lines in Decatur. Photograph by Jim West; courtesy of photographer.

The Company and the Union

The turbulent labor-management relations at the Decatur Staley plant in the 1990s could not have been foretold from either the company's history or the union's. For six decades the A. E. Staley Manufacturing Company was a family-run business with good labor and community relations. The workforce organized to join a union during World War II, but relations were relatively peaceful for the next two decades. In the 1970s the Staley family relinquished control of the company, and in the 1980s, with corporations across America demanding give-backs, Local 837 felt helpless as working conditions deteriorated under new management.

A. E. Staley

As you drive any of the four-lane highways into Decatur, vast cornfields line the road and extend to the horizon. Your nose tells you that you're nearing town, for the sickening-sweet smell of processed corn fills the air. When the wind is strong, the odor permeates the entire town.

"Most of the people from Decatur are proud of their city, while they know that, to people driving through, it's a . . . smelly" industrial town, writes Decatur essayist Becky Bradway. "It might seem the sort of place that people work hard to leave, except that most residents have lived in this area for generations. They only leave when they can't get jobs." Decatur "maintains the character of an old southern city; the downtown stores reside in turn-of-the-century buildings." There's a "sense of trapped time, [an] embrace of tradition, dialect, roots."[1]

In the early 1990s nearly 5,000 employees in a town of 84,000 worked in three corn- and soy-processing plants, the Staley plant and two owned by Archer Daniels Midland. Decatur, the self-proclaimed "Pride of the Prairie," is all about corn—growing it, processing it, and selling it. And no company is more identified with Decatur than A. E. Staley, the first to bring corn processing to the town.

The story of the A. E. Staley Manufacturing Company begins with Augustus Eugene "Gene" Staley, who was born into a North Carolina farm family in 1867. Because of the farm's demands, Gene Staley received less than a third-grade education in a one-room schoolhouse. Ambitious to see the world, at fourteen he set out for nearby towns to sell the farm's produce. In 1898, at the age of thirty-one, Staley established a business repackaging and selling cornstarch to grocers in Baltimore. Cornstarch was a popular household item, often used in cooking and in laundering clothes. Within eight years he had incorporated his business and had sixteen people on his payroll.

Dissatisfied with retailing, Staley wanted to produce the starch himself and started shopping around for a plant. In 1909 he paid $45,000 for a Decatur cornstarch plant that had been inoperative for thirteen years. An appraisal engineer gave Staley the confirmation he needed: "Coal is at your doorstep, all the corn you ever need is within 75 miles of Decatur, Decatur is served by five railroads, and labor is plentiful."[2] After an additional $150,000 investment to upgrade the plant, the first corn was ground in March 1912. Within three years Gene Staley had doubled the worth of the plant, and the A. E. Staley Manufacturing Company was prospering. By 1919 pretax profits had jumped to $2 million.

Gene Staley was also a huge sports fan, and he founded what would become one of America's premier professional teams. In the late 1910s some industrial plants in Ohio and Pennsylvania were sponsoring worker baseball teams, and in 1917 Staley followed suit; after their shifts workers played baseball on Staley Field, next to the plant. Staley grew dissatisfied with amateur athletics, however, and sent a company executive to Chicago to meet with George Halas. Halas had become a football hero at the University of Illinois, but when he graduated in 1917, with no professional teams yet established, Halas found himself working as a bridge engineer for the Burlington and Quincy Railroad.

Halas was asked to establish a Staley football team and to be its recruiter and coach, as well as a player. Team members would be paid for an eight-hour day: six hours in the plant and two hours of paid practice time. Halas eagerly agreed and moved to Decatur in March 1920. After a baseball season working in the plant as a scale-house clerk and playing shortstop on the Staley baseball team, Halas set off for "the first professional football recruiting journey in history." When he returned to Decatur, Halas told Staley, "I assured the players that they would get paid at the end of the season for their football, depending on the size of the gate, and I also told them they'd get paid weekly wages for the various duties they'd have in the plant. They all seemed to like the prospect of stability in a corporate set-up."[3]

The Decatur Staleys were ready to go—but they lacked opponents. Halas quickly contacted other industrial football team managers, and they met in an automobile showroom in September 1920 in Canton, Ohio—now home to the Football Hall of Fame. They created the American Professional Football Association (later renamed the National Football League). Franchises were issued to twelve teams in the Midwest for one hundred dollars each and a playing schedule was set.

In the league's first season in 1920, the Decatur Staleys were the champions, with a record of 10-1-2. In 1921 they repeated, with a 9-1-1 record. Gene Staley was elated, and the players gave an elegant dinner in his honor. Staley Field was too small for the growing crowds, however, and in 1921 only two of the eleven games were played at home. Gene Staley decided that his players were costing too much; at the same time, he realized that his boys needed a big city and a big stadium. With Staley's blessing, Halas moved his nineteen teammates to Chicago in October 1921, where they began playing at Cubs Park (later named Wrigley Field), home of the Chicago Cubs. Staley gave Halas five thousand dollars to get the team established, and he kept the workers on the plant payroll for a while. By agreement the team would be known as the Staley Football Club for the first season, but in 1922 Halas renamed the team the Chicago Bears.

Halas played eleven seasons and coached the Bears until 1955. A football legend, Halas was inducted into the Football Hall of Fame in 1963 and remained owner of the Bears until his death in 1983. He and Gene Staley remained friends, and Staley would occasionally attend a Bears game, calling the team "the transplants." "Without Gene Staley, there never would have been the Chicago Bears," said Halas many years later. "The Staley company was indirectly and partially responsible for the founding of the National Football League."[4]

With his beloved Decatur Staleys football team gone, in 1922 Gene Staley turned his full attention back to running the business. Two new projects captured Staley's attention, ones that would greatly impact the Decatur community and establish the reciprocal relationship between the company and the community that lasted for decades.

Staley's first project was to create Lake Decatur, with thirty-six miles of shoreline, to meet the plant's need for 10 million gallons of water a day. Pressuring the city council and the mayor by threatening to leave Decatur, Staley convinced city officials to create the artificial lake. The council then sold the idea to Decatur's citizens with the argument that the expanding city population and its industries needed the lake. With its 2,800 acres entirely within the city limits, Lake Decatur quickly became a showpiece for the city leaders and for Staley. While Decatur citizens had initially reserved judgment on the East Coast stranger, they now embraced Gene Staley. Henceforth the people of Decatur would often say, "What is good for Decatur has usually been good for Staley and what is good for Staley has been good for Decatur."[5]

Staley's second major project was to expand his business. In the mid-1920s he gambled on a new venture: processing soybeans, an excellent source of protein and (as tofu) a food staple in the Far East but virtually unknown in the United States. Staley convinced some Illinois farmers to plant soybeans, since rotating crops was beneficial to the land. When most farmers were reluctant to forsake their predictable corn, Staley chartered a private train dubbed the "Soybean Special," which traveled throughout central Illinois to educate farmers. In less than a month over 33,000 people passed through the six-car train filled with exhibits, lectures, and film showings.

Soybeans were difficult to process, but Staley, with the help of the U.S. Department of Agriculture and the University of Illinois, pressed researchers to find better methods and more ways for the American household to use the bean. By the late 1920s the investment began paying off, and within a decade other companies followed Staley into the business, most notably Archer Daniels Midland, which also established its home base in Decatur. By 1950 Decatur proudly claimed the title of "Soy Bean Capital of the World."

In 1929 Gene Staley oversaw the building of a new headquarters, an ornate fourteen-story structure of Indiana limestone with a gold-crowned dome. The office building is Decatur's most notable architectural landmark.

In 1932, when the sixty-five-year-old Staley was feeling the effects of age and diabetes, he turned over daily operations to his oldest son, Augustus Eugene "Gus" Staley Jr. The sprawling plant had grown to fifty-six buildings covering three hundred acres, employing over three thousand people, and producing cornstarch, corn oil, corn sugar, soybean flour, soy sauce, soy oil, and animal feed. Eighty products were now marketed by, as the company proclaimed itself, "the world's largest independent corn products company."

Gus Jr. did not have the same charisma as his father. Both were considered honorable and trustworthy men, but where Gene had been daring, friendly, and persuasive, Gus Jr. was more cautious, aloof, and shy. Gene had received his third-grade education in a one-room schoolhouse; Gus Jr. attended the Wharton School of Business. The father struggled to gather $1,500 to incorporate in 1906; Gus Jr. inherited a company with $28 million in sales in 1932. While Gene would often say, "I'm just an overgrown North Carolina country boy," Gus Jr. fancied gourmet meals and boasted of his wine collection.

Gene and Gus Jr. also had different styles of relating to their workers. Homer Altevogt, who worked at Staley for thirty-nine years, explained, "before my time Gene Staley, Sr. would go out in the plant. . . . He would talk to his employees. He would ask them what they needed. Sometimes it would be pay advancement, food, or coal, and when that employee got home, he had his food and coal delivered."[6]

Whether fact or folklore, a story commonly told around the plant had the company facing a cash-flow problem during the Great Depression and unable to make its payroll. "Old Man Staley" (the workers' affectionate name for their boss, of which Gene approved) asked whether the workers would agree to hold off on receiving their paychecks for a month. Out of loyalty to Gene, many workers agreed. Years later a supervisor threatened to fire one of these workers, but Staley said to the supervisor, "That guy has a job here as long as I'm here, and if he doesn't have a job then *you* don't have a job." Old Man Staley, it was said, appreciated the sacrifices his workers made and was loyal to them.

In contrast, Gus Jr. did not come into the plant or ask the workers about their families. He even opposed coffee drinking by management and plant workers because, he said, it resulted in lost production. He sometimes sent out "coffee police" to make note of violators. But Gus Jr. did display some social responsibility as Decatur's most powerful executive. He once told a worker that providing jobs and income—even when there was an excess of workers—was part of Staley's reason for being.[7] Reportedly, Gus Jr. was gazing out his window during his tenure as president and saw a destitute man walking by. He ran out of the building, handed the man a broom, and instantly put him on the payroll. Bill Strohl, president of the local in the 1970s and 1980s, recalled, "Gus Staley was an exceptional employer. People were willing to go to bat for him and people were willing to do things for him."[8]

Gene Staley died in 1940 at the age of seventy-three. As was his wish, his pallbearers were production workers from the plant. Under Gus Jr.'s tutelage the Staley family continued to control 70 percent of the company's privately owned stock. The plant thrived during World War II, providing food to Allied troops, and Gus Jr. served as the U.S. Corn Chief in the federal government's Food Supply Branch.

Local 837

As were all his corporate counterparts, Gus Staley Jr. was adamantly opposed to union representation. Nonetheless, on November 11, 1943, the workers voted in favor of union representation and became Local 837 of the American Federation of Labor's United Auto Workers. Gus Jr. was forced into a "grudging acceptance" that a union in his plant was an inevitable fact, said a union organizer.[9]

The local's origins lay in a split in the progressive United Auto Workers (UAW), one of the foremost unions in the militant Congress of Industrial Organizations (CIO), which led the 1930s labor upsurge.[10] The UAW was headed by Homer Martin, a fiery Baptist pastor who equated union organizing to worship, union halls to churches, and unions to Christ. "No other man," said a 1930s labor organizer, "could pierce the hearts of Southern-born workers as [Martin] could. He made men feel that in organizing a union they were going forth to battle for righteousness and the word of God."[11] The UAW won its first huge victory in February 1937 when it negotiated a contract with General Motors after a forty-four-day sit-in by autoworkers in Flint, Michigan. By the late 1930s, however, the union was faltering, and many workers blamed Martin, who had become increasingly unstable and dictatorial. Delegates at the 1939 UAW convention voted to oust Martin by a twenty-to-one margin, leading Martin and his supporters to leave the CIO and form a more conservative union affiliated with the American Federation of Labor.

For the next sixteen years the labor movement endured the bizarre situation of two unions calling themselves the United Auto Workers—the well-known UAW-CIO, which grew to well over one million members, and the relatively unknown UAW-AFL, which peaked at 93,000. Martin's erratic behavior continued, and within a year he lost his bid for reelection to the UAW-AFL presidency and left the labor movement. The UAW-AFL found modest success organizing workers in Illinois, Indiana, and Wisconsin. Decatur turned out to be one of its greatest success stories. In 1943 an organizer sent to Decatur rapidly succeeded in organizing seven plants.[12]

As the cold war began in the late 1940s and the country was swept up in anticommunist hysteria, the CIO moved to the right. By 1955, with few substantial differences, the CIO and the AFL merged to form the AFL-CIO.[13] This meant that one of the autoworkers unions had to change its name, and so the UAW-AFL became the Allied Industrial Workers (AIW). AIW organizing drives continued in Decatur, and by the 1970s the AIW had organized seventeen local unions there.[14]

For the most part, Local 837's first two decades were peaceful. The plant operations and workforce expanded as the demand for corn products grew. The union called a one-day strike in 1958 and struck for two weeks over economic issues in 1964 but otherwise had a good relationship with management.[15]

When the big factories in Decatur were all hiring, many workers chose to work at Staley even though other plants paid a higher wage. There was pride in working at "Staley's," as Decatur residents called the plant. "In Decatur, A. E. Staley Manufacturing Company is not just another industry," editorialized the *Decatur Herald and Review* on July 11, 1992. "In an almost symbiotic way, Staley is Decatur." Gary Lamb, who worked at Staley for twenty-seven years, explained why he turned down a better-paid job at Caterpillar in 1969: "When I was young I worked at Staley one day a week, in the garage or office building. When Mr. Staley would come walking out the door, I'd say 'Good morning!' and he'd say 'Good morning!' It made you feel a part of the operation. You weren't necessarily a number. Staley was the hub of Decatur."[16]

"These workers felt a real tie to that company and to the history of that plant," echoed Glenn Poshard, U.S. representative from central Illinois from 1988 to 1998. "Generations worked there, and wanted to work there. I had never seen a plant where the workers felt more loyal. Those guys at Staley's would have done anything to make that company successful."

The pride the Staley workers felt in their company was extended into the Decatur community when profits were channeled into supporting community resources. The family endowed a library at Decatur's private Millikin University, and it donated an entire wing, which bears the Staley name, to Decatur Memorial Hospital. The company also contributed to youth athletics, local charities, and community events. A. E. Staley was Decatur's leading corporate philanthropist.

In the 1950s and 1960s most Decatur citizens felt that the benefits of the Staley plant were shared equally among the company, its workers, and the people of Decatur. It seemed that the company and the town would be forever linked.

"Community in Decatur Is Factories"

Consumption of corn products dramatically increased in the post–World War II decades, and the company's profits grew. Nevertheless, the 1970s saw the end of an era for the Staley family's relationship with the company. Mike Griffin, a unionist in the plant since 1966, described the events: "Gus Staley got sick, had a severe heart attack, and signed over power of attorney to Don Nordlund, a lawyer. [Gus Jr.] told me one time, when I took something over to put in his car, 'I want you to know that I think I made a terrible mistake in turning the power of this company over to others. But I was sick and I just hope that we don't all regret it.' He recognized that something was changing dramatically."

By the time Gus Jr. died in 1975, the name "Staley" no longer referred to a family-run company; now it was simply the name of a corporation.

Success followed the company into the 1980s, when corn syrup replaced sugar as the sweetener of choice for soft drinks and thousands of processed foods, such as fruit drinks, ice cream, canned fruit, candy, snack foods, and beer. An American consumer could not go through a day without using or eating dozens of products that originally came from corn. "Corn was once something that people ate directly, fed to animals, or dried so that it could be either ground for tortillas and cornbread or stored for long periods before being used for either animal or human consumption," noted one study of the industry. "Now corn is one of the basic agricultural raw materials out of which almost anything, it seems, can be made."[17]

Cornstarches and corn sweeteners were essential in food-processing innovations such as frozen and microwaveable foods, instant mixes, shelf-stable products, and low-calorie, low-fat products.[18] Companies producing paper, cardboard, textiles, gypsum, and plaster board became major users of cornstarch.

The development of high-fructose corn syrup revolutionized the corn wet-milling industry and led the industry to unprecedented growth. As CEO Donald Nordlund said in 1980, "High fructose corn syrup was as much of a technological breakthrough as the transistor and videotape."[19] Makers of soft drinks such as Coke and Pepsi quickly became Staley's primary customers. High demand brought expansion; in 1981 a nonunion plant was established in Louden, Tennessee, and two more plants sprouted up in Lafayette, Indiana, in 1982, one of which unionized. The Decatur plant, however, remained the company's flagship, with 130 buildings spread over 440 acres.

It's likely that Old Man Staley never dreamed how expansive his business would become, with $400 million in profits in 1992. Staley and his workers helped boost the U.S. corn-refining industry into one of the most profitable industries in the world. By 1992 the United States had become the world's largest corn-growing country, with roughly 70 million acres under cultivation, twenty-seven processing plants nationwide, and sales exceeding $7.5 billion. Nearly half the annual purchases from the corn-refining industry came from the industry's ten Illinois plants, with the Staley plant among the top producers.[20]

The success of the Staley plant drew more people and industries into Decatur. From 1910 to 1980 the population more than tripled, from 31,000 to 100,000. Decatur drew a portion of its population from central and southern Illinois, as small family farms lost the ability to sustain themselves and younger generations clamored to move to the cities. Many southern Illinois coal miners drifted northward to Decatur, which was seen as a place where a high-school graduate could make a decent wage. Many African American families also migrated north and made their homes in Decatur, constituting 15 percent of the population by 1990.

Following the success of Gene Staley, three other major corporations came to Decatur. Archer Daniels Midland (ADM), also a producer of corn and soy products, grew astronomically. By the 1990s ADM was the world's largest corn and soybean processor, employed 2,600 people at its two Decatur plants, and had over two hundred plants across the globe.[21]

After World War II the Firestone Company bought a Decatur plant that had produced tanks, and the United Rubber Workers quickly organized it. In 1988 Firestone merged with the Bridgestone tire company to form the largest rubber company and the second-largest tire company in the world. By 1993 the Decatur Bridgestone/Firestone plant, located one mile north of Staley, employed 1,600 union workers.

In 1956 Caterpillar, the largest earthmoving-equipment producer in the world, came to Decatur. With its home office in nearby Peoria, "Cat" established its Decatur location two miles northeast of the Staley plant. The Cat workers soon joined the United Auto Workers, and by 1993 the plant employed 1,800 union members.

Decatur's strategic location between two manufacturing cities—Chicago, 180 miles northeast, and St. Louis, 120 miles southwest—and its central location in some of America's best agricultural land helped to establish it as an industrial and agribusiness center. In 1993 fully 30 percent of Decatur's workforce was in manufacturing, over twice the national figure. Blue-collar Decatur became a "miniature Chicago," said Kevin Breheny of the city's chamber of commerce.[22] Congressman Glenn Poshard aptly characterized the Decatur workers' sense of identity:

> This is the way I saw central Illinois: You've got Champaign [45 miles northeast of Decatur], with its great university [University of Illinois], and that's sort of the head. And you've got Springfield [40 miles west of Decatur], with the legislature and home of Abraham Lincoln, and that's sort of the heart and the soul. And you've got Decatur right in the middle, and that's the brawn. That's the sinew and the muscle. That's what the workers took pride in. They felt like that was their contribution. . . . You look around Decatur, that's a blue-collar community. . . . Community in Decatur is factories. . . . People take pride in that. . . . Somebody has to build this country through the *sweat*. And that's what the union makes people proud of: We have a *contribution* here to make. We're the builders of this nation.

Labor-Management Relations Cool

In 1970 Local 837 launched a bitter eighty-two-day strike when Staley demanded that the union relinquish the right to strike over grievances, as most unions had already done, and instead send unresolved grievances to a neutral third party for binding arbitration. Although the union was defeated, its members maintained some pride because not one striker crossed the picket line. The company fired seven strikers, however, claiming they had damaged property while on the picket line.[23] Although labor-management relations returned to normal through the rest of the decade, the memory of the union's defeat in the 1970 strike would play a role in the 1990s.

During the 1970s, as the corn industry increasingly turned to the use of chemicals to speed corn processing, workers were constantly handling a vast number of toxic and volatile substances, including sulphuric acid, ethylene oxide, propylene oxide, and chlorine. "When you get in the refinery and starch areas it's either all white and dusty and very explosive," noted Dave Watts, the local's president in the early 1990s, "or in some areas like the refinery, where they do the sweeteners and the syrup, it's sticky and extremely hot."[24]

In the mid-1970s Staley was losing money in its soybean operations, and there were serious safety problems. "The union went to management," said Watts, "and told them that we're going to get together on a safety program or we'll all go down. We didn't want to die in this plant." Dan Lane recalled the conditions in the soybean department that led to the creation of a union-management cooperation program:

> It was a dirty, filthy place: hotter than a son of a buck, dust all over the place, rats everywhere. The workers would set the electrical breakers, and they would take a broomstick to reset it because the electrical stuff was so screwed up. The breakers would blow out, and a big ball of fire would come out. I've actually seen guys catch on fire. Then there was the explosion incident and all the process workers bid out [i.e., requested department transfers]. The company didn't know what to do. These were guys with a lot of experience. . . . The company wouldn't let them bid out.

Bill Strohl, AIW 837's chief steward and then president in the 1970s, said of the soybean department explosions of 1976 and 1977: "People were scared to death. . . . The company said they needed our help. That's how we got into the 'Quality of Work Life Cooperative.'" Under this plan, union members and supervisors in the soybean department met regularly to discuss improving safety, productivity, and product quality.[25] Many workers felt the cooperation improved conditions in the department. "We would try to head off little problems before they become big problems," said Bill Strohl in 1981. "The important thing is that the company has respect for the union's rights to function properly and the union has respect for management's rights. . . . We treat each other as equals."[26]

Sales of Staley's soybean line continued to slump, however, because of the U.S. grain embargo against the Soviet Union in 1980 and a sag in the U.S. economy, and the company sold its soybean operations to Archer Daniels Midland.

By 1983 the company was pushing the union to expand the cooperation program to the rest of the plant. The union agreed, but through the 1980s members debated the program. Many workers were initially hopeful. "We thought by helping them make more money," recalled Lane, who was elected to the bargaining committee in 1986, "that it would secure our position, that we would share in that wealth; it would be better for the community . . . and it would be better for [management]. . . . Working conditions in the plant should have improved—but they didn't."[27] Others felt the union should never have joined the cooperation scheme and was failing to represent its members. "Staley had a plantation mentality," recalled Mike Griffin. "The cooperation effort was always a trap. Management uses [cooperation schemes] to downsize, and they get you to help them do it, and make you think you have ownership in the downsizing, that you're part of it."

By the mid-1980s opponents of the cooperation program pointed to the company's new policy of drastically cutting the number of mechanics, from seven hundred to fewer than two hundred. The company demanded and got changes in job classifications and work rules that merged jobs. Pipefitters, electricians, boilermakers, and other skilled workers now did multiple jobs outside their trained crafts. As with many operations that underwent deskilling in the 1980s, the plant became extremely hazardous and accidents became more frequent. At the same time, production demands were more strenuous than ever before.

The Decatur plant peaked at around 2,200 union employees in the late 1960s but dropped to 1,600 in 1975 and to 1,250 in the early 1980s. By 1992 the plant had just 850 union members. In the same period the corn grind rate steadily increased. Management was able to cut jobs through speedup, excessive overtime, and new technology, all of which were typical in the industry. "If ever there was an industry which illustrated the 'overworked American,' it was wet corn," noted Laurie Clements, a labor scholar who studied the industry.[28]

The 1980s were a difficult time for AIW 837, but unions across the country were suffering major setbacks. Massive wage and benefit concessions began with the UAW's Chrysler workers when Chrysler threatened bankruptcy and was bailed out in 1979 by the federal government on the condition that autoworkers cut their wages and benefits. This action opened the floodgates on corporate demands for union givebacks. Virtually every large manufacturer in the country downsized its workforce while demanding more work from those remaining. Other corporations moved their plants south to escape unions. When President Reagan fired eleven thousand striking air-traffic controllers and destroyed their union (PATCO) in 1981, he sent a message to corporate America that the federal government would support efforts to bust unions. Across the country workers faced deteriorating wages, benefits, and working conditions. Labor's numbers and political influence steadily declined.[29]

AFL-CIO leaders offered no resistance, and the AIW International responded to the attacks on unions with the same timidity. In contract after contract, recalled member Barrie Williams, when the company demanded that Local 837 accept concessions, "What you heard from the [union's] international representative was, 'Boys, there ain't no more there. You had better take it.'" The workers were angry, said Dan Lane, but "weren't sure about what to do about it. There's a whole mind-set out there: You're in a community that was hit severely—not as bad as Flint, Michigan, but severely. Decatur's population fell from 100,000 to 85,000, a 15 percent drop in population, and this was because we had all these plants closed down and people were just leaving."

In 1985 A. E. Staley merged with Continental Foods and became Staley-Continental. The next three years were among the worst workers had ever experienced. The company pleaded hard times, and the union agreed to freeze base pay at $10.80 an hour and take an annual lump-sum bonus rather than a wage increase. This saved Staley substantial money, but "during that time the plant was sucked dry," recalled Lane. "There was no money put into the plant. The workforce was being cut. Overtime hours were extreme because of the lack of workforce. Safety was just getting worse and worse."

Union members and their leaders felt helpless and demoralized. "We had a locomotive going downhill," said Local 837 president Bill Strohl. "If we step in front of it, we're not going to stop it." When it was announced that Staley-Continental was looking for a buyer, rumors surfaced that Archer Daniels Midland would purchase the plant. The workers were relieved when the rumor proved false, because ADM management was bitterly antiunion. The Staley workers didn't know what to expect, but they figured that whoever bought the plant couldn't be worse than Continental or ADM.

2

Tate & Lyle Comes to Decatur

When Tate & Lyle announced it was buying A. E. Staley, the workers were thrilled. Their joy rapidly turned to anger, however, as the new management made changes that led to deteriorating working conditions. Jim Beals's death in 1990 galvanized the local but didn't halt the company's assault. Workers realized that management was laying the groundwork to force a strike in 1992, bring in scabs, and cripple or eliminate the union.

The World's Largest Sugar Conglomerate

On April 13, 1988, Tate & Lyle CEO Sir Neil Shaw stepped into the expansive Allied Industrial Workers union hall on Dineen Street in Decatur. In the lobby he passed pop machines, encased bowling trophies, and plaques that commemorated AIW members who had died on the job, some at the Staley plant. Shaw entered the main hall, where rectangular tables with brown folding chairs were aligned in rows from wall to wall. The massive union hall easily seated eight hundred people. At the front of the room a circular AIW insignia was sewn into a blue velvet curtain that served as the backdrop for the speaker's podium. To the left was a black banner honoring Vietnam soldiers who were missing in action or prisoners of war.

In 1943 four UAW-AFL locals had jointly purchased the Vic and Fritz Hall and turned it into the largest union hall in Decatur. Along with other Decatur AIW locals, Local 837 held all its meetings there and had a small office on the second floor. A tavern occupying part of the first floor was open to the public. The unions rented out the popular hall for wedding receptions, semiweekly bingo games, and a host of other community gatherings.[1]

Shaw, the CEO of London-based Tate & Lyle since 1985, was in Decatur for a two-day visit to meet with Staley management, Illinois state legislators, and Decatur city officials about his plans for the Staley plant. A few weeks later Tate & Lyle's $1.5 billion purchase of Staley's four U.S. plants was finalized.[2] Shaw's visit to the union hall resulted in an impromptu invitation to lunch with about fifteen of the union's officials. Dave Watts, then the local's vice president, described the meeting with Shaw:

> Neil Shaw and a few others on Tate & Lyle's board of directors came out to the union hall with their starched white shirts on. They took off their coats and rolled up their sleeves. We cooked hamburgers in the grill and drank Miller Lite. They were measuring us, just as we were measuring them. . . . They said, "Let's drink beer and talk about this. What would you guys like to see the future of this place be?" [We told them that] we had gone through a hell of a period in the 1980s, and that we'd lost half of our membership through technology and downsizing. We were hopeful with Tate & Lyle.[3]

Shaw assured the local leaders that "they would notice very little change in their life at Staley."[4] The unionists were pleased to hear that he intended to move the company's headquarters back to Decatur from Rolling Meadows, Illinois, where it had moved after the Continental buyout in 1985. Shaw gained union members' confidence when he told the *Decatur Herald and Review*, "I see no problem with the union if we take over. It would improve the morale among those people 100 percent if we just met with them and talked about what we are going to do."[5] When the news spread around the plant, recalled Dan Lane, "people were going nuts, saying 'This is great!'"

By 1992 Tate & Lyle was the world's leading sugar company, with operations in twenty-seven countries. Its most notable label in the U.S. market is Domino Sugar. The corporation also has extensive interests in shipbuilding, finance, insurance, rum, and bulk-storage facilities.[6] Buying out Staley allowed Tate & Lyle entry into the corn-syrup market, eliminated a competitor, and gave it a strong base in the United States. According to a 1995 study conducted by the University of Illinois at Chicago, "In an industry already remarkably non-competitive, Tate & Lyle reduced the competition further in order to tighten its control of world markets."[7] Now four companies—Staley/Tate & Lyle, ADM, Cargill, and CPC International—controlled the American market in three product lines: high-fructose corn sweetener; citric acid, used in processed foods; and lysine, used in feed grains.[8]

At the same time, Decatur-based Archer Daniels Midland was closely linked with the industry's other leading companies. ADM owned 28 percent of American Maize, the fifth-largest U.S. maker of corn sweeteners; ADM had filled corn-syrup orders for CPC International when that company ran out of product; and, through a subsidiary, ADM controlled 7.4 percent of Tate & Lyle stock, giving the company considerable influence over Decatur's Staley plant. ADM and Staley also had a joint venture in Guadalajara, Mexico, to produce corn sweeteners.[9]

ADM board chairman Duane Andreas, who led the company's growth into a multinational giant in the 1980s, was known to say often, "The competitor is our friend and the customer is our enemy."[10] The corn-processing firms had a long history of price fixing, which was revealed in 1995 when ADM executive Mark Whitacre became an undercover informer for an FBI probe. "It doesn't take a rocket scientist to see that these companies—and the industry—work with a certain kind of harmony" that does not exist in most industries, noted Tom Pirko, president of BevMark, a New York consulting firm in the beverage industry. "It would be unimaginable for Coke to own stock in Pepsi or vice versa."[11]

The Informant (2009), directed by Steven Soderbergh and starring Matt Damon as Mark Whitacre, details the ADM price-fixing scandal. Most of the filming was done in Decatur. The film is based on Kurt Eichenwald's *The Informant: A True Story* (2001).

"We Will Get You Next Time"

The new management made radical changes in plant operations. Recalled Dave Watts, managers "made promises . . . about improving safety, job security, growth, and introducing different product lines. In fact, it was the complete opposite with every one of their promises."

"Our purpose," declared Staley executive vice president J. Patrick Mohan, "was to make changes in the work rules which would make the Decatur plant competitive with the three other corn-processing plants Staley operates in the U.S. and with facilities operated by our competitors."[12] Tate & Lyle had enjoyed thirteen straight years of rising profits, however, dating from 1979. Between 1984 and 1992 net profits increased fourfold, with the Staley subsidiary, the biggest profit center after 1988, accounting for 30 percent of the net. Profits in 1991 reached $400 million on sales of $5.5 billion, and profits over the three-year period from 1991 through 1993 were $2 billion.[13]

The corn-processing industry achieves such remarkable profits because it has one of the highest "value-added" rates of any industry. This figure refers to the value each worker adds to the product minus his or her wages. In 1988 the average value added per worker in the corn wet-milling industry was over a quarter-million dollars. By 1991 the figure had doubled to a towering $527,000. The entire industry boomed in the 1980s and 1990s as food and beverage companies switched from sugar to corn syrup. Shipments doubled between 1969 and 1979 and doubled again between 1979 and 1992. The handful of corporations dominating the sweetener industry achieved some of the highest productivity growth rates in the United States. Average revenue in the corn wet-milling industry grew at a rate of 8.8 percent per year from 1973 to 1991, near the very top of U.S. industries.[14]

Just one year after Tate & Lyle took over, negotiations for a new three-year contract began. In the summer of 1989, union members had just completed four years of a wage freeze and were expecting, at a minimum, that their wages would rise to keep pace with inflation. They were also adamant about shoring up safety practices. The bargaining committee, however, was stunned to find that Shaw had ordered his Decatur managers to demand rotating shifts, the deskilling of jobs, the elimination of most safety procedures, and other major concessions. The union moved quickly to educate workers about the company's demands and to unite the workforce. Dave Watts mobilized members to rally outside Decatur's Ambassador Hotel, where bargaining sessions were being held. The company realized that it was not in a position to force acceptance of such severe concessions. "The company basically was not prepared to negotiate, as they'd just taken the company over," recalled Dan Lane. As a result, "they walked in the room and told the union committee, 'Take what you've got. We're not changing anything from the 1986 contract.'" In October 1989 the two parties signed an agreement that mirrored the 1986 agreement.[15]

Before leaving the bargaining table, however, a Tate & Lyle manager swore to the committee, "We couldn't get you this time. But we will get you next time." If the union did not capitulate, management threatened, the plant would close. The 1989 negotiations were "a real wake-up call," said Watts. "We knew there were going to be challenges because Tate & Lyle was so aggressive."

Shaw's first step was to eliminate managers who had a good working relationship with the union and to organize a top leadership team with experience in busting unions. In November 1990 Richard "Red" Geurts was hired as director of operations, and in September 1991 John Phillips was hired as vice president of operations. Both men had acquired antiunion reputations, at Conagra and Proctor and Gamble, respectively. In 1991 the company brought in Glen Zalkin as labor-relations director. Zalkin was notorious for his union-busting efforts as a top manager at International Paper in Jay, Maine, when the company crushed a 1988 United Paperworkers strike, permanently replaced 1,200 unionists, and decertified the union. J. Patrick Mohan, an attorney who had been with the Staley company since 1979, became the company's chief spokesperson. Finally, in August 1992 Shaw chose Larry Pillard as CEO for the Staley operations. Pillard had twenty-three years of experience at Cargill, one of the four corn wet-milling giants, and a strong antiunion background. Pillard would head the company through the coming labor conflict.[16]

Before hiring Pillard the company had gone through four CEOs during its first four years in Decatur. The most notable turnover came when Larry Cunningham, who had twenty-five years with the company, resigned in July 1990 after just twenty months as CEO. Cunningham cited a "serious difference in philosophy" with the new corporate owners "about what Staley should do, how it should be managed, and how we should close ranks and pull together toward common goals." His superiors responded that under his leadership Staley operations "had not been aggressively managed." In a statement that could have been made by union officials, Cunningham told the *Decatur Herald and Review* in 1991, "I don't think Tate & Lyle understood the slippage in safety and housekeeping that occurred after they acquired Staley. A faction of Staley management concentrated far too much on production quantity at the expense of some of these other areas." Cunningham added that he was disturbed that Tate & Lyle was firing so many good managers with decades of experience.[17]

The company fired many of its vice presidents, then laid off middle management, and finally fired frontline supervisors. Local 837 vice president Bob Hull worked in the storeroom and watched as managers walked up the stairs. "They actually had meetings scheduled eight minutes apart. . . . They called them up and told them if they had a job. . . . Then they had guards in another room and they would escort them out. They would not even let these people go get their coats or go back to their office." Over the next two years, one-fourth of the company's white-collar workforce was replaced. By 1992 an additional quarter of the lower-level supervisors were fired. Tate & Lyle officials made it clear to the remaining managers: demonstrate complete adherence to the Tate & Lyle style or be terminated.

"Very few of our immediate supervisors are from Decatur any more," said executive board member John Lehew. "It used to be your supervisor had more experience than you. Now they have as much experience as your teen-age kid at McDonalds."[18] Added Gary Lamb, "I asked my supervisor what he did before he came to Staley's. He said, 'I sold vacuum cleaners.' And now he's a supervisor over the wet mill!"

"We Are Going to Hit You Hard All at Once"

From 1990 through 1992 managers worsened working conditions and assailed the union.

Safety conditions continued to deteriorate. Supervisors forced workers to ignore OSHA standards as they worked with hazardous chemicals. When workers refused, they were verbally abused, usually disciplined, and sometimes fired. Nonunion contractors, whose workers were untrained in safety procedures and regularly violated OSHA regulations, were hired to do union work. The plant's safety team was slashed from twenty-four to three.

So when Jim Beals was killed on the job on May 15, 1990, the entire union workforce reacted with rage. If the company were still being run by the Staley family, said the workers, Jim Beals would never have been forced to clean that tank, because he wasn't trained for that work. The propylene oxide fumes that killed Beals never would have seeped into the tank because the adjoining reactor would have been shut down, even if it meant lower production. The supervisor would have monitored the work to make sure safety procedures were followed. And the oxygen tanks for the emergency masks would have been properly filled. When OSHA settled with Tate & Lyle over Jim Beals's death, the union was stunned to find that the company would be fined only $4,000 for its gross negligence. "The law is inadequate to deal with serious violators, repetitive violators, situations where people are put at risk day after day," says OSHA official Charles Jeffress. "The penalties in the OSHA Act are inadequate to deal with people that don't take their safety responsibility seriously. A serious violation, something that might lead to someone's death, carries a maximum penalty of $7,000."[19]

In a letter to the company posted on union bulletin boards, Local 837 officers denounced the worsening safety standards and withdrew from all safety training and record keeping. "Our plant-wide safety system has turned into a company dog-and-pony show with little attention to the health and safety concerns that many of you know are still out there," declared the union leadership.[20]

In July 1991 the company announced a new attendance policy: any worker with more than seven absences per year would be fired, and the number of allowed absences would decrease each year. Combining that with derogatory statements from supervisors, the union understood the policy as directed at removing older workers from the plant. Then, beginning on October 14, 1991, Tate & Lyle instituted harsh disciplinary measures designed to intimidate the workers into bowing to the company's demands.

Union workers have far more protection from arbitrary management actions than do workers in a nonunion workplace. Every union contract in the United States provides management with the right to discipline workers only if the company can prove "just cause." In most cases management must exercise "progressive discipline"—workers cannot be discharged for first offenses but must receive gradually increasing punishments. Exceptions where immediate discharge is permissible include such egregious offenses as intoxication or violence on the job.

In October 1991, however, management notified the union that it would now consider a long list of offenses grounds for immediate discharge, including "smoking outside of designated areas; loafing; dishonesty; sleeping on duty; insubordination; refusal to work overtime as directed; unauthorized possession of a camera; and use of abusive or threatening language."[21] The union was stunned. This was a complete violation of the union contract and fifty years of cordial labor-management relations. Even most nonunion employers did not immediately discharge employees for such offenses.

As a result, from October 1991 through September 1992 fifteen employees received disciplinary suspensions and nine were fired. There were more discharges in that one year than in the previous twenty years combined.[22] In just the five-month period from October through February 1992 the union filed 172 grievances. The union also filed fifteen NLRB charges in the seven months before March 1992—more than it had filed in the previous twenty years. Whereas grievances had often been quickly settled under the previous management, in the early 1990s some one thousand grievances were not settled on the shop floor.

"Before 1989, I liked running my job," said twenty-year Staley veteran Michael Stewart, but "after the 1989 contract, people just didn't feel like going into work. They put foremen over us who absolutely knew nothing about our jobs . . . making decisions that a lot of times made our jobs worse."[23] In a sentiment that was echoed by the entire workforce, twenty-three-year Staley unionist Guy O'Brien stated, "This isn't Staley. Staley's gone. This is Tate & Lyle now."[24]

From 1991 through the spring of 1992, management made clear that it was preparing for an expected strike when the contract expired on September 30, 1992.

First, in early 1991 Tate & Lyle replaced its longstanding Decatur-based union contractors with the nonunion, Louisiana-based Harmony Construction Company, nationally known for its track record of supplying replacements to companies whose workers went on strike.

Second, in June 1992 Tate & Lyle and ADM announced that the two companies, in an act of corporate solidarity, would build a 3.5-mile, $600,000 pipeline between their Decatur corn-processing plants. The pipeline was designed to carry twelve thousand gallons of starch slurry per minute in either direction.[25] Despite both companies' denials, it was obvious to the Staley workers that the purpose of the pipeline was to supply Staley during a strike.[26]

Third, in early 1992, most of the Staley workers began to notice outsiders who were assigned to watch them do their jobs on the shop floor. At the same time, under the guise of the labor-management cooperation plan and a "job safety analysis," Staley ordered workers to develop written procedure manuals that detailed how they did their jobs. Many members presciently believed that the "nannies," as the workers derisively called them, were there to learn the jobs so that they could run the plant in the event of a strike. "All along they had plans to use that against us," said Dave Watts, "input after input, page after page of detailed instructions, clear directives for training scabs." "The company's plan all along was to force a strike," said Royal Plankenhorn, voicing sentiments expressed by most workers. "They'd hand your 'safety manual' along to the scab that replaces you. You've told him how to do your job, and there's no glitch in production. They don't miss a beat."[27]

Fourth, in March 1992 the company began mandatory monthly "state of the plant" meetings, which the workers quickly labeled "plant propaganda" sessions. The unionists were ordered to sit quietly and listen while upper management harangued them over the plant's supposed low productivity. Workers were told that extreme measures would have to be taken to completely reorganize the plant and to change work rules if the plant was to remain competitive and stay in business.

Fifth, labor-relations director Glen Zalkin boasted constantly of helping to destroy the Paperworkers union in Jay, Maine, by hiring permanent replacements when the union went on strike. And operations director Red Geurts repeatedly made clear that he had hired Zalkin based on his union-busting experience and that he shared Zalkin's philosophy.[28]

Finally, the company retained Seyfarth, Shaw, Fairweather, and Geraldson to lead its bargaining team. In previous negotiations the company's top officials had led its team. The Chicago-based partnership, with over three hundred lawyers on its payroll, was one of the most infamous union-busting law firms in the country. The union-busting consulting industry had grown rapidly since the early 1980s into a $2 billion a year business, and Seyfarth was a leader in that expansion.[29]

By spring 1992 the signs were clear to the Staley workers: Tate & Lyle was intent on ruthlessly eliminating the gains the union had won in fifty years of collective bargaining. At a June 8, 1992, meeting vice president for operations John Phillips finally put into words what the workers had long known: "We are going to hit you hard all at once, rather than have people pissed off for several contracts and years."[30]

It appeared that the union had two equally odious choices: capitulate or strike.

3

The Union Prepares to Resist

Under the leadership of their newly elected president, Dave Watts, Local 837 invited labor educators to the union hall to help them understand what they were facing and how they could resist Tate & Lyle's aggression. As a result of those discussions, in the summer of 1992 the local hired Ray Rogers to launch a nationwide corporate campaign to pressure the company to bargain a fair contract. In early October, faced with a company proposal that Watts called "an insult . . . , one management rights clause from beginning to end," the members overwhelmingly voted to reject the contract.[1]

President Dave Watts

When the Staley workers found their world turned upside down under the new Tate & Lyle management, they quickly realized that they would have to look for new strategies if the union were to survive. In December 1989 the members elected Dave Watts as their president.

Watts was born in Decatur in 1947. His father was a railroad worker, and his mother was a housewife whose parents were Belgian immigrants. Watts took the path of many of his high-school classmates, entering the navy in 1965 at age seventeen. A few days after getting out, recalls Watts, "I walked into the Staley employment office, never dreaming I could get a job there. But lo and behold, the guy doing the hiring was my old basketball coach from elementary school, and he gave me a job."[2]

At age twenty-one Watts became one of the company's youngest carpenter apprentices. He was soon elected shop steward and earnestly studied the union contract. "I had that inner drive to do something different rather than just go through the compound every day," he recalled. In 1980, when the company demanded concessions, Watts felt motivated to become more active. "The 1980 contract left a sour taste. . . . From that point forward I took a stronger interest and planned to run for office." Elected to the union's executive board as a trustee in 1981 and as vice president in 1984, Watts observed the president, Gene Sharp, closely. "There were some things he did very well. The things that he didn't do well always stuck in my craw. . . . He wouldn't get into the fire. He stood in the shadows and watched the fire. . . . I swore I wouldn't [do that]."

Watts voraciously read labor history and attended leadership training at the AFL-CIO's George Meany Center for Labor Studies, in Maryland. "I could not get enough reading material, enough education," said Watts. "I really felt connected to the purpose of the labor movement." Watts's passion for the rights of working people was later reinforced when his older brother, who lived in Kansas City, died at the age of forty-eight. Watts related: "His company was demanding concession after concession. Then they laid him off after twenty-two years with the company. Here he was, with two kids, struggling to survive. He really suffered, lost his house, ended up getting a divorce, and then collapsed from a heart attack. And it was all due to the tragedy of his job."

Watts worked on the shop floor, with some time off allowed for conducting union business. Some unions of comparable size have a full-time president, but Local 837 was a no-frills organization. Only the bargaining committee chairperson worked full-time for the union; in periods between contract negotiations, the chair worked as a chief steward, handling grievances from a small union office within the plant.

Running the union extended far beyond a forty-hour workweek for Watts, but he gave his time freely. With their children from previous marriages both raised, Dave and his wife, Pat, a highly respected nurse manager at a local hospital, were committed to Watts's pursuing his dream of serving the membership. He received a token monthly check for twenty-five dollars, which he automatically signed back to the union treasury.

Watts was greatly influenced by Bill Strohl, who had served seven years as the local's president and four years as an AIW regional representative. Strohl made the unusual decision to return to the plant, preferring his work as a mechanic and the camaraderie of the shop floor over the prestige and higher pay of working for the AIW International. "I really looked up to Bill," said Watts. "He taught me a great deal."

U.S. Congressman Glenn Poshard, who came from a United Mine Workers family in southern Illinois, described Watts as having the same fighting spirit as his family: "Dave really believed in that union. He was a person that held real deep convictions, and was willing to put everything on the line. When you believe in the union, you literally see it as a heritage, as your role in building the country, and defending your children and your family. Dave was that kind of person."

Throughout his presidency an overwhelming majority of the union's membership admired Watts for his tenacity, innovative ideas, integrity, and democratic leadership style. "I couldn't see anybody else doing what Dave did," said Royal Plankenhorn. "Nobody else would have had the guts. . . . He wanted everybody to be involved. He wanted everybody's voice to be heard."

When Watts was sworn into office in January 1990, he knew he had his work cut out for him. As in many locals across the country, generally fewer than 5 percent of the members attended the monthly meetings, except when there was an officers' election or a contract vote. So that workers on all three shifts could attend, the local held meetings on both Tuesday nights and Wednesday mornings. "At the night meetings you might have about twenty," said member Richard Brummett; at the morning meetings, "maybe six or eight."[3]

Watts knew that most Staley workers gave only passive support to the union. They knew that having the union gave them rights, but for them "the union" meant the union leadership, not the membership. The union was something they supported and paid dues to but not part of their daily lives. When the workers had a complaint about a supervisor's actions, they expected the steward to take care of the problem *for* them rather than work *with* the steward to resolve the problem.

During the 1980s, recalled Watts, the Staley local was like most of the other fifty thousand AFL-CIO locals across the country: "We were living in a cloud, living in a dream world. It wasn't really obvious to most of the leadership or membership what was happening at that time, like with PATCO and a lot of other disputes and struggles where labor was being hit. There wasn't a lot of education being brought into the local by the leadership. . . . At that time we were losing a lot of jobs at Staley, and it was just the lack of education of what was going on in the real world that kept people uninvolved."

After watching his own local endure layoffs and concessions throughout the 1980s, and through his studies at the AFL-CIO labor center, Watts knew that the labor movement was steadily losing ground but also that leaders were not offering a strategy to defend workers' jobs, wages, or rights. The AIW International continually advised Local 837 that it should accept whatever contract the company was offering and be grateful for having survived negotiations.[4]

This answer did not satisfy Watts, yet he recognized that the AIW was weak and didn't have the resources to stand up to the corporations. The AIW was one of the smallest internationals in the AFL-CIO, peaking at ninety-four thousand members in 1979 but dropping to forty-eight thousand members by 1992, spread over 298 local unions. Eighty-five percent of its membership was in Illinois, Indiana, Wisconsin, and Michigan. Moreover, the international was in a serious financial crisis and had been forced to cut back to a bare-bones staff.[5]

In the early 1990s the Staley workforce fell into three hiring clusters.[6] Those in the first group, about a hundred workers, had thirty or more years of seniority. Those in the second group, three-quarters of the workforce (including Dave Watts), were hired during the Vietnam War era. Many of these older workers were second- or third-generation Staley workers.

Then, after a fifteen-year hiring drought, Tate & Lyle began accepting applications in 1990 and hired eighty-six workers within a year. This third group, constituting an eighth of the workforce, had been subjected to intense scrutiny from management. In violation of the law, applicants underwent a barrage of questions about loyalty to the company and their willingness to betray a union member. Management told the new employees "that they were there to get the union in line," recalled Lorell Patterson, who was hired in 1990, and that "the union workers were lazy and didn't want to work; that [the new employees] were [being hired] to show them how to do the work."

The Staley workers, like those in many other unions, were also facing divisions along skill, race, and gender lines.

Workers fell into two skill categories at the Staley plant. Twenty-five percent were maintenance workers, who had completed long apprenticeships and held special skills, such as carpenters, pipefitters, and electricians. They received higher wages than other workers, traveled throughout the plant to maintain and repair the equipment, and enjoyed more autonomy on the job. The remaining 75 percent were mostly semiskilled "process workers," who engaged in the less-desirable work of turning out product, and a small number were "service workers," who did janitorial and transportation work.

The maintenance workers had long dominated the union's elected offices, and many process workers felt unwelcome at the union hall. Many process workers believed the maintenance workers negotiated extra gains for themselves. The division was so sharp that in the December 1985 elections the process workers organized to vote all the maintenance workers off the executive board. While maintenance workers returned to the board in the next election, the tension lingered into the 1990s.

Throughout its history, the Staley workforce had largely consisted of white, male workers whose families had been Democrats since the days of Franklin Roosevelt. A high percentage of those working under Tate & Lyle had served in Vietnam and held a strong distaste for the 1960s antiwar movement. By the 1980s many had become "Reagan Democrats"—a political stance that swept the country as a backlash against the antiwar, civil rights, and women's movements. These tensions were played out inside the plant as well.

Whereas 15 percent of Decatur's population was African American in 1990, only 7 percent of Staley's workforce was.[7] The local had never elected an African American to its leadership bodies. As we will discuss in chapter 11, many black Staley workers saw Local 837 as a white-led union that looked out only for whites, so they rarely attended union meetings. Racist comments and graffiti by white workers and supervisors were common in the 1970s and 1980s.[8]

Decatur politics have long been dominated by Republicans, and whites held nearly every position of power in town, from the school board to the city council to the corporate boardrooms. Decatur was run by a "closed club," said Mayor Eric Brechnitz; a half-dozen wealthy white men called the shots there.[9] Whites with the means sent their children to private schools; nearly 45 percent of the children in Decatur's public schools were African Americans, whose families held the lowest-paid jobs in town.[10] In the 1980s and 1990s Decatur neighborhoods, like those in most American cities, were heavily segregated. Blacks were kept out of the white side of town; the small towns surrounding Decatur were virtually all white—by design, as James Loewen documents in *Sundown Towns*.[11]

Much of the male workforce exhibited traditionally sexist attitudes toward the roughly three dozen women working in the plant. Many believed that women didn't belong in manufacturing and that they were taking away jobs from men who needed to support their families. As we will also discuss in chapter 11, women regularly faced sexual harassment on the job and, like the black workers, were not active in the union. The local had elected only one woman officer in its fifty-year history, and then only as recording secretary.

When Dave Watts took the oath as president in 1990, he knew he had a tremendous task. Not only was his small local forced to challenge a giant multinational corporation; Watts also had to help the local mend its internal divisions.

The Failed Caterpillar Strike and the Labor Movement in Crisis

As the unionists began to discuss their situation, it was clear that they faced a dilemma. If they struck, permanent replacements could be brought in, and they stood to lose their jobs forever. If they didn't strike, management would continue to assail working conditions, and fifty years of union gains would be washed away. "We either stood up, as smartly as we could, to the aggression that was coming in our direction," said Dave Watts, "or we lay down and let it happen. Nobody wanted to let it happen."

Watts sought the advice of Larry Solomon, president of Decatur's United Auto Workers Local 751, representing the Caterpillar workers, and invited him to Local 837's board meetings. A labor activist for three decades who had read scores of books on labor history, Solomon could draw on his experience to help chart the Staley workers' course.

Solomon had hired into the Caterpillar plant in 1963 and soon became active in the UAW. He was stunned when, throughout the 1980s, one employer after another demanded and received major wage and benefit concessions from industrial unions. In 1986 he was in St. Louis when UAW International staff and representatives from the Caterpillar locals were bargaining a contract. "The international started giving some things away, and it just broke my heart," recalled Solomon. At 4:00 A.M., unable to sleep, Solomon got out of his hotel bed and wrote an anguished letter denouncing the concessions to Jerry Tucker, head of the New Directions reform caucus within the UAW. After Tucker and Solomon met, Solomon decided to join New Directions, which opposed the international's policy of labor-management cooperation. The whole point of the cooperation programs, said Solomon, "was to prepare the workers to take things away from them." Influenced by Tucker, Solomon ran an aggressive campaign and was elected president of UAW Local 751 in 1987.

In December 1991, 1,870 Decatur Caterpillar workers began a five-month strike. Nationwide 13,400 Cat workers, most of them in Illinois, walked the picket lines for 163 days. Earlier that year the UAW had negotiated a contract with John Deere and then approached its major domestic competitor. But Caterpillar shocked the union by demanding huge concessions: freedom to subcontract work to low-wage, nonunion workers; twelve-hour rotating shifts; flexible work assignments and schedules; a much weaker grievance procedure; laxer safety rules; and a two-tier pay scale, with some new hires making only seven dollars an hour. These demands flew in the face of the pattern-bargaining model, which had been central to labor-management relations in steel, rubber, auto, and agricultural implements since the 1950s. Under pattern bargaining, a union negotiated a contract with one company in an industry, and the others quickly signed similar deals. Wages and benefits were thus taken out of competition, forcing corporations to compete solely on product quality and service.

When the union rejected Caterpillar's demands and struck in 1991, it was the tenth work stoppage there in forty-three years. It quickly became clear to the UAW strikers that this time Caterpillar was out to cripple or break the union. No corporation the size of Caterpillar had launched such an attack on its unionized workforce since the 1930s.

By the spring of 1992, six hundred UAW members were crossing picket lines (the company claimed twice that many), and the union was weakening. Decatur's Local 751 was perhaps the strongest Cat local, with only ten or twelve of its members crossing the lines.[12] On April 3 CEO Donald Fites sent letters to striking workers declaring that unless they returned to work within the week, the company would hire scabs to run the plants, and UAW members would be permanently replaced. The UAW International ordered members to return to work without a contract and work under the terms of the company's final offer. The Cat workers had suffered a major defeat. Union members regrouped and continued their fight for a fair contract inside the plants.

Throughout the spring and summer of 1992 the Staley workers intently discussed why the Caterpillar strike had failed and what that failure said about their chances of winning a strike against Tate & Lyle. They ultimately realized that the defeat at Caterpillar and their own union's dire situation reflected the crisis of the U.S. labor movement as a whole. Once a stronghold, organized labor was rapidly losing its power.

For a century and a half of American labor history, the strike constituted the unions' primary weapon. From the formation of the first unions and the first major strikes in the early 1800s through the labor upsurge of the 1930s, employers often called on the government to send in the police, the national guard, or even the U.S. Army to help scabs cross picket lines to break strikes. Courts assisted by issuing injunctions against unions. To defend their jobs, strikers often found themselves fighting to keep scabs out of their factories.

Until the U.S. Congress responded to the 1930s workers' upsurge and passed the Wagner Act in 1935, unions had no legal standing. The Wagner Act legalized unions, banned company-dominated unions, outlined workers' legal rights as they attempted to organize a union, and set up the National Labor Relations Board to fairly monitor union certification elections and to enforce the law. Even with the Wagner Act, however, it took a virtual national uprising to force big business to recognize labor and institutionalize unions into the American mosaic.

In 1946, 4.5 million workers successfully struck for wage increases, but labor's victory resulted in a backlash. A majority of Americans became convinced that "Big Labor," as it would henceforth be labeled by labor's corporate and political opponents, had gained too much power and didn't care about the needs of nonunion workers or the country as a whole. As the country shifted to the right with the rise of the cold war and anticommunism, the labor movement was politically isolated. The CIO purged eleven of its international unions for having communists among their elected leaderships. In 1947 Congress passed the Taft-Hartley Act, which amended the Wagner Act by severely restricting unionists' rights. With the union movement in retreat—and with the United States emerging from World War II as the dominant global economic power, producing half of the world's goods—most large manufacturing employers were willing to live with the moderated unions. Thus the postwar "social contract" between labor and management was born.[13] By 1954, 35 percent of American workers were unionized, and by 1956, nearly 50 percent of all manufacturing workers were in unions.[14] From 1950 through the early 1970s, the wages and benefits of unionized workers soared. Real income for American workers doubled in a generation. When agreement could not be reached at the bargaining table, unions sometimes went on strike, but they were rarely met with the intense violence of past decades. In heavily unionized cities in industrial states, most large employers no longer sought to bring in scabs. Instead most strikes became battles of attrition, with each side waiting out the other to see who would compromise first. This strategy worked for labor in the sense that each contract brought substantially higher wages and improved benefits.

In the late 1970s and early 1980s the rules began to change. New competition from abroad, combined with the unprecedented economic power of the ever-larger multinational corporations, led companies to reevaluate their social contract with organized labor, which they viewed as having grown weak and bureaucratic. Then, in 1980, America elected its most antiunion president since the 1920s. In 1981 President Reagan swiftly smashed a strike of eleven thousand air-traffic controllers, organized in the PATCO union, firing the strikers and replacing them with scabs. This was the first time the U.S. government had crushed a union of government employees, and the nation hadn't seen the complete destruction of a union since the 1890s. The government's action was a signal to corporate America that it was open season on unions.[15]

With "competitiveness" and "the new global economy" as mantras, big business demanded and received major concessions in wages, benefits, and work rules during the 1980s. Major employers began to force their workers out on strike and then break their unions, bringing in scabs under police protection. In most strikes the law allowed an employer to retain scabs after the union signed a contract, bringing back the union members only as positions became available. And if a strike lasted a year, employers were allowed to permanently replace the entire union workforce.[16] Phelps Dodge, Brown & Sharpe, Greyhound, the Tribune Company, Hormel, International Paper, Eastern Airlines—the list of companies that broke strikes in the 1980s marks a graveyard of labor defeats. An estimated 300,000 strikers lost their jobs to permanent replacements in that decade.[17]

The percentage of unionized workers dropped steadily from the 1955 peak of 35 percent to 16 percent in 1990, and unionized manufacturing workers fell even more sharply, from 50 percent in the 1950s to just 19 percent in 1993.[18] At the same time, corporations were automating and downsizing their plants, increasing overtime hours and the pace of work, and moving their operations abroad. As a result, the percentage of manufacturing workers in the workforce steadily fell. From 1979 to 1995, the United States lost at least 43 million jobs.[19] As a result of all these factors, real wages (adjusted for inflation) for all U.S. workers fell 12 percent between 1973 and 1998, despite the so-called "economic boom" of the 1990s.[20]

Unions felt too weak to strike. In the 1960s and 1970s an average of 186 large strikes (those involving 1,000 or more workers) took place each year; in the 1980s the number fell to 83; in 1992 there were just 35.[21] To be sure, some unions still struck briefly without being permanently replaced, but as happened with the Caterpillar workers, increasingly unions were dismayed to find that what they had thought would be a quick strike ending in compromise had turned into a war for their very existence. There were new rules, and those who ignored them did so at their peril.

Educating the Membership

The failure of the UAW's 1991–92 strike weighed heavily on the minds of the Staley workers as they debated their response to Tate & Lyle's harsh demands. "It was clear Tate & Lyle would take us on in a big way in 1992," said Dave Watts, "and we tried to figure how we would take them on."[22] Having seen what had happened at Caterpillar, noted Staley worker Emery Scrimpsher, "we were fairly convinced that they would bring the replacement workers in right after we left if we went on strike."[23]

Union officers decided that the union needed extensive education about Tate & Lyle, the state of the corn-milling industry, and ways to fight back. Members voted by an overwhelming majority to increase their dues from eighteen to thirty-four dollars a month in order to hire university-based labor educators. The local brought in Mark Crouch, a professor of labor studies at Indiana University's Fort Wayne campus, to lead an all-day seminar on January 25, 1992. "We just weren't sure where to go," recalled Dan Lane. "Strike, can't strike, what do we do? . . . Mark was brought in to talk to us specifically about that." Crouch discussed the need to transform the local by educating and involving the membership. He returned on February 8 and March 18 to lead discussions on Tate & Lyle's intentions and on alternatives to striking, such as work-to-rule and corporate campaigns (we discuss both in later chapters). At a fourth education session, on July 18, Crouch invited Laurie Clements, director of the University of Iowa Labor Center, to make a presentation about the corn wet-milling industry, Tate & Lyle's global strategy, and bargaining trends in the industry. In addition, Indiana University labor studies professor Paul Rainsberger spoke to the workers about legal issues involving strikes, lockouts, and permanent replacements.[24]

Through these discussions, the Staley workers came to understand that Tate & Lyle and the entire corn wet-milling industry were highly profitable, that what was happening to them was not unique but part of a national and global trend, and that all the signs pointed to a Tate & Lyle strategy of provoking a strike in order to replace the workers and eliminate the union. The company's proposals for the 1992 contract, said Clements, were not the "industry standard," as management claimed, but the worst in the industry. When Clements surveyed other unions in the industry about the Staley proposals, "their reaction was just horror," he said.[25]

In February, shortly after Crouch's first meeting with the workers, the local formed solidarity and publications committees, which began monthly meetings to organize and educate the members, and the monthly steward meetings were opened up to all workers. "We were trying to feed information down through the system," says Watts, "but it wasn't enough. We couldn't operate on a monthly basis. It was too slow." So the local began weekly "solidarity meetings" to discuss strategy. "The inverted triangle was the basic principle I operated on," said Watts. "In corporate America everything comes down from the top. With the union, it's the other way around. It's the bottom up." In Local 837, said Watts, "all the direction comes from the floor [as the Staley workers called the union membership]. Not the international, not the president, not the union leadership. The *floor* governs."

In addition, occasionally at first and then as a regular practice, the local did what few unions have done: open up the meetings to the spouses and children of the workers and to sympathetic friends and other unionists. Discussions about what the union should do in the face of Staley's assault would involve not just the workers but their families. That decision, said Dave Watts, "broke with tradition and walked over our local bylaws and international bylaws." If a fight was to be waged and won, however, "it just made all the sense in the world to have the workers' families attend the union meetings. If your spouse is going to fight you, we're going to lose half the troops. They have to be educated right along with us."

The weekly solidarity meetings regularly filled the huge union hall. "You'll get the majority of our regular membership at the meeting, and by the time you bring in the spouses and children and girlfriends and boyfriends, you're looking at eight hundred, nine hundred, sometimes a thousand people at a Tuesday night meeting," said Richard Brummett.[26] Congressman Glenn Poshard was one of many supporters who attended a Tuesday-night meeting and came away in awe. "Those meetings were community," recalled Poshard. "There was an absolute steel will to survive. It was a whole family thing. Those families felt that those workers were doing the right thing, and they were willing to endure the hardship because it was a matter of principle."

As the Staley unionists analyzed the corporate assault on unions, said Dave Watts, "it became clear . . . that this damn thing was going to become a major battle."[27] He asked the national AFL-CIO in Washington, D.C., for help, but its president, Lane Kirkland, had provided little leadership as major strikes were repeatedly broken, the number of workers in unions steadily declined, and the federation failed to get proworker legislation passed. "Over and over," Watts lamented, "we tried to get somebody in some authority position in the AFL-CIO to give us some help. We wrote letters, we made calls, and it just never happened. The AFL-CIO had the resources, they had the numbers, but they never had the desire." As Watts reported on the lack of response at the local's weekly meetings, the workers were baffled by the AFL-CIO's complacency.[28]

Larry Solomon and Mark Crouch had raised two possible strategies to fight Tate & Lyle: an in-plant campaign to pressure the company on the shop floor and a corporate campaign to mobilize popular pressure. Watts told AIW International president Nick Serraglio that the union was considering bringing in advisers to fight Tate & Lyle with these strategies. With retirement just months away, Serraglio spoke candidly. "I've got to tell you that you cannot hire outside advisers," said Serraglio, "and that's what the AFL-CIO recommends I tell you. But off the record, you gotta do what you gotta do. You're not going to get any grief out of me. . . . The AIW union doesn't have any money and we don't have any resources. But you do whatever you gotta do."[29]

"His saying that," recalled Watts, "gave me the incentive to continue on. . . . Had we waited for the AFL-CIO to help us, we would've been a union in the past tense."[30] AIW 837 was determined to make a stand against Tate & Lyle. "If it takes a hard-line approach to fight a hard-line business out to destroy unions, then so be it," declared Watts. "We'll take a hard-line approach."[31] Watts also got advice from AIW regional director Danny Wirges. "There is no question that this company is out to do you," Wirges said. "If you want to do them back, there is only one person, and that is Ray Rogers."[32] Rogers, director of his own New York–based consulting firm, Corporate Campaign Incorporated, had a reputation for bringing tremendous passion, commitment, and twenty years of experience to his campaigns against corporations. Watts called Rogers and requested he meet with Local 837's executive board.

Ray Rogers

Ray Rogers was born in 1944 into a working-class family in Beverly, Massachusetts. His father was a union machinist employed by General Electric, and his mother worked as an assembler in an electronics plant. After studying sociology and astronomy at the University of Massachusetts, Rogers served in VISTA, building housing for the poor in Appalachia; campaigned with reformer Arnold Miller in his successful bid for the United Mine Workers presidency; and then joined the staff of the Amalgamated Clothing and Textile Workers Union (ACTWU).[33]

Rogers first came into the labor spotlight when he led a four-year national pressure campaign that forced the J. P. Stevens Company of Roanoke Rapids, North Carolina, to negotiate a contract with its textile workers.[34] The union had previously won a hard-fought union recognition vote in 1974, as portrayed in the film *Norma Rae,* but only after the union launched a national corporate campaign did the company finally agree to sign a union contract in 1980.[35] In 1981 Rogers left the ACTWU staff and formed Corporate Campaign (CCI). He worked with unions in the successful battles of farmworkers against Campbell Soup (1985–86) and flight attendants against American Airlines (1986–87 and 1990–91) and in the failed strikes at the Austin, Minnesota, Hormel meatpacking plant in 1985–86 and International Paper in Jay, Maine, in 1988.[36]

Rogers researched the corn-processing industry and a few weeks later flew to Decatur to meet with the local's executive board. "You have a chance, a very slim chance," Rogers told them. "It's kind of like David and Goliath. The only thing is, you're David, they're Goliath, and you're about ten feet in a hole."[37] But, Rogers insisted, he had a strategy to get the union out of the hole.

That night Rogers spoke to a large, attentive audience of workers and spouses. A dynamic speaker, Rogers possesses a great power to inspire and motivate. Rogers explained that the only way to defeat a multinational such as Tate & Lyle was to launch a member-driven national and global corporate campaign. A corporate campaign is a mobilization of the labor movement and the community to tarnish a corporation's image and to inflict serious damage on the company to pressure management to negotiate a fair contract.[38] All the activities in a corporate campaign—reaching out to other workers, unions, and community groups locally, nationally, and internationally; organizing national boycotts; engaging in visible protests; putting public pressure on the corporation's financial allies—would require a mobilized union membership.

A corporate campaign hits the company from every conceivable angle, Rogers told the workers. As AFL-CIO secretary-treasurer Rich Trumka explains it, "You fire fifty arrows out of the quiver. Each one of them has some effect, but you don't know how much. But collectively they achieve the result you want to get to. And you keep firing arrows" until the employer concedes. If a corporation has received tax subsidies from local governments, this may be an opening to ally with homeowners burdened with high property taxes. If a corporation has damaged the environment, then neighborhood groups, civic leaders, and environmental organizations may be natural allies.

In Rogers's analysis the most important target of a corporate campaign is the corporation's financial relationships. "You have to dissect a corporation and break it down into its components," said Rogers. "Who really can wield the power to the point of control? A corporation is really a coalition of individual and institutional interests, some more vital and vulnerable than others, that can be challenged, attacked, divided, and conquered." Rogers argued that Tate & Lyle could be pressured into negotiating a just contract through four targets. First, the union would target Archer Daniels Midland, which through a subsidiary held 7 percent of Tate & Lyle stock. Second, the union would pressure the State Farm Insurance Company, which was a significant stockholder in ADM. The union's third target would be Tate & Lyle itself, through a boycott campaign against its best-known product, Domino Sugar. Finally, the union would pressure banks that had Staley officials on their boards or were Staley creditors. "A major goal of a corporate campaign," said Rogers, "is to turn the power structure supporting the company against management."[39]

Impressed with his presentation, experience, and enthusiasm, Local 837 hired Ray Rogers and his firm on June 27, 1992. The price was high: twenty-eight thousand dollars a month plus expenses and 15 percent of all money CCI raised through its mass mailings. At the July 14 union meeting the Staley workers voted by a 96 percent margin to raise their dues from thirty-four to one hundred dollars a month in order to pay Rogers. Within a year the workers had raised their dues by 500 percent. "Ray was a very hyper, enthusiastic guy," said Dan Lane. "If [Rogers had asked me for] two hundred dollars a month, I would have been willing to write the check every month. That's how desperate all of us were feeling. . . . It was a lot of money, but to me, it was an investment."

"It Was a Total Obliteration of the Union"

On August 4, 1992, Jim Shinall pushed his chair in to the bargaining table to begin ironing out a three-year contract that would be acceptable to the AIW 837 membership. Shinall, who had worked at Staley since 1964, had helped negotiate the 1986 and 1989 contracts and was considered a skilled negotiator. In 1990 the five members of the bargaining committee elected him committee chair. Like Dave Watts, Shinall had attended courses at the George Meany Center to strengthen his skills. Next to Shinall on the union's side of the table were committee members Bill Strohl, Dan Lane, Denton Larrimore, and Allain "Dike" Ferris. Dave Watts, AIW International representative Bill Coleman, and AIW regional director Danny Wirges rounded out the union team.

In 1986, when Dan Lane joined the bargaining committee, he and Shinall became good friends. Only one member of the committee, Strohl, was elected at-large by the entire membership. Larrimore was elected by the service workers in the plant; Ferris, by the maintenance workers; and Lane and Shinall, by the process workers. Lane and Shinall felt a heavy responsibility to bring the concerns of the process workers to the table. Many felt that the mechanics, who had long dominated the union leadership, did not give process workers adequate respect or fair treatment in negotiations.

As neighbors, Shinall and Lane often rode to work together and regularly discussed union issues as well as their personal lives. Shinall had encouraged Lane to run for the bargaining committee, knowing that Lane would not let the process workers be neglected. "I had a lot of respect for Jim," Lane recalled. "I think he worked very hard as bargaining committee chair." For the 1992 negotiations, it was Lane's vote along with Denton Larrimore's that had elected Jim Shinall to the chair over Bill Strohl.

As he looked across the table at management, Shinall felt his anxiety deepen. In all previous negotiations the company's officers, with whom the union had long-standing relationships, had led its bargaining team, but this time Tate & Lyle had retained Brad Livingston from the Seyfarth, Shaw law firm. The workers had dealt with Seyfarth, Shaw just once before—during the 1970 strike, which the union lost, resulting in the firing of seven workers. Also across the table was Glen Zalkin, Staley's new union-busting director of labor relations.

Shinall knew that the union bargainers were in for a rough two months. The company had attempted to start talking in March, six months before the contract expired, a move characteristic of corporations intent on weakening a union, but the union refused the ploy. On May 15 Tate & Lyle had submitted a long list of concession demands and even attempted to bypass the bargaining committee by communicating its demands directly to the members.

But Shinall and the bargaining committee were fortified by the membership's strong stance. AIW Local 837 was rebuilding and rejuvenating itself through education and rank-and-file participation. It had not waited passively for this moment.

When the union bargainers sat down, they brought with them the 1989 contract. The protocol at Staley—as at every unionized company—was for both union and management to make proposals to modify the existing contract. To the unionists' shock, however, Tate & Lyle did not use the 116-page contract as a starting point. Instead, company officials handed over an entirely new contract, just seventeen pages long. Management sought to radically weaken the grievance procedure; impose a rotating, twelve-hour shift schedule; eliminate the union safety committee; impose all costs of arbitrations solely on the union; gut the seniority system; escalate its contracting out of union jobs to nonunion firms; substantially increase workers' health-care payments; expand company work rules; and give supervisors far more flexibility in assigning jobs to workers. The company offered modest hourly wage increases, but with the new shift schedule, workers would lose an average of six thousand dollars each year in overtime.

"I've never in my life seen a company totally obliterate an agreement to the extent they did and expect the membership to accept it," said Danny Wirges. "It went far beyond concessions. It was a total obliteration of the union and the labor agreement all at one time. You might as well have gone back to the company's handbook before the plant was unionized."

Union and management met thirty-one times in August and September. Each time the union offered to make changes to the 1989 contract, and each time the company insisted that the old contract was gone and that any negotiations must be based on its seventeen-page proposal. "We are convinced that the only way this plant can remain viable," said the company over and over, "is to create an entirely new labor agreement to reflect a complete change in the way work is done."[40]

At each weekly union meeting Dave Watts called upon Shinall to give a report. The usual practice, at Staley and elsewhere, was for union and management to keep everything that happened in negotiations a secret until a contract was submitted to members for a vote. As a result, "in past negotiations the rumor mills would go like crazy," recalled Richard Brummett, "and no one really knew what was going on."[41] For the 1992 negotiations the leadership decided that members would receive detailed reports on the negotiations at each weekly solidarity meeting.

Shinall distributed a copy of Tate & Lyle's proposal to each member, provoking outrage. "We could see everything we worked for going down the drain," said Walter Maus.[42] What the company is apparently saying, said Mike Griffin, is "I can treat my employees worse than my competitor and I can take more rights away from my employees, pay them less, make them suffer more, have less job safety, [and thus] have a larger profit margin. The margin is good now, but there is always more if I take away more from my employees."[43]

The company complained that the union was immovable. "This is an issue over change," said its vice president, J. Patrick Mohan. The financial returns from the Decatur plant were "inadequate," requiring a radically revised contract to allow "Staley in Decatur to be competitive."[44]

The union responded that it was willing to make changes to improve productivity but would not agree to a wholesale scrapping of the long-standing contract. "We were willing to make concessions," said unionist Gary Lamb, and "to stop some of the things that management thought were very wasteful. We were willing to meet in the middle of the road, but Tate & Lyle looked like they wanted all of the road." Watts wrote of the union's willingness to change in the *Local 837 News*:

> We want a corporate/manager system that works collectively with all employees to build a stronger competitive edge with rewards going throughout the system, not just to a few at the top. We want a system that promotes hard work, decent wages and benefits, and a sound long-term organization, not one that underestimates, harasses, and bullies the very souls responsible for this company's success. If times are tough, then let's deal with those problems together. If things can be better, then let's all share in the rewards of our input and labor. We encourage change.[45]

"Crisis in Decatur"

In early September 1992—just weeks before the Staley workers were to vote on a contract—Ray Rogers and AIW 837 formally launched the public campaign to expose the company and build broad support for the Staley workers' drive for a fair contract and safe working conditions. Rogers and his staff wrote a four-page brochure titled "Crisis in Decatur" that detailed Tate & Lyle's assault and its attempts to instigate a strike: "Supervisors seem to believe they are running a prison camp: Employees are severely disciplined for minor infractions. Over twenty workers have been penalized with the loss of five to eight days' pay . . . , numerous workers have been reprimanded . . . , and there have been ten firings. . . . Staley is doing everything possible to instigate a strike, and if that doesn't happen, the company is ready to impose a contract or lock the workers out."[46]

"Crisis in Decatur" outlined the safety violations documented in the 1991 OSHA investigation and the $1.6 million in fines levied against the company. It detailed the enormous amount of toxic substances that the company poured into Decatur's water and air. The brochure exposed Staley's huge profits, along with its "sky-high executive salaries and lavish perks" and revealed the ties between Staley and its "competitor" and neighbor, ADM.

When Rogers brought "Crisis in Decatur" to the weekly solidarity meeting, the workers and their families were enthusiastic. "Once you read Ray's literature," said Bill Strohl, "you just become infected with [the campaign]." Hundreds of workers and family members agreed to deliver the material door-to-door. It took several weeks to reach every Decatur doorstep, but fifty thousand brochures were delivered to homes and small businesses across the town. It was like we were "getting *my story* out" to the people, said Art Dhermy. The workers felt that now the people of Decatur would understand and support the union's stand against Tate & Lyle.

Rogers then turned to his database, which reportedly contained sixty-two thousand names of unions and labor activists. The workers soon completed what would turn out to be the first of dozens of such national mailings over the next three years. The mailing received an overwhelming response, with supporters sending the requested letters of protest to Tate & Lyle's CEO and donations to Local 837. Both official declarations and handwritten notes of support accompanied the donations. Feeling that their fate was tied to the success of the Staley workers' campaign, the Decatur ADM workers in Grainmillers Local 103 began a monthly contribution of five hundred dollars to Local 837.

"It's Totally Destructive to Our Collective Bargaining"

By late September, when the contract was about to expire, Local 837 and Tate & Lyle management were just as far apart as when bargaining had begun two months before.

The unionists were willing to compromise but not to surrender all their rights. The company's proposal "clearly destroys years of human rights that are much more important than wages," wrote Dave Watts in the union's newsletter. "It contains destruction of our voice and participation in safety and health programs. And our workplace is one of the most dangerous, not only to us, but to our community. It's totally destructive to our collective bargaining—it is our demise!"[47]

Staley worker Barrie Williams described how the majority of workers felt about the offer: "They put our back right into that corner. And there wasn't any other way to go: you had to fight to get out." On September 30, as the contract expired, over a thousand unionists and supporters, including a large contingent of Caterpillar workers, held a spirited rally. Facing company headquarters, members and supporters wore black armbands in memory of the members of Paperworkers Local 14 in Jay, Maine, who had been permanently replaced in 1988. The armbands were to tell labor relations director Glen Zalkin that workers would not sit by passively while he tried to do in Decatur what he had done in Maine.[48]

At 5:00 P.M. that day negotiations ended and the company had not budged. Shinall told the members that the executive board and bargaining committee unanimously recommended rejection of the contract. Said Watts, "If this is approved, decertification of the union is only a few years away."[49] Members were given six days to consider their vote. In an attempt to buy votes, the company included a two-thousand-dollar bonus for each member if the contract was ratified.

Three days later the local ran a half-page ad in the *Decatur Herald and Review* titled "Don't Take the Sucker Bait." The ad outlined Local 837's position and stated that no other company in the corn industry had asked for such harsh concessions.[50] In a letter to the editor, Staley worker Michael Stewart called the contract a "travesty" and spelled out ten examples of ways the union, through "dedication and hard work," had made financial gains for the company, including a near tripling of profits since 1985.[51]

On October 6, members voted down the company's contract 687 to 29—a 96 percent no vote. Even older workers who were close to retirement put their individual interests aside and stood by their union. In the local's newsletter shortly afterward, special thanks were given to "those 86 members, aged 55 or older, who voted 'no.'"[52]

The war had begun.

"We Just Got That Much Stronger"

With the workers still in the plant and the company's hopes for a strike dashed, Tate & Lyle unilaterally imposed most of its contract upon the workers, evicted the union from its office in the plant, and abolished "excused time" for officers to handle grievances. Said Watts: "Everyone was infuriated with this management that was kicking us around, treating you like a dog, and showing you: 'I'm the boss and you're nothing, and that's the way it's going to be.' The company tried and hoped that they could intimidate us enough to get us mad enough to lose our cool and to strike."[53]

Union officers declared that the company had "crossed the line" from "a war of words" to "direct action against" the workers.[54] The membership "should prepare for the long haul," wrote Watts in the October *Local 837 News*:

This will not be finished quickly. But certainly we can say to ourselves and others that we knew it was coming. We can proudly and solidly say we have unified as a union with support of many family members as well as the community. Take much pride and let's do what we must—outside the plant as well as inside. Solidarity is the answer. They cannot destroy a union that sticks together. . . . Thanks, membership—you truly are a union to be reckoned with, and they know it![55]

In early October the company informed the union that it was ending "dues check-off," the long-established practice in unionized workplaces whereby the company deducts union dues from each workers' paycheck and turns the money over to the union. For fifty years, every month, Local 837 had received members' dues from the company. Now the local had to go back to collecting dues one-on-one on the shop floor and at union meetings.

At the first union meeting after the elimination of check off, a startling 80 percent of union dues were collected. The remaining dues were then collected by hand in the plant. By the October 14 union meeting it was reported that 96 percent had been paid. At each subsequent meeting dues were collected, and the names of those few who weren't paying were read along with their building numbers, so that their co-workers could encourage them to participate. During the nine months they worked without a contract, 97 percent of the local's members voluntarily paid their dues. "Ending dues check-off was one of Staley's major threats over us, that they thought would be our demise," said Watts. "But every time they hammered us with a major threat, we just got that much stronger. They thought it would tear us down, but it built us up."

Despite rejecting the contract, the workers had no intention of striking and being permanently replaced. The local adopted a second strategy to take on Tate & Lyle: in addition to the external, public campaign, workers would also begin a pressure campaign inside the plant.

4

Work-to-Rule

In addition to conducting the corporate campaign, AIW 837 members mobilized on the job to confront management. Led by the seasoned union activist Jerry Tucker, the nine-month in-plant campaign involved hindering production by "working to rule": workers did only what their supervisors told them to do while carrying out shop-floor actions to confront management with a unified membership. Many Staley workers spoke of the work-to-rule campaign as one of the most liberating times of their lives. The campaign not only lowered production, recalled Mike Griffin, a union activist with twenty-seven years at Staley, but also "galvanized the membership and gave them courage, faith, and hope."

Jerry Tucker

It was UAW Local 751 president Larry Solomon who suggested Jerry Tucker to the Staley workers.[1] Tucker is the labor movement's foremost expert on work-to-rule campaigns where, instead of striking, workers organize on-the-job actions to pressure the company to bargain a fair contract. In August 1992 Dave Watts asked Ray Rogers to call Tucker. Rogers and Tucker had known each other for years, though they had never worked together on a campaign. Rogers explained the local's situation, and Tucker was intrigued, so Watts invited him to Decatur to meet with the union's leadership.

Tucker was born in 1938 and raised in a working-class neighborhood in St. Louis. His father was a tool-and-die maker and belonged to the progressive United Electrical Workers union. In 1960 Tucker went to work at General Motors and joined the UAW. When he was laid off in 1962, Tucker hired in at Carter Carburetor, then the largest carburetor company in the world, where he developed the skills he would later use at Staley. After just a year on the job, he was elected shop steward and to the bargaining committee for the three-thousand-member UAW Local 819. In 1965, when he was just twenty-six years old, he became the local's bargaining committee chairperson.

UAW 819 was "a very active local," recalled Tucker; "we always favored the workers' involvement. There were two union meetings each month to cover all three shifts, and the day-shift meeting alone would see 20 percent of the members show up," a much higher involvement than most unions. As with AIW 837 until the defeated strike of 1970, the local had the right to strike over grievances during the term of the contract. "We had a strike every six months just to clear out the grievances" and get them settled fairly, said Tucker. "It gave the workers control. There's no doubt that my experiences at that plant flowed into how I've been able to conduct myself. When you grow up in a spirit of freedom, you operate differently than when you grow up under confining circumstances."

In 1968 Tucker led his first in-plant campaign at Carter Carburetor. Its success opened his eyes to new strategies; it was "a shaping experience." The in-plant strategy was so effective that the Carter local negotiated a better contract that year than the UAW had negotiated with the "Big Three" auto companies, GM, Ford, and Chrysler.

In 1970 the UAW International, impressed with Tucker's talents, hired him onto its St. Louis–based Region 5 staff to coordinate the union's work on legislative and community issues across four states. Through the 1980s, Tucker also continued perfecting the in-plant strategy. Fourteen hundred workers at Moog Automotive in Missouri faced a demand for harsh concessions in 1981, a time when thousands of unemployed workers caught in a national recession would willingly take the jobs of striking workers. Tucker advised the local to keep working after the contract expired and helped members organize inside the plant. After an intense six-month campaign that mobilized the members and drastically slashed production, the company relented and gave the union a good contract without concessions. Tucker led more successful in-plant campaigns in 1983 at Schwitzer Manufacturing in Rolla, Missouri; in 1984 at Bell Helicopter in Fort Worth, Texas; and again in 1984 at LTV Steel in Grand Prairie, Texas.[2]

In 1986, distressed at the concessions the UAW International was negotiating with the auto companies, Tucker helped to form the New Directions reform caucus in UAW Region 5 and ran for regional director. He lost by a hair but appealed to federal court, which ruled in 1988 that the election had suffered serious irregularities. Tucker won the court-ordered rerun. He lost his 1989 reelection bid but continued to help lead the New Directions caucus. In September 1992, when Tucker agreed to come to Decatur, he had just concluded a symbolic run for the UAW presidency to raise the issues of fighting concessions, opposing labor-management cooperation schemes, and broadening union democracy. He was ready to take on a new challenge.[3]

Before leaving for Decatur, Tucker sent the AIW 837 leadership literature on work-to-rule campaigns, most notably a chapter from Dan La Botz's 1991 book *A Troublemakers' Handbook,* which detailed the successful Moog, Schwitzer, LTV, and other in-plant campaigns.[4] Tucker drove from his St. Louis home to Decatur on September 8, 1992. The stretch of road would become very familiar, for he would make this 240-mile round-trip on a weekly basis for the next forty months.

Tucker led a two-hour discussion at a combined meeting of AIW 837's executive board, bargaining committee, and stewards. Their situation, said Tucker, "was almost cookie-cutter. Management had big concessions on the table. They were less economic and more work-rule concessions, but that was becoming the trend."

Tucker also validated the workers' perception that if they struck, they would quickly be permanently replaced. The union leaders hung on every word as Tucker outlined the basics of a work-to-rule campaign, fielded questions, and gave examples from his extensive experience. "Work-to-rule is not walking away from a fight," said Tucker, "but a *different* way to fight." A work-to-rule, he said, is the ultimate member-driven campaign for a just contract. The goal is to show the company that the plant cannot be run successfully without the knowledge and skills of the workers; that the union membership is a unified, determined force with which the company must deal fairly; and that if management refuses to bargain reasonably, then productivity, quality, and thus profits will be severely diminished.[5]

Over the years, explained Tucker, factory workers develop skills that help increase production and turn out a quality product, such as twisting a knob when a machine makes a worrisome sound or knowing when to oil a gear. In a work-to-rule campaign the workers stop bringing their knowledge and experience into their daily work life. They follow company rules to the letter, take no initiative, work at a normal rate of speed, and give no advice or help to supervisors. Workers refuse overtime if the contract permits, grieve every management contract violation, and refuse to work under dangerous health or safety conditions. They show management that the union membership is unified and determined through organized actions such as plant-gate rallies, union T-shirt days, and group grievance hearings to confront management about deteriorating working conditions.

While work-to-rule as a labor tactic largely dropped out of use in the United States after World War II, the concept has long roots in the labor movement. When the Industrial Workers of the World—the Wobblies, a radical union of unskilled workers—was formed in 1905, its members perfected what they called "the conscious withdrawal of efficiency."[6] The strategy was again visible during the rise of industrial unionism led by the Congress of Industrial Organizations in the late 1930s.

Tucker told the AIW 837 leaders that he had never lost a work-to-rule campaign, never failed to win a fair contract, and never failed to get illegally fired activists back on the job with back pay. "When Jerry Tucker came in," said Dan Lane, "there was a lot of credibility there. Jerry was a *worker*; this is a guy who knew what the hell he was talking about. People started clicking. 'This makes *sense*. This can *work*.'"

At the same time, Tucker was gauging the union's level of commitment. "My question to the leadership was, 'What kind of struggle do you really want to engage in?'" recalled Tucker. "My questions were as much of them as they were of me. The leadership convinced me that they were serious."

After meeting with the local's leaders, Tucker stepped up to the podium in the union hall to explain to the members how work-to-rule could succeed. "The idea of a hierarchy, of a vertical leadership, will not work," Tucker told the Staley workers.

> You don't top-down this program; you bottom-up this program. You stimulate workers to use their brains and their hands in ways that will help the union win the struggle. The word *leadership* means something entirely different in the context of a work-to-rule campaign. The local's president is still going to be the president; the top officers remain the officers. But you're going to have a whole lot of people working with you now. You're going to have a whole lot of hands on the oars. You can't manage an effective in-plant strategy from the union hall. You have to broaden the leadership. It has to become very horizontal. The members have to get away from the "call the hall to tell us what to do" mentality. The executive board and the bargaining committee offer basic direction, but *everyone* is a leader. The members have to stop saying "I" and start saying "We."

AIW 837 president Dave Watts understood the need for the membership to play a far bigger role than it had in decades. "Dave realized that a fight of this magnitude is not fought and won by the leadership," said Staley worker Royal Plankenhorn. "It takes the whole union to fight back. Unions at the local level are more democratic than at any other level . . . because we *are* the union. . . . We *run* this show."[7]

Tucker explained the risks—some workers could get fired, and the company might lock out the workforce. "I make a point to say that this is not a painless process," Tucker related. "This is a protected, legal activity, but they could select some of you to fire." Under the 1935 National Labor Relations Act, workers have the right to engage in "concerted activities for the purpose of collective bargaining or other mutual aid or protection." A worker cannot legally be fired for engaging in protected union activity, but employers illegally fire thousands of workers every year.

Tucker observed one strength of AIW Local 837 that would bode well for the members in a work-to-rule campaign: "Every member is a worker, and there were no union bureaucrats who sat around the office all day waiting for the phone to ring. They work. They all felt like the rank-and-file."[8]

In mid-September the membership hired Tucker as an adviser at the modest cost of one hundred dollars for each day he spent in Decatur. Mike Griffin recalled that the workers "wanted to do something, but the overwhelming majority were not comfortable with a strike at that point. When the in-plant strategy was put before them, they saw that there was a hope there, a way of fighting back." The idea that they could keep drawing wages while escalating the fight had a strong appeal.

"Trying to Have a Real Strategy"

After the members overwhelmingly rejected the contract on October 6, Tucker urged formation of a "solidarity team" that would meet with him weekly, and seventy workers quickly responded to his call. While it was a good start, a successful campaign could not be built with only 10 percent of the workforce involved. "You always saw the same seventy-five to eighty at the meetings," recalled Art Dhermy. At first, said Tucker, "We didn't have a critical mass in the whole plant. . . . It would be mythical to say the rank-and-file were ready to go; they needed guidance."

Workers had to fully understand the proposed contract's long-term effects on their individual lives and on their union before they could be convinced to work to rule. The solidarity team organized one-on-one meetings with each worker to explain the seventeen-page contract line by line. Team member Dan Lane recalled: "Part of this is from my military training: you don't send green troops out to fight the battles. There had to be some kind of training; you have to create a mind-set. So I would sit down with union members and go through the contract. . . . We were actually educating people right in the plant. We would take an issue at a time. It was more than, 'This is what the contract language says.' We made sure that people understood that, but we also tried to be broader."[9]

After receiving a comprehensive education about the company's demands and struggling to live with the harsh reality of the imposed contract, more workers became receptive to participating in the campaign. The solidarity team then turned its efforts to educating members about the nuances of working to rule. They explained that work-to-rule is not a slowdown or sabotage, which are not legally protected union activities. "Don't confuse sabotage with working-to-rule," said a shop-floor newsletter. "Let the company people make the decisions!! They will sabotage the company on their own!!"[10]

Learning from the solidarity team how the corn-processing plant was laid out and how the workers made the products, Tucker began to map out the plant. It became clear that there were four key departments—the refinery, dry starch, the mill, and cogeneration—plus the maintenance department, whose members worked throughout the plant. Tucker solicited information about the workers in each key department. Shift by shift, workers tracked each person's involvement in the campaign. Who was participating fully, who was partway in, and who was not yet involved? Where were the union's strengths and weaknesses? Where was the company harassing or disciplining workers? How were the workers in each department responding to company intimidation? Which workers were emerging as leaders in their departments?

To broaden the organizing effort, in November Tucker began to hold departmental meetings, a necessary but time-consuming process. He recalled: "We put notices out in every department calling for the meetings for the purpose of analyzing the contract and shop problems that the members had in each area. It was a marathon. I stayed there for two weeks, one meeting after another. It was important because until we reached the larger membership and got a critical mass, [work-to-rule] wouldn't work."

Tucker guided the meetings, but his major purpose was to hear from the workers. "You don't get up and have big speeches, or have the president harangue people, or tell the people what they should do and give them orders," said Tucker. "You ask people what's going on. . . . You get them to convey the information. . . . You get them talking." The departmental meetings were vital to educating and solidifying the union. When they rejected the contract, some members had advocated for a traditional strike, but now the departmental meetings convinced them that work-to-rule was a viable alternative. Jeanette Hawkins recalled that many workers she talked to wanted to strike: "They were ready to strike, and they didn't want to take another contract rammed down our throat. A lot of the people thought the union was backing down. When work-to-rule was introduced, a lot of people were thinking it was another way the union was getting ready to ram something down our throat. But then, after we got more into it, we found out that they were trying to have a real strategy."

The solidarity team learned how to patiently talk with each worker to educate, steadily increase involvement, and develop leaders. Said Tucker:

> The workers have to buy in—but they do buy in because it's a rational strategy. If they don't immediately understand how empowering it is, they come to understand it. You could see that at Staley. You could see the evolution of the workers, to see them emerge, and develop, and take responsibility, and take charge. It's a process. Some workers are born leaders and throw themselves into the campaign. But for most, there was a threshold moment when they went from passive to active in the struggle. They went from being a relatively good, docile, following-orders employee to somebody who was going to find a way to resist.

The departmental meetings helped to identify the key people, the "go-to" people, as Tucker called them—those who were most reliable, were most willing to take risks to challenge the company on the job, and had the most complete information about their departments. For Tucker these were the "key people, the operational cadre." Although a handful of the elected union leaders were go-to people, the majority were rank-and-file members.

In many ways the Decatur Staley plant was ideal for working to rule. It was an old plant with decades-old machinery run by an experienced workforce. "You know what it is?" posed Staley worker Richard Brummett, who had twenty-four years in the plant. "Everybody knows you got to kick a Model A to get it to start. But it takes twenty years to know where to kick it."[11]

Brummett quickly became one of the shop-floor leaders. When there is a problem in your area, said Brummett, "you call up the boss and say, 'This piece of equipment is doing such-and-such.' And he says, 'What do you think we ought to do?' And you tell him, 'You come up here and you tell *me* what to do. That's what they pay you for.' And if he tells you to do something and you know it's wrong, you do it anyway."[12]

"You just did what you had to do to get by," explained Mike Dulaney. "The little extras that you might have done on your own to make things run smoother, we didn't do that. And the problem was nobody knew what to tell you to do. The supervisors didn't know. They didn't work the job. Most of them had not been there for more than three, four years at the most. I've been in the plant *twenty-five years!*"[13]

Most Staley workers had more than two decades in the plant, often working the same job, but the newly hired supervisors were ignorant about the idiosyncrasies of the aging factory. The new supervisors were engineers straight out of college or, as Barrie Williams said, "people straight out of Dairy Queen or the lumberyards—know-nothings."[14]

"The thing that scared the company the most was when they realized that we started using this [our heads] instead of this [our backs]," said nineteen-year Staley veteran Danny Rhodes. "They looked over and said, 'Hey, they're using their minds. We have lost control. If they start using their mind and target it towards us, we've lost control of that plant.' . . . That's what this is all about, control. And we took that power and control away from them."[15] Bill Scheibly put it succinctly: "We are just letting them know that they need us to run that plant."[16]

Even as they asserted their control over daily operations, however, the Staley workers exercised great caution in their volatile chemical plant. They were careful not to put themselves, other employees, or the Decatur community at risk. "We *made sure* it was safe," explained Bill Strohl.

As Tucker's department meetings continued, attendance grew and the rank-and-file's sense of ownership in the campaign blossomed. The meetings allowed them to turn their rage into action. "Don't get mad—Get involved—Fight back!" the local urged. "The important thing for us is to avoid acting on our anger alone. We've been fighting smart for many months, and we've got to continue to do the same."[17]

During their Tuesday night union meetings the workers shared stories, laughed together at tales of management's ineptness, discussed successes and setbacks, and built up one another's courage and determination to escalate the fight. The workers' audacity and leadership skills were developing at exponential rates. At the meetings, recalled Tucker, "a worker—not a leader used to giving speeches—would get up and give a report on their area. When they sat down they would feel a little more powerful, feel a sense of satisfaction. The idea is to pull people out, get them to convey information, get them talking. You start where workers are at and you bring them along. My role was to help develop leaders."

The workers heard success stories from other departments and discussed how to adapt the tactics to their own work sites. The meetings always ended with the question, "What creative actions can the union take next?" In addition, the workers began to meet inside the plant in each department. "We started having union meetings in the plant at lunch, breaks, shift changes," said Bob Miller.[18]

"You Are Your Brother's Keeper"

The in-plant campaign involved more than just actions to decrease production. The workers also launched a series of creative actions that demonstrated to management the magnitude of their solidarity and resolve. Both types of actions were fundamental to the campaign and served to fuel each other.

The Staley workers regularly wore red union T-shirts to work, along with union caps and an extensive array of union buttons. Workers honked their horns as they drove out of the parking lot after their shifts. At times the leadership called for an action where hundreds of workers would gather at the plant gate before they marched en masse into work.[19]

These actions built a spirit of solidarity, lifted morale, and taught the idea of collective action. "The elation of solidarity becomes addictive," said Jerry Fargusson.[20] Beyond that, the job actions built friendships and camaraderie, and that strengthened unity. Moreover, the workers became more aggressive as they felt support from one another. "You are your brother's keeper in an in-plant strategy," noted Barrie Williams.[21]

In the massive plant more than half the workers carried company-furnished radios to provide production updates or report machine breakdowns. During the work-to-rule the workers transformed the radios into a weapon of solidarity. "We used radios to communicate throughout the plant," recalled Emery Scrimpsher.

You started hearing "Solidarity Forever" [the labor anthem] being sung. . . . There was a preacher that came on and preached sermons [calling on the company to repent]. There were whistles being blown on the radio. It was childish stuff. But a lot of these supervisors did nothing but run around trying to find these radios. A lot of them would broadcast outside of their particular departments, so the supervisors didn't know [where the broadcasts were coming from]. . . . Those radios drove them nuts. They hated the radios![22]

Dan Lane explained how the radios helped unify the members:

In Five and Ten Building there had been divisions between process workers and the mechanics, between the older and younger workers, men and women, black and white. So when the radio use was broadened, people read things like Martin Luther King's "I Have a Dream" speech. It brought people together. . . . This grew from a one-person thing to all of a sudden guests were coming on. And as this radio show is going on, we were meeting in our department with people one-on-one to discuss the issues. People started getting more involved. People started to feel like maybe we can challenge Tate & Lyle.

The grievance procedure had become less and less effective since Tate & Lyle's takeover, but under the imposed contract the official grievance procedure became virtually worthless. So, with Jerry Tucker's guidance on their legal latitude, workers began to hold mass, on-the-spot grievance hearings. "Under normal circumstances," noted Tucker, "if you've got a problem, you call your steward. Your steward says, 'Okay, I'll check into it and get back to you,' and then maybe he files a grievance. Then in a few weeks, if it's not settled, the steward takes it to the chairman of the Bargaining Committee or the Chief Steward. Under the in-plant strategy, you teach the art of collective confrontation at the shop level."[23]

Tucker explained how the confrontations spread:

Two workers have both decided to make a commitment that they are going to do the best they can to work to rule. They look at each other and say, "Now how can we reinforce each other? Let's get five other people and go see the boss," which is something that hasn't been done. . . . They step over a threshold. Then somewhere down the line a half-dozen other people say, "Did you see what those crazy fools did? Maybe we ought to try that." . . . People take a certain step and they bounce off each other. It's a synergy. . . . These group grievances all have to do with telling the boss, "You don't run this place—we do."

In the local's in-plant newsletter, members were told, "Remember you have the right to have as many union people present as you feel comfortable with when confronting a company or salaried person with any issue or dispute. Never go in one-on-one. You will lose!!!"[24] Many carried a laminated copy of their

"Weingarten rights"—protections the law gives to unionists—in their hard hats. If a supervisor reprimanded a worker, he or she would read to the foreman: "If the discussion I am being asked to enter could in any way lead to my discipline or termination or impact on my personal working conditions, I ask that a union steward, representative, or officer be present. Unless I have this union representation I respectfully choose not to participate in this discussion."[25]

Many times, when a worker was called into a supervisor's office to be reprimanded, large numbers would stop their work and pile in after the worker. In some cases an entire department would stop work to join a worker in the office. Sometimes whistles would be blown to signal that a worker was in trouble. As the work-to-rule campaign unfolded, the workers were devising their own, on-the-spot method of resolving complaints. Of course, workers had to return to work when ordered or else risk discipline or discharge. But even then the few minutes off the job affected productivity, and the boss got the message that the workers were unified.

Mike Griffin, who had been repeatedly singled out and harassed, described how he and others transformed the Twenty-nine Building: "We decided we needed a grievance hearing. . . . [We made the boss come in] at three o'clock in the morning. I had thirty guys in there, almost the whole night-shift maintenance crew and half the process people, and he about panicked. He said, 'What is this?' I said, 'It's called a grievance hearing. This is where we're going to tell you what we think you're doing wrong.' And the war was on. It lasted about two hours. He was so mad he couldn't see straight."

The workers developed a monthly newsletter, *Local 837 News*, edited by Jerry Dilbeck and Robert Luka Jr. and mailed to every member. It included reports by Dave Watts, Jim Shinall, and other leaders on the status of negotiations and on the corporate campaign.

The workers on the shop floor also wrote and distributed an underground weekly newsletter that became a mainstay of the in-plant fight. The *Midnight Express* detailed, in unsigned articles, the errors and accidents of the nonunion contract workers, management's harassment of union activists, and the bumbling of Staley supervisors and top management. Once a week on the midnight shift, a member would walk to the plant gate to pick up his lunch from his wife and secretly retrieve bundles of the *Midnight Express*. Copies of the one- or two-page handwritten newsletter were then distributed to key activists throughout the plant, who would circulate it in their departments and leave stacks in break rooms. "The *Midnight Express* was very important," recalled Tucker. "It's taking steps against authority. . . . The more empowerment you feel, then the more ready you are for other things." The clandestine activities surrounding the newspaper were never uncovered by management and were known to only a handful of workers.

Union members and supervisors alike anticipated the weekly arrival of the *Midnight Express*, for it often detailed management's laziness and ineptness. "The supervisors really sweated the publication of their names," said Gary Lamb.[26] The paper hammered away against unsafe working conditions and reported on the danger posed by the untrained nonunion workers brought in by the Harmony Construction Company. As Tate & Lyle managers harassed and bullied the workers, *Midnight Express* exposed and ridiculed them.

"Grabbing the Bull"

Not all the union's 762 members participated in the work-to-rule, and some contributed more than others. One difficulty was that it ran counter to the members' natural work ethic. As Dick Schable explained, "The work ethics and the knowledge of this group of people are probably some of the best in Illinois . . . , so [working to rule] was really hard for a lot of people to do. In addition, many workers were reluctant to play a leading role because it meant constant confrontation with their supervisors. Tucker insisted,

> If you think [work-to-rule] is easier than striking, then you are all wet. Because if you think it is easier to stand in front of your boss, day in and day out, and tell him you are not going to do it the way he *says* for you to do it at that moment, but that you are going to do it the way the *rules* say to do it, . . . if you think it is easier to hold mass grievances, . . . if you think that is easier than walking a picket line once or twice a week—then you are full of stuff. Everybody started dealing with that.

And although the union had set up a casualty fund to provide full pay to any worker fired as a result of union activity, the fear of discharge was still there. "The first thought that comes to your mind," recalled Dike Ferris, "is, 'How many people are going to get fired?' because the company is going to start accusing you of doing a slowdown." "Some of us . . . saw this as, 'Hey, we're going to be in a fight,'" recalled Dan Lane. "There were others thinking that by flashing Ray Rogers and Jerry Tucker out there . . . the company might capitulate and offer enough back that we could get an agreement. There were others looking at retirement that said, 'Hey, maybe I can get out of here. I don't want to mess with this.' There were all kind of different agendas there."

Art Dhermy estimated that about one-third of the workforce was aggressively working to rule, while many others were supportive but not taking the lead. Dhermy, who worked in the boiler room, vividly described the levels of participation:

> My department was like everybody else's. You had the ones that were going to grab the bull. You had the ones that might grab the tail and be drug along. And

then you had the ones on the other side of the fence to make sure the bull wasn't going to get them. Ninety percent of the time, my hands were on the bull's horns. It made me feel good to know that I had somebody next to me at my shoulder, grabbing the bull's tail. I had no animosity to the ones not grabbing the horns. We needed some standing out in the pasture watching our backs. Just because you don't run up there and grab the bull doesn't mean you can't do your thing your way. And then there are those who were in the pasture but were on the other side of the fence, but they often came to the union meeting—at least they're in the pasture. You probably had 75 to 80 workers grabbing the bull, 150 to 200 workers grabbing the tail, and about 75 to 80 in the pasture. And everybody else was on the other side of the fence, but still in the pasture.

As time passed Dhermy added, "that fence got expanded some," and more people stepped up their participation. "There was peer pressure that forced some of the less inclined to get on board," recalled Ferris. "Even the less inclined were put in the position that, 'Wait a minute; all the rest of my people are doing this, and here I am still helping this company out.'"

For the core of workers who aggressively led the work-to-rule campaign, "it was almost a spiritual thing," said Dan Lane.

> People started moving together, starting to understand better who the company was. It was like you were peeling away these layers, that this image that the company tried to paint as this wonderful grandfather that was there to take care of his grandchildren, that all of a sudden was being seen for who he really was, this huge ugly ogre that had no feelings, no concern. . . . It was like undressing this company for the first time, understanding as workers who we really were, that we need each other, that our interests weren't with the company but with one another. When I say spiritual . . . a worker's color, their sex, or their age no longer became important. What was important was the unity in order for us and our families to survive. . . . To me that was a liberation. It was like reidentifying your soul.

By March 1993, five months into the campaign, the work-to-rule effort was steadily building steam, and the number of workers participating was growing. The workers' sense of their power had dramatically increased, and their confidence was strong. As Bob Willoughby said, "This is the most solid group of people I've ever seen in my life. . . . It's almost like a school of fish. When one turns, they all turn."[27]

Local 837 members learned that Staley's customers were hit hard by the work-to-rule. Deliveries were often too little, too late, and lacked their usual quality, resulting in a steady stream of complaints and returns. "In-plant tactics were very effective," said Jerry Tucker, "and customer concern was rising apace with that."[28] The Staley workers could also see the company's desperate measures to fill orders. Jeanette Hawkins knew that with soy sauce, for instance, "you couldn't have sediment in it. [But] the supervisors were new, and they would get cocky. I brought it to the supervisor and showed him all the sediment. He said, 'Ship it. The truck is out there; ship it.' I let it go."

"Production was down from 140,000 bushels [of ground corn] a day to 80 to 90,000," recalled Ferris. "The company let us know how terrible things were going. . . . They were trying to find instances to fire people." By spring the union estimated that production had fallen 50 percent, but Staley spokesperson Mohan would admit to only 32 percent.[29] "For every day you fall behind, it takes two days to catch up," said Tucker. "Management could see that they could never catch up. The bottom line is to put that production in the ditch."

"Things were going the way we wanted to," said Dan Lane in 1993. "It was getting to be like a real strike *in* the plant."[30] "We're fighting the battle of our lives," declared Dave Watts, "and through this, the entire membership of this local knows what class consciousness and class struggle are all about."[31]

5

The Temperature Rises

In the fall of 1992 the union's corporate campaign began to heat up as workers repeatedly distributed brochures door-to-door in Decatur and organized demonstrations against two banks with Staley officers on their boards. In early 1993, however, responding to the work-to-rule campaign, the company began a counteroffensive by implementing rotating twelve-hour shifts, harassing the workers at mandatory meetings, and firing leading activists. The union retaliated by escalating its tactics with a plantwide walkout.

"It's Our Solidarity versus Theirs!"

Beginning with the "Crisis in Decatur" brochure, Ray Rogers and his Corporate Campaign firm produced many flyers and brochures for workers to distribute locally and through national mailings. The literature conveyed three themes. First, the Staley workers' fight was about dignity, respect, and safety on the job. A flyer distributed throughout Decatur noted:

> This dispute is not about wages—it's about rights in the workplace. It's about control—Staley/Tate & Lyle want total control. It's also about dignity, both on and off the job. Imagine if you worked in a plant with hazardous materials and dangerous equipment that has killed, maimed, and severely wounded workers. Wouldn't you want protection at that job? If you were injured, wouldn't you want adequate medical care? Wouldn't you want to know that when you left your home to go to work, you were going to come back in one piece? Well, we do, too, and that's why we can't accept what Staley is trying to do to our jobs.[1]

Second, the fight was not just to defend the Staley workers but to protect their whole community against a multinational corporation that disregarded

Decatur citizens. "Corporate Greed Is Tearing Decatur Apart" proclaimed the union's banners and placards. The literature detailed the corporate allies supporting Tate & Lyle's union-busting strategy, especially Decatur-based Archer Daniels Midland. A flyer addressed to Decatur citizens read:

> This is your community and you have a stake in the Staley dispute. For months, we have been asking the question: Is Decatur the "Pride of the Prairie" or a Company Town? Everyone in this town depends on a solid industrial base to have a good life. If you own a small business, you depend on customers with money to spend. If you have children, you depend on unions to protect decent paying jobs when it's time for them to work. If you live or work in the "Pride of the Prairie," you depend on unions to maintain wages, protect jobs, and give workers a voice in how this town is run; to provide a balance between the haves and the have-nots. We are not fighting for ourselves alone. If we were, we would have quit long ago. This fight is about our future and our children's future.[2]

Third, the issues at stake extended beyond the local community to include *all* working people. Tate & Lyle was intent on union-busting, and if it succeeded, then corporate America would gain an edge in its assault on all workers, union and nonunion. "Workers everywhere have a stake in the Staley struggle," proclaimed one flyer: "Given the high profile of this fight a Staley victory in Decatur will become a rallying point for big business everywhere. Corporate America understands the importance of the Staley battle and is answering Staley's call for corporate solidarity. . . . That's why the slogan of Local 837 is 'It's Our Solidarity versus Theirs! Help us Fight the Union-Busters!'"[3]

After the first "Crisis in Decatur" national mailing was completed and the workers had gone door-to-door, Rogers proposed banks as the focal point for the corporate campaign. On November 19, 1992, the union held a press conference to call for a boycott of First of America, a chain with 551 branches in the Midwest, including one in Decatur. The union demanded that Staley board chair Robert Powers be removed from First of America's board of directors.

Rogers's strategy to target banks stemmed from his research on the interlocking relationships between banks and corporations. Banks, Rogers asserted, are a corporation's lifeline, supplying short- and long-term loans. "When the bank receives pressure, it will put pressure on the targeted company. When the bank starts getting phone calls and letters, and people start asking questions and threaten to withdraw their accounts, and when unions start withdrawing their large accounts—then that captures the banks' attention. . . . And the bank will tell the company, 'Get this thing settled, or you get off our board and we'll get off your board.' Now that's divide and conquer!"[4]

By moving the fight into the corporate boardrooms, Rogers argued, the union's strategy was to "let them begin to beat each other up." Rogers's research also demonstrated a connection, via First of America's board of directors, between the Staley and Caterpillar companies. In their second door-to-door distribution to fifty thousand Decatur homes and businesses, the Staley workers delivered a four-page brochure, "They Get the Gold, We Get the Grief," which explained the Staley-Cat connection:

> Staley and Caterpillar are leaders of the management attack on the rights of working people. Rather than shunning these corporate outlaws, First of America has allied itself with them. James Wogsland, vice chairman of Caterpillar, serves on First of America's board of directors, while Robert Powers, chairman of Staley, sits on the board of First of America–Decatur. In other words, key architects of the union-busting policies of these companies are also top policymakers of First of America.

After leafleting the Decatur community, carloads of AIW 837 members began to travel regularly to surrounding cities to distribute brochures in front of bank branches. "In all the towns where the bank has branches we're getting the daily and weekly newspapers to write stories about the Staley struggle," explained Rogers. "The bank boycotts gave the local news a reason to come out and interview you."

The Staley workers also brought their message to union halls. Because of Caterpillar's connection to First of America, and with the Cat workers still stinging from their April 1992 strike defeat, the biggest supporters of the bank boycott were UAW locals 974 and 751, representing thousands of Caterpillar workers in Peoria and Decatur. These locals distributed the Staley flyers at all Caterpillar plant gates—including twenty-seven gates in East Peoria alone—and joined the door-to-door canvassing in Decatur.

The campaign against First of America resulted in thousands of protest letters and many withdrawals. International Brotherhood of Electrical Workers Local 146 in Decatur withdrew $900,000; UAW Local 724 in Lansing, Michigan, $500,000; Laborers Local 159 in Decatur, $180,000; UAW Local 2488 in Bloomington, Illinois, $35,000; Amalgamated Transit Union Local 859 in Decatur, $7,000; and the 30,000-member United Food and Commercial Workers Local 951 in Grand Rapids, Michigan, withdrew an undisclosed amount.[5]

Less than two months after the union launched its boycott, the corporate campaign won its first victory. On January 7, 1993, Bob Powers was forced to resign from the board of directors of First of America Bank–Decatur. "We all should be proud of the support from our community," declared the *Midnight Express.* "We are winning whether the company admits it or not!"[6]

On February 10, 1993, Rogers launched a campaign targeting St. Louis–based Magna Bank, which had $3.6 billion in assets and eighty-five branches in Illinois and Missouri. The campaign involved hundreds of Staley workers again distributing boycott materials locally door-to-door and at banks and union events across the region. Campaign literature focused on Staley officer J. Patrick Mohan, who sat on Magna's board of directors. Mohan wore many hats at Staley: executive vice president, general counsel, secretary, and director. As the corporation's most prominent spokesperson, Mohan quickly became its most identified and most resented official.

At Rogers's suggestion the union organized demonstrations at the homes of Mohan and the newly appointed CEO for the Decatur plant, Larry Pillard. On March 10, 1993, some two hundred and fifty workers stood outside Mohan's home and sang solidarity songs. "Mohan has a fine spread," said Dave Watts, "three or four acres with a massive palace . . . , yet they [claim they] need all of these concessions from us, the ones who made the profits they live off."[7] Within the next month the workers staged two protests at banquets where Mohan and Pillard were speaking and then organized a march to Pillard's home, even though the county sheriff and state's attorney had warned the union not to come.

On May 14 Mohan resigned from Magna's board. "It's a tremendous victory and it shows the potential labor has in using its economic strength," declared Rogers.[8] The Staley workers were energized; it was a "confidence builder," said Barrie Williams. "Our people were really overjoyed when we got Mohan off the board," recalled Dike Ferris. "That was kind of a baby step with the bank campaign. We could get a board member off and show a little bit of pressure. We were thinking maybe there's some hope out there. . . . It kind of rejuvenated our people."

In April, for the fourth time in seven months, the workers went door-to-door distributing a new brochure. The six-page "Deadly Corn" brochure detailed several personal, compelling accounts of the extreme hazards of work at Staley and the new management's "lost concern for human life." The centerpiece was the story of Jim Beals's death on the job. The brochure explained that, contrary to company assertions, the safety issue was the number-one reason for the labor dispute:

> "You've got to die sometime." This is how a supervisor at Staley responded when a worker complained about being asked to handle hazardous materials without proper safety equipment. Such an attitude is typical of the company's lack of concern for the well-being of its workers. . . . To an outsider, corn processing sounds like a safe and benign industry. What could be less threatening than ears of corn? It turns out, however, that the production of sweeteners, starches and other corn products . . . is anything but harmless—both for Staley's workers and for the residents of the surrounding community.

For the Staley workers, handing out literature door-to-door, outside grocery stores, and at other unions' plant gates was a new experience. Traveling to other cities to discuss their situation with complete strangers, handling the media, and building a network of support required an aggressive and adventurous spirit. Despite the initial awkwardness most of them felt, their goal of a fair contract superseded any qualms, and the bank campaigns and work-to-rule fueled their confidence.

"We Both Have Headaches All the Time from Lack of Sleep"

In the summer of 1992 Staley management had expected a demoralized Local 837 membership to accept the company's concession-laden contract. Failing that, they expected the workers to strike in October 1992, and they prepared to run the plant with scabs. The union's decision not to strike, and then its aggressive work-to-rule campaign, caught management completely off guard. By early 1993, however, in the face of declining productivity and rising worker morale and resistance, the company regrouped to attack the union more forcefully. Its plan was three-pronged: to impose the rest of its contract; to escalate discipline, including the firing of leading activists; and to hold mandatory departmental meetings to intimidate and threaten the workers.

On February 18, 1993, operations director Red Geurts announced that the company intended to fully impose its contract, including twelve-hour shifts, with workers rotating from days to nights and back again every thirty days. The next day he sent a memo to salaried employees:

> Unfortunately the [bargaining] committee clearly and repeatedly advised us that they would never accept work teams and rotating shifts. It is clear from what happened today at the meeting that the differences between the company and the union are growing wider. This is exemplified by [committee chairperson] Jim Shinall's statement this morning, "You can do whatever you want. We are not agreeing or helping. We don't care if there is no plant left here at all, and that includes you guys on that side of the table." . . . Regardless of the obstacles we face, we remain committed to do what is necessary to make this plant competitive.[9]

At the union meeting the following Tuesday, Shinall reported Geurts's threats and his own retort. He was met with deafening applause. The company could legally impose its contract, however, and mandatory twelve-hour rotating shifts would begin on March 15.

Shortly after the new schedule began, Rose Feurer and the St. Louis–based Labor Vision cable television crew went to Decatur to produce a compelling thirty-minute video titled *Deadly Corn*. In the film, Dee and Rudy Scott discussed what the rotating shifts had done to their lives. Rudy had started at Staley in 1969 and Dee in 1990. With the toxic chemicals and the amount of physical labor and mental concentration involved in their jobs, they were worried about the toll the extra four hours would take. Dee explained that she and her co-workers were now scheduled to work from 6 A.M. to 6 P.M. for three days and then had three days off. After a month of working the day shift, she rotated to nights, again with three days on and three days off. After another month, she returned to the day shift. Dee felt that this complete disruption of her life and sleep meant she had surrendered her life to the company. If she refused to come in when a supervisor called her to work on her days off, she risked being discharged.

Dee Scott described her life under rotating shifts as constant grogginess, particularly when she was on nights. She wanted to keep a more-or-less normal sleep cycle during her days off, so on her first off day during a night rotation, she would try to stay up but inevitably fell asleep, exhausted. The second off day she often felt dazed as she tried to adjust to being awake during the day and sleeping at night. She would enjoy her third day off, but by then it was time to go to work again on the night shift and stay awake for twenty-four hours. "We both have headaches all the time from lack of sleep," Dee said. "Everything is disturbed. . . . Even your bodily functions are disturbed. You're not as alert; your reaction time slows down."[10]

Dee and Rudy Scott had taken some comfort from the company's promise that the Scotts, as well as the other eleven married couples in the plant, would be assigned to the same shifts. But when rotating shifts began, the Scotts and the other eleven couples were all assigned to opposite shifts and days off.

Virtually every worker in the plant suffered sleep problems and a resulting onslaught of other physical problems. Rick Brummett, who had been in the plant since 1969, echoed the Scotts' experience:

> You don't get any sleep on your time off. I've asked guys that work on my shift— we all wake up the same time in the night; we all get about two or three hours of sleep. Then, if you have to work overtime, that's on your day off. And if it's the middle day of your three days off, then you have no time off. . . . You get to the point where, if you don't have the date on your watch, you don't know what day it is. . . . Before the [imposed] contract, we had voluntary overtime, and I had been forced to work maybe eight or ten times in twenty years. But now, if it's on your day off, they can nail you.[11]

Rick's wife, Mary, recalled that Rick became sick and lost thirty days of work as a result of the new schedule:

> Rick was worn out. He couldn't sleep. One night I met Rick at the parking lot of the union hall. He was literally laying across the fender of the car because he was so sick. He said, "We can't go to the union meeting because you have to take me to the hospital." So I took him, and they diagnosed him as having pneumonia. . . . The doctor got real upset and said he was going to send a letter to Staley telling them what he thought of them with their twelve-hour rotating shifts.

Dave Hays, too, was featured in the *Deadly Corn* video, for he had contracted lung cancer from breathing dangerous dusts and chemicals in the twenty-five years he had worked at the plant. The labor movement, Hays said, had "fought for years to get 8-hour shifts and the 40-hour workweek. Now it seems to me that we're going right back to the way it was in the 1920s."[12]

Marie Sigmon, the wife of thirty-three-year worker Don Sigmon, described the impact on families:

> We didn't have a family life with them working 12-hour shifts. They'd go to work at six in the morning and come home at six at night. By the time they were through with everything it was about nine o'clock and time to go to bed. People couldn't go to church on Sundays. The people with young kids couldn't be at their children's school functions. It was devastating for the families. And that's supposed to be our way of life, the family unit. But not anymore. Not with this.[13]

Henry Kramer said that his children had to get professional counseling to cope with the stress: "When I'm working I can see my kids one hour a day. My boy plays basketball—I can't see any of his games. My daughter is on the drill team—I can't see her perform. She's a senior this year, and I have to work on her graduation night."[14] "I can't be involved in church activities, scouting, or even bowling league," said Denton Larrimore. "I can't be involved in anything outside of work. It's like we're tools the company uses and then stores in a toolbox when it doesn't need us."[15]

On June 20, three months after rotating shifts were introduced, the *Decatur Herald and Review* finally ran a story on their debilitating effects. "You never get in a groove," Bob Jelks, a twenty-seven-year employee, told the paper. "You never sleep well. . . . It's like you're not part of the family." Jelks said that once he had driven home on the wrong side of the road. Added Mike Griffin, "Your sex life goes out the window, and I'm too young for that!"[16]

Under the revised schedule, Staley was able to add one hundred hours of work per worker per year—yet workers forfeited up to six thousand dollars a year in lost overtime pay. For many workers it felt as if their whole lives had been reduced to the wallet-sized company-issued calendar that marked their days on and off.

The workers appealed to the company and offered research proving that twelve-hour rotating shifts were dangerous to workers' health, led to more job accidents, and destroyed family life and participation in the community. But the company was unyielding. Management argued that twelve-hour shifts were necessary to save money, and rotating shifts was more "fair" for all. If it's so fair, retorted Local 837, why not put it to a vote? Leaders knew that the members would vote against the new schedule because it had been a major reason for the 96 percent contract rejection vote in October 1992. "It is touching to read that management is concerned about fairness," union leaders wrote to the company. "Your claim that rotating shifts would be fairer is classic doubletalk. The fact is that seniority is the fair system. . . . There is nothing fair about mistreating everyone equally."[17]

Under the union's old contract, workers chose their shifts by seniority. Now workers with over twenty years were forced to rotate from days to nights. The imposed contract also allowed the company virtually total control over job assignments and created a new two-tiered arrangement, with process jobs newly classified as "support operators" or "regular operators." Workers with decades of seniority could now be classified support operators and paid two dollars less an hour, while low-seniority workers could be assigned as regular operators. Jeanette Hawkins, with nineteen years in the plant, described the tension that she felt with lower-seniority workers:

> I wanted Sunday off [to go to church], and this other girl wanted Sunday off so she could go dancing. She was friends with Mike, the supervisor. So the supervisor said, "You know, Jeanette, you don't have seniority no more, so you can't [take off] Sunday." [The other woman] had three or four years in the plant, and I had nineteen. The supervisor said, "No, Jeanette, you got to work." I said, "You ain't Jesus and I won't be here." . . . [Loss of seniority] took us back to the "good old buddy" days.

Hawkins was forced to use personal time to go to church. She and the other workers knew that the company had set a trap, trying to pit them against one another. The workers addressed it at their union meetings, encouraging all to remain united and not turn against one another. As the union later said to the citizens of Decatur in a flyer, "The loss of basic rights, the cruel and pointless twelve hour shifts, and the on-the-job harassment were unbearable. It was as if, when we went to work, we went back 100 years to the days of sweatshops and robber barons. We made a great deal of money for Staley and we deserve better than this—we deserve to be treated like people, not slaves to management's wish list. Profit is all that matters to them—not 20, 30, or even 40 years of loyalty."[18]

Management again brought in more than two hundred supervisors and non-union workers from its other factories—the hated "nannies" first introduced in June 1992—to monitor the workers. As was mentioned previously, union members believed they were there to act as scabs in the event of a strike or lockout. The union reported that the company had rented twenty-six apartments at nine hundred dollars a month to house the nannies.[19] Members discussed the matter and determined they would refuse to share information with the nannies. Rosie Brown recalled, "They would learn our jobs, so they could lock us out and do our jobs. We're not going to give them any training when we know what they're going to do! A couple of times we got into it with the bosses over this. I said, 'I ain't training him! He can walk along, but I ain't got nothing to say to him.'"

As weeks went by and the workers stuck to their work-to-rule and again refused to strike, the company sent the nannies home.

Initially, the rotating shifts disrupted the work-to-rule campaign. The workers were in a constant state of exhaustion, and departmental solidarity was hindered. "Communication became more difficult because of rotating shifts," recalled Dan Lane. "We had people who had worked their shifts together for years. They trusted each other. All of a sudden, management took that whole thing and shook it up, and you're with different people. It took a period of re-learning and retrusting. There was still a sense of slowing down production, but production wasn't hit as hard as it had been in late 1992 and early 1993."

"The Company Couldn't Deal with It"

As part of its aggressive response to the union's successful work-to-rule, in April 1993 the company renewed its mandatory "state of the plant" departmental meetings. These meetings, which had first been held the previous summer before the contract expired, were meant to intimidate workers with antiunion rhetoric and procompany platitudes. "The company was trying to force feed us all the lies that they could," relayed Staley worker Dick Schable. "They even went to the point to say that we needed behavior modification classes. That just frosted me." "The mandatory meetings," recalled Barrie Williams, "were designed to try to negotiate with individual groups and take [power] away from the union leadership."

When the meetings started up again in 1993, however, workers were determined to take control. They strategized several possible responses. One popular idea was the "hear no, see no, speak no" approach, where no one said a word. Each worker sat silently with a stoic face as management gave an antiunion presentation and asked for comments. Art Dhermy told one story:

> My boss was a presenter. [When he was finished,] he asked if there were any questions. I stood up and asked each of the managers how well they slept at night. "Is your conscience bothering you?" Only one answered. I said, "Okay, that's my question," and I turned around and walked out. I was in the front row and everyone else followed me. My boss said, "We haven't dismissed you!" I said, "You asked for questions. There are no more questions. So we're out of here."

Another strategy was the blitz. The minute managers walked into a meeting, the workers all started shouting at once: "I've got a safety problem in my work area!" "The nonunion contractors are violating OSHA regulations!" "The toilet doesn't work!" The blitz caused the managers to storm out, prematurely ending the meeting.

As each department designed its own tactics, a friendly competition developed as to who could come up with the most creative resistance. At one meeting, in the midst of management's presentation the workers suddenly stood and sang "God Bless America." At another meeting they recited the Pledge of Allegiance. At other meetings the workers chanted, "No contract, no peace!" and "Union, union, union!" In all cases, the stunned Staley managers stopped the meetings.

Dan Lane recalled a creative effort in the Five and Ten Building: "Everyone was going to wear red T-shirts and not say anything. One worker [Nancy Hanna] had bought Groucho Marx masks at a novelty store and distributed them as people walked in. Management started to talk, and all at once we all put on the masks. Of course management's eyes are going like this [bulging]! Then everybody got up and walked out."

"When the union retaliated at the meetings, the company saw that they couldn't deal with it," said Frankie Travis. Seven unionists were suspended without pay because they were "disruptive" at a state of the plant meeting, but members in their department came to the rescue. "We said, 'Look, if they get time off, we all get time off,'" said Barrie Williams. "If you suspend one of us for insubordination, you suspend all of us."[20] Management abruptly ended the suspension and returned the seven workers to the plant.

Before the in-plant campaign began, Jerry Tucker had advised the workers that the company would pick out union activists and illegally fire them in an effort to decapitate the campaign. In March 1993 the firings began and continued for the next three months.

Also that March the company ordered workers to remove all union stickers or signs they had put up during the work-to-rule, except those on the union bulletin board (which the law requires companies to permit). Some workers then pasted the stickers on their clothes and hats. When workers were ordered to take union logos off plant windows, some painted "AIW 837" on the entire window. Dan Lane described the events leading to his firing in the midst of this:

> There was still a sign up inside Five and Ten Building with the AIW and Staley logos, and all the customers' logos around them. They're really proud of it. . . . It was located so customers could see the sign. We unbolted the sign and took it down. It was plywood, so we cut off the AIW logo. There were four workers holding the sign and I was cutting. A foreman walked in and started screaming at the top of his voice, going nuts. They sent me home, and I was discharged the next day.

The next edition of the *Midnight Express* printed a five-by-seven picture of Lane with his wife, Donna, and five children; a warning accompanied the image: "Look at this picture. Look real close because this could be a picture of you and your family. This is Dan Lane, process bargaining committeeman. He was discharged for following his supervisor's instructions." Lane's nickname in the plant was "Bronco." In the months after he was fired, when the call "Bronco" went out over the radio, it was a code to alert unionists that someone was being fired and to rally to that worker's side. Lane's was just the first in what became a steady stream of firings.

On May 21 the outspoken maintenance worker Mike Griffin became the third. Griffin had twenty-six years in the plant and had served as steward and bargaining committee member. His wife, Jan, recounted the campaign to harass her husband, typical of the way the company was pressuring leading activists in late 1992 and early 1993: "Mike constantly had to watch his back, making sure he did nothing wrong. They made him work Christmas Eve and Christmas Day in a building that was shut down. That year was hell for both of us. . . . They created a shift just for him and isolated him from the other employees. He was put in the basement of a filthy building by himself, and he had to do jobs that were two- and three-man jobs by himself."[21]

"I was on permanent midnights," added Mike. "I couldn't seem to get off that rotation. The company gave me job assignments that were more than any one guy could do, then they'd write me up."[22] Undeterred, Griffin continued to play a leading role in the work-to-rule and in organizing mass grievance hearings. Every time the company violated the contract, Griffin responded with a grievance. He liked to get under management's skin by sending copies of all his grievances directly to CEO Larry Pillard, which infuriated his supervisors. Rosie Brown had nothing but praise for Griffin, who was her steward: "If I felt like something wasn't safe, [and] the union steward said don't do it, then I don't do it. That's why they hated Mike Griffin so much. Because he was on his job! . . . Mike Griffin was always there for you. They did everything they could to get rid of him because he stood up so much for the union. They said, 'He's a troublemaker!' I didn't see that. I saw a man standing up for his fellow workers."

Jan Griffin continued the story of Mike's discharge: "They said he took too long fixing a pump and sent him home for ten days with a warning. We knew it was just a matter of days. Mike was put with a person that he didn't want to work with because, as Mike put it, 'He'll either get me killed or fired.' He got Mike fired. He fell into a hole they were working over. The company said it was Mike's fault because he didn't have the hole covered."

In July 1992 the Staley workers had overwhelmingly voted to raise their monthly dues to one hundred dollars for three months to fund the corporate campaign. In October the local voted to reduce dues to seventy-five dollars but established the casualty fund, where workers could voluntarily contribute an additional twenty-five dollars a month to support workers targeted by the company. The idea was that workers suspended or fired for union activity would be paid their salaries as they continued the fight outside the plant. The casualty fund, remembered Dike Ferris, "wasn't mandatory. But the pressure by your peers was definitely strong enough to make it almost *seem* mandatory." Those who donated got stickers to put on their union caps, reading "I gave to the Casualty Fund." Upwards of 90 percent of the workers gave.

The casualty fund was a "trust factor," said Barrie Williams. It was a statement by the entire union membership that they would stand by each other. Linked to the casualty fund was the clear declaration by the union that no contract would be approved until every fired worker was given amnesty. No one would be left behind.[23] "Every time [Tate & Lyle] fired somebody, they disciplined somebody, or they took away some of our quality of life inside that plant," said Dave Watts, "they thought they could turn us around. And every time they did it, we just got stronger. And it blew their mind."

"Your Heart's Pumping a Mile a Minute"

By May 1993, eight months into the work-to-rule campaign, the local was preparing to take even bolder steps. The workers had been escalating their in-plant actions week by week, but the debilitating impact of the rotating twelve-hour shifts had sapped some momentum. An in-plant campaign "is an uneven process," said Jerry Tucker. "You're moving along, you think you're making progress, and all of a sudden it flattens out. And you know if it stays flat, it's going to start going downhill. So you try to figure out ways to give it a boost."

In mid-May the members initiated a grievance blitz. Across the plant, unionists in every building gathered together and marched to the supervisor's office to confront management over working conditions. The action lifted the workers' morale, but it was clear to Tucker that something more was needed.

On May 19 a serious chlorine bleach spill occurred inside the plant. Dangerous conditions such as this were commonplace, and if one were to strictly follow OSHA guidelines, the spill could require that virtually the entire plant be shut down. The union, however, didn't jump on the opportunity. Instead, as during past safety incidents, Watts negotiated a safe cleanup with the plant manager.

At the next union meeting Tucker discussed the chlorine spill to show how the workers could escalate the fight: the next time there was a safety incident, they could walk off the job in a "safety stand-down." "A safety stand-down is when something becomes significantly unsafe in the minds of the workers," explained Tucker. "Then a worker should take the necessary steps to stand down and take himself out of harm's way. It was time to look for those safety problems where a stand-down might occur. Then everyone on the shift would join the worker that was having the problem, and workers would converge on the union hall to discuss the safety crisis in the plant."

Dan Lane recalled that Tucker told the workers, "Twenty years from now, you are all going to be sitting back in a rocking chair; the grandkids will be on your knee. It is not a question whether this is history. It already is. But the question is: What are you going to tell your children? Whose side are you on?" After Tucker spoke, "There was a stillness out there," said Lane. "It had a chilling effect. We are *in* this thing."

On June 16 workers walked off the job. It began in the morning with a minor incident: union recording secretary Ron VanScyoc refused his foreman's order to change a burned-out lightbulb. In past years this would have been a simple task any worker would agree to do. But now, following company work rules, an electrician was required to do the task. Recalled VanScyoc,

> The company's safety manual said that a safety condition must be reported to management, and *management* would write the safety work order before work is done. The supervisor told me that *I* should write the safety work order for changing a lightbulb. I explained to him that if I wrote the safety work order, then I would be violating the safety manual, which had been set up for everybody's safety. I would be subjecting myself to possible discipline, including discharge, for disregarding the manual. Different supervisors kept coming to me and saying you have to write the safety work order. . . . This went on for four or five hours. Finally they said, "You're going home."

Gary Taylor jumped on the in-plant radio, declaring "Code Bronco P-3," signifying that a worker was being fired. "About twelve or fifteen workers appeared instantly in the control room," remembered VanScyoc. "Every one of them was on the supervisor's back. [Management] called plant security." A supervisor then fired Taylor for "improper use of company property" (the radio) and threatened to suspend eleven other workers who came to support VanScyoc. The workers called the union hall and consulted Tucker and bargaining committee chair Jim Shinall. Tucker said, "This is the right time for the safety stand-down." Shinall replied, "I think you're right."

Word rapidly spread throughout the plant. Workers excitedly spread the news that the union had called a safety stand-down, and if they wanted to know what the safety problem was, they had to come to the union hall immediately. An overwhelming majority of the 270 workers on the day shift walked off the job. Former union president Bill Strohl recalled that some of his co-workers struggled with their decision: "I was working with [treasurer] Mike Grandon when we heard the news, and he says to me, 'Well, what are we going to do?' I told him we are going to meet out at the union hall. And they sat there and sat there and finally they were coming. It was a touchy thing because nothing like that had ever been done before. I went to change my clothes, and the boss said to a group of workers nearby, 'If he leaves, he's fired. If any of you leave, you're all fired.'"

Strohl shrugged his shoulders at the boss's threats and left the plant. When Dike Ferris heard that Taylor had been fired and that a safety stand-down had been called, he knew instantly that he was walking out. "I decided to put my tools away, lock my locker, and head for the gate. I was stopped by a supervisor. 'Where you going?' I told him that we had a safety issue and I was going to the union hall to find out what was going on. Your heart's pumping a mile a minute; your heart's praying that you're doing the right thing." As Ferris was leaving, he was confronted by a couple of workers. "I'm not leaving here," declared one. "You may cause me to get fired." "We're either in this thing together or we can take our separate paths," answered Ferris, "but that's where I'm headed."

While some workers were shutting down their machines, others were deciding what they would do. "Everyone was calling down to 111 Building and asking what I was going to do," said Jeanette Hawkins. "Al [her husband] came down and got me, and we walked out together, holding hands. It was tough for a lot of people to make that decision."

Art Dhermy was disappointed that five workers from his area remained in the plant. "Three of the five were over fifty-five, and they feared for their pensions. I felt they let me down. 'They can't fire the whole plant' is what I tried to get across to them."

At 1:00 P.M. the workers met in a mass safety meeting at the union hall. The hall was abuzz with conversations. Ron VanScyoc and Gary Taylor went to the microphone and told the members what had happened. The excitement in the air was palpable, and many workers were in awe of what they had achieved. Gary Lamb recalled the jubilation:

> As you're going out the gate, people were saying, "Is anybody going to follow me?" "Are you going?" "I'm going!" "Is anybody else behind us?" Finally they all went. Even guys within years or months of retirement walked out. Gosh, was that great! It said so much! It had to make the company really wonder how that many middle-aged souls, tied up in a job that long, could have that much courage to just individually walk out that gate. That was one of the singularly most courageous times in the whole fight.

The supervisors were dumbfounded. Management scrambled around, placing calls to the home office in London for advice. They called the union office and demanded to know whether the union was going to order everybody back to work. The leaders said they would formally respond after a 6:00 P.M. union meeting with the next shift. Second-shift workers were reached through a phone tree and told to report to the union hall rather than to work. At a packed meeting that evening, the membership voted to stay out till the next day. In an act of further defiance, they would report at 7:00 A.M.—an hour later than they were due at work—since this had been their starting time before twelve-hour shifts were imposed.

At six o'clock the next morning, over one thousand workers and family members held a spirited one-hour rally outside the plant. Wearing their red union

T-shirts and carrying banners and homemade signs, members shouted "Union!" and "Solidarity!" Spouses and children cheered the workers on as they headed back into work.

Staley management stopped the workers from entering the plant, however, declaring that each would be required to sign a statement agreeing to the terms in the contract the members had overwhelmingly rejected. The workers refused to sign and returned to the union hall, with the exception of two lone workers who entered the plant. Union leaders formally notified the company that the workforce was ready to return to work, but under no circumstances would they sign individual statements.

Advised by their lawyers that the agreements were blatantly illegal under the National Labor Relations Act—which prohibits employers from bargaining directly with individuals rather than with the union—the company relented. After thirty-two hours off the job, the unionists returned to the plant at 6:00 P.M. on June 17. The entire shift marched into the plant singing "Solidarity Forever" at the top of their lungs. "You would have thought we were all Johnny Cash," recalled Dave Watts, "the way we were singing. We were really bellowing her out."[24] When the workers marched into work, it "looked like the opening ceremony of a Chicago Bulls game," said CCI staffer Kip Voytek.[25] The workers were filled with pride; they felt their collective power.

A week later a ruling from the National Labor Relations Board forced the company to reinstate Gary Taylor and cancel the eleven suspensions.

During the workers' thirty-two-hour absence from the plant, management moved ahead with its plans to bring in replacement workers by soliciting the Red Cross for cots. In a move it would soon regret, the Decatur chapter of the Red Cross loaned cots to the company. The union was furious and protested vehemently. "Union members . . . have contributed hard-earned dollars to what we thought was emergency relief charity only to have the Red Cross betray us," wrote Kenneth Long in a letter to the *Decatur Herald and Review*. The Red Cross quickly apologized and withdrew the cots.[26]

Meanwhile, for weeks the Staley workers and UAW 751 had been planning a June 26 demonstration in which a 2.6-mile human chain would extend from the Staley plant to the Caterpillar plant. The success of the walkout the week before gave new energy to the demonstration. On that Saturday, Staley and Cat workers and family members were joined by a fifty-car caravan of Caterpillar workers from Peoria; over one hundred AIW workers from the Milwaukee Harley-Davidson plant, who roared into town in a motorcycle caravan; Oil, Chemical, and Atomic Workers members from St. Paul, Minnesota; unionists from Chicago; and striking mine workers.

Four thousand people formed a human billboard of solidarity. The workers were "on a high, all the people together for one cause," recalled Nancy Hanna.

A twenty-foot banner declaring simply "Solidarity" was unfurled from a tall Staley building by a unionist working the weekend shift. AIW International president Nick Serraglio and regional director Danny Wirges spoke, encouraging the workers to continue their struggle. Dave Watts declared, "Today is the day that we send the union-busters . . . a message: You don't belong in central Illinois. Go back to where you belong. This is our turf and we're going to keep it that way." Watts praised the solidarity of the spouses and families, declaring their courage "one-half of our battle."[27]

Within twenty-four hours, however, the lives of the Staley workers and their families would be forever changed.

6

Locked Out

At 3:00 A.M. on Sunday, June 27, 1993, Tate & Lyle management locked out the members of AIW Local 837 at the Decatur plant. The local immediately began to organize a series of demonstrations. Many in the community, including local unions, rallied to the workers' side, providing both moral and financial support, while others sided with the company. To combat the heavy emotional toll, a number of the women formed a support and activist group.

The workers struggled to survive on the sixty dollars a week they received from the AIW International, but soon additional aid arrived. The local launched a food program to give workers the bare necessities each week and initiated an "adopt-a-family" program through which supporters across the country could make monthly donations to a locked-out family. The local also mobilized to demand unemployment benefits from the state—and won.

"A Shocker"

After the "Hands across Decatur" rally on June 26, Gary Lamb went home exhilarated by the display of solidarity from unionists across the Midwest. Lamb's wife of thirteen years, Cheryl, and their ten-year-old son, Josh, listened as Lamb told them about the turnout. "I started at Staley's when I was eighteen," Lamb later related. "I was never away from there for more than two and a half weeks in twenty-seven years. That was my life. That was what I knew."[1] While he was relaxing in his easy chair, the phone rang. Lamb was scheduled to work the next day, but now a supervisor was calling to say that he needed a mechanic for the night shift. Lamb reluctantly agreed to go in.

As he entered the plant at six o'clock that Saturday night, he braced himself for a twenty-four-hour shift. After midnight, however, he began receiving calls on the plant radio that something peculiar was happening.

I got calls telling me a whole bunch of cars were coming in the gate, four to six people in a car. Nobody recognized any of the faces. . . . As it all started to unfold, the [internal] phones weren't working. . . . I thought, "I'll go to a pay phone and call Dave Watts." I was met there by two company people. They said, "What are you doing?" I said, "I'm making a phone call, calling home." I told a little fib there. They said, "At two in the morning?" . . . I dialed, and they reached in and tapped the phone down. They said, "Phone booths are out of bounds."

Lamb's duties as a mechanic allowed him to travel throughout the compound. He went to the front gate, and when he saw the carloads of people coming in, he wondered why so many people would be entering the plant in the middle of the night. A supervisor called Lamb on the plant radio and told him to go to the dry starch department. Recalled Lamb,

He said "I got a real quick job for you, five minutes tops." . . . When I went back there, there was no work to be done. I said to the supervisor, "I caught you in a lie, didn't I? There's no work for me back here, is there?" He read to me from a piece of paper, "You are being locked out. I'll escort you to your locker. You will get your personal belongings but you will not shower or change your clothes. I will escort you to the gate or a holding area." . . . I put my tools in the locker, got my street clothes, and he escorted me clear to the gate.[2]

When the company came to expel the employees who monitored consoles and other key machinery, the workers were told to gently back away from their machines. Standing behind them were company personnel who then slid into position. Lamb reflected, "I've laughed about it over the years. Staley has bumbled up a lot of things over the years. But that they carried off very, very skillfully."

Mike Odeneal too was working the night shift. "I pride myself on not missing days and being absent," said Odeneal. "I had a perfect record." This night marked his twenty-sixth anniversary of working at the Staley plant. By two in the morning, Odeneal recalled,

I knew something was unusual, to see so many [supervisors] at that late hour. [I thought to myself] "Something is wrong here. You never see this guy here at this time." . . . They said, "We've been instructed to walk you to the gate." . . . They wanted everything running. They didn't want anything shut down. I had stuff in my locker that I was going to get. I said, "If you want to come with me to my locker, that's fine with me." . . . I got what I wanted and left. The guy walked us out to the gate.

Although Lamb and Odeneal were allowed to go to their lockers for their personal belongings, many workers were not. Some workers were subjected to strip searches. Recounted L. M. Ballard: "Imagine being herded out of the plant at 3:00 A.M., no phone calls, no gathering of tools or personal items from lockers, and no showers. But several employees [who were] allowed to change into street clothes had to strip naked while being constantly observed by management, and all were videotaped while leaving the plant.[3]

Gary Lamb angrily noted the irony of being called to work on his day off only to be locked out. "Of all the times I had walked into that plant, and was dead tired or sick . . . , after all we gave to Staley's . . . , they threw us out. . . . It hurt my feelings a lot. I was very mad." "The lockout for me was a major betrayal," echoed Duwayne Williams. "I had given over twenty years of service to the company, and I felt I did my best to be an asset to help them succeed."[4]

Workers who reported for the day shift at 6 A.M. were turned back at the gates. "A lot of us didn't know we were locked out," recalled Jeanette Hawkins. At the plant gate, security guards "told us we were locked out and to get off their property. A lot of people couldn't believe it. It was a very sad, hurtful thing. We were standing around talking about it . . . , and they ran us off."

Hawkins rushed home to tell her husband, Al, who had sixteen years in the plant. "I was ready to call a mover," recalled Jeanette. "I said to Al, 'We don't have any ties here—let's move.' He said, 'We are going to stay and see what happens.' Then I told him that a lot of families break up when they don't have anything, but we are going to take this opportunity to get closer to one another and to Christ. We've got to work together as a family."

Dike Ferris said he knew that if the company continued to insist on the seventeen-page contract, then "sooner or later it was imminent that they would lock us out. . . . Some of the supervisors said to some workers, 'Something's coming up, and you're not going to like it.' We said, 'Bring it on!' We knew it was getting to them, so no better time than now."

Even though they realized that a lockout was always a possibility, Dick Schable and many others said "it was a shocker." Nevertheless, after the long months of tolerating management's barrage of antiunion actions, recounted Jeanette Hawkins, "A lot of people said, 'Well, I'm glad it's here.' They were living from one day until the next, not knowing what was going to happen. . . . Let's get on with it!"

When the lockout happened, said Dan Lane, "It was scary. But still, it's that kind of exhilaration, and you are exceeding all power that you ever thought you had. It was like being free. You broke the shackles. It was an emancipation. I am *not* a part of that grind. I have to be treated better than that and I am doing something about it."

In the first three decades after World War II American corporations rarely used lockouts as a weapon against unions. Since the 1980s, however, they have increasingly used them, aided by a 1965 U.S. Supreme Court ruling that legalized temporary lockouts after negotiations have reached an impasse. "Although lockouts account for only about 5 to 8 percent of all work stoppages," wrote Paul D. Staudohar in 1990, "their frequency is rising." The first big postwar lockout in the United States occurred in 1986, when USX (formerly US Steel) in Gary, Indiana, locked out its union workforce. The German chemical giant BASF locked out workers (members of the Oil, Chemical and Atomic Workers) at its Geismar, Louisiana, plant from 1984 to 1989, the longest lockout in U.S. history. The Staley lockout was the sixth in the United States in the first six months of 1993.[5]

On the day of the lockout Illinois governor Jim Edgar was in Decatur to attend one of his favorite pastimes, horse racing. While on his way to the grandstand, Edgar responded to a reporter's questions about the lockout and Illinois's being a center of labor strife by asserting, "I don't think we have that many labor problems around the state."[6] The Republican governor of Wisconsin, Tommy Thompson, was in Decatur that same weekend, however, and commented to a local Republican activist, "Every time I pick up the *Wall Street Journal* and see this area mentioned, it has to do with labor."[7]

Many members went straight to the union hall after being escorted out of the plant, while other bleary-eyed workers, having received a startling phone call from their fellow union members, began streaming in. Bill Strohl described the mixed mood as somewhere between a funeral and a party. There was "disbelief and relief that it finally happened. . . . We're there!"

From that day forward the union hall became the anchor, the rallying place where workers would come together to strategize, to support one another, to hold debates, and to make decisions.

Leaders immediately set union meetings for noon and 7:00 P.M. During those two meetings Local 837 quickly decided on several actions and set a brisk pace for a campaign against the company. Within minutes after the lockout, some astute workers began picketing at the main plant gates. At the noon union meeting, with input from the floor, union vice president Bob Hull organized a picketing schedule. Five entrances to the plant would have picketers twenty-four hours a day, seven days a week. Each site would host an average of five union members, with each taking a four-hour shift once a week. By establishing a picket line, AIW 837 hoped that workers from other unions who had business in the plant—such as carpenters, electricians, and truck drivers—would not enter the plant. Crossing their picket line would violate a time-honored morality among unionists.

The picket lines would also pick up information about the ebb and flow of company operations. The seasoned workforce could easily determine the scope of the plant's productivity simply by smelling the plant's fumes, monitoring the smokestacks, and watching truck and rail deliveries.

A center was established to coordinate picket activity. A retired member donated use of his two-car garage, strategically situated across from the plant's west gate. Harking back to their experiences in Vietnam, workers painted their own billboard above the garage announcing it as the "AIW Local 837 War Room Command Center." Picketers signed in and out for their picket shifts at the command center and received hot coffee and snacks there. Each picket site was given a two-way radio so that production glitches, unusual activity, and out-of-state license plates could be reported to the center. The site also became the informal news center, for other Decatur workers and supporters would often drop by to catch up.

When Jerry Tucker got the call that the workers had been locked out, he jumped in his car and drove to Decatur. When he spoke at the union meeting that Sunday evening, he encouraged the workers to stay united and build support for their cause. Tucker advised each member to file for unemployment benefits, informing them that some states paid benefits to locked-out workers and that, despite bad precedents in Illinois, theirs might be a test case. Since employers ultimately pay for unemployment benefits, the company might be forced to pay its locked-out workers for the next six months. The unionists made such an overwhelming response to Tucker's suggestion that by Tuesday the Illinois Department of Employment Security had established a satellite location in the union hall to assist workers in filing claims.[8]

The union immediately organized a series of rallies. Ray Rogers, who was still in town from the "Hands across Decatur" rally, moved quickly to help. On Monday over one thousand workers, family members, and supporters demonstrated outside the Staley plant. The rally spanned over four city blocks between the east and west gates, with the huge company office building in between. "Hey, Hey, Ho, Ho, Larry Pillard has got to go!" "No contract, no peace," and other shouts of protest were pitched from the streets into company officials' offices.

On Tuesday Staley workers filled fifteen buses and dozens of cars as they descended upon the Illinois state capitol in Springfield. They were joined by locked-out workers from two other unions who welcomed AIW 837's invitation to join the protest. The Central Illinois Public Service Company (CIPSCO) had locked out its two unions in May—fifteen hundred members of International Brotherhood of Electrical Workers (IBEW) Local 702 and two hundred members of Operating Engineers Local 148. Over two thousand protesters stood on the steps of the state capitol demanding unemployment benefits. The raucous workers and their supporters then moved inside the rotunda. Their numbers and the sheer volume of their chants forced the Senate to suspend its business, and the workers then lobbied each state representative. "We chanted labor chants and sang 'Solidarity' several times in the rotunda," said Dave Watts. "This really got the attention of the legislators, their staff, and visitors. People tell us we were the loudest demonstrators they've ever had there, and the best organized."[9]

On Wednesday fourteen buses filled with 350 Staley workers drove to Bloomington, Illinois, to demonstrate at the home office of the State Farm Insurance Company. State Farm, an investor in Tate & Lyle, was chosen by Ray Rogers to be the next target for the Staley workers' corporate campaign.

On July 4 the Staley workers joined members of the United Mine Workers for a parade in nearby Mattoon, Illinois. Thirty-five hundred Illinois mine workers had been striking since February over a contract dispute with the Bituminous Coal Operators Association, and many had turned out for the "Hands across Decatur" rally. Together the unionists made their presence known in the Independence Day parade, as over one thousand workers marched, cheered on by a supportive crowd along the parade route. The marchers carried union signs, chanted, and threw their fists in the air.

Over four hundred Staley and CIPSCO workers held a second demonstration in the state capital on July 7. Just one day after their earlier rally the CIPSCO workers were told that their claim for benefits had been denied, but the workers were undeterred. After each speech on the capitol steps, every worker threw an arm in the air with clenched fist and yelled "Solidarity!" three times. This militant ritual was to become standard practice at every labor rally in central Illinois throughout the 1990s. The workers passionately sang "Solidarity Forever" four times, both outside the capitol and inside, where they continued the demonstration. The workers repeatedly roared their chants, "We will win!" "War Zone!" and "Solidarity!"

With the AIW Staley workers, the UAW Caterpillar workers, the UMWA mineworkers, and the IBEW CIPSCO workers all engaged in labor conflicts, the workers' slogan was "Illinois is a War Zone!" A fiercely united labor movement was burgeoning in central Illinois, and the Staley workers were the igniting spark.

The Company's Postlockout Campaign

The lockout did not end Staley's harassment of its workers. The company painted a yellow line across each gate entrance, marking property boundaries. Any member of AIW 837 who crossed the line would be arrested for trespassing. Security guards checked the identification of anyone entering the plant.

At both the east and west gates, mobile shacks for the newly hired Vance security guards appeared. Video cameras pointed directly at the picket lines were mounted on the corners of the shacks. Security guards gave office employees disposable cameras to record "any hostile event directed at you or your vehicle." The idea came from the head of company security, a former FBI agent. "When more than two of our people got together, the cameras immediately popped out," said Watts. The workers felt "harassed and spied upon. It infuriated them and intimidated them." The union filed charges with the NLRB, and in October the company claimed that it would stop the practice, although the workers noted bitterly that it continued.[10]

Three days after the lockout Tate & Lyle announced that it had discontinued company-paid health care for union members. Workers could continue their coverage for eighteen months under the federal COBRA law, but a single worker would pay $131 a month and a worker with a family, $345. Most families could not afford the coverage and were left without health insurance.[11]

Since several hundred workers were home asleep at the time of the lockout, they were eager to retrieve their personal possessions from their lockers and work areas. Many had brought their own tools from home and didn't want managers or scabs using them. Eventually, the company succumbed to union pressure and, six weeks after the lockout, scheduled the workers to come into the plant to retrieve their possessions. While doing so, the workers were under tight scrutiny by supervisors and guards.

On July 3 Staley began running ads for temporary replacement workers in the *Decatur Herald and Review,* nine other central Illinois newspapers, and one in neighboring Indiana, and on July 9 the company announced it would hire three hundred workers. Because the workers were locked out, the company could not legally offer replacement workers permanent jobs. Staley spokesperson Mohan declared that the company could "run this plant indefinitely with management personnel and temporary replacements." Mohan said seventy people had been brought into the plant from Staley's white-collar personnel in Decatur and from Staley plants elsewhere to help the supervisors run the plant.[12] On August 5 Karen Forbes, writing to the *Herald and Review,* said that a supervisor had told her that the company personnel were exhausted from "working 12 hour days, seven days a week," and would speak out against "what the company is doing [but] they fear for their jobs."[13]

By early August the company announced that it had hired 150 replacements. In mid-August it ran another ad stating that applications would be accepted by phone. Large numbers of the scabs were recruited from out of state. If workers on the picket lines saw a car with out-of-state plates coming into the plant, usually from the South, they would know instantly who its occupants were. Dick Schable volunteered to make Judy Dulaney a sign to put in her son's car when he visited from out of state, reading "This is a scab-free car. My Dad is locked-out at Staley."

The union leadership and its advisers counseled the workers not to let scabs or security guards provoke them. "Violence on the picket line would only play into the company's hands," said Watts. "We are not going to let them portray us as thugs."[14] As with any strike or lockout, however, it was a struggle for the workers to control their anger. Diana Marquis, the spouse of a Staley worker, wrote the *Decatur Herald and Review*: "As I read the article about the workers (scabs) crossing picket lines, my blood pressure rose. These people cross because of their families—what selfish people! . . . Shame on you, there will be no future for your kids!"[15] "I couldn't understand why another person would cross the picket line," said Jeanette Hawkins. "I don't know how they can sleep with themselves. I have a problem with a Christian crossing a picket line."

When scab Sharon Tripp wrote a letter to the *Decatur Herald and Review* claiming the plant was "a country club" and that the unionists had "bled this company for all it's worth," workers and family members flooded the paper with angry letters. Tripp's attitude "stinks," wrote teenager Angela Williams, denouncing Tripp and the other scabs for "stealing other peoples' jobs and livelihoods from them. . . . If anyone's being treated to that kind of (country club) atmosphere it is you people who are in there eating steak dinners provided by the company and catered by Shaw's Restaurant." Mona Williams, whose husband Duwayne was locked-out, angrily wrote "that job does not belong to you or any other scab out there!"[16]

In an effort to sway public opinion, the company ran a full-page ad the day after the lockout. Headlined "Why a Lock-out?" the ad stated that the union had given management "no other choice" but to "take a defensive action" in order to "save our Decatur business" and that unionists had "engaged in acts designed to minimize production, harm quality and endanger the environment."[17] The ad ran again on June 30.

On July 16 the company and union met, but management spent half the bargaining session complaining about the work-to-rule and charging the union with acts of "sabotage." "This is the first time the company has approached the union with these allegations," Jerry Tucker told the *Decatur Herald and Review*. "They admit that the actions are probably caused by—their words—'a few bad apples,' but they are unable to show where individuals have been disciplined or discharged over illegal conduct. Instead they have locked out 750 workers when they admit only a few deserve punishment."[18]

Nearly four weeks after the lockout, Staley management invited television and newspaper reporters to tour the plant and witness the union's alleged sabotage. The union adamantly denied sabotage and once again reasserted that its actions were legal, concerted union activity. "In the last nine months," said Dave Watts, "there has not been a single reprimand or even mention of sabotage in the plant."[19] Richard Brummett hotly disputed the company's sabotage charge: "What they showed on TV as 'sabotage' was . . . my machine. I had started taking it apart after I shut it down and I got to a certain stage and [the supervisor] put me on another job, and that's the way it's been since the first of May. It looked terrible. They also showed an elevator, showing how the back of it was all bashed up and the top was bent. Well, I've been in that department for ten years, and it's been that way ever since I've been there."[20]

In a press release Jim Shinall asserted, "The company's attempt to blame misconduct by workers for its production problems is a smoke screen. Production fell because workers followed Staley's own rules and procedures to the letter in a lawful and protected manner. If the company is looking for people to blame, it should start with its own supervisors and with the unskilled contract-workers it brought in."[21]

Local merchants in Decatur were both courted and threatened by Staley. In early August the company sent out several hundred letters to business and community leaders, attempting to justify the lockout and to discredit Ray Rogers. When Tom Gillum, a retired Staley worker, went to a local company to rent a trailer for the food bank, his business was refused. Bill Strohl recalled, "The company that rented trailers told Tom Gillum and I that they were threatened by Staley, that if they did anything for [the union] they would lose Staley's trucking business."

In July and August the company announced plans to eliminate 284 union jobs. Eighty-eight jobs in the corn-oil refinery were to be cut in July, and 196 other jobs by October.[22] Union leaders responded that the layoffs were negotiable and that the jobs could be retained if the union won a fair contract. The company, they argued, was attempting to divide the union by telling low-seniority workers that they didn't have a stake in the fight. The union was unwilling to discuss the job cuts as long as the company refused to bargain in good faith. "We will not aid in downsizing the plant and eliminating bargaining unit jobs through a false process," declared Shinall.[23]

The local newspaper endorsed the Tate & Lyle position in an August 2 editorial. In words that could have written by the company itself, the *Decatur Herald and Review* stated that the plant must remain competitive or it would close. The editors further stated, "Watts must change the union's methods and move away from confrontation as a tactic. . . . Local 837 should end its affiliation with Rogers and Tucker. . . . Rank-and-file members of Local 837 must make certain their leaders are acting in the best interest of the membership and not just accepting the mantra of a consultant who will make money even if the union loses. They must push their leadership to change course while there is still time to change."

The editorial went on to support twelve-hour shifts, albeit without the rotation, and hefty increases to workers' contributions for their health insurance. Tate & Lyle had found a strong collaborator in its project to divide the members from their leaders. Four days later Local 837 wrote a guest opinion piece to rebut the editorial:

> Staley seems to think that repeating the word competitiveness will justify gutting our ability to grieve unsafe working conditions, remove the privileges of seniority, force us into rotating shifts and weaken our union to the point of uselessness. A similar argument underlies the H&R editorial. . . . Who says Staley isn't competitive? . . . In the last two fiscal years, Tate & Lyle has had profits of more than $700 million . . . , with Staley earning more than one-fourth of Tate & Lyle's operating profits. . . .
>
> We do feel it is ironic and unfair for the Herald and Review to make an issue of Jerry Tucker and Ray Rogers, who have won the respect of our members, without once questioning: the role of the union-busting law firm Seyfarth, Shaw,

Fairweather, and Geraldson; the hiring of Glen Zalkin . . . , who engineered the replacement of 1,200 workers in Jay, Maine; the use of Harmony construction, a company known for providing replacement workers to companies in labor disputes; and the purpose of ADM's pipeline to the Staley plant.[24]

"The Unions in This Town Had Better Stick Together"

Decatur's blue-collar workers—25 percent of the city's workforce—had a strong sense that if AIW 837 won, they would see a positive ripple effect on other unionized workplaces throughout town. Likewise, if they lost, Decatur workers foresaw negative repercussions on their own working conditions.

The Caterpillar workers held a collection at their plant gates three weeks after the lockout. As the Staley workers stood in their signature red T-shirts holding large white buckets, Cat unionists expressed their solidarity by throwing in ten-, twenty-, and fifty-dollar bills. The one-day "bucket drop" yielded nine thousand dollars. Over the next months UAW 751 repeated the plant gate collections four more times, each time yielding over ten thousand dollars. In early September, United Rubber Workers Local 713 followed suit and raised ten thousand dollars at the Firestone gates, as well as food donations worth another thousand. Grainmillers Local 103, one of two unions at the Archer Daniels Midland plant, continued its monthly donation of five hundred dollars, a contribution started months before the lockout. Finally, in a show of solidarity that would later develop an ironic twist, the Decatur police union donated fifteen hundred dollars to Local 837.[25]

"The unions in this town had better stick together and help each other out," wrote Skeet White to the *Decatur Herald and Review*. "My Local (AIW 838) takes up a gate collection every two weeks for the locked-out Local 837 employees. . . . Several locals in Decatur have contributed to them. If your local hasn't, I challenge you to do so. We may all have this same problem in the future."[26]

On a rainy Labor Day, September 1, 1993, more than four thousand unionists held an exuberant demonstration in downtown Decatur. Virtually every local union in the area turned out for the parade, and hundreds of people on the sidewalks cheered the workers as they passed by. The Staley workers were by far the loudest contingent and received the greatest applause.

The Staley workers also received much generosity and support from the larger Decatur community. The locally owned Lakeview grocery store discounted all Staley workers' purchases by 5 percent, with its owner stating that his customers had been there for him and now it was his turn to support them. Other grocers donated day-old bread and sweet rolls for distribution at the weekly union meeting. Stoney's, an upscale restaurant, regularly donated ground steak. Several Decatur churches donated food.

Local doctors and merchants offered price breaks and donated supplies and services. A pediatrician donated two truckloads of baby food and nonprescription drugs. Jimmy Peck, who owned Simms Lumber Company, "gave us all the plywood we needed for signs and paint," recalled Gary Lamb. Peck said, "Come back if you need more. People don't understand that you guys have got to win. You have to have people making a living wage for them to worry about the condition of their house."

Strangers stopped by the picket lines with coffee and soft drinks. At night workers from Kentucky Fried Chicken and Hardee's drove to the lines and dropped off leftovers. Boisterous honking and supportive waving became a daily ritual for many people who drove by. Picketing the Staley gates was a sacred trust, said Larry Pearse. "If we left, that would be like a soldier leaving the Tomb of the Unknown Soldier. It'd be like sacrilege, an abomination."[27]

When Local 837 printed fifteen hundred yard signs that read "We Support Locked Out AIW Local 837," the signs appeared all over town in front yards and store windows. Richard Brummett and his wife, Mary, who lived on a heavily traveled street, added to their sign by tallying the number of days of the lockout. "Every day I went out and changed it," said Mary.

Some acts of support were anonymous. Marcia Duncan, wife of Dave Duncan, recalled running a twenty-minute errand one day. When she returned home, she found that her "kitchen was stocked with food. I don't know where it came from. Nobody I know will take the responsibility. I just know there was about $75 worth of food overflowing my pantry."[28] Another locked-out member received a substantial monthly donation from an unidentified member in her church.

Both the Macon County Board and Congressman Glenn Poshard offered to mediate between the company and the union, but the company abruptly declined. The Democratic candidates for governor and lieutenant governor, Dawn Clark Netsch and Penny Severns (herself a former union member) visited the picket lines and offered workers their unwavering support.

During the summer of 1993 a flood of letters appeared in the *Decatur Herald and Review* carrying supportive messages for the workers and condemnation of Tate & Lyle. While a few came from locked-out workers, the overwhelming majority came from others among the Decatur citizenry. "In the '30s our grandfathers found themselves exploited by their employers," wrote Shari Grider. "Unions were formed out of necessity, not a fringe benefit. . . . [Local 837] is fighting for more than their jobs, they are fighting for the principles that make this country unique. . . . If we Americans allow the corporate greed of Tate & Lyle to get by with this lock-out, we are allowing future companies to feel they can do the same." "The salaried employees that I have talked to do not agree with any of the management practices that have been implemented," wrote Gene Wooters. "The people who are now locked-out are good, conscientious, and loyal employees."[29]

Tate & Lyle have proven that they "don't care about our people at all," wrote Karl Brownlee. "They just want the almighty dollar. . . . [Tate & Lyle's] and ADM's trouble is you've got good employees, but you don't give a damn. Having been a business owner here for twenty-five years, I know most of the men employed in companies here are pretty damn loyal employees. . . . [Tate & Lyle's] negotiations are as phony as a three dollar bill with my picture on it. . . . We don't need your kind in our great country."[30] Many pro-union letter writers made references to Britain's defeat in the American Revolution.

"We've had a lot of support in the community," said union president Dave Watts. Decatur citizens "understand the issues," he added, referring to the local's four door-to-door literature distributions. "They've got the education as to the reality of Staley's destructive, dictatorial policy."[31] To further solidify their standing in the community, the Staley workers widely distributed the video *Deadly Corn* to local media, politicians, and clergy.

The Emotional Toll

Like many Americans, the Staley workers defined their identities through their work. Some felt that without a job, life had lost its meaning. Most had not experienced an event of this magnitude. Many unionists and family members privately reported having bouts of depression. They expressed their despair in many ways. While some shared their deepest feelings with their spouses or close friends, others turned to alcohol or gambling. Some wandered around their houses aimlessly, and still others took to their beds or couches for weeks, feeling paralyzed. Many workers and spouses experienced anxiety attacks and nightmares. It was no longer unusual at a union meeting to hear that a fellow worker had suffered a stroke or heart attack.

Their spouses' attitudes made a difference in how the workers handled the emotional pain of the lockout. Many felt great compassion for their husbands or wives. The plant was "like a second home" to her husband, said Cheryl Lamb. Gary "spent so much of his life there; he put in overtime all the time. He gave it everything he had, and then they tell him, 'Get out of here!' How humiliating is that? I really felt bad for him." "I just had to be much more supportive, understanding, and motivated to do more to keep my husband from feeling like he was not to blame for not having a job," said Mona Williams of her husband, Duwayne. "Our family grew closer together."[32]

But "a lot of wives did not support their husbands," said Susan Hull, whose husband, Bob, was the local's vice president. They said, "'He is just laying at home on the couch. He's not out making money.' . . . I would tell the wives, 'Support your husband! Let him be on the picket line, doing what he needs to be doing!'"

Some family relationships and friendships were strained as well. The labor studies scholar Mark Crouch had warned the workers that taking on the company would lead to divorces and familial rifts. "I didn't really believe it," recalled Richard Brummett in 1994. "Well, my mother and I don't talk over this one issue. We're at an impasse on this. We have got some members that their wives are on them, giving up: 'Go find a job. Let it go.' . . . We have people on the verge of losing their houses. Some have lost their cars."[33]

"When we had family get-togethers," elaborated Mary Brummett, "it was awful. We had part of the family that was sympathetic and supportive, but you didn't want to tell them too much because then they would worry too much. . . . And then there were other parts of the family that were so oblivious to you." "All the people we thought were our friends," said Jeanette Hawkins, "when we didn't have a job, they stayed away from us because they thought, 'Hmm. Their money is going to run out here soon, and they might want some money.' . . . It taught us who our friends were."

Things became most tense, however, when a family member or friend became a replacement worker or worked for a firm that did business inside the plant. This was the ultimate betrayal. In either case, the workers considered the line-crossers to be scabs. "We had some very good friends whose son was a scab at Staley," recalled Judy Dulaney. "They told everybody not to tell Mike and me. A good friend of mine finally told me. Mike called the guy and asked if Doug was really working there. They said, 'Yeah, it's the best job he has ever had. We're really happy that he's got a job. Now he can get somewhere.' Needless to say, that ended that friendship."

"I had one brother who was a scab. I told him, 'When you see me on the street, don't talk to me,'" said Jeanette Hawkins. When a cousin scabbed, said Royal Plankenhorn's wife, Rhonda,

> that caused big tension in the family. I haven't spoken to him in years because of it. . . . My cousin who scabbed got fired, and my mother said, "Poor Bill lost his job and car." I said, "Oh? Poor Bill? I ain't going to shed any tears over poor Bill!" My mother got quite angry at me. . . . I had a brother-in-law who worked for a company that was in the plant before the lockout. His company continued to go in and out of the plant. For the sake of my sister, I decided that this is not going to affect us. But to this day [my husband] Royal and my brother-in-law do not speak. He will not come to our house, and we will not go to his.

Eventually it became common knowledge that the son of Decatur mayor Eric Brechnitz was a Staley scab.[34] For this and other reasons, Brechnitz would not see another term in office.

Women's Support Group

Many of the wives of Staley workers welcomed the union's decision to open the doors of the union hall for the Tuesday-night meetings. Now the women could learn firsthand where negotiations stood and how the union's strategies were unfolding.[35] Union leaders were aware, said Pat Watts, that "if women don't have the understanding, . . . the men will be going back to work because the wife says you have to." Attending the meetings "made me realize that Mike was not the only one who was going through all the problems and stress," recalled Jan Griffin. "It woke me up to what was going on in the plant."

"I think there were some wives who were not encouraged to attend," said Ethel Fargusson. "A few men were too macho to have their wife there," echoed Pat Watts. "And some of the women said it's not my battle; it's my husband's battle," added Judy Dulaney. "But for those who were there, week after week, we got involved in so much more than just coming to the meetings," said Fargusson. "Personally, if I hadn't gone, I would have gone nuts at home. Jerry was never one to be very articulate, and I would not have known three-quarters of what was going on."

Many wives also walked the picket lines, volunteered with the food bank, and joined prayer groups with other spouses and workers. They came to the union's rallies, and many wore the red solidarity T-shirt everywhere they went. But many of the women wanted to get even more active. They began by holding a bake sale at the union's November 6, 1993, rally, which netted over one thousand dollars to buy Christmas toys. Some started to help out with mailings, go door-to-door distributing flyers, or join their husbands on out-of-town trips to build solidarity.

The wives also began to meet informally in groups of two or three to talk about stress and financial problems. "I had anxiety attacks. Those three years were pure hell," said Jan Griffin. "I think most of us dealt with depression," added Ethel Fargusson. "There was no way we could not have."

In early 1994 a dozen wives determined that they needed something more and organized the Women's Support Group, which met every other week for the duration of the lockout. Here the women found a place to speak openly and honestly. "I didn't have anybody I could talk to," said Sandy Gosnell. "I couldn't talk to Tim [who was locked out]. I couldn't talk to anybody at work." But with the Women's Support Group, said Mary Brummett, "you didn't have to sit and explain how you felt because everybody was going through the same thing."

Jeanette Hawkins, one of the few women working at Staley to join the group, said of the meetings, "We could take out our frustrations. Rhonda use to get frustrated that Royal was out being a Road Warrior [discussed in chapter 7], and we tried to convince her, 'Hey, he's doing it for all of us. We appreciate what he's doing. Don't take it out on your spouse.'" Rhonda Plankenhorn readily agreed. "They kept me from strangling Royal," she said, laughing. "He'd go to Boston and other cities, and he'd come home with these wonderful stories. I really knew that he wasn't on vacation, but he was going places and doing things. And I was stuck working in the day-care center, taking care of the babies who were screaming all day long. And at night, I wasn't able to sleep because I was worrying about how we were going to pay the bills."

"The friendships that were formed because of the lockout, nobody can take those away from us," reflected Ethel Fargusson, "and we're not about to give them up."

While they appreciated their spouses' support, the locked-out workers faced the overriding concern of their families' financial survival. International unions set aside a percentage of their members' dues in a fund to assist striking or locked-out members. The UAW, for example, provided "picket pay" of one hundred dollars a week to the Caterpillar workers during their 1991–92 strike. The financially beleaguered Allied Industrial Workers paid just sixty dollars a week, with no additional funds to cover health insurance.[36]

In the days and months after the lockout, in household after household, Staley workers and their spouses gathered around their kitchen tables to assess their financial situations. Terri Garren summed up what many families faced: "It was very stressful—not knowing where we were going to get the money to pay the bills, when and if your spouse would be going back to work. . . . Coming so close to losing our house and bankruptcy, not having health insurance, not knowing where the money would come from for next week's groceries . . . it was a terrible time.[37]

Single parents' problems were worse. "I had three kids at home," recalled Rosie Brown. "I started to worry about losing my house and my car. All I dreamed of was this house. It was like my whole world was falling apart."

The financial situations of the Staley workers ran the gamut. Some had saved money; some had not. Some were debt-free, but most had to make house and car payments. Some families had massive debts. "There were some families who were in trouble the first week," said steward Nancy Hanna, who provided financial counseling to members. "I've got a wife who's had cancer and open-heart surgery," said Ray Walters, who had worked in the plant twenty-four years. "If we have any more illness, we're just sunk. I'm gonna be bankrupt." The Walterses were forced to disconnect their phone within a month.[38]

Two Staley wives, Shawna Dunn (married to Michael) and Gina Wilson (married to Shawn), gave birth, two days and six weeks, respectively, after the lockout—with no health insurance. Executive board member Steve Haseley reported that he owed twenty thousand dollars in credit card debt. Many families began to drain their savings accounts and make early withdrawals from their 401Ks, for which they encountered severe penalties. The employee-run Staley Credit Union allowed workers a substantial grace period before having to resume their monthly loan payments.

Some families could hold on for a while, especially those with a spouse who had a full-time job with medical benefits. But as the lockout continued, even these families began to buckle. Almost every family received pressing calls from bill collectors. Cheryl Lamb, herself employed full-time, summarized: "We could pay the bills with my income but we could not buy clothes for the kids or an extra pack of chewing gum. There was no leeway whatsoever! . . . I ran up the charge cards. . . . They were calling to collect payments on stuff and I was behind. . . . I remember crying when they called about the house. I went into the bathroom, shut the door, and I was just bawling."

Since Decatur-area employers believed the lockout would be short, few would hire Staley workers for full-time jobs, forcing many workers to take low-paying, part-time jobs. Dan Lane began a paper route, rising at four o'clock each morning. Bob Sheibly went to work at a bowling alley. Art Dhermy joined his wife in baking wedding cakes. Nancy Hanna and her husband, Bill, both locked out, gave pony rides at carnivals and birthday parties. Some got temporary work from friends who owned small businesses, painting houses, hauling trash, or pumping gas.

Many African American workers had a harder time finding side jobs because only a handful of African Americans owned businesses in Decatur. Al Hawkins described his situation: "I started to feel like I was never going to get a job because of my age, my color, or because of [my being from] Staley. . . . It really got my head all messed up because I felt like I was not good for anything. . . . They could have paid me ten dollars less an hour and it would have been okay because at least I would have had a job."

It quickly became clear that the worker's spouse, usually the wife, was more employable. Many wives increased their hours or went job hunting, some for the first time, often seeking full-time jobs with medical benefits. Donna Lane increased her hours to full-time at her retail job, and Pat Watts, a nurse, took a second job. Janet Winter worked two jobs, up to seventy hours a week, to keep her family from going under. Sandy Schable worked three low-paying part-time jobs, and Rhonda Plankenhorn began her first paid job. "I did housework for elderly clients," recalled Judy Dulaney. "But that was just spending money. Now we were living on it!" Judy expanded her cleaning business.

To sustain the families, Local 837 began two programs—the food bank and "adopt a family."

The Union Organizes Assistance

In July 1993 the members of AIW Local 837 voted to use incoming donations to buy food at sharply discounted bulk prices. Bargaining committee member Bill Strohl and retiree Tom Gillum took on the enormous task of running the food program. Strohl and Gillum rented trucks to bring the food from nearby Springfield, where they picked it up from Come Share, administered by Catholic Charities, and Second Harvest, a program of the Central Illinois Food Bank. Purchasers were obliged to satisfy Catholic Charities' requirement of donating time for community service, and a number of Staley unionists met the requirement by volunteering at the Central Illinois Food Bank in Springfield.

The food had to be sorted, bagged, and stored once it was brought to the union hall. When Strohl announced that volunteers, trailers, refrigerators, and freezers were needed, members responded generously. Electricians wired the trailers that stored the food, and carpenters fortified them. A Decatur Teamsters local covered the monthly cost of renting one of the trailers. Whatever was not donated, the union purchased at discount prices. Eventually four long trailers occupied the ground next to the union hall, some holding the ten refrigerators and freezers.

The food bank became a hub of activity, with members and spouses often donating long hours each week to the effort. Many volunteers "worked a minimum of forty hours, [starting at] 7 A.M.," recalled Strohl. "Sometimes people worked Saturdays and Sundays, a lot of hours. . . . It was like a little village out there." As did so many of the union's activities, the food bank became an opportunity for members to serve their union, to form friendships, and to boost one another's morale. In the summer of 1993, *Stand Fast in Liberty,* a new weekly newsletter written by spouse Paula Hawthorne and distributed at the weekly solidarity meetings, described the atmosphere as volunteers sorted food: "More and more food was carried into the hall to be sorted. . . . The evening progresses and the [thirty] tables begin to swell to maximum proportions. . . . It was amazing to see the effort that had been made. . . . It is a real pleasure to work with friends. . . . The pride that we shared during the sorting process was tremendous. And for anyone who was a participant, they'll agree that *we were smok'n.* Solidarity is always a great thing to share with one another."[39]

Gillum kept meticulous financial records. The local, said Strohl, "spent seven to ten thousand dollars a month on food . . . If it hadn't been for the food program, I don't know how our people would have gotten through the lockout as long as they did."

Union members waited for a decision on their applications for unemployment benefits. Workers on strike are generally not allowed such benefits, but state laws covering locked-out workers are often vague. Tate & Lyle quickly contested the workers' claims. Since the locked-out Central Illinois Public Service Company workers had been denied, the *Decatur Herald and Review* reporter Gary Minich wrote that it "appeared unlikely" the Staley workers would receive a different response.[40]

But Local 837 took on the uphill battle. After they twice marched on the Illinois capitol in Springfield, a group of 125 supporters and members held a spirited demonstration outside the State of Illinois Center in downtown Chicago. Even some of the more conservative lawmakers could not tolerate the brutality of the lockout. Republican state representative Duane Noland commented that "the current law allows the companies to use [a lockout] unfairly."[41] Noland joined sixty-one cosponsors of a new measure with liberal guidelines on awarding benefits to locked-out workers. Proponents of the bill decided to delay a vote until they were more sure of victory. In reaction, the Illinois Chamber of Commerce produced a statewide mailing to its members, urging them to lobby lawmakers to vote no.

Jerry Tucker guided the union through the legal steps to pursue the benefits. Local 837 asked to meet with the company in the presence of a federal mediator, prompting a July 2 meeting. The company was legally required to give an explanation for the lockout. Twice Tucker posed the question, but the company refused to respond, strengthening the union's case for unemployment benefits. Notably, the company did not claim sabotage to be a reason.

Tate & Lyle then discovered that Illinois law required locked-out workers be paid unemployment benefits once plant operations returned to normal. Tate & Lyle did not want to admit that operations were *not* back to normal, for fear of alienating customers. If the company claimed that production had returned to normal, however, then benefits would have to be awarded. The company chose the latter course. On August 11 the Illinois Department of Employment Security announced that the Staley workers would draw unemployment benefits for the next twenty-six weeks. Each worker's weekly amount would be determined by salary and number of dependents, with a cap of three hundred dollars.

The Staley workers were jubilant over the six-month reprieve from economic devastation. (They later won an extension of benefits through March 1994.)

Immediately after the lockout some donated funds were given to a handful of families whose extremely critical needs were evaluated by the local's community service committee, headed by Bob Hull. The committee also provided financial and peer counseling. Nonetheless, even with weekly unemployment checks, sixty dollars a week in AIW picket pay, free groceries from the food bank, and emergency aid available from the local, many families were in financial distress, without health insurance, and vulnerable to losing their cars and homes. To provide further relief, in August 1993 the local organized an "adopt-a-family" program, in which groups of supporters would send a monthly check of six hundred dollars directly to locked-out families. Ray Rogers had helped United Food and Commercial Workers Local P-9 establish such a program during its 1985–86 strike against Hormel in Austin, Minnesota, and suggested that Local 837 do the same.

Barrie Williams volunteered to coordinate the program.[42] Williams knew that many people would say they were too proud to participate, so he told the unionists, "You're not receiving charity. These are groups out there that someday are going to be in the same fight, and if they can stop the fight here by supporting you, then that's what they're doing." Initially 240 workers applied to be adopted. Williams had them fill out two forms, one an identification containing the worker's name, address, and phone number and the other an anonymous financial statement listing bills and medical and special needs. The two sheets for each application were assigned a single identifying number, and workers dropped them into separate locked boxes.

A small committee of individuals from Decatur Auto Workers, Rubber Workers, and Electrical Workers unions evaluated the financial statements, prioritizing the families with the greatest needs. No AIW 837 member was allowed to serve on the committee, not even Williams. The committee then gave Williams the ranked list of code numbers. Williams now knew who should be adopted and in what priority, but the specifics of each family's financial situation remained confidential. Only Williams and Ethel Fargusson, who managed the database on the computer, knew which families were adopted.

Rogers's CCI staff produced a flyer for the program, complete with pictures and personal stories of families who volunteered to appear there. The flyer's headline read, "When you adopt a locked-out family, you're investing in solidarity . . . , family stability . . . , workplace rights . . . , and the future." The *Wall Street Journal* eventually gave the program front-page coverage but added a demeaning description, saying it looked "like a typical financial appeal for an impoverished child in a developing nation."[43]

As the workers traversed the country, they took the adopt-a-family flyers with them. The bulk of the adoptions came through these one-on-one connections. As support groups were established in city after city, those committees and affiliated unions also began to adopt Staley workers. The union's *War Zone* newsletter, which began in December 1993, regularly featured the program.

Some large unions were extraordinarily generous and adopted more than one family. The Caterpillar workers of Peoria's UAW Local 974, led by Jerry Brown, adopted nine families; the Springfield office of the American Federation of State, County, and Municipal Employees (AFSCME) Council 31, led by its regional director, Buddy Maupin, adopted five; and Chicago's Service Employees International Union (SEIU) Local 73, led by Tom Balanoff, adopted four. Many smaller unions also adopted Staley families, some voting to raise their dues to do so. Some individual supporters wrote to Williams that they didn't have much money, but sent one, five, or ten dollars every month. Williams pieced together such cases to bring a family up to six hundred dollars.

The workers' employment and financial status fluctuated as the individuals sought temporary work during the lockout. Recalled Williams, "People would come to me and say, 'I don't need it anymore: I'm working now, or my wife has a good job. Pass it along to someone who needs it.' . . . Time after time that happened. It was made clear that, at any time, you could come back to the program." When an adoption was made, the adoptee was asked to volunteer at least four hours a week, excluding picket duty, on behalf of the union.

To speed disbursement and to foster ongoing relationships, the adopters sent the monthly stipend directly to the home of the locked-out worker; the adoptee would regularly write letters back to give supporters a firsthand account of the struggle. Walter Maus, a Staley worker of twenty-eight years, wrote in 1994 to a group of supporters who had adopted his family: "I was very proud to learn today that my family was the next needy one to be adopted. . . . The financial support comes at a time when we wondered how much longer we could survive without losing something. . . . [Your support] is what will sustain us in this fight."[44]

Judy Dulaney wrote in 1995: "Your support . . . always seems to come at just the right time and we always get emotional at the thought of people caring for us. . . . In the same mail with your check came a doctor bill. . . . We cannot tell you how blessed we feel. . . . One day we will all be getting together for a victory celebration! When that day comes, we will all know that we didn't get there alone!"[45]

The personal connections made through the adopt-a-family program fostered deep friendships and strengthened the national solidarity effort. When donors came to Decatur for a rally, the union set up an adopt-a-family booth. Williams would discreetly bring donors together with their adopted Staley worker. Years later, said Williams, "there are still people exchanging Christmas cards."

The program, recalled Williams, "was more successful than I ever really dreamed it would be." Within the first year, several dozen families were adopted. By the end of 1994 participants included more than 660 unions and groups from California to Connecticut. During the thirty-month lockout 126 Staley workers were adopted for periods ranging from a few months to over two years. About 85 percent received the full six hundred dollars a month, and others a bit less. All told, an estimated $1.25 million was contributed through the program.[46]

The assistance helped families survive as the locked-out workers took to the road to build a broader network of worker-to-worker solidarity.

7

Road Warriors and Solidarity Committees

Within a week of the lockout AIW Local 837 established one of the most vital components of its campaign. Rank-and-file workers, quickly dubbed "Road Warriors," became the local's traveling ambassadors, traversing the country to build solidarity and raise funds. From late 1992 through 1995, the local raised over $3.5 million from unions and sympathetic individuals, much of it through the Road Warriors.[1] One of the warriors' main tasks was to form local support groups of unionists, students, and progressives. Within months of the lockout the Staley fight was fast becoming "a rank-and-file fight that really . . . did have the potential of revitalizing the union movement," said Communication Workers (CWA) vice president Jan Pierce.

"Transfer the Energy"

Before the lockout a few members of Local 837's executive board had spoken to audiences outside Decatur, but after the lockout a large group of rank-and-file members were charged up to bring their struggle to the labor movement. Jerry Tucker was the first to see the need to organize a national outreach program: "When the workers were locked out, I recognized that we had to immediately transfer the energy from the shop-floor fight into the external fight and build worker-to-worker solidarity."[2]

At the union meeting the night of the lockout Tucker called for a special meeting four days later to organize a new outreach program. Sixty-two people came, primarily the leading activists during the in-plant campaign. Tucker coached them in public speaking and honing the message of their struggle. He conducted role-playing exercises and fielded questions from an enthusiastic but apprehensive audience. The unionists weren't sure whether they could talk in front of an audience or how they would be received.

The workers decided to establish two groups of speakers, one that would travel within a seventy-five-mile radius and could thus be home at night and the other for overnight trips. The local told its members, "You provide the car, and we'll provide the gas." Dan Lane recalled that Ron VanScyoc, Dwayne Carlyle, and he coined the name "Road Warriors" in a van on the way to Chicago on the first overnight trip. The name stuck—and has since been adopted by workers including Detroit newspaper strikers, locked-out West Coast longshore workers, and striking Kaiser Aluminum workers.

Other local unions under siege had put members on the road to build support. The workers at Hormel in Austin, Minnesota, in 1985–86 and at International Paper in Jay, Maine, in 1988 had made such trips. The United Mine Workers had done it during the 1978 national coal strike and again during the 1989–90 Pittston strike. Nonetheless, no other union in U.S. history has sent so many rank-and-file workers to speak in so many cities and to garner support over such a prolonged period as did the Staley workers.

"How do you make a local fight into a bigger fight for the whole labor movement?" asked Milwaukee Central Labor Council president Bruce Colburn. "That's where the Road Warriors become so important—through the Road Warriors, people can see [the struggle], touch it, feel it." The AFL-CIO strategist Joe Uehlein viewed the Staley emissaries as a model. "Those Staley Road Warriors did an unbelievable amount of good to the labor movement," said Uehlein. "When Road Warriors go out in any campaign, they touch people in a way that union newsletters don't, magazines don't, phone calls don't, staff to staff don't, staff speaking to members don't. These Road Warriors . . . touch people in their heart and soul, not just in their head, and it makes a very big difference. . . . We learned a lot from the Staley workers about Road Warriors: what they do, why they do it, and what role they contribute in campaigns."

Local 837 was keeping a frenetic pace with its myriad activities, and members were tripping over one another in their tiny two-phone office on the second floor of the AIW hall on Dineen Street. Kip Voytek of the CCI was as frustrated as the members were. "I found a message that someone wanted to give ten thousand dollars but there was no number, no name, no union! How do you follow up? You can't run the kind of campaign we need to run out of this space. We need more space!"

In August 1993 the executive board rented additional space in an office park two blocks from the union hall. A large wooden sign with the AIW logo and the new office's official title, "Campaign for Justice," was painted and placed over the entrance. Unionists soon nicknamed the office "Kandy Lane," however, after its street address. Union president Dave Watts and vice president Bob Hull remained at the Dineen office, while Kandy Lane became the hub for the Road Warriors and the corporate-campaign effort. Desks, tables, chairs, and file cabinets were donated or scrounged at low cost, and seven phones were installed. Shelves were built to hold literature, T-shirts, and videos. A circulating library filled with books and videos about labor history was established. "The circulation of books in and out of the library," said Kip Voytek, led to "very real changes" in the workers' consciousness.

A large map of the United States adorned one wall of the Kandy Lane office. Red yarn pinned between Decatur and the towns where Road Warriors had spoken soon covered the map. Across the room, a large calendar was always filled with notes about upcoming union rallies and Road Warrior speaking engagements. A few long tables, where the almost weekly bulk mailings were processed, stood in the middle of the room.

A small back room held two donated computers and printers. Ethel Fargusson managed the growing database, typed correspondence, and ran mailing labels. Recalled Ethel, "I had quit my job . . . and I knew I had computer skills they needed, so I volunteered. . . . Wives that sat home with spouses that never told them anything, I don't know how they made it through. . . . Going out to Kandy Lane and working, I was doing something not only to help Jerry but to help the union, and it was helping me. It bonded us, that I was doing something for him."

Between their work at Kandy Lane and weekly picket duty, on which Ethel accompanied Jerry, the Fargussons each gave over sixty hours a week to the union, not an uncommon occurrence for those who anchored their work at the Kandy Lane office. "Kandy Lane was the workers who were the best organizers," recalled Barrie Williams, "the people who weren't afraid to speak their mind. It got pretty electric in there at times. Thank goodness everyone in there was pretty good humored."

An important tool throughout the campaign was the *War Zone* newsletter, edited by Jerry Tucker, which was produced at and mailed from Kandy Lane. The Road Warriors would bring bundles of *War Zone* on every trip, and it was mailed to the growing list of supporters who donated money or signed a mailing list. While Rogers's corporate campaign and adopt-a-family mailings continued, *War Zone* became the main vehicle to publicize and report on demonstrations, the corporate campaign, the activities of the solidarity committees, and the unproductive negotiations with the company.[3]

Road Warrior coordinators Mike Griffin and Gary Lamb, along with other Kandy Lane workers, worked the phones, making cold calls to organize speaking engagements. Nine months into the lockout, Road Warriors had already spoken to tens of thousands of people in twenty states. Over 120 members and spouses served as Road Warriors at least once. The core group, those who went out repeatedly and for extended periods, consisted of about forty activists.

When the activists began to place calls looking for speaking engagements at union halls, they abruptly stumbled across issues of protocol. At the top of labor's house stood the AFL-CIO, an umbrella organization based in Washington, D.C., and comprising all but a few U.S. unions.[4] Within each of the fifty states, AFL-CIO–affiliated unions form a state federation. The state federations have small staffs that primarily lobby state legislators. In 1993 there were six hundred central labor councils (CLCs) throughout the United States. The CLCs are regional bodies consisting of delegates from local unions. These are voluntary associations; not all local unions in a geographic area join and pay dues to them. The CLCs work primarily on lobbying and electoral campaigns, but some are actively involved in labor-community coalitions and grassroots solidarity for union organizing drives or strikes.

While the state federations and CLCs come under the auspices of the AFL-CIO, the federation has no official power over them. By the 1980s most CLCs "weren't mobilized or active," said Joe Uehlein, even though organized labor experienced its most devastating losses during that decade. In 1987 leaders of the AFL-CIO's major industrial and service-sector unions inaugurated regional chapters of Jobs with Justice (JwJ), labor-community coalitions that advocated for workers' rights but did not come under the rubric of the AFL-CIO. "One of the reasons the industrial unions developed a group like Jobs with Justice," said United Paperworkers special projects coordinator Mark Brooks, "is because the central labor councils were not doing what they were supposed to be doing."[5] For some newly emerging JwJ chapters, solidarity work for the Staley workers became a focal point.

The Staley workers received passive support from the AFL-CIO executive council on August 4, 1993, just five weeks after the lockout. The AFL-CIO stated that Tate & Lyle "clearly intended to bust the union . . . [and was] poisoning the relationship between labor and management." It called on the company to "end the lock-out and begin good-faith bargaining." The federation "declares its solidarity . . . and calls upon its member affiliates to provide the Allied Industrial Workers with all appropriate assistance."[6]

After developing a deeper understanding of labor's formalities and with the AFL-CIO's endorsement in hand, the Staley workers were now ready to follow the protocol. Road Warrior Gary Lamb explained: "When you go to a new town, you have to go through the Trades and Labor [aka the central labor council]. . . . We would plead our case with the [CLC] president and the board, saying, 'Can we have your blessing to go speak at this UAW local or this Ironworkers local?' I don't think we ever got turned down. Then we could go ahead and firm the calls up [to local unions]. But . . . if you stepped out of that line . . . , the trip was a bust."

Using the list of unions that had sent donations thus far, Ray Rogers's and Jerry Tucker's contacts, and a mailing list provided by the reform magazine *Labor Notes,* the Kandy Lane activists started making calls. This was a new and humbling task that required enormous persistence. "This is not our forte," said Dan Lane. "We're usually the guys pounding out sheet metal and running heavy equipment."

The Staley workers began by explaining that they were locked out and not on strike. Then they described their struggle with Tate & Lyle, detailing their in-plant and corporate campaigns. "At first," recalled Mike Griffin, "it was pretty tough. We didn't have that many contacts, [so] we were making cold calls. It was like selling foot powder or something. But after a period of time, you develop a sense about who is going to help you and who is not."

Most CLCs and unions rarely received phone calls asking them to get involved in a struggle outside their cities or regions. Their responses were mixed. Some opened their doors to the Staley workers, inviting them to speak at CLC and union meetings and offering to mobilize for the corporate campaign and upcoming Decatur rallies. After the Staley workers spoke, the host union would take up a collection, write a check out of the treasury, and sometimes even authorize monthly contributions.

But other CLCs and locals turned down the callers. "A lot of unions have an agenda that makes them see only part of the overall picture," said Ron VanScyoc. "What we're doing goes to the grassroots of labor and activists."[7] When a CLC gave the workers the runaround or flat-out declined, they turned to a Jobs with Justice chapter in that city. If a JwJ chapter didn't exist, individual supporters were encouraged to independently spread the word and to form a solidarity committee.

Most of the workers had one problem in common: stagefright. Mike Griffin, who eventually logged tens of thousands of miles in his truck making road trips, said, "I wasn't very comfortable with public speaking. It was not something that I wanted to do, but it was something that had to be done." Lorell Patterson, a Road Warrior known for her no-nonsense style, recalled: "I was nervous: how will people react to you? What to expect? The first time I spoke, I was shaking like a leaf! I would take big breaths, calm myself down, not try to impress people, just tell people what happened to me. . . . People were impressed that a young person was fighting for the union [because] I had less than five years in the plant."

Royal Plankenhorn, who ultimately covered thirty states and three Canadian provinces over the course of the fight, admitted his initial terror: "The first time I spoke, I was scared out of my mind, but over time it got a lot easier. . . . I'd tell how we got locked out, the 762 families, how we were drawing a line in the sand, if we lost what it would mean for labor. . . . And to my surprise, people would come back telling me how impressed they were with how I spoke." "People in America are getting tired of people getting up and fluently speaking, fluently cynical, and full of bullshit," reflected Frankie Travis. "They're tired of it and they want to hear honesty."[8]

"It was fun. It was an eye-opener. I got a chance to work with a lot of good people," said Barrie Williams. "But sometimes it got really intimidating. I remember one time in Detroit, there were six or seven thousand postal workers at their convention at the Joe Louis Convention Center. Little old me was up on the stand, you look out and see all these big screen TVs and see yourself, and beside you is someone doing sign language. It's the most intimidating thing I've ever done, but it came off pretty well."

On the Road

Each time they spoke, the Road Warriors explained that for decades their working conditions at the Staley plant had been essentially good but that their lives were turned upside down in 1988 when the multinational Tate & Lyle arrived in Decatur. They spoke about Jim Beals's death and the deteriorating safety conditions in the plant. They described how the company attempted to strip them of fifty years of collective bargaining gains by implementing twelve-hour rotating shifts, gutting safety and seniority, and moving from a 116-page contract to a 17-page one. They explained that Tate & Lyle was trying to eradicate their union, where a worker, on average, had twenty-one years in the plant and made $12.40 an hour.[9]

Many audiences felt as if the Road Warriors were telling their own stories. The Road Warriors argued that it was time for workers to stand up, to return to the assertive strategies of the labor movement's roots, and to fight back against corporate greed. "The corporations have a common strategy to decimate the labor movement," said the Road Warriors. "They're coming after us now, but you're next. This fight is your fight, too. This fight is about all workers, everywhere." They told their audiences about the slogan they carried on placards at demonstrations: "It's Their Solidarity versus Ours." "We have to break down the walls that divide us," said Royal Plankenhorn, "because his battle is my battle, my battle is his battle, and your battle is my battle. We can't succeed any other way."[10]

The Road Warriors learned to shape their message to fit an audience. Barrie Williams remembered: "If I was talking to teachers, everything was how it affected the teachers, students, and parents. You start telling them, 'You wonder why you can't get parents into your teacher's meetings and why they don't have time to spend with their kids? It's because they're working twelve-hour shifts in their plant.' Something they could relate to."

The enthusiastic response astounded the Road Warriors. Many people in the audiences were searching for a renewal within their own unions and saw the Staley workers' struggle as a model for labor's revitalization. Workers registered for Local 837's mailings, made plans to come to the next Decatur demonstration, and vowed to boycott corporate-campaign targets. Unionists repeatedly asked Road Warriors questions about bringing a work-to-rule campaign to their own workplaces.

The audiences' applause and admiration were backed up by substantial donations. Gary Lamb recalled his amazement while driving back to Decatur after a road trip: "I couldn't believe it! Why did all those people give us all that money? Maybe there's a chance!" Added Lamb, "We were counting as we went down the road, and I said to the others, 'My God, if the law stops us, they'll think we've been selling drugs!'" Some small locals donated hundreds of dollars. One small union in Illinois paid its stewards twelve dollars for attending stewards meetings; the attendees voted to turn the money over to the Staley workers for the duration of the lockout. Some large unions gave sizable donations. The Canadian Auto Workers, who were contacted through Tucker, invited Road Warriors to speak and then contributed ten thousand dollars.

The Road Warriors were invigorated by the profound solidarity they experienced. "These are people who never met you, who invite you into their home, put you up, feed you, and take you where you need to go," recalled Lorell Patterson. "Once you got out there, you found people willing to help. You just had to go out there and find them." Bill Winter recalled one trip to West Hartford, Connecticut, where a Machinists local raised $1,700 and the union sent another $2,000 two months later. That level of generosity was not unusual. But that night, as the event was winding down, remembers Winter, "one of the gals who had been doing the bartending came to me with an envelope and told me that all the volunteer bartenders had agreed to donate their tips for the night. The envelope contained over $200, which those girls had been on their feet all evening to earn. That donation touched me as much as any we received on that trip."[11]

The Road Warriors would often show *Deadly Corn,* the compelling documentary with testimonies from workers about hazardous conditions, the history of the dispute, and the work-to-rule. The video also illustrated the financial ties among Staley, ADM, and State Farm. One of the workers featured in *Deadly Corn* was Dave Hays, who hired into Staley in 1968. As a result of breathing toxic chemicals and asbestos in the plant, he contracted a rare form of lung cancer in 1991. After the biopsy showed cancer, said Hays, the doctor asked whether he had been exposed to asbestos at work. "When I said that I had, they didn't seem to want to discuss it any further."[12] Doctors took out one of Hays's lungs, but when Staley cut off his disability benefits, he was forced to return to work. Management assigned him back to the asbestos-contaminated boiler room and to the chemical-filled wastewater-treatment building.

While he had not been a union leader before the lockout, Dave Hays devoted himself to the union's cause. Hays, said the Detroit solidarity activist Simone Sagovac, was rejuvenated by being a Road Warrior, which gave him the strength to carry on even while his body was giving out. "He wasn't expected to live long, and his involvement in the struggle brought him back to life," recalled Sagovac. "It's people that really change our lives. . . . Dave Hays deeply touched my life."

Dave Hays and Gary Lamb grew very close during the struggle. Recalled Lamb:

> One day Dave called me and said, "Gary, come to the [Decatur] hospital." I thought he was in Kansas City on a Road Warrior trip. I went to his hospital room; Dave handed me his notebook, and said, "I'm done, I can't go anymore. I only have a short while to live." He said to me from his hospital bed, "Can you do the rest of these speaking engagements I've got in my datebook?" . . . At the first one, there were a few hundred people, and I talked about Dave. . . . He could have been doing a lot of things, but the gravity of the fight was so important to him, he chose to spend his last days on this earth going on the road for the union.

In a conversation shortly before he died on July 25, 1995, Hays remarked that his primary concern was that, whatever the outcome of the Staley workers' fight, the lessons of the battle not be lost. "We can't start from scratch when another big fight comes along," he said. "We need to build on all the grassroots organizing and the work of the solidarity committees and keep it going. This fight goes far beyond the conflict between A. E. Staley and its workers."[13]

The Road Warriors were notorious for watching every penny. Before leaving Decatur, one worker would be designated the trip's treasurer and given cash for gas and food. "We'd go to the grocery store the night before," recalled Mary Brummett. "We'd buy a loaf of bread and a bag of potato chips and bologna, and you'd bring the mustard from home and maybe some cookies and pop, and fix up a cooler and they would head out." Royal Plankenhorn, who rounded out the frequent Road Warrior trio with Brummett and Bob Sheibley, always brought along the paper plates.

Barrie Williams related an exchange that took place on a trip to Michigan: "Royal Plankenhorn was treasurer. The air conditioner was out on the van and it was over a hundred degrees. We were hot! We pulled over at a rest stop, and there was a little ice-cream stand. I went over and got some, the others did, but Dick Schable was broke. He said to Royal, 'The union ought to buy us ice-cream cones.' Royal said 'No. You don't need that ice-cream cone. You can do without it. . . . We don't waste union money on stupid shit.' . . . We almost had to get between them to stop the blows."

Plankenhorn recalled another story about frugality during a seven-hour trip to Minnesota:

> Dave Watts, [Staley spouse] Janie McKinney, and I were headed up to Austin, Minnesota, and we stopped for gas. Dave says, "When are we stopping to eat?" Janie says, "You must not be in on the program. We don't stop. We'll eat this evening when we get there. We're on the union funds." And Dave says, "When

you're hungry, you eat." Janie says, "No." Dave looked my way. I said, "That's right. We don't waste union money if we don't have to. We eat as little as possible; we spend as little as possible." And we didn't stop until we got to Austin. Not even for Dave Watts, the president! Dave couldn't believe it!

Road Warriors usually supplied their own cars, but if a trip required a flight, the host union paid the airfare. For the most part, staying in hotels was an extravagance that Road Warriors shunned. When making arrangements they asked to stay in supporters' homes, where they were often enveloped in hospitality. Pat Watts recalled how one couple gave Pat and Dave their bed while their hosts slept on the pull-out sofa, a scenario that repeated itself dozens of times. Jeanette Hawkins was stunned at the trust strangers showed in her: "These people had big, beautiful homes, and they would leave the key in the mailbox or under the mat and say, 'Make yourself at home and go in!'"

Occasionally the accommodations were abysmal, and Road Warriors had to adapt. Art Dhermy was unprepared for his first trip, taken with four other warriors: "Nobody was told to bring anything. The guy we stayed with had maybe three blankets and two sheets and a couple of pillows. I rolled up my coat as a pillow and only had a sheet as a blanket. It was rather cool, sleeping there on the floor. That was all right, I've camped out before. We learned from that experience."

"You get used to it after a while, and you don't care where you sleep," said Barrie Williams, "as long as it's warm and dry. . . . One time, we were in New York City at a cheap hotel. New York was a hoot! What kind of hotel do you get in the middle of New York City for twenty-five dollars a night? We were there for five days, and not one day did we have hot water. Their lounge downstairs was a sheet hanging on the wall where they showed old eight-millimeter movies, like Charlie Chaplin movies. The bar was two orange crates with a board across it."

Everyone was aware that collecting thousands of dollars in cash called for the highest integrity. Donations were counted by two or more people and given to the trip's treasurer. Recalled Lamb,

> The Road Warriors were a testament to humanity. At first I thought, give a fellow X amount of hundreds in their hand, and they're living on sixty dollars a week, their tendency is going to be, "The car's not paid for; I've got the bill collector biting at me." But I'd stake my name on it: the money that was collected made it back to the people. The Road Warriors were dedicated to winning the fight. The trip treasurers diligently collected, accurately counted, and turned the money over to me in, of all things, a paper bag. I kept the paper bag in a file cabinet with a ten-cent lock on it, until we could turn it over to treasurer [Mike] Grandon.

The Road Warriors were also keenly aware that, while on the road, they reflected the integrity of their union. "I never saw anybody misbehave," said Barrie

Williams. "I never saw a Road Warrior drunk. Road Warriors, if they wanted a drink with a meal, they bought it themselves. It didn't go on the union bill."

While the support from their families was immense, the days and weeks spent away from home provoked tensions. "We had to be both parents when our spouses went out on the road," said Janet Winter.[14] Gary Lamb pushed Dick Schable to the limit at times, although he had regrets about doing it, because Schable's daughter had recently died. "Dick would be gone for two, three weeks at a time. He shouldn't have been on the road that much. Just before the lockout he and Sandy had lost their twelve-year-old daughter, Beth, to cancer. Dick should have been with Sandy more. Some of the guys I knew the best, I pushed the hardest. I knew them better, knew how good a job they would do."

In a few cases, the spouses became Road Warriors themselves. Jan Griffin recalled that the only time she and her husband had spent a night apart in their twenty-seven years of marriage occurred when she was in the hospital giving birth. Now, however, she suddenly found herself alone: "I didn't like what was happening to our lives. We seemed, all of a sudden, to be going our separate ways. I felt left out. I knew if I asked Mike to give it all up and go get a job, he would, but he would never be happy and I'd lose him for sure then. So I did what any loving wife would do—I joined him. It was hard. I worked days and traveled with Mike at night and on weekends. The generosity and love we received from strangers brought me to tears many times."[15]

Staley Workers Solidarity Committees

One of the Road Warriors' primary tasks was to help supporters from across the country form Staley workers solidarity committees. The committees were largely made up of union activists but welcomed campus, community, and religious activists as well. The committees organized local speaking events for the Road Warriors, raised money, adopted Staley families and encouraged local unions to do the same, brought people to Local 837's demonstrations in Decatur, and mobilized support for the corporate campaign.

The first group formed in Chicago. On June 26, 1993, the day before the lockout, local activist Rust Gilbert traveled downstate to participate in the "Hands across Decatur" rally. Gilbert, impressed by the energy and militancy of the union members, shared his enthusiasm with his friends Earl Silbar and Steven Ashby. On July 6 Silbar, a teacher and vice president of his AFSCME local, and Ashby, a labor activist, drove 175 miles to Decatur to talk with the Staley workers and participate in the union's second demonstration for unemployment benefits in Springfield. Inspired by the workers' militancy, they met with Dave Watts and asked if they could form a local solidarity committee. Watts responded enthusiastically. "It was obvious we needed all the support we could get," recalled Watts about that first meeting with the Chicagoans. "I was always enthusiastic about the idea of solidarity committees."

Local 837's posture was the exception, not the rule, in the labor movement. Most unions on strike or locked out do not welcome independent organizing on their behalf. They invite allies to attend their rallies but fear they could not control the day-to-day activism of independent committees.

Back in Chicago, Silbar, Ashby, and Gilbert were joined by the seasoned unionist Jack Spiegel, who began his labor activism organizing shoe workers in the 1930s. Together the foursome decided to launch the Chicago Staley Workers Solidarity Committee (SWSC), and on July 17, eighty-five people attended the founding meeting. Staley workers Dan Lane, Wayne Carlyle, and Ron Van-Scyoc spoke at the meeting. Following the Chicago model, within nine months of the lockout the Road Warriors initiated committees in a dozen cities. Over the course of the 2½-year lockout, groups in eighty cities, including a few in Europe, organized support for the workers.

To most Staley workers and their families, the idea that complete strangers who lived hundreds of miles away would devote endless hours to working on their behalf was mind-boggling. A handful were suspicious of supporters' motives, but for the big majority the solidarity committees strengthened morale and their resolve to expand their campaign against Tate & Lyle.

At any time there are always a host of struggles for social or economic justice to draw the attention of politically active people. Why, then, did folks across the country volunteer thousands of hours to help workers in a small town in central Illinois? The answer lies in the character of the Staley fight. Activists were drawn into building support for the Staley workers when they heard of the intensive membership participation in the work-to-rule campaign. They were inspired when they learned that the local had overwhelmingly voted to raise dues from eighteen to one hundred dollars a month and successfully collected the union dues by hand. "I was paying twenty-seven dollars a month for dues," said Chicago supporter Mike Sacco, "and everyone I worked with bitched about it. Here were people making thirteen dollars an hour, almost half of what a telephone worker makes, that went to the hall and raised their dues to one hundred dollars a month!"

The union's weekly meetings attended by five hundred to a thousand workers and family members impressed activists such as Jon Baker, a representative with Machinists Local 701 in Chicago. Baker visited the local during the work-to-rule campaign and came away awed: "The fact that the union ran on such a democratic basis—the decisions were made at mass meetings. Family members were encouraged to participate. There was a strong level of militancy and amazing amount of unity . . . , husbands and wives there working together.

I saw how close the leadership was with the ranks. These are things different from what I see in day-to-day life."

Supporters were excited by the repeated door-to-door canvassing to elicit support from the Decatur community and by the national corporate campaign. And they were inspired when they met the Road Warriors. For many unionists and other progressives, Local 837's fight was no ordinary labor-management conflict. "The Staley fight opened my eyes, opened people's eyes to class issues," said Chicago activist David Klein. To the solidarity committee members, the Staley workers were in the forefront of the struggle to revive the labor movement. Members of the Chicago group asserted in early 1994, "A victory for [AIW 837] will be an encouragement to other workers that it is possible, even under today's adverse conditions for labor, to fight back and win. It will be a victory for new strategies and tactics; a victory for actively involving the membership in the affairs of the union; and a victory for building bridges between labor and its allies. It will show others what can be done—what must be done—to win."

Members of the Minneapolis–St. Paul solidarity group echoed this perspective in a letter to the Decatur local: "Your just struggle has engendered nationwide support and has become one of the most important labor battles of the last decade. Your victory will be a victory for all working people and send a signal to employers that their union-busting tactics will backfire."[16]

Jim Cavanaugh, the labor council president in Madison, Wisconsin, explained why labor activists in south central Wisconsin got involved:

> We feel that the primary purpose of the CLC is solidarity. Our labor council from time to time takes on a strike or lockout from outside our area and puts a lot of energy into it. We kind of look for a struggle where the workers are putting on a courageous and creative battle with a lot at stake. I guess one unwritten requirement is that the union have a Road Warrior component so that we can make these often distant struggles real for workers in our area. . . . I was intrigued with their aggressive stance and with the way they reached out for assistance from Jerry Tucker and Ray Rogers. . . . The Staley struggle was compelling.

Milwaukee CLC president Bruce Colburn was one of the first to rally to the Staley workers' side:

> It was certainly one of the more militant fights in terms of people standing up for their rights. They seemed to have an extreme amount of solidarity within their organization. They had what at least looked like a plan and some strategy to really fight over these issues of concessions. And they were a part of what seemed like a tremendous amount of attacks in the Decatur area. The Road Warriors were another reason people got involved: a very engaging group of people who would go around the country—extremely dedicated, good unionists, militant—and that helped spread the word.

For some unionists the Staley fight was also a tool to rejuvenate their *own* local labor movements. Chicago-area IBEW member Mike Sacco noted in 1994 that as "word got around, subsequent union meetings showed increased attendance. Everyone I spoke to was glad they came, and many felt that they had taken away something from the meeting. For some of the younger sisters and brothers, this was the first time they had *felt* solidarity. A month later, the AIW brothers' talks [were] still discussed, especially their work-to-rule campaign. In my view, our local received far more spiritually than we gave to the AIW materially."[17]

"When we do these kinds of things," said Jim Cavanaugh, "we see it as an educational opportunity as well as a solidarity activity. . . . Here it is real; it's not just theory." Adds Bruce Colburn, "As our people picked up on the [Staley workers'] willingness to sacrifice, their commitment to making change—it helped our people develop their *own* commitment and leadership."[18]

Students and others outside unions were similarly inspired as the Staley fight became a tangible example of the corporate war on workers' rights and the rising resistance to corporate-driven globalization. Each solidarity committee had student members, and a number of campuses spawned their own solidarity committees. "I'd always try to get a [Road Warrior] speaking engagement at local colleges," said Mike Griffin. "I love the universities. The kids are the best warriors you could ask for. Many times when I left a university, I'd think, 'God, I wish these were my kids.'"

Large universities were new territory to most of the Road Warriors, but they consistently found a welcoming audience. Over the course of the struggle the warriors spoke at more than three dozen universities across the country. During the Boston-area tour, for example, they spoke at Harvard, Clark, Smith, and the University of Massachusetts at Amherst. Royal Plankenhorn was initially terrified. But after receiving an enthusiastic response, he reflected, "Now I like to tell people I lectured at Harvard."

The Staley workers' struggle sparked the formation of a national student group, the Student Labor Action Coalition, which originated in Madison, Wisconsin. Steve Hinds, a graduate student at the University of Wisconsin, showed the *Deadly Corn* video to his undergraduate sociology class of mostly freshmen in February 1994. "Having that imagery about what is it like to work in a plant became this really great vehicle when we reached out to students," said Detroit activist Simone Sagovac. "This is what it is like to be a working person in a plant and to make products that we all use and we never think about."

Many of the Madison students felt compelled to take action and formed the Staley Solidarity Action Coalition (SSAC). Several graduate students who belonged to Madison's Teaching Assistants Association joined the SSAC. As the group took up the corporate campaigns, it became a notable presence on campus. During the spring 1994 semester a large contingent of SSAC members came to a Decatur rally and walked a picket line, many for the first time. In the fall the group changed its name to the Student Labor Action Coalition (SLAC) and advised a similar group of students at the University of Michigan in Ann Arbor on organizing Staley support work. A year later young activists from eight college campuses met in Ann Arbor to coordinate nationwide actions for the Staley workers and other labor struggles. Ultimately, SLAC built chapters on several Midwest and Northeast campuses and recruited new graduates to train as organizers at the AFL-CIO's Organizing Institute.

Aware of the growing student interest in labor, in 1996 newly elected AFL-CIO leaders initiated Union Summer, a program to bring college students onto union organizing drives as interns. Veterans of those experiences contributed to the formation in 1998 of United Students against Sweatshops, which grew to have chapters on over two hundred campuses. In many ways today's campus movement against sweatshops and for a living wage for campus workers was born in the Staley workers' solidarity movement.

Solidarity Committees at Work

In late autumn 1993, working from his desk at the Kandy Lane office, Mike Griffin took primary responsibility for forming new solidarity committees. In spring 1994, when Local 837 had established a dozen solidarity committees, mostly in the Midwest, Dave Watts reflected on the committees' growing impact in *War Zone*: "We cannot wage this battle, one that we think affects all workers, alone. . . . Union-led Staley worker solidarity groups can make our customer pressure program work. They can be the difference between survival and victory, or submission by starvation for us. We need a labor movement on the march in this country if the wave of unprovoked attacks on the jobs and standard of living of all workers is going to be turned back."[19]

Each time Road Warriors visited a city they counted on the solidarity committees to fill every free moment with speaking engagements. For example, in October 1994 the Boston committee, led by International Union of Electrical Workers Local 201 activist Russ Davis and the Jobs with Justice chapter, organized forty-six speaking engagements in ten days in Massachusetts and Rhode Island for Road Warriors Dick Schable and Royal Plankenhorn, raising over fourteen thousand dollars.

Whenever a central labor council sponsored a Labor Day parade or a rally, the solidarity committees would try to secure an invitation for Staley workers to speak and sell T-shirts. On five occasions Local 837 issued a call for a national rally, asking supporters to come to Decatur, and the solidarity committees were the main vehicles for publicizing the rallies and bringing supporters to them, often renting buses or vans. Committees sometimes sponsored their own rallies and forums as well. The Chicago committee, for example, held a picket line of 125 people, including a dozen Staley workers, at the State of Illinois Center to demand unemployment benefits. Through the invitation of International Brotherhood of Electrical Workers Local 134, eighty Staley workers and spouses joined in the Chicago Labor Day parade, forming the most vocal contingent. For Decatur's Labor Day parade three days later, fifty Chicagoans traveled to Decatur.[20]

In September over fifty Chicago labor leaders squeezed into a private room at a Greek restaurant, paid for their own dinners, and heard from the Road Warriors. The group was energized, and the unionists promised to host Road Warriors at their union halls, raise funds, and publicize upcoming rallies in Chicago and Decatur. And on a cold and snowy October 30, 1993, over four hundred unionists and supporters attended a rousing solidarity rally at Chicago's downtown Methodist Temple. The rally, which was endorsed by twenty-seven union and community groups, had speakers from Chicago-area unions under siege, as well as Decatur union presidents Dave Watts and Larry Solomon and downstate striking mineworkers. After donations and a closing, the rally moved outside and marched through the downtown streets to the office of Tate & Lyle's union-busting law firm, Seyfarth, Shaw. Another solidarity rally, attended by over seven hundred supporters, was held at the Chicago Teamsters hall in March 1994.

In November 1994 United Auto Workers activist Caroline Lund and labor activist Steve Zeltzer became cochairs of California's Bay Area Solidarity Committee after organizing a benefit dinner attended by eighty people. The proceeds were given to Decatur's Staley workers, but the Cat workers' fight was presented as equally important, for they had gone on strike in June 1994. "I always saw the Staley struggle in partnership with the Cat struggle," stated Lund. "I thought this was the central labor struggle that should have been embraced by the whole movement." Two months later the committee organized an extensive speaking tour for the Road Warriors and rallies for the Decatur locals and striking San Francisco newspaper workers.

A key task of the solidarity committees was to mobilize support for Local 837's grassroots corporate campaign. While activism around State Farm and Domino's Sugar was slow, when the campaign targets switched to Staley customers Miller Brewing in early 1994 and PepsiCo a year later, the committees became much more engaged (see chapter 8). Miller and Pepsi frequently sponsor festivals, concerts, and fairs across the country, so the committees handed out thousands of flyers asking people to call Staley's customers and tell them to stop purchasing Staley corn sweetener. The committees also distributed thousands of copies of the union's *Deadly Corn* and *Struggle in the Heartland* videos.

Intense, lifelong friendships were formed between solidarity activists and Staley workers. Perhaps the most beloved and easily recognizable supporter was the Chicago committee's Jack Spiegel. Spiegel was immortalized in the *Struggle in the Heartland* video, both for being one of the forty-eight people arrested for blocking Staley's plant gate on June 4, 1994 (his twenty-ninth arrest in his seven decades of labor and social justice activism) and for his rousing speech at the conclusion of the June 25 demonstration (see chapter 12). The untiring activism of the eighty-nine-year-old Spiegel was a source of enormous inspiration to the Staley workers. "The moment you met him, you knew he was special," wrote Mike Griffin in a tribute to Spiegel, who died in 2000. "Jack was a teacher, a fighter, a scholar by experience; Jack *was* labor history."[21]

The Minneapolis–St. Paul support group had first come together in 1985–86 to build solidarity for the striking Hormel workers in nearby Austin. The Hormel and Staley workers were connected through both struggles' association with Ray Rogers, but Staley workers also felt a strong connection to the Hormel fight because many had become avid readers of Peter Rachleff's *Hard-Pressed in the Heartland: The Hormel Strike and the Future of the Labor Movement.* The book outlined Hormel workers' formation of solidarity groups across the country and served as a guidebook for the Staley workers and their burgeoning solidarity committees.

To raise funds, solidarity committees in many cities asked musicians to give benefit concerts. The St. Louis committee organized an event they called "Rock Out the Lock-out Blues" and a concert by the folksinger Anne Feeney. Feeney, a labor troubadour, wrote a song about the Staley workers, "War on the Workers," which was featured on the soundtrack of the *Struggle in the Heartland* video. The Chicago committee held a benefit with the bluegrass band Whiskey Hollow. In northwest Indiana supporters organized an event titled "Christmas in the War Zone Rock Benefit."

One of the more remarkable displays of solidarity came from symphony musicians. Through the request of Chicago committee member Joel Finkel, musicians with the Chicago Symphony Orchestra (CSO) held a benefit concert. "It might surprise people to hear that members of an orchestra would give support to blue-collar workers," the violist and American Federation of Musicians member Max Raimi explained when he and two other musicians performed and were interviewed on the Studs Terkel radio show in late 1993 to promote the benefit. "But we realize that the fight of the Staley workers is about all working people, including us. . . . When workers are not allowed to strike or to bargain collectively, it has very grave ramifications for us as well."[22]

In the fall of 1993 four CSO labor activists organized themselves as the Mallarmé Quartet, and then, as more CSO musicians joined their effort for 1994 and 1995 benefit concerts, as the Solidarity Chamber Players. The three concerts raised seventeen thousand dollars. At each concert Road Warriors updated the audience on their struggle. When the CSO was scheduled to play at Millikin University, in Decatur, tuxedo-clad CSO members leafleted arriving concertgoers with flyers expressing their solidarity with the locked-out workers. Although it was a highly unusual action, members of Chicago AFM Local 10–208 voted overwhelmingly to sanction the leafleting. When the Decatur police ordered the musicians off the entryway to the auditorium, they went out in the pouring rain to the public sidewalk to give flyers to concertgoers as they drove into the parking lot.

Inspired by this example, activists in Detroit initiated a benefit concert by members of the Detroit Symphony Orchestra in January 1995 and raised five thousand dollars. Not only did each concert raise money for the Staley workers, but, because of the unusual character of the benefits, activists were able to get more than the usual organizations to volunteer their mailing lists to publicize the concerts.

In his book about the 1985–86 Hormel strike, Peter Rachleff recounts how solidarity activists organized a Christmas caravan for the strikers' children. In October 1993 Chicago solidarity activist C. J. Hawking borrowed the idea and volunteered to coordinate the effort. As Chicago unions announced the food and toy drive in their newsletters and at membership meetings, donations poured in. The 1993 "Holiday Caravan" brought hundreds of toys for the 145 children of AIW 837 workers and thousands of pounds of food for the families.

The caravan was greeted by a large group of Staley workers who unloaded the packed cars and minivans—and by local television and newspaper reporters. Spirits were high as people laughed and hugged one another. Then supporters moved into the packed union hall to attend the weekly AIW 837 solidarity meeting, and checks were presented to the union. One wife told a Chicago activist that she cried throughout the meeting. "You know, every time I get discouraged and think about what this company is doing to us," she said, "I then think about all of you in Chicago and all the work you're doing for us. . . . Thank you for bringing us Christmas."[23]

In 1994 the holiday solidarity effort grew to include fourteen cities in seven states. Hundreds of local unions collected toys and food and wrote checks, and unions, churches, and bookstores agreed to be drop-off sites for donations. A few days before Christmas that year, a caravan of eighty people in twenty-eight vehicles, including a forty-foot tractor-trailer filled with toys and food, pulled into the local's parking lot. The Holiday Solidarity Caravan was met by three hundred cheering Staley workers and family members.[24] "When I saw the caravan pulling into the parking lot with the semitrailer leading the way, and all the blinkers flashing and horns honking, I knew that the true spirit of Christmas and solidarity was alive and here for us," exclaimed Ethel Fargusson. "To think that so many people took a day off to drive down here to make sure that we had a good Christmas, it's overwhelming."

A human chain spontaneously formed to unload the trailer and cars. Toys were brought into the union hall to be sorted according to the children's age groups. The number of toys was so vast that the workers were also able to give presents to their grandchildren. Supporters then were treated to a dinner provided by the local and afterward attended the weekly solidarity meeting in the packed union hall, where it was announced that the caravan had also brought checks totaling nearly forty-one thousand dollars for the union's solidarity fund, and another twenty-thousand dollars for the Caterpillar workers and the Bridgestone/Firestone workers, who went on strike in the summer of 1994.[25] Decatur congregations contributed over five thousand dollars, the third collection from local churches. "Many people understand what is happening in the Decatur community," said Father Martin Mangan, of St. James Church. "They know they have to be with the workers because it's the side of justice. Helping these workers is God's work."

"I can't believe all the work people have done for us," said Barrie Williams while shaking his head in disbelief. "We know that we have a lot of supporters out there, but we don't always get to see who they are. . . . To see those people hanging out of car windows, waving to us as they came into the parking lot, shouting 'Solidarity,' bringing carload after carload of toys—well, it brought tears to just about everyone's eyes." Thirteen-year-old Joey VanScyoc told a television reporter, "People might think that this is going to be our worst Christmas ever. They're wrong. We may not have much, but this is the best Christmas I've ever had!"

"We wanted to show our solidarity to these workers during a time of year that otherwise might be bleak for them," said Lorenzo Crowell, vice president of SEIU 1199 in Gary and a vice president of the Northwest Indiana Federation of Labor. "We used this [caravan] to educate our own members about how one union is fighting back against a multimillion dollar corporation. More and more, our members are seeing the Staley fight as their fight, too."

8

Debating the
Corporate Campaign

With its membership locked out, said Dave Watts, AIW 837 would have a "fighting force of 760 full-time activists" who would bring the company's union-busting practices into the national spotlight. "When you lock-out a well-organized membership," declared Ray Rogers, "you give the union a full-time army of campaigners . . . who will fan out into the community and across the country to campaign against Staley's actions."[1]

After the success of the two bank campaigns, Rogers chose Domino Sugar and State Farm Insurance as the next two corporate-campaign targets. However, a debate soon emerged over the choice of targets, with the Kandy Lane activists arguing that a focus on customers, not Tate & Lyle's financial allies, would be more effective. By March 1994 the local had shifted its target to the Miller Brewing Company, and the Road Warriors and solidarity committees enthusiastically took up the new campaign. Seven months later Miller announced it was severing ties with Staley.

Domino Sugar and State Farm

Because Domino sugar was the most recognized Tate & Lyle product sold in the United States, Rogers argued that a boycott campaign would muddy the name of Tate & Lyle.[2] "I may pick a target not because it may be the thing that is going to necessarily force an issue," said Rogers, "but because it gives the opportunity to expand the visibility of the campaign and to educate a much greater audience. Domino—especially in New York City and other cities—is like an institution. Everybody uses it in restaurants. No one can identify Staley or Tate & Lyle, but they know Domino sugar."[3]

A Domino boycott raised questions for the local, because the Staley plant did not make the product. Leaders discussed the issue with Rogers and Jerry

Tucker, in particular the risk that unionized Domino workers at the other plants might be hostile to a boycott. Dave Watts concluded: "The 760 locked-out Staley workers have thought long and hard about the impact of our boycotts on other people's jobs. And we know that the Domino-GW boycott will win us a fair contract long before any Tate & Lyle sugar workers are hurt. . . . Tate & Lyle's workers can't be lulled into a false sense of security because the company is focusing its attack on Decatur. Once they're done in Decatur, if they win, they're going after some other Tate & Lyle workers."[4]

Supporters were therefore asked to write letters of protest to Domino's CEO, to talk with supermarket and restaurant managers about dropping Domino sugar, and to spread news of the boycott. AIW 837 workers and solidarity committees distributed flyers at supermarkets, street fairs, and community gatherings. In Decatur one independent grocer took Domino off his shelves, but the other grocers, most often chain stores whose upper management dictated policies from afar, did not follow suit.

The Domino campaign, however, was to be secondary. Rogers selected State Farm as the primary target. State Farm was the largest stockholder in Decatur-based Archer Daniels Midland (ADM), with 7.2 percent of the corporation's stock. State Farm also held $101 million in ADM bonds, making it the largest ADM bondholder. Archer Daniels Midland, an $8.5 billion agribusiness multinational, was supposedly a competitor of Tate & Lyle, but through a British subsidiary, it was in actuality the largest Tate & Lyle stockholder, with 7.4 percent of its shares. As was discussed previously, in 1992 ADM joined Staley in building a 3.5-mile pipeline to allow it to ship starch slurry to Staley's facility in the event of a labor conflict.[5]

Rogers had another reason for going after State Farm: it was one of the largest insurance company bondholders and the tenth-largest stockholder in Caterpillar, whose union workers were also fighting for a fair contract. Before announcing the campaign, Rogers and Watts won the support of Larry Solomon, the president of UAW Local 751, which represented 1,850 Caterpillar workers in Decatur, and Jerry Brown, head of the 5,000-member UAW Local 974, in Peoria. Brown warned, "State Farm cannot be allowed to collect insurance premiums from union members with one hand and then beat up on their unions with the other."[6]

At union meetings in Decatur, said Rogers, a show of hands revealed that large numbers of members held State Farm policies, making State Farm susceptible to a boycott. The corporate-campaign flyer addressed its message to American workers:

> For years, the State Farm Insurance Companies have tried to convince us that "like a good neighbor, State Farm is there." But the 760 members of Allied Industrial Workers Local 837 have experienced State Farm's neighborliness through its ties to our employer, the A. E. Staley Manufacturing Company. And in State Farm we see

a company that is engaged in corporate America's war against workers. We're asking you to join our consumer boycott of State Farm and send our "good neighbor" a powerful message: act responsibly toward workers—or lose lots of business.[7]

Kip Voytek, Roger's assistant who spent many days in Decatur in 1993, explained why he thought the State Farm campaign was winnable:

If you can get hundreds of people canceling their insurance policies, you're quickly costing the company a million dollars, and people don't easily come back to their insurance companies once they switch. State Farm was vulnerable because State Farm didn't have enough of a stake in Staley destroying their union. Certainly State Farm would like to see that, because it would be more profitable for them—but it wouldn't be profitable enough to make up for those one thousand customers that were not going to come back.

Three days after the lockout, the union brought fourteen busloads and many carloads of workers and family members to Bloomington, Illinois, to launch the State Farm boycott. A boisterous crowd of seven hundred people demonstrated outside the company's headquarters. In July 1993 Rogers mailed sixty thousand brochures to union supporters across the country, calling on them to contact their State Farm agent to threaten to cancel their policies unless State Farm pressured Staley to end the lockout.

In August and September the Staley workers fanned out to the nearby Illinois cities of Bloomington, Champaign, and Peoria to meet with dozens of State Farm insurance agents. Rogers counted on panic-stricken agents flooding the home office with calls. Road Warriors spoke in dozens of cities in the summer and fall of 1993, calling on activists to write to their State Farm agents. The new solidarity committees passed out flyers in front of State Farm offices and at labor and community gatherings. At the weekly union meetings Rogers read letters from supporters who had canceled their policies; by late 1993 supporters in ten states had made calls or sent letters of protest to the company.

State Farm agents were bewildered by the sudden protests. Executives wrote to their sixteen thousand offices and to concerned customers that the company did hold 7 percent of ADM but that it was not, as the union claimed, "a controlling interest." Furthermore, State Farm did not "attempt to pick sides in labor disputes." The company tried to reassure customers that it was not antiunion and was in fact "one of the largest purchaser of union made automobiles."[8]

Dissent over the State Farm Campaign

The State Farm campaign took place during a critical time for the locked-out workers. The union had fought for and won unemployment benefits in August 1993. This victory not only strengthened the workers' resolve and lifted their hopes but also allowed them to pay most of their bills. As a result, many workers decided to become more active in the union's campaign. It was during this time that the largest number of members participated as Road Warriors. As they made their trips, however, they soon discovered multiple problems with the State Farm campaign.

First, the State Farm connection was too indirect and cumbersome to explain. Clearly ADM was aligned with Tate & Lyle to cripple unions, but the State Farm connection was more tenuous. The Road Warriors, given only a short time to make their presentations at union meetings, tried to explain that State Farm owned part of ADM, which in turn had a British subsidiary, which owned part of Tate & Lyle, which in turn owned Staley. Dan Lane recalled,

> People were having too hard a time connecting, "What the hell does State Farm have to do with this struggle in Decatur?" Our *own workers* did not understand it and were not buying into it. Rogers went through his whole presentation, and people got hyped about it, but once people stepped away from it and started processing it, they were saying, "Wait a minute. You want me to do this to A so he'll do something to B to do something to C to do something to D? That seems like an awful long, indirect way to get something done." . . . We started losing momentum. We went from a whole lot of people involved in the in-plant to all of a sudden people . . . saying, "I haven't got time for that."

"While the early victories of [Staley officials] Powers and Mohan stepping down from their respective bank boards fueled our belief in our efforts," recalled Bill Winter, "victories after that were hard to come by. . . . We had no real way of gauging our effects on the sales of Domino sugar, nor could we discern how many people had dropped State Farm Insurance. The fact that we could not see any concrete results of these efforts led many to believe that they weren't effective. Once visible results of Ray Rogers's efforts weren't forthcoming, he seemed to lose favor with the rank-and-file."

Second, the membership found that large numbers of people could not be persuaded to change their insurance policies. Consumers received discounts for being longtime customers, and most people didn't want to undergo the arduous process of finding another company. The corporate campaign, said Lorell Patterson, "stalled around that State Farm thing. Why are you telling people to dump their insurance? They're not going to do it. . . . Most people just stayed where they were. But Rogers just kept hammering that State Farm thing."

Third, the Road Warriors heard harsh words about the State Farm campaign from the solidarity committees, echoing the criticism that the connection was obscure. When they handed out flyers in front of State Farm branch offices in their cities, they found only a trickle of traffic, since most insurance business was done over the phone. Supporters felt they were wasting their time.

Central labor council presidents Jim Cavanaugh in Madison and Bruce Colburn in Milwaukee were frustrated. "We didn't do much around State Farm," Cavanaugh recalled. "We thought that was quite a reach and a really hard sell." Colburn echoed, "We weren't able to make a very clear connection to the general public. We didn't have any way to put much pressure on State Farm. It seemed like it was a pretty ineffective campaign."

Informal discussions at the union hall, picket lines, food bank, and the Kandy Lane office led members to call for a change in corporate campaign targets. But Rogers insisted on keeping the focus on State Farm. A corporation's financial backers were its lifeline, argued Rogers; cutting off Tate & Lyle's ties to the financial community would rapidly bring the company back to the bargaining table with a decent contract. Pressure on Staley's customers wouldn't work. "You don't win boycotts by getting people not to buy the product," said Rogers. "We live in a society where everyone is after your attention. . . . They hear the [boycott] message one month, [and] the next month they think it's off." Rogers continually reminded members that isolating J. P. Stevens from its financial backers had been the key to victory in 1980.[9]

Rogers's aggressiveness and boisterous self-confidence generally served him well, but some of the members felt intimidated by his zealous defense of his strategy. "There were a lot of people saying that they didn't think [the corporate campaign] was working," said Lorell Patterson, "and it seemed like they were blown off."[10] Recalled Voytek, sometimes "people would have legitimate tactical questions: 'I don't understand this? Why are we doing this?' But Ray would answer it as if it was a hostile question."

Voytek later reflected on the members' doubts: "If [the workers] weren't going to buy into it, then maybe we should have stepped back from it. Putting resources into a half-hearted pursuit of State Farm might have been a waste of resources, however good a target it was, since not everyone was in agreement, and in a lot of cases people were doing it just because they had faith in Ray."

When the Allied Industrial Workers voted to merge with the United Paperworkers International Union in September 1993 (see chapter 14), UPIU special projects coordinator Mark Brooks began working with the local. (The Allied Industrial Workers merged with the United Paperworkers International Union in January 1994, and AIW Local 837 became UPIU Local 7837. The manuscript alternates between the two names, depending on the time frame being discussed.) Brooks saw no merit in the State Farm campaign and favored pressuring customers instead, but he stayed quiet, viewing it as the local's call to make. Said Brooks, "State Farm owned 7 percent of ADM, which owned 7 percent of Tate & Lyle. I wish someone had asked the question, 'What is 7 percent of 7 percent?' It's 49/10,000ths of indirect influence. It struck me as [a target] that was not going to produce anything. You can take the view that there was no real harm done, but it seems to me that any amount of effort that we could have poured early on into other avenues would have helped a great deal."

But Rogers was unequivocal about State Farm's being the path to victory. "I thought it was a great target," said Rogers years later. "State Farm had millions of policyholders. The first mailing we did [in July 1993] brought in a *lot* of money from supporters." In 1994 Rogers told a Decatur reporter, "I raised $100,000 within two months of the lock-out and $400,000 within six months."[11]

Rogers had indisputable dynamism, but to many he seemed to exert inordinate influence. "It was hard to get Dave [Watts] to do anything that was contrary to Ray Rogers's program," observed Brooks. He added, however, "I'm not sure the local was in a position to know what a better approach might be." Jerry Tucker concurred, observing that the local "had invested so much, it would have looked like a defeat to the rank-and-file if all of a sudden somebody had said, '[State Farm] was a fool's errand.'" But Tucker had never been happy with Rogers's choice of targets.

The two advisers had known each other for several years. Rogers had hosted a fundraising party in New York City when Tucker launched his reform campaign for the United Auto Workers presidency in early 1992. Tucker appreciated Rogers's ability to garner publicity, raise funds, and put the local on the map, and Rogers acknowledged that there wasn't "anybody better than Jerry Tucker on organizing internal campaigns." But there had always been an underlying tension. Rogers felt that Tucker took the in-plant campaign too far and was critical of the safety stand-down. There was a "fairly big division over this tactical issue," recalled Voytek.

For his part, Tucker had never been happy with Rogers's corporate-campaign targets. "The bank campaigns," said Tucker, "virtually had no impact": "If we were talking about [the old] Staley—homegrown, family-run, its top executives spread out in the community—then that would have been a whole different ball game. There was potential for embarrassment. But when you're being run from London by a group of people who didn't care if they lost the whole management [team] tomorrow, it doesn't matter."

In Tucker's view, delineating the State Farm connection to Tate & Lyle involved a "tortured description," and the campaign was a "weak strategy" whose chances of success were "extremely remote." During the in-plant campaign Tucker felt he shouldn't openly fight for a shift in targets. The workers had hired Rogers to strategize a corporate campaign and had placed their trust in his leadership. Now they were locked out, however, and the stakes were higher.

Miller Beer

At first quietly and then more forcefully, Tucker began to assert that the local should target customers who purchased Staley product from the plant. Staley's biggest product, high-fructose corn syrup, is found in hundreds of popular food items. Tucker talked with the workers who knew the destinations of deliveries. He made a list of the companies that purchased large quantities, including PepsiCo, Coca-Cola, Miller Brewing, the J.M. Smucker Company, and Brach's Confections. A customer, Tucker argued, could be pressured to purchase corn syrup from one of Staley's competitors. As Staley lost customers and income, it would be forced to begin bargaining fairly. Such a target would also be easier to explain and more appealing to supporters than was the complicated web of Staley's financial allies.

Tucker argued for targeting the Miller Brewing Company, which accounted for 11 percent of Staley's income. In 1994 Miller was the second-largest brewing company in the United States, with annual sales of more than $4 billion. The beer industry, with 1994 sales of $49 billion, is highly competitive. Beer companies spend tens of millions of dollars on advertising every year. When one beer tops the sales chart in a major city, the company highlights that fact in local advertising in an effort to solidify its dominance. Just a 1 percent drop in market share causes tremors in the boardrooms of the three companies that dominate the U.S. market, Miller, Anheuser-Busch, and Adolph Coors.

Miller was thus vulnerable to a mass campaign. "Miller would be the easiest to roll," said Tucker, "and we needed a victory. Just like in the in-plant campaign, you need something new happening every week." Tucker argued for focusing on key cities with active solidarity committees. For example, research showed that Miller Lite and Miller Genuine Draft were the best-selling beers in Chicago, followed by Old Style and Budweiser. In 1994 Anheuser-Busch, which makes Budweiser, the national best-seller, had launched an advertising blitz in the Chicago market with the avowed goal of toppling Miller. "It's very much a dogfight," said Anheuser-Busch vice president Bob Lachky in August 1994.[12] In response, Miller made deals to have its beer be the only one sold at every sporting event possible, including Bulls and White Sox games and World Cup soccer matches. Miller had similar deals for Chicago's premier festivals, including Taste of Chicago, the Blues Festival, and Venetian Night, each drawing over a million people, as well as dozens of smaller neighborhood festivals.

Tucker further contended that Miller would be particularly vulnerable to a labor campaign since a primary customer base was blue-collar workers and it frequently advertised its products as union-made beer. Finally, there was an important precedent. In 1992 Miller had succumbed to a campaign organized by the United Steel Workers when Ravenswood Aluminum of West Virginia— which sold aluminum to Miller for its cans—locked out its 1,700 workers. The USWA's successful corporate campaign targeting Miller was a factor in the Ravenswood workers' victory.

Before the Miller versus State Farm debate crystallized, a few Road Warriors had already begun to establish connections with the unionized Miller workers in Milwaukee. CLC president Bruce Colburn talked to these workers about getting involved. On July 17, 1993, Dan Lane, Ron VanScyoc, and Wayne Carlyle met with leaders of the two unions, UAW Local 9 and IAM Local 66, that represented workers at Miller's Milwaukee breweries. Colburn recalled: "We were trying to use the support of the union there to push the company so it wasn't confrontational; to let Miller know that workers in Milwaukee and their own union wanted them to take some action. . . . There is always an issue when you ask union workers to do something around their own company. But people still went ahead even though they have lost a lot of jobs themselves over a period of years."

After a long and friendly meeting, the Road Warriors were promised support from both unions, with Local 9 being particularly cooperative. Road Warriors made repeated trips to the Miller plant gates to hand out the "Crisis in Decatur" brochure, give away *Deadly Corn* videos, and conduct bucket drops at the plant gate to ask workers for donations.

In early August, however, the solidarity work with Miller unionists was called to an abrupt halt. On their second trip to Milwaukee Road Warriors were mysteriously called back to Decatur by Dave Watts and AIW representative Bill Coleman. Shortly thereafter, on August 18, Watts, Coleman, bargaining chair Jim Shinall, and Road Warrior Roger Tucker made their own trip to Milwaukee to meet with Miller union leaders. They also met with two Miller executives.

Watts, Shinall, and Coleman were fearful that if Staley lost Miller as a customer, management might have to lay workers off after the lockout ended. Unions that pressure customers to stop doing business with their employers assume this risk, for the goal is to immediately affect the company's bottom line. Unions generally gauge the risk to be manageable, since the company can regain the business after a fair contract is signed. Watts gave an optimistic report at the next Tuesday-night meeting: "[It] went very well. . . . We opened the meeting [with the corporate executives] with a very, very sincere statement. 'We are not here to drive Miller Brewing away. We are here to put them on notice of what could possibly happen to them.'" Watts reported that the executives said they would sample Staley product to verify quality, since it was now being made by scabs.[13]

Based on Watts's report, Dan Lane, who had been the chief coordinator with the Miller workers, continued his efforts to communicate with them, but he now received a chilly reception. "All of a sudden when I called up [to Milwaukee]," recalled Lane, "nobody wanted to talk with us. [They said], 'You're on a whole different rhythm than what your leadership is. We don't want to get in between this.' . . . Bang! It was done! . . . As a result, everything on the Miller campaign was shut down."

The shift had a demoralizing effect on Roger Tucker, who had been the only rank-and-filer on the Milwaukee trip with Watts. Roger Tucker had been very active in the in-plant campaign and was a valuable Road Warrior. He now believed that his union leadership had backed down too quickly and soon stopped his Road Warrior trips, barely attending subsequent union meetings.

To Dan Lane, Roger Tucker, and most of the union's activists, targeting Miller held great promise. As Jerry Tucker observed, however, a large percentage of the workers found the selection of corporate-campaign targets to be "mystical," something that they little understood. Since Ray Rogers was supposed to be "the expert," they deferred to him. Tucker summarized, "[The workers] didn't have the same feeling of control as with the in-plant."

The corporate-campaign focus, therefore, remained on State Farm and Domino. Miller was given only tertiary coverage in campaign literature as one of many Staley customers. The brochures asked supporters to write to these customers expressing concern that they were supporting union busting by purchasing Staley syrup.

At the local's first big postlockout demonstration its contradictory stance toward Miller became clear to supporters. The November 6, 1993, rally marked the fiftieth anniversary of the birth of AIW Local 837. Fifteen hundred workers and supporters braved subfreezing temperatures and blizzardlike conditions to hear speakers rail against corporate greed. Soon-to-retire AIW president Nick Serraglio expressed his solidarity. Because delegates at the AIW convention had voted two months before to merge with the United Paperworkers, the UPIU sent two vice presidents. Boyd Young declared, "A. E. Staley is a modern-day sweatshop. For those who say unions are not needed, let them come to Decatur!"[14] "We are at your command," declared Glenn Goss.[15] Galen Garrett, an IBEW member, sang a song he had written, "I'd Walk a Mile . . . to Beat Tate & Lyle." The Reverend Tim McDonald, national director of Operation Breakbasket, traveled from Atlanta to call on "all people of goodwill to join together," saying, "We can unlock the lock-out—the spirit of the workers is the locksmith that will unlock it."[16]

The rally was held outside the union hall, but the freezing weather and snow soon drove most protesters inside. Out-of-town supporters were stunned to discover that Miller beer was still being served at the bar. How could the local allow Miller in its union hall while it simultaneously asked supporters to write protest letters to the company? Ray Rogers, Jerry Tucker, and the Kandy Lane activists had pleaded that Miller not be sold, but a majority on the executive board overruled them. Gary Lamb later explained that the union hall belonged to all of Decatur's AIW locals and that the hall's building board refused to pull Miller beer: "Their rationalization was that Miller beer was a union beer, sold very well from the bar, and they got a good deal from the distributor. . . . If they switched to a lesser-name beer they were afraid that the revenue would drop off, and they would have to do more bingos and other things to keep the revenue flowing for the board. That was it—money."

Local 837 treasurer Mike Grandon, who also served as treasurer of the building board, reportedly said, "We've got customers coming in here and they want Miller." Greg Hill and a majority of executive board members agreed with Grandon. "Miller is the beer we all like to drink," they stated matter-of-factly.[17]

The executive board's unwillingness to launch a campaign against Miller and the shocking sight of Miller in the union hall provided most supporters the first signals that the Decatur local might not be fully unified in its fight.

"It's Miller Time!"

Two months later, however, bowing to the pressure of the activists who were expressing rising dissatisfaction over the ineffective State Farm campaign, Watts and the executive board finally agreed to add Miller as a primary target. At the January 11, 1994, union meeting Tucker spoke about the change of course:

> The leadership has approved a decision to turn up the burners and spend a lot more effort on Miller beer. . . . Miller brewery stopped buying from Ravenswood a few years ago, and that decision almost turned that struggle around. . . . There are only so many things you can do, and one of them is to cut off [the company's] access to customers. . . . We talked today about promoting dozens and dozens more solidarity committees. Support committees can carry this fight for you and with you, if we build them.

Ray Rogers argued strenuously and won assent that State Farm remain a main target. Nonetheless, Miller quickly emerged as the principal focus of the local's corporate campaign and of the activities of the solidarity committees across the country, with State Farm falling by the wayside. By March 1994 the Road Warriors were emphasizing Miller in their speeches and found a receptive audience. "When we would talk about the campaign," recalled Royal Plankenhorn, "people said 'I'll never drink another Miller beer again.'" A flyer about Miller was produced by CCI and mailed to the sixty thousand sympathetic people and unions on the consulting firm's mailing list.

The campaign slogan in the April *War Zone* and on the initial mass-distributed flyer was "Miller Beer: Boycott Staley!" The language was chosen carefully. The campaigns against Miller (and later PepsiCo) were never officially boycotts. Unions engaged in corporate campaigns have to walk a legal tightrope. Under the 1947 Taft-Hartley Act, a union engaged in a strike or lockout can legally call for a boycott only of products made by its own company. "Secondary" boycotts of a company's customers or suppliers are against the law.

To avoid being hit with a big fine should Staley or its customers take the union to court, the local wanted to be clear that it was not technically advocating a consumer boycott of Miller products. Rather, it was urging supporters to "pressure"—not "boycott"—Staley's customers. Walking that fine line, the flyer called for Miller to boycott Staley, not for customers to boycott Miller. Nevertheless, the flyer used the word *boycott* with the hope of making Miller executives nervous.[18] It was the UPIU's attorneys who got nervous, however. They ordered Local 7837 to alter the language. The lawyers—Lynn Agee and special projects coordinator Mark Brooks—feared that Miller would sue the UPIU, alleging that *any* use of the term constituted a secondary boycott. The UPIU staff insisted on the slogan "Miller: Dump Staley."[19]

The solidarity committees enthusiastically moved into high gear on the Miller campaign, and local newspapers, the labor press, and campus newspapers began to feature the arguments against Miller. The committees organized mass leafleting at dozens of musical, cultural, and sporting events in cities across the Midwest where Miller was a corporate sponsor. Committee members often set up literature tables next to Miller beer tents and distributed flyers with a detachable coupon addressed to Miller headquarters and requesting that Miller dump Staley. Miller representatives sometimes asked the police to arrest Staley workers and their supporters, but knowing that the distribution of flyers on public property is a legally protected activity under the First Amendment, committee members were undeterred.

In Chicago, which boasts a large Irish American population and celebrates an annual tradition of dyeing the Chicago River green for St. Patrick's Day, a group of seventy-five unionists, community activists, and Road Warriors filled Miller bottles filled with red dye (signifying the Staley workers' blood) and then poured the contents into the Chicago River after the parade. The action was widely reported on local radio and television news that day.

Student Labor Action Committee activists at the University of Wisconsin targeted the on-campus UW Memorial Union—the largest beer distributor in Madison. "College students drink a lot of beer, so this is a case where students will be listened to," said SLAC leader Steve Hinds. "Miller must take responsibility for the products they use. If they don't then we are asking [students] to take their business elsewhere."[20]

The support groups also focused on local beer distributors. Breweries have distribution centers in large cities, and truck drivers making deliveries are often members of the Teamsters union. The committees in St. Louis and Chicago got lucky breaks. Teamsters in St. Louis were already fighting a Miller distributor that was trying to break the union in that city and had won the support of many tavern owners; in Chicago the association of beer distributors had broken a strike by truck drivers just a few years before. Activists leafleted the truck drivers, brought Road Warriors to their terminals, and distributed the Staley video. Road Warriors also returned to Miller breweries to talk to union officials and leaflet workers at plant gates. "It's a result of Miller's business that Staley is making a profit and they can continue to pursue this war," said Dan Lane on March 17, 1994, as he and a dozen others flyered Miller workers in Milwaukee.[21]

Still, whenever the Staley workers targeted a Staley customer—Domino, Miller, or Pepsi—whose workforce was represented by unions, those unions were often cool if not outright hostile to Local 7837's corporate campaign. The unions representing the brewery workers argued that the campaign against Miller, if successful, would lead to a decrease in Miller sales and therefore potentially to layoffs of union workers. The Staley workers argued that a boycott would hurt the company enough for it to drop Staley but not enough to force layoffs and that a victory for Local 7837 would benefit all unions. Despite many discussions with local and national union leaders, throughout the thirty-month lockout this tension with unions representing targeted companies was never resolved.

Nevertheless, when Teamsters Local 200, at Jacob Leinenkugel Brewing Company in Chippewa Falls, Wisconsin, heard about the campaign, union leaders got management to stop purchasing Staley corn syrup. "All of a sudden we got a letter from Leinenkugel saying they would pull out," recalled UPIU staffer Dick Blinn, "and it gave us hope." Leinenkugel had been purchased by Miller in 1988, so the victory gave impetus to press on against Miller itself.

Eight months after the campaign had officially begun, Miller announced that it would cease doing business with Staley when its contract expired three months later, on January 1, 1995. Miller stated that its decision was based on "cost considerations," and Staley spokesperson J. Patrick Mohan dismissed the loss of a major customer by casually remarking, "Customers come and go."[22]

But the Staley workers were convinced that their campaign had won the desired effect. Miller had felt the heat and was abandoning Staley. Workers and supporters were exuberant. It had been a year since the last victory—knocking Staley officials off the boards of two banks—and this was a success that hit A. E. Staley directly in the pocketbook. Unionists speculated that the timing of Miller's announcement was tied to a national rally set for Decatur on October 15, 1994, at which a major escalation of the Miller campaign would have been announced.[23] "Union solidarity across the country turned Miller around," said Dave Watts, "and the same thing can happen to Staley's other major customers if they don't move to end this bitter dispute and get us a fair contract!"

9

Peacetime Soldiers
and Wartime Soldiers

Although the lockout had been a shock to the Staley workers, they responded with both anger and a determination to escalate the fight to win a fair contract. The intensity of the in-plant campaign was transferred to the picket line, the Kandy Lane organizing center, the national corporate campaign, and the Road Warriors' trips across the country.

But the union and its leaders were not united. Some members of the executive board and the bargaining committee quickly grew wary of the grassroots activism and the militant tone of the fight. They began to maneuver to reassert control over the activists and to moderate the union. The activists, in turn, believed that many of the union's top leaders were an obstacle to winning. Union president Dave Watts struggled to mediate this division, fearing that disunity would cripple the fight against the company.

The Old Guard versus the Activists

Division over leadership first emerged during the in-plant campaign. Although they had endorsed hiring Jerry Tucker to lead the campaign, some members of the executive board and bargaining committee did not fully engage in the work-to-rule, and others did not participate at all. Work-to-rule "was kind of a time when people got to evaluate their union loyalty and those who they had picked for leadership," recalled Dike Ferris, a bargaining committee member for fourteen years and a leader of the in-plant campaign. "There were people who professed to really be union people who didn't stick their necks out at all. . . . We found them out pretty quickly."[1]

The divisions were clear early on, said bargaining committee member Dan Lane:

There was no question in my mind from the get-go that the executive board was *so* uncomfortable with the in-plant. They got *really* uncomfortable when people started walking in the company offices and started taking over meetings. They were *really* uncomfortable when all these demonstrations were going on. And they got *really* uncomfortable when we walked out of the plant that morning [June 17]. In fact, in two buildings the executive board member was the last person to leave. He was just sitting there alone in both cases.

The in-plant campaign succeeded brilliantly in broadening the leadership beyond the local's elected officials. Up to a quarter of the plant's workers were aggressively leading on-the-job actions, and another half were actively participating. Tucker had told the workers that they must begin to see themselves as leaders if the in-plant campaign was to succeed, and scores of workers had taken the challenge to heart. "It was just amazing that [rank-and-file] people, who I never thought in my wildest dreams [would become active], all of a sudden started surfacing during the in-plant," said Lane. "These were people who very seldom went to a union meeting and who had not really been involved in union politics."

One incident that poignantly revealed the inverse authority—the rank-and-file leading much of the elected leadership—occurred shortly before the lockout, when Gary Lamb and executive board member Greg Hill were assigned to work together in the plant. Lamb remembered, "I was going around promoting solidarity, and Greg was saying, 'Lamb, you're going to get us fired.' I said, "No, I'm not. Just stay in tow, buddy."

While the in-plant campaign had transformed the way the membership thought about unionism, it hadn't affected the majority on the executive board. Seven of the union's top leaders—executive board members Greg Hill, Terry Hale, Mike Grandon, John Lehew, and Steve Haseley and bargaining committee members Jim Shinall and Denton Larrimore—quickly came together in an informal conservative caucus. They believed that they, the elected leaders, should make all decisions affecting the union. Haseley, who had been elected to leadership positions for over a decade, expressed these officers' growing disdain toward the activists and Road Warriors by calling the Kandy Lane volunteers "wannabes" who sought the status of the union's elected leaders. The seven leaders resented the newly empowered membership and feared that the direction and tenor of the fight, as portrayed to the public from Kandy Lane, were too radical. Danny Wirges, formerly the AIW regional director and now UPIU assistant regional director, and AIW/UPIU representative Bill Coleman aligned themselves with the seven conservative leaders.

The *Decatur Herald and Review*, which had condemned the local's struggle since 1992, gave ammunition to the old-guard leaders by publicizing the fact that the Road Warriors never turned down a speaking engagement, including those with left-wing groups. When the *Herald and Review* reported that Road Warrior Dan Lane was to speak in Chicago at a "Labor Militant Forum" sponsored by the Socialist Workers Party, the old guard repeatedly chastised Lane as a radical or a socialist.[2]

The old guard directed their criticism toward Jerry Tucker, too. While they would not make their accusations openly at a union meeting, privately they blamed Tucker for the lockout. This murmured accusation came even though in 1992 Tucker had repeatedly raised the possibility that the company could respond to a successful work-to-rule with a lockout, as had the labor educator Mark Crouch, and the members had been fully aware of the risks when they determined to try the tactic. The old-guard leaders also deeply resented Tucker's close association with the Kandy Lane activists.

They increasingly began to believe that Tucker, whom the membership strongly backed as the local's lead negotiator, was hurting the leadership's efforts to make major concessions and end the lockout. It was uncommon for the lead negotiator not to be a member of the union, but the Staley workers felt that since a member of a union-busting law firm was heading negotiations for Staley, then surely the union was entitled to have the expertise of Jerry Tucker on its side of the table. "It didn't take us long to see the worth of having Jerry Tucker on board," Dike Ferris related, "because he was the source of immense knowledge." Tucker followed the mandate from the membership and did not yield on any of their key issues, including the rotating twelve-hour shifts, subcontracting, and gutting the grievance and health and safety procedures.

As negotiations continued fruitlessly, it was apparent to most workers that the company was at the table merely to avoid NLRB charges for refusing to bargain in good faith and was intent on destroying the union. But bargaining chair Jim Shinall saw Tucker as the major barrier to securing a contract. Shinall thought that if *he* could be in charge, he could deliver an acceptable contract, even if it meant sacrificing on key issues."[Shinall] is a gullible cat," reflected Gary Lamb. "He [thought], 'I'm going to be the hero of this whole thing. I'm going to break it open.'"

In direct opposition to the mandate from the membership and to the bargaining committee's agreed strategy, Shinall would sometimes direct the bargaining sessions to the topic of retirement and severance packages, which was clearly in his self-interest, since he was hoping to retire soon. In their debriefing sessions Tucker would chide Shinall for his actions. Lamb, who was elected to the board in December 1993, recalled an incident that occurred shortly after he was elected: "I watched Jerry Tucker chastise [Shinall] like you would a little boy. I was new on the board, so I kept my mouth shut and listened. . . . Jerry Tucker said, 'I *told* you, Jim, *not* to do that! You approach it *this* way. This way works!' He said it quite loudly, clear across the room. I thought then, 'Boy, Shinall, you are taking it pretty hard in front of everybody.'... Later on, as I grew in confidence in Jerry Tucker ... I [understood] why [Shinall] was getting the chastising."

Meanwhile, the activists began to resent the inactivity of the seven officers, since they never came to Kandy Lane or organized outreach efforts. While the conservatives made a handful of trips during the work-to-rule and immediately after the lockout, none became Road Warriors.

When the Kandy Lane office was set up in August 1993, Dave Watts had assigned executive board member John Lehew to work there as the leadership's liaison. But Lehew walked the two blocks from the union hall to the Kandy Lane office only a couple of times. As for the others, Watts lamented, "I tried my damnedest to get Denton Larrimore, Steve Haseley, [and the others] to be part of [the Kandy Lane] office, to be the overseers as executive board members. None of them would ever do it."

All the while, the activists worked nonstop. Many volunteered sixty, seventy, or eighty hours a week, and the Road Warriors would leave their families for days. Among elected leaders, bargaining committee members Dan Lane and Dike Ferris became Road Warriors, and Bill Strohl contributed endless hours coordinating the food program. Neither did anyone doubt the long hours put into the fight by the local's president and vice president, Dave Watts and Bob Hull.

By the winter of 1993–94 the activists no longer viewed the conservatives as leaders. In the full-scale war with the company, most of their elected leaders were not rising to the occasion. As the conservatives began to bad-mouth the Kandy Lane volunteers and Road Warriors, the activists got steadily angrier at the officers who never left the Dineen Street office. Some Kandy Laners called the executive board majority the "extra board," a reference to new hires in the Staley plant who did the most menial work. Gary Lamb noted that the majority of the elected leadership were "good peacetime soldiers" but just didn't make "good wartime soldiers."

Watts's Dilemma

Dave Watts was torn between the two camps: the conservatives, who held a majority on the executive board and two of five seats on the bargaining committee, and the activists organizing out of the Kandy Lane office. The division was personally painful to him. He had served on the executive board since 1981, and long-standing board members Hill, Hale, Grandon, Lehew, and Haseley were his friends. Throughout the 1980s and early 1990s, this leadership team had conducted union business, made trips to conventions, and attended classes at the AFL-CIO–sponsored school outside Washington. When he moved from the local's vice presidency to become president in 1990, Watts depended on these officials to help him lead.

"With most of them," recalled Watts, "I had a pretty good friendship. I had worked with all these guys for years. . . . We'd have a few backyarders [barbecues], not a lot but a few, through the years. I thought we shared a devotion to the labor movement. . . . In the beginning, we brought labor educators in and everyone was on the same page." Watts assumed that the leadership team that had led the local to reject the contract and mobilize against the company would stay unified until a fair contract could be won.

Now, however, his old friends regularly complained to Watts that, because of the Road Warriors and Kandy Lane, their authority had dissipated. The board members wanted to reassert their authority over the union's operations and decisions because *they* were the elected leaders. Watts was sensitive to this position and keenly aware that this faction also had sympathizers among the membership.

At the same time, Watts wanted to see the grassroots activism expand. His primary goal was to get the best possible contract for the members, and an aggressive campaign for such a contract was being effectively organized out of Kandy Lane. Since the spring of 1992, thought Watts, when they had invited the labor educators to the hall to prepare the groundwork for a fight, the board had sought just this level of activism.

Dave Watts knew that he wasn't the same person he had been in the 1980s; he had grown in his education and he had grown as a leader. Watts wholeheartedly believed, as the union's corporate campaign literature said, that Local 837 was waging a fight for all working people, not just for its own members. Labor activists from around the country repeatedly told Watts that he and Local 837 had set a new standard for grassroots union activism, which was key to the labor movement's revival. People were trusting Local 837 to lead the fight for workers' rights, Watts knew, and they were looking to him to lead the local.

So, the forty-six-year-old Dave Watts, in office for three years, had two priorities. First, he faced the monumental task of leading the union's campaign against Tate & Lyle, and second, he had to referee the mounting animosity between the executive board and Kandy Lane. Watts felt tremendous responsibility to hold the fight together.

One thorn in Watts's side throughout the struggle was the union hall's bar. Each Staley worker had to grapple with the financial and emotional devastation inflicted by the company. Some channeled their anger into organizing, but others increased their use of alcohol or other addictive activities, such as gambling. It became evident to much of the membership that some officials were losing control of their drinking.

With a tavern in the union hall, the local had established a "no-alcohol" policy that was strictly enforced during its weekly Tuesday-night union meetings. There was no such rule, however, for the executive board meetings held just before each union meeting. The board met in a room directly across the hallway from the tavern to plan the agenda for the union meeting. Gary Lamb described his disgust at what he encountered in early 1994: "[Some executive board] guys couldn't get the gist of the motion because they would be gone, running beers back and forth [across the hallway]. . . . A lot of times they drank before they got there and their reasoning was shot in the head, and they only worsened it. They would sit in there and get soused and still make motions and vote on them and take them back to the floor. They would have been better off if they had just passed out in the chair."

Lamb made a motion to ban drinking at board meetings. "This wasn't business as usual," Lamb told the officers. "These were tumultuous times. Our decision-making should be at its very best, for everybody. There is no need for us to drink." Watts shared Lamb's frustration and backed the motion, but it was quickly voted down. Disgusted, Lamb walked out and went home, too angry to stay for the membership meeting.

Watts reflected that when "a handful of members who get their courage from the bar" try to participate in union meetings, it creates an "acrimonious environment."[3] For example, as the split within the union widened, a drunken member of the old guard twice shouted from the union floor, "We oughta burn down Kandy Lane."[4] When asked why the board members had refused Watts's request to work in the Kandy Lane office, union member Tammy McCartney, who assisted Watts at the union's main office, responded, "There was no bar on Kandy Lane—cut and dry."

Said Watts, "I like a glass of beer as much as anybody, [but one thing] I would *never* do again is be an official of any union that had a union hall with a bar in it."

Jim Shinall and Dan Lane

For some members the emergence of two camps was imperceptible. The division began to come into focus, however, during one of the most dramatic of all union meetings, when two former friends, Jim Shinall and Dan Lane, publicly squared off in January 1994.

Shinall often expressed a tough stance against the company's concession demands. "As long as everyone sticks together," he declared in December 1992, "we will get a fair contract. It is going to take time, effort, and money, but *we will prevail!* Solidarity is the answer." Writing in the local's newsletter a month later, Shinall declared, "Make no mistake about it, we are winning this battle. The question is not *will* we win, but *when* will we win."[5] In February 1993 he defiantly told the company's bargaining team, "You can do whatever you want. We are not agreeing or helping. We don't care if there is no plant left here at all, and that includes you guys on that side of the table."[6] Finally, at the local's November 1993 rally, after the lockout, Shinall told a reporter, "I think we have given the labor movement a good shot in the arm in showing workers how and when you can stand up and fight," and he declared that American workers needed a labor party.[7]

Despite his high position in the union, however, Shinall played a minimal role in the nine-month work-to-rule campaign, and after the lockout he never joined the Road Warriors or volunteered at Kandy Lane. By late 1993 Shinall had begun speaking informally to members against the growing militancy of the local's fight. He had reached the conclusion that the fight had been lost and that the local should take what it could get from the company.

As bargaining committee chair, Shinall felt enormous pressure. He saw himself as responsible for the lives of 762 members and their families. His wife, Sharon, worried about the fight's effect on his health. Shinall, then fifty-five, had already had a heart attack, and the toll of chairing the bargaining committee was showing on his face. In addition, as were all the locked-out families, the Shinalls were struggling financially. Most significantly, though, Shinall had made it known well before the lockout that he planned to retire on April 4, 1994, when he became eligible, or sooner if new contract language allowed early retirement with full benefits.

Shinall had always been a trusted union man, so the members were shocked when it was revealed in December 1993 that he had quietly held an unofficial meeting with Staley vice president of operations John Phillips, who was taking a position with another company. Shinall described his version of the events:

> A few weeks after John Phillips left the company he called me and suggested an informal meeting to talk about ways the dispute might be settled. Watts was out of town and so was Bob Hull, so I called [international representative] Bill Coleman, and [executive board member] Greg Hill and [bargaining committee member] Denton Larrimore. All said they didn't see anything wrong with talking to Phillips, particularly since he was no longer with Staley. A group of us met with him at an apartment the union had rented and basically listened to him tell us that he thought there were items the company would move on if we could move some.[8]

Even though they were on the bargaining committee, Dan Lane, Dick Ferris, and Bill Strohl had not been consulted and were furious. Shinall, Larrimore, Hill, and Coleman had broken a basic principle of collective bargaining—namely, that any meeting with company officials include the bargaining committee or at the very least be authorized by a vote from that body. Lane recalled his anger: "When Shinall had the meeting, we found out and took him to task. The bargaining committee was very clear: there wouldn't be any deals made on the side. We've got too much invested in this thing for someone to go off on the side and make a deal. . . . But Shinall said, 'I don't give a shit. I'll do what I want. I'll meet with the company whenever I want to.' Which is *not* the way that committee operates. He is a spokesman, period. That's all he is."

At the December 10, 1993, union meeting Shinall began his weekly report by describing what had occurred. After careful deliberation, said Shinall, "it was a consensus of the bargaining committee and the executive board that when any member gets a call and is asked to be at a meeting" with the company, the decision whether to meet, and who would meet, would be sent to "the committee and the executive board before [a meeting] happens." Concluded Shinall, "whether you believe what I did was right, or whether you disagreed with it, let's lay it to bed."[9] The membership wholeheartedly backed the affirmation of the long-standing prohibition on backroom meetings with management.

Now the chasm within the bargaining committee was becoming more public. On one side, Jim Shinall and Denton Larrimore were ready to make whatever concessions necessary to settle with the company. On the other side were Dike Ferris, Dan Lane, and Bill Strohl. Strohl, a former local president and AIW International rep, summarized the evolution of his attitude toward Shinall:

> At one time I had a lot of respect for Jim Shinall, but it went downhill. [The fight] opened our eyes to a lot of people who we thought were a lot stronger than they were. Jim and Denton were not in the fight. Jim made the statement that he would do everything and anything to solve it. If it meant he would meet privately with the company, then that's what he would do. . . . They weren't interested in winning. They wanted the thing over. . . . They didn't give a damn about the kind of [contract] language that people went back in the plant with. . . . I had twenty-seven years in the plant [and could have taken early retirement], but I made up my mind I wanted to win, *nothing* less than a win—we all go back in the plant with our heads held high.

While Shinall's December backroom meeting was now known to the entire membership, additional damning facts were known only to the five members of the bargaining committee. Shinall was advocating that the union give in to the company's demand to negotiate off management's 17-page proposal rather than the union's original 116-page contract. To Ferris, Lane, and Strohl, it was clear that Shinall needed to be replaced as committee chair.

According to the union's bylaws, the five bargaining committee members had sole authority to decide their chairperson. Neither Ferris nor Strohl was willing to accept the post, so Lane reluctantly agreed to serve as chair. Lane knew that while the members wanted him on the committee, many thought him too radical to chair it. Many people expressed the notion that, as Lane recalled it, "Dan is good to have on the committee because he's this kind of radical guy, not afraid to speak his mind. But we don't want a whole bargaining committee of Dans." Lane also knew that some workers might argue that the bargaining chair should not be a worker who had been fired and therefore might be accused of putting his personal animosity toward the company and his own need for amnesty above the needs of the majority. Despite his deep reservations, Lane agreed to put his name forward, and in early January 1994, by a vote of three to two, he was elected chair.

As had most Staley workers, Lane had been born and raised in Decatur. After graduating from high school, he served as a squad leader for the U.S. Marines in Vietnam. After two tours of duty, he returned to Decatur, got married, and raised five children with his wife, Donna. His life typified those of many Decatur citizens—Lane was active in his church, attended his children's school and sporting events, and coached his daughter's softball team. He hired on at Staley in February 1974 as a process operator in the syrup-refinery department and later became a steward.

As discussed earlier, Lane and Shinall enjoyed a friendship and were neighbors who often rode to work together. Shinall took Lane under his wing, supported his election to the bargaining committee in 1986, and coached him in the art of negotiations. Shinall and Lane, both process workers, had vigorously advocated for the lower-paid, less-skilled workers they represented.

Lane was a creative leader during the in-plant campaign. He and his coworkers rightfully boasted that his "Five and Ten" department was the most militant in the plant. When Lane was fired in March 1993, hundreds of workers throughout the plant donned "Bring Back Dan Lane" buttons. He was one of the first Road Warriors, took scores of overnight trips, coached dozens of others on their first trips, helped establish many solidarity committees, and was recognized as the most fiery speechmaker in the local. Lane's determination to win a fair contract was unsurpassed, even though he harbored few hopes of ever returning to work. In Lane's mind, either the company or the more conservative members in the local would likely keep him out. Lane, nicknamed "Bronco" by his co-workers, described a conversation with Denton Larrimore: "After I was fired, Denton Larrimore told me a few weeks later, 'Bronco, you'll never get your job back. I don't see the company ever giving you your job back, and I don't see this floor ever giving you your job back.' It was very clear to me that the leadership had a very distinct difference of opinion about what was going to happen during this struggle."

Lane believed in amnesty for himself and the other six fired workers as a principle of solidarity, but this was not his motivation in accepting the position of bargaining chair. Together with Ferris and Strohl, Lane simply did not want to see Shinall lead a union surrender to the company.

Pandemonium

Bob Hull presided at the January 11, 1994, union meeting because Watts had laryngitis. Every seat in the huge hall was filled, and workers stood against the walls, for virtually every member had heard the news of Shinall's ouster. Prior to the meeting Shinall and his supporters had talked to scores of workers to solidify opposition to Lane. They vilified Lane as a "radical." Speaking to whoever would listen, they made remarks such as "Should a guy be up there that doesn't have a job, trying to get us a contract, when he doesn't have a job to go back to? Lane's just interested in his job. He doesn't care about the rest of us; otherwise, we'd have a contract."[10]

As Lane stepped to the podium, he was greeted with hisses, boos, and shouts of "bullshit!" Hull called for order, and for the next forty-five minutes the members heatedly debated Lane's election. Hull explained that there was no procedure to recall the chair; the bylaws gave the committee the right to elect their own. Many workers rose to speak from the microphone, but others continued to shout "Bullshit!" and "We want Jim!"

Lane, Strohl, and Ferris had expected that a segment of the membership would be upset, but the attack was more ferocious and had deeper support than they had predicted. "It was very scary," recalled Lane. "I wasn't sure what was going to happen. I tried to put on the stiffest face I could, tried to pretend it wasn't fazing me or anything. Any time they'd let down, I'd try again [to speak]. And as soon as they'd start, I'd just step back. I've got all night, too."

One of Shinall's spokespersons was Henry Kramer, who repeatedly spoke to the crowd from the floor microphone. He argued that Lane, Strohl, and Ferris had violated the members' trust and broken a consensus that there would be no contested elections during the fight. "We had an unsigned agreement that no member of the union would challenge anybody on the bargaining committee," declared Kramer. "We agreed: we're not going to change in midstream. We're fighting one hell of a battle right now. We don't need a change."[11]

Since the contract had been rejected in October 1992, workers had often spoken of a consensus not to unseat any officers. Several of the December 1993 elections had been contested, however, and there hadn't been any outcry, so Lane, Ferris, and Strohl had felt justified in having taken their action.[12] Now, however, a majority of members at the meeting opposed any changes to the bargaining committee. "You did this democratically," argued another worker from the floor, "but we had a gentlemen's agreement, and you threw it in our face. Not that you can't do a good job, Danny, but you threw the switch on us, and we don't appreciate it!"

Bill Strohl was called to the podium to explain his vote for Lane:

> During this last year, we stopped functioning as a committee, and then I think it is time for a change. It has a lot to do with [Shinall's meeting with] John Phillips. . . . It's time for a change when one man sets himself up and makes it clear he's going to do it again, and the floor overruled him, but he still feels what he did in his heart was right. . . . I felt the bargaining committee needed to come together and move in a different direction. We have not compromised on anything, and we don't intend to. That's exactly why I did what I did.

Shinall spoke to great applause from his supporters.

> I've got a clear conscience. I have nothing to apologize for. I made a decision to meet with John Phillips. . . . I spoke to the floor and said that I would never [again] do what I did before without talking to the executive board and bargaining committee. And when I say I'll do something, I'll do it. I have never lied to you people. I've never misled anyone in private conversation or on this floor. . . . [My stance has been] "Is there any way to get proposals [from the company] and move them forward?"

A number of workers challenged the committee to explain why Shinall should be removed for making one mistake. Many denounced the insinuation that Shinall was not fighting aggressively in negotiations. Said one worker to loud applause, "I've known Jim for a number of years. We haven't always seen eye to eye. But shame on anyone that questions his integrity." Most of the members didn't see the issue as the conservatives versus the activists. They thought the committee should put aside their differences and work together. After more Shinall supporters spoke, member Mike Manning said that he was "putting the floor on notice" that he would circulate a petition to unseat Lane as chair.

Eventually Lane came to the microphone again, defending the replacement of Shinall: "Jim Shinall is not promoting [the fight]. I don't want to get into a mudslinging contest. . . . It is time to look at a new direction. It has to do with preserving jobs. It has to do with keeping subcontractors out. It has to do with *not* accepting rotating shifts. . . . [In the December election] the floor *did* decide to change other officers [and no one complained]."

Lane then gave a brief bargaining committee report. Meanwhile, AIW/UPIU representative Bill Coleman and board member Steve Haseley left the hall to phone a United Paperworkers official at the union's headquarters in Nashville, since the AIW's merger with them had gone into effect just ten days before, on

January 1. Over the next hour, members gave routine reports, and Tucker and Rogers reported on the corporate campaign. Then, however, Coleman unexpectedly returned to the podium to make a shocking announcement: "If some of you are wondering why Jim left the hall, he had severe chest pains. I walked him outside, and we stood outside for a while, and it didn't ease up. . . . [Sharon] got in the van to take Jim to the hospital. He has had a heart attack. They got his blood pressure back up and are trying to stabilize him."

A collective gasp came from the floor. The meeting ended with a prayer. Shinall's supporters were now even more furious with Lane. By the next day Shinall's condition was stable, and four days later he was discharged from the hospital with orders to rest for two months.

The next Tuesday-night meeting was switched to a members-only business meeting. After the members recited the Pledge of Allegiance, a hush permeated the packed hall. Dave Watts announced that Lane and Strohl had resigned their positions of chair and assistant chair, and recording secretary Greg Hill read their resignation letters. Lane wrote that he had resigned "after careful consideration, and in order to keep solidarity and unity." He expressed his desire that he remain on the committee and that "energy be focused on the enemy of the union, Tate & Lyle."[13]

Even with all the Staley workers had been through together, there had never been such a heavy, somber air in the union hall. The usual laughter and the collective synergy had evaporated. Dee Scott requested that a prayer be said, and all stood in reverence.

A solemn Dave Watts then continued, "Many of us have not slept well since last Tuesday." To ensure that union bylaws were followed, Watts had requested an interpretation from the international, which he now explained. There was no procedure to unseat the chair of the bargaining committee. The only recourse was to recall someone from the committee, and Lane's opponents had filed a petition to do just that. Even though Lane had resigned as chair and been replaced by Shinall, there would now be an election by secret ballot to determine whether Lane would stay on the committee at all. The process workers that Lane represented would be the only members eligible to vote. Greg Hill read a statement from the executive board and the bargaining committee in support of Lane's remaining on. Even Shinall, writing from his sickbed, expressed his opposition to recalling Lane. Despite their divisions, the leadership was unanimous in recognizing that only the company would benefit if Lane were thrown off and the schism deepened. The vote went in Lane's favor.

To members who were not fully involved in the struggle, the Shinall versus Lane dispute may have looked like petty bickering. For the local's officers and the activists, however, it was now apparent that Shinall had emerged as the figurehead for those who wanted to end the struggle by negotiating a concessionary contract and that this group could be organized into action. A few months after recovering from his heart attack, Shinall took a full-time job as a truck driver, and at the end of the summer he resigned from the bargaining committee. As will be described in chapter 16, however, in late 1994 he and his supporters renewed their efforts to end the struggle on the company's terms.

Meanwhile, with the tensions of the January union meeting simmering beneath the surface, the union's activists renewed their efforts to build national solidarity and debated whether the union should organize demonstrations to block the plant gates. In Decatur, supporters among the clergy and African American Staley workers stepped up their activities to win a fair contract.

10

God as Outside Agitator

A vital part of Local 837's outreach was directed toward Decatur's religious community. A clergy group was formed, building bridges between congregations and unions and strengthening bonds within the religious community itself. The group's leader, Father Martin Mangan, became a highly visible advocate for the workers' cause. The Staley fight also catalyzed an effort for workers' rights among clergy across the nation and around the world. Religious backing for the locked-out unionists heightened support and media coverage and encouraged the workers that their cause was righteous.[1]

"What They Are Trying to Accomplish Is Immoral"

In March 1992, over a year before the lockout, Tate & Lyle hired Jennifer Bean as a communications officer to launch a company newsletter. While the newsletter aimed to convince union employees to accept the company's demands, it had a broader purpose, too. Distributed to the media, local politicians, and community and religious leaders, *Keynotes* pressed home the argument that the Decatur plant needed to be completely reorganized, with "antiquated" work rules tossed aside, if Decatur was to remain globally competitive.

After the workers rejected the contract in October 1992, Tate & Lyle invited the Decatur clergy to a meeting alerting them to the forthcoming pastoral care needs of the three hundred white-collar workers who were to be laid off. The company used the opportunity to explain its drastic workplace changes and to defend the rejected contract offer, but the clergy were not convinced. Company vice president J. Patrick Mohan "warned us to be ready because there was a great deal of 'ministering ahead,'" said Father Dennis Kollross of St. Thomas Catholic Church. "He was so arrogant in saying it. . . . One meeting with Mohan cleared it up for me that what they are trying to accomplish is immoral."[2]

In late 1992 and early 1993 the union began its own tentative efforts to reach out to the clergy. During the four door-to-door operations when workers distributed fifty thousand copies of the "Crisis in Decatur," "Deadly Corn," and bank boycott brochures, workers were encouraged to give copies to their pastors, too. Shortly after the lockout, in July 1993, a group led by Mike Landacre organized a well-attended outdoor gospel festival that raised about seven hundred dollars.

In August 1993 C. J. Hawking visited the AIW 837 hall, along with several other members of the newly formed Chicago Staley Workers Solidarity Committee. Hawking, a United Methodist pastor and hospice chaplain, met with Landacre to discuss religious outreach. Once back in Chicago, she sought the advice of Kim Bobo, an educator and organizer with the Midwest Academy, a community organizer training center. In 1991 Bobo had established the Religious Committee for Workplace Fairness, a Chicago-area group that supported unions in labor battles. In spring 1992 the group had organized clergy support for the striking Caterpillar workers.

Bobo's Religious Committee for Workplace Fairness drafted a letter in support of the Decatur workers. When Local 837 wrote to Decatur clergy and invited them to sign it, however, only a handful replied. The Decatur clergy needed an opportunity to hear directly from the locked-out workers and their families—and religious support could not be expanded until the local clergy first took their own collective action.

Virtually all the largest faith communities in the United States—including Protestant, Catholic, Jewish, Muslim, and Buddhist—have issued strong statements in support of workers' right to organize unions and bargain collectively. Nevertheless, many clergy resist getting involved in labor disputes. They have generally not viewed contentious labor-management disputes as part of congregational life.

In Decatur, many clergy felt ambivalent or received pressure to remain neutral, as evidenced by one pastor's experience. Shortly after the lockout, Rev. Dale Downs of Decatur's Foursquare Church attended a rally at the invitation of the union. His remarks, which drew the cheers of members, were quoted extensively in the newspaper. "The evangelical community supports you," declared the pastor. "Greed spoils [Decatur] unity." He urged workers to maintain faith in God and their union.[3] Ten days later, however, Downs reversed himself. He wrote a letter to the *Decatur Herald and Review* stating that he did not mean to imply support for the union and that he was neutral in the labor conflict.[4]

In November 1993 Bobo sent an intern from Lutheran Volunteer Services to Decatur, and Hawking accompanied her. With the assistance of Staley worker Dike Ferris, they set up a clergy meeting. Six pastors attended and talked frankly about the impact of the lockout on their congregations. The Reverend Levi Mc-Clendon, pastor of Ebenezer Missionary Baptist, a prominent African American church, said that he had begun to notice before the lockout that some of his flock were missing on Sundays because of mandatory weekend shifts. "I have one woman in my church," said McClendon, "whose husband is a locked-out worker. Last Sunday she sat in the pew and cried throughout the whole service. I know that she was crying because they don't have any money and the bills are piling up. But I felt helpless. I don't know what to tell her."[5]

The pastors decided to offer themselves as mediators between the company and the union, in hopes that they could lend their moral authority to bring about a fair solution. The Reverend George Harjes, a United Methodist pastor, said, "Somehow, we've got to be able to build some sort of bridge. We've got to be reconcilers."[6]

The Decatur Clergy Group

In December Hawking organized a second meeting, this one attended by nineteen clergy members. Most were unfamiliar with collective bargaining issues and lockouts, and they peppered Dike Ferris with questions. Ferris explained the needless death of Jim Beals and the dangerous deterioration of safety conditions, the necessity of defending the eight-hour workday, and the difference between a lockout and a strike. Ferris emphasized the union's willingness to make compromises to negotiate a fair contract but noted that the company's proposal obliterated the workers' dignity and was rejected by 97 percent of the workforce. The pastors discussed their distaste for Staley's October 1992 clergy meeting and decided to initiate their own meeting with management. They sketched out an agenda where the clergy would guide the discussion, with each person covering a specific topic. The date was set for two weeks later, and the company was notified.

The group held another meeting in the interim, on December 14. The numbers continued to climb: twenty-five members of the clergy attended. Harjes presented a draft of an open letter to the Decatur community. The group made minor changes and decided to publish it in the *Decatur Herald and Review*; those present chipped in to pay for running the letter as an ad in the Sunday edition. With the newspaper's deadline two days away, Harjes drove the letter around to other colleagues and gathered sixty signatures, nearly half the city's clergy, with an impressive cross-section of denominations.

The letter appeared on December 19 as a half-page ad, with the name of the congregation listed below each signer. Much to the disappointment of the signers, the editors buried it near the back of the "Home" section, which had more to do with lawns than with lockouts. In contrast, the clergy noted with displeasure, Staley's ads justifying the lockout ran in the front section. Although most of the signers considered the letter fairly neutral, it did address twelve-hour shifts as being disruptive to family life and explained that segments of the community were hurting from the lockout. It called upon the company and the local to "sit down and reason together." The company made no formal response.

As the fourth clergy meeting convened at the Decatur Civic Center on December 21, anticipation was high. Thirty members of the clergy gathered to hear Tate & Lyle executives' explanation of the lockout. Astutely, they wanted to ascertain who had decision-making power—London-based Tate & Lyle executives or Decatur's Staley management. To the complete dismay of those present, however, management did not show up. "The least [Staley management] could do is come out and listen," Rev. Eugene Green of Trinity CME Church told the *Decatur Herald and Review*. "To me, as a clergy person in the community, it's like a slap in the face."[7]

Managers offered the excuse that they had insufficient time to prepare for the meeting, and further, the "appropriate people" were not available. They refused to propose a date for another meeting but instead suggested that they begin meeting clergy one-on-one or in small groups. In an internal newsletter that was meant only for supervisors and scabs but that found its way to the union and to the clergy, the company falsely stated that the clergy meeting "was never scheduled" and declared, "We will not be a party to media events designed to pit ministers and priests against Staley. These actions merely continue to tear the community apart."[8]

The pastors were insulted to be accused of organizing a "media event." If anyone was "tearing the community apart," they felt, it was the company, which had imposed the lockout, not the pastors, who were seeking reconciliation. In a letter to the editor a few days later, Father Martin Mangan of St. James Catholic Church expressed his dismay that even though the clergy had answered the company's call to attend a meeting the year before, management would refuse to attend a clergy-sponsored gathering. "Could not the Staley management have returned the same courtesy we showed them? Apparently with Staley management, it is either their way or no way."[9]

The unifying effect of these first four clergy meetings reached beyond the labor issues involved. The clergy meetings and Tate & Lyle's arrogant response were creating bonds of friendship and connecting Decatur clergy in new ways. Prior to these meetings Decatur had three ministerial associations, collections of religious leaders who regularly met for collegial support. The three groups were divided along theological and racial lines and had virtually no contact with one another. The clergy group's efforts to end the lockout, said Sister Glenda Bourgeois proudly, had created "the first-ever ecumenical experience in Decatur."[10]

In December 1993 Hawking spoke with Dave Watts, volunteering to assist full-time in the local's outreach to the religious community. Watts embraced

Hawking's offer, gave her a desk at the Kandy Lane office, and allowed her to join the union's food-assistance program. Hawking became the first of five full-time volunteer organizers who would move to Decatur to assist the local.

A Labor Priest

One Decatur religious leader soon became a central figure in the clergy group. Father Martin Mangan had been deeply moved by the sight of locked-out workers picketing at the Staley gates. He would often stop by the line to offer his support and prayers and to ask questions about the union's stance. When he heard that the union was planning a rally, he would stop by to listen and give support. Soon he was asked to lead prayers and to speak at union events, and he began to give invocations at the weekly meetings at the union hall.

"The Catholic church has always had a strong written history in support of workers," said Mangan, referring both to the Vatican encyclicals Rerum Novarum and Quadragesimo Anno and to the writings of Pope John Paul II. "I believe Jesus would appear more often in union halls than in the boardrooms of multinational companies because Jesus identified with those less powerful."[11] Added Mangan, "The Roman Catholic Church has taught that workers have the right to organize, the right to collective bargaining, and the right to a just contract. I felt these rights could be in jeopardy, not only here in Decatur, but elsewhere. It is our duty in the church to defend these rights. I have to stand on the side of the union."[12]

One of eight children, Mangan was born and raised in Springfield and studied at Mundelein Seminary, in Mundelein, Illinois. Having studied pro-union Catholic teachings, he refused to go to a nonunion barber shop during his seminary days. Mangan was ordained on May 1, 1957, the Feast of St. Joseph, the patron saint of the worker. He studied canon law in Rome and was once considered to be a candidate for bishop, but close observers concluded that his support for women's ordination and the civil rights movement, along with his opposition to the Vietnam War, precluded him. For the next thirty years Mangan pastored churches throughout central Illinois.

Mangan arrived in Decatur in 1991 to pastor at St. James, a Gothic structure in the city center with 550 congregants, mostly blue-collar workers of German descent. The church had built a private school on its property that for decades was filled with German immigrants. The school evolved with the neighborhood and by 1991 served mostly non-Catholic, African American children, many of whom attended on scholarships funded by parishioners. Mangan had been drawn to St. James parish primarily because of the school. He also became active in the Southside Improvement Association and DOVE, a social services agency with programs to support victims of domestic violence.[13]

When Mangan arrived at St. James at the age of sixty, recalled Rev. Jim Montgomery, "some wondered whether this elderly priest, who had studied Canon Law at the Vatican, would be satisfied in a struggling parish. But the assignment [Mangan said], was 'a dream come true.' He was so glad to be in a section of town where people were workers, rich and poor and black and white."[14]

Mangan hired Sister Glenda Bourgeois as a full-time pastoral associate shortly after the lockout. An Ursuline nun originally from New Orleans, Bourgeois had previously taught children in the Dominican Republic and had served as prioress at the Ursuline convent in Decatur. Although neither Mangan nor Bourgeois had previously been active in the labor movement, they both felt a strong conviction to stand with the workers and their families. "I find great consistency in my life right now and it's due to the Spirit being alive in people who are suffering through this," Bourgeois reflected in late 1994. "I find myself a part of the living Gospel here in Decatur and solidarity to me [becomes] the Word [in] the flesh."[15]

At each weekly Local 837 solidarity meeting, the Pledge of Allegiance was followed by a prayer. On their frequent visits Mangan and Bourgeois received standing ovations and cheers of gratitude as they sought to inspire the workers with prayers and provide blessings for strength.

After their refusal to attend the December 21 clergy meeting, Tate & Lyle managers soon regretted the public-relations disaster and made an attempt to repair their reputation by requesting a meeting in February 1994 at a downtown church. Only eight pastors attended. J. Patrick Mohan claimed that the lockout was the "only way" the company could protect itself, asserting that the workers had "sabotaged" the plant and caused environmental damage that brought city fines. He claimed that before the lockout, the waste-water discharge from the plant was contaminated beyond the usual amounts allowed by the city. Later, an astute union officer, Art Dhermy, retrieved the city records and found no appreciable changes.

Mohan told the religious leaders that the lockout was a local decision made by Staley CEO Larry Pillard. When asked which company proposals were negotiable, he couldn't provide specific answers. When questioned about placing profits before people, Mohan responded, "We're looking to grow a business. This will create new jobs."[16] Rev. Bob Wiedrich, a United Methodist pastor, told Mohan that he understood the need to make a profit, but as a Christian, he recognized another bottom line, and that was people. "I don't think he had the faintest clue to what I was talking about," Wiedrich reflected.[17]

Father Mangan, by now well-versed in the dispute, drew the comparison between multinational corporations such as Tate & Lyle and Nazi Germany. He later recounted the interchange to *U.S. Catholic* magazine: "In Germany there was a systematic destruction of people called the Holocaust, and I really believe that there is also a systematic process going on now to destroy the economic lives of people. In Germany, the ministers were silent; I'm not planning to be this time." "I said this to Mohan," recounted Mangan, "and he said, 'I really, really resent that.' And I said, 'You should!'"[18]

Father Mangan opened the doors of his rectory to the union, especially when the Kandy Lane activists wanted to hold strategy sessions but suspected that the union hall was bugged. Midwest solidarity activists dubbed the rectory "Hotel Solidarity" when Mangan repeatedly welcomed them to spend the night. When Doug Kandt, a *Labor Notes* intern, moved from Detroit to Decatur in the summer of 1994, Mangan allowed him to live at the rectory. And when Dan Lane launched a sixty-five-day hunger strike in September 1995 (see chapter 17), he accepted Mangan's invitation to make the rectory his haven.

For the duration of the 2½-year lockout, and throughout the 1994–95 Caterpillar and Bridgestone/Firestone strikes, Father Mangan was as much the public face of the workers' struggle as were the presidents of the three embattled locals. "I really hope Decatur can be the Stalingrad of the labor movement," he declared, "where they dig in and say: 'Enough is enough is enough.'"[19]

In September 1994 several thousand people marched through downtown Decatur, culminating with a rally at the county courthouse featuring speeches from union leaders. At the end Father Mangan asked the crowd to kneel before he prayed. This became one of the most emotionally powerful moments in Decatur labor history, etched in the memories of those who were there. Father Mangan recounted the events:

> All the Caterpillar, Firestone, and Staley people came together in front of the courthouse. They were all in bright red solidarity shirts. Leadership knew what was going to happen, but the people didn't. The police were nervously looking around. It started with short talks from the leaders. Then they asked me to say a prayer. I said, "I'd like this to be an action prayer. First, I'd like you to all kneel down in front of God to ask his blessing on our struggle." Well, I didn't know that five thousand people would kneel down in red shirts. But they did. "The second prayer action," I said, "is to raise your right hand if your are willing to lay down your life for your brothers and sisters in the union struggle." They all raised their hands. "The third action is to join your hands as brothers and sisters in the struggle." They did. "The fourth and final prayer action is to please stand and walk in silence from this rally as a sign of our solidarity." Some five thousand people got up, and all you could hear was the shuffle of feet. They just walked by the police in silence.

The thousands of unionists, so used to chanting at the tops of their voices, stood as one, turned, and walked away without a word. "They thought we were going to be violent," said Mangan. "But you can't deal with life by violence of any kind. So we stood and walked away."[20] Everyone who participated was deeply moved by the event. "I could feel the pain and the *hope* of so many," recalled Staley spouse Terri Garren.[21] "Only [Father Mangan] could have gotten that many people to walk away silently," said Judy Dulaney. "The police did not know what to do. He is the only person in the world that many people would have done that for."[22]

Support Broadens

As the weekly clergy meetings continued, most of the attendees committed themselves to offering Sunday prayers calling for a just end to the lockout. Some churches that had locked-out workers in their congregations invited the workers to speak on Sunday or in religious classes. Awareness of the workers' plight often led to collections for the families, with some receiving monthly gifts. "Our church gave us money to help with living expenses," said Rhonda Plankenhorn. "And one day a lady from our church paid for my groceries at the supermarket. She said she couldn't do much, but she wanted to help."[23] Several locked-out workers were offered part-time jobs at their churches as custodians.

Some local churches began sending food and money to the union hall on a regular basis. Father Dennis Kollross of St. Thomas Catholic Church discussed the ease with which his congregation accepted his appeals for the Staley workers. Members of his congregation were "experiencing a number of workplace take-aways [of rights] that have taken years to achieve. They also see a company that won't budge—won't talk—and they see a grave injustice in that."[24] When Kollross mailed personal appeals to his congregants, his efforts raised over six thousand dollars. With the help of a grocer who was a parishioner, Kollross personally purchased food and paper products and drove them to the union hall. George Harjes's United Methodist congregation offered families free used clothing for their children. Several pastors began frequenting the union hall and the picket lines, talking with the workers and offering prayers of support.

In March 1994 the clergy group called upon the Decatur community to engage in a day of prayer and fasting over the Palm Sunday weekend. The fast was to begin Saturday afternoon at 3:00 and would close with a rally in front of the corporate offices on Sunday at 2:30. During their worship services several churches collected food and money earmarked for the Staley workers. Each participating pastor donated one hundred dollars out of his or her own pocket. Over five hundred people attended the rally, many of them in their Sunday clothes. Several pastors offered fervent prayers, including Rev. Doug Lowery, of the large Maranatha Assembly of God Church: "God, you know how to move things that seem to be barriers. Make a way where there seems to be no way."[25] During the gathering the participants held hands and sang "Amazing Grace" and "The Battle Hymn of the Republic."

While the service dealt primarily with themes of faith and social justice, its conclusion left no doubt that it was also a union rally, as participants sang "Solidarity Forever."[26] From the rally dozens of fasters traveled to a nearby United Methodist church basement where some of the workers had prepared a meal of soup and bread. While participants broke the fast together, more prayers were offered and donations from churches were announced. The *Decatur Herald and Review* gave the prayer rally positive coverage.

Meanwhile, back in Chicago, Kim Bobo's group, now renamed the Chicago Interfaith Committee on Worker Issues, put out its first newsletter in January 1994; the publication included a story urging clergy to actively support the Decatur workers.[27] The newsletter was mailed to supportive clergy in Chicago and across the country, and coverage in regional denominational newspapers followed. Invitations for workers to speak to ministerial associations, regional social-justice committees, and denominational meetings in nearby communities were actively pursued. This resulted in many letters to CEO Pillard reaffirming the righteousness of the workers' cause.

Some clergy statements were strongly worded. The Commission on Human Rights of the Catholic Archdiocese of St. Louis issued a statement "in solidarity with the locked-out Staley workers as they seek to restore both their dignity and their jobs."[28] The Springfield Religious Leaders Association called on both company and union to "bargain in good faith and end the lock-out."[29] Even as religious bodies professed neutrality, however, the company was informed of the broader community's concern.

Inquiries from the clergy across the Midwest became a regular occurrence, many wanting to know how they could support the union. In response, the Decatur clergy group sponsored a Midwest Clergy Day on May 17, 1994. Hosted by Father Mangan and Sister Bourgeois, the day included workers' presentations, discussions, a meal, and a prayer rally in front of the corporate office. Forty clergy from throughout the Midwest, representing a range of denominations, listened to the workers attentively. They also expressed enthusiasm about their own emerging network.

Standing on Staley's front lawn for the concluding prayer rally, Father Tom Joyce of the Catholic Eighth Day Center for Justice in Chicago reflected on the lockout as a moral and ethical issue. "You're dealing with the quality of human life. The corporate strategy is being pushed by profit, by people very removed from this community. Can people be used this way?" Calling the twelve-hour shifts "ridiculous," Joyce further asserted that such shifts are "destructive to the whole quality of human life."[30]

Linda Bushong, whose husband was locked out, expressed the sentiments of many unionists and family members: "It feels good to have that type of spiritual and emotional support. I have for the last nine months taken refuge in the knowledge that Jesus was a people-person who was often amidst the downtrodden and outcast—which is what Tate & Lyle are trying to do to us."[31]

Civil Disobedience

As the lockout passed its sixth month, the workers began to discuss nonviolent civil disobedience, specifically, blocking the Staley gates. As the workers discussed and then engaged in this tactic (see chapter 12), many did so within a spiritual framework.

The Eighth Day Center for Justice in Chicago was called upon to help workers understand the tactic. Tracing the historical roots of civil disobedience, four nuns and a priest from the center gave a compelling presentation at a Saturday seminar in April and again at the union's weekly Tuesday-night solidarity meeting on May 3, 1994. Although no date was set for an action, becoming familiar with the ideological, spiritual, and practical concepts helped to allay many unionists' fears.

At five o'clock the following evening, while on their way to be honored at a cookout hosted by the Women's Support Group, the five religious leaders from Eighth Day—Sisters Delores Brooks, Mary Kay Flanigan, Jean Hughes, and Kathleen Desautels and Father Bob Bossie—decided to stop at Staley's east gate. They wanted to greet the picketers and request a meeting with management to discuss the lockout. The previous night they had visited the west gate picketers but were turned away when they audaciously asked the security guard for a plant tour. The guards at the east gate were quite friendly, however, and one even posed for a photo with Sister Kathleen, who was two feet shorter than he was. When another guard told them that the Staley executives did not want them on the property, the five started to leave. As they neared the edge of the driveway, however, a paddy wagon arrived, and Decatur police arrested them. Despite repeated requests, the police would not specify the charges to the Chicagoans.

The women at the cookout were summoned, and soon three dozen people appeared in the lobby of the police station, chanting a line from Exodus: "Let our people go." The five "outlaws" were fingerprinted and had their mug shots taken. Chagrined to learn that they had arrested four nuns and a priest with no cause, one of the officers invited the five to join another officer's birthday celebration and offered them cake. Within two hours of their arrests, all five were released without posting bail, and a court date was set for June 7. Sister Delores Brooks suggested to the *Decatur Herald and Review* that the police commanders and city leaders were in league with the company.[32]

Dave Watts, outraged by the arrests, called a press conference the next day. With Father Mangan at his side, he declared, "This is just another example of how Decatur is at risk of becoming a company town," adding, "The laws of this town are being bent to serve the whims of companies, at the expense of people's rights."[33] Mangan, who understood that the five had come to teach about civil disobedience but had harbored no desire to be arrested during this visit, told the media that the visitors were upset because clearly they had done nothing wrong.[34] Although the charges were eventually dropped, the arrests became significant to many workers and their families. They vividly demonstrated the police department's willingness to carry out irrational demands made by the company, even when no charges were viable.

When union leaders decided to adopt civil disobedience as a tactic, the clergy played a prominent role. The first such action at the gates, the union decided, would involve not Staley workers but other unionists, spouses, and community supporters. The representatives from Eighth Day returned to lead an organiz- ing meeting with Hawking on the morning of the June 4, 1994, demonstration. Flanigan, Hughes, and Desautels again outlined the principles of nonviolent civil disobedience. They were able to draw a commitment from all present that nonviolent guidelines would be followed. Most participants, the overwhelming majority of whom had never participated in or even witnessed civil disobedi- ence, experienced a broad range of emotions, ranging from fear to invigoration. Asked how he felt just before leaving the safety of the union hall to go to the plant gate, Father Mangan candidly admitted, "I want to throw up."

Interviewed by a Labor Vision film crew before blocking the gates on June 4, Rev. Darren Cushman-Wood, a United Methodist pastor from Indianapolis who had been seasoned by the Pittston mineworkers' civil disobedience in 1989, articulated the call he felt to participate: "Jesus is not in a crystal cathedral or a stained-glass window," said Cushman-Wood. "He is walking the picket line with these workers. That's how he lived his life, and that's where his spirit abides. If I want to follow Jesus, this is where I need to be."[35] Staley wife Judy Dulaney expressed the impact Cushman-Wood had on her: "I'll always remember what he said. . . . People like that gave us a lot of strength. People that didn't even know us but really put their butts on the line for us."[36]

At the June 4 action Rev. George Harjes was assisted by the VanScyocs, a locked-out family, who carried a ten-foot cross to lead the procession of over six hundred people from the front of the Staley office building to the west gate. In a disciplined fashion, waves of union supporters crossed the Staley property line and sat down. Three pastors, seeing the calmness of the action and wit- nessing the devotion of the people who supported the workers, spontaneously joined the action. Bob White, Levi McClendon, and Lloyd Jackson, all African American pastors, sat on the front lines. "There is a higher law involved in this," Rev. Lloyd Jackson, of Shiloh Missionary Baptist Church, told reporters. "Our city has suffered enough. We are here for our community."[37]

A fourth pastor, United Methodist minister Bob Wiedrich, had told colleagues the day before that such a protest was "not for him." Nevertheless, when he saw his parishioner Sandy Schable on the front line, he experienced a transformation. "It suddenly dawned on me that if I were to preach the meaning of the significance of the cross, that if I were to truly accept Christ and the love of the Lord, then I had to stand with her and ache with her," said Wiedrich. "It seemed to me at that precise time that the cross needed to be shored up."[38] Wiedrich sat down next to Schable and waited his turn to be arrested. Seven of the forty-eight arrested that day were members of the clergy.

That night, after being arrested and released, Father Mangan had a nightmare. He dreamed that when he entered his church for services the next morning, there were no people in the pews. His anxiety was furthered when he awoke to see that the Sunday *Herald and Review* had run a large photo of him sitting with his legs crossed in the middle of the protesters. Behind him loomed a huge semi blocked from exiting the plant. Mangan had a confident smile on his face and was giving a "thumbs up" gesture to someone outside camera range.

As it turned out, when Father Mangan nervously processed into the church for his three masses that morning, many parishioners smiled and playfully extended a thumbs up as he passed their pews. He released an audible sigh. The money collected in the offering that Sunday was the highest ever, twice the norm. Although only three of Mangan's parishioners were actually locked out, it became obvious that most in his congregation supported his work on behalf of the besieged workers.

Nonetheless, other pastors retreated from the struggle for various reasons. Some held the theological view that religious leaders are called upon to be mediators, not advocates. Some received pressure from their congregations. In more than one case, a key donor threatened to withdraw contributions if the pastor continued to speak out. Others were keenly aware that corporations donated to their social-service agencies and that these and other projects were threatened.

"When we were doing the fasting and the chaining," recalled Judy Dulaney, referring to a later demonstration initiated by clergy, "I was calling around to see who would do it. I called a prominent minister in town. He said, 'Yes, I'll do it—but can I do it at night so nobody has to know?'" Stunned, Dulaney wondered what the point would be. The pastor decided not to participate, since the action might be publicized and his congregation would find out.

In the history of church-union relations, pressure from wealthy congregants and donors is not unique to Decatur. And with few exceptions, seminary education does not cover workers' rights. For many Staley workers, however, their pastors' apathy and sometimes even outright hostility came as a painful shock. "We lost our church," recalled Jan Griffin. "That hurt us the most. After 27 years and raising six children in that church, they would not support our struggle."[39] Gary Lamb also stopped going to his church when his pastor refused to speak up on the workers' behalf. "I went on a hiatus and didn't go to church for years," said Lamb. "If I can't find support, don't let me find anything." Said Cheryl Lamb, "They would pray that people would have jobs, but they didn't want to discuss [the lockout] because they had both sides there and they didn't want to have to take sides. A pastor in my opinion should be standing for the rights of the people. . . . What they were concerned with was the pocketbook. . . . For this to be such a widespread thing in the city, and for them not to take a stand, it was upsetting."

The Decatur pastors who maintained their commitment to the Staley workers came largely from independent African American congregations or from the ranks of Roman Catholics and United Methodists. The moral fortitude provided by these clergy members was immeasurable to the Staley workers and their families, as it was to the Caterpillar and Bridgestone/Firestone workers, too, when they were forced on strike in the summer of 1994. Faith was becoming a framework within which the workers came to understand their struggle for justice.

National and International Clergy Outreach

In May 1994 Hawking contacted Rev. Michael Szpak, the AFL-CIO's labor-religion coordinator and a United Methodist pastor, to seek national support. Szpak had traversed the country to gain support from congregations for workers in labor disputes. The labor movement and religious congregations, said Szpak, "have values in common: Respect for the individual, solidarity, social and economic justice, and justice in the workplace."[40]

Szpak informed Hawking that the AFL-CIO's protocol required that UPIU president Wayne Glenn first make a written request to AFL-CIO president Lane Kirkland. Within a month, Szpak was on board, bringing with him a national network of prolabor religious leaders. Through Szpak's efforts, over four hundred Catholic, Protestant, and Jewish leaders signed a statement calling on Tate & Lyle to end the lockout and treat workers fairly.

A contingent of religious leaders greeted Father Mangan when, in January 1995, the priest accompanied a Local 7837 delegation to London to attend the Tate & Lyle stockholders meeting. Mangan insisted on paying his own expenses, and before the trip he bought one share of Tate & Lyle stock to gain speaking rights. Mangan presented the national clergy statement at the meeting, and as he read his own statement, the room was hushed. His voice quivering slightly, Mangan began, "Mr. Chairman, I come from a broken city and you can do something to heal it. . . . Tate & Lyle has ignored the pain this lock-out has brought to families in Decatur for too long. I call upon management to live up to its responsibility to the wider community . . . and bring hope and peace to a hurting community."[41]

Although Mangan was later besieged by a clamoring media, his plea had no apparent effect on CEO Shaw, who sat stone-faced. "They patted me on the top of the head rather patronizingly," said Mangan, "and said, in effect, 'Father, you go take care of the spiritual needs of your people. We'll take care of the economic needs of Tate & Lyle.'"[42] "You could sense the icicles; people were cold," observed Dike Ferris. Several London newspapers covered the speech, running a profile and a photo of Mangan in front of Tate & Lyle headquarters.

The national and global clergy outreach was aided by a four-page spread in the January 1995 issue of the UPIU newspaper *The Paperworker*. Dick Blinn, its editor, interviewed Decatur clergy for the article, and the UPIU reprinted it as a glossy handout for national and global distribution.

Throughout 1995 religious leaders continued to build on the momentum of the London trip, largely because of Szpak's efforts. The Reverend Raymond Singh, a colleague of Szpak's in the United Kingdom, mobilized his network of religious leaders, most of whom were deeply familiar with Tate & Lyle's antiworker practices. Through Singh's efforts, over two hundred Britons added their names to the "Religious Leaders for Justice at A. E. Staley" statement.

In June 1995, marking the two-year anniversary of the lockout, a solemn delegation of British religious leaders stood outside the company's London office, holding placards with the names of all 762 locked-out Staley workers. Simultaneously, a delegation of religious leaders held vigil in front of a Toronto bank where Tate & Lyle CEO Shaw was a director. Dioceses, synagogue federations, conferences, ministerial associations, and presidents of denominations from across the country issued statements on behalf of the Staley workers, urging their clergy and congregations to become involved. In an attempt to squelch such efforts, J. Patrick Mohan wrote to the religious leaders, "It is regrettable that you are signatories to a false and misleading letter. . . . We urge you to verify information before creating a public document."[43] But clergy across the United States and the globe remain undeterred. Decatur's Rev. Bob Wiedrich accompanied the Staley workers to London in October 1995. In conjunction with a civil-disobedience action in Decatur where workers took twelve-hour shifts chaining themselves to the Staley fence, Wiedrich led a delegation whose members chained themselves to a kiosk outside Tate & Lyle's London headquarters. Singh and a group of London pastors joined the Decatur pastor.

Many workers gained spiritual strength from the involvement of the clergy, reinforcing the profound moral issues surrounding their struggle. Some also began to understand God in new ways—as one who stands with the marginalized, the locked-out of society.

11

The African American Workers

A large number of the sixty African American Staley workers were active in the struggle, and some became Road Warriors. They formed their own union caucus to aggressively educate Decatur's black community, organized a civil rights march, and brought Jesse Jackson to speak at a rally. Jeanette Hawkins, Lorell Patterson, and Frankie Travis were among the local's most active members and became nationally recognized leaders of the fight. In the course of the struggle and in reaction to the black workers' efforts, many white Staley workers underwent a personal transformation on racial issues. White workers who hadn't associated with black workers developed lasting friendships in the course of the conflict. A year and a half into the lockout, black and white unionists united to elect Jeanette Hawkins to the bargaining committee, making her the first African American to serve there.

Nonetheless, the decision of the black workers to throw themselves into the fight was a difficult one and surprised many of the workers themselves. The African American workers had suffered decades of racism both from white supervisors and from union members.[1]

"We Had to Take Care of Ourselves"

Generations of families worked at Staley—it was not uncommon for workers' parents and grandparents to have been employed there. But this was true only of white workers. For decades, the only black workers employed by Staley were the family's cooks and chauffeurs. Until the 1960s, just a handful of African Americans worked in the plant, all of them relegated to the "extra board"— seasonal workers who did the most menial work in the plant. Before the 1960s, that is, blacks were excluded from production jobs.

The civil rights movement transformed the nation in the 1950s and 1960s, but few in Decatur participated. While there was a local NAACP chapter, there were no protests in the city. Nevertheless, the 1964 Civil Rights Act, which prohibits discrimination in employment, forced Staley to hire a few dozen black men as production workers beginning in the late 1960s. They in turn pressured the company to hire black women beginning in the mid-1970s. By the early 1990s about 15 percent of Decatur's 84,000 people were African Americans. At the Staley plant, however, only 7 percent were African American.[2]

The end to hiring discrimination did not translate into equality on the job. African American workers endured racism from both management and white union members. Most considered the majority of the white workers to have "sold out" to the company, and they saw Local 837 as a "white man's union."[3]

In November 1974 Jeanette Hawkins's brother asked her to join him in applying for a job at Staley. Being an African American woman, Hawkins thought she didn't have the slightest chance. In addition, her brother and his two friends who were also applying had some college, but Hawkins had not completed high school. Staley gave Hawkins the standard test to see whether she could lift, walk with, and throw one-hundred-pound bags of corn. Jeanette Hawkins stands over six feet tall with a large, muscular frame. When she easily demonstrated her strength, she became only the second African American woman to be hired at Staley and the first to become a process worker.[4]

Hawkins had worked hard all her life, hiring on as a hotel maid at age thirteen. She turned over her paychecks to her mother and helped care for her younger siblings. Hawkins married at sixteen, and by the time she was twenty-one she had four children. Her husband was physically abusive, but she stayed with him for several years for the sake of their children. Hawkins's assignments at the plant were the dirtiest and hottest, as was typical for new hires, and she accepted that. But she was stunned by the racial harassment. She was first assigned to a building where a white secretary declared that she wasn't going "to use no toilet behind some nigger." Although segregation had been illegal for over nine years, the Staley plant, like many factories across the nation, was still highly segregated. Hawkins was forced to use the men's bathroom, yelling "Is anybody in here?" before entering.

When Hawkins brought this blatant discrimination to a union official, she was told, "You hired on to do a man's job, so you can use a man's restroom." She was furious when the union refused to take any action. "I was really positive about the union," said Hawkins, "until it didn't do anything for me. When I first went to a union meeting, it was like a white country club, and they didn't want no blacks out there. Nobody from process went to the union hall. . . . They made me feel like I was intruding." So Hawkins did not get involved in union activities, and neither did any of her African American co-workers.

Many of the white men were angry that there were blacks and women working in the plant. Hardly a day went by that Hawkins didn't hear a racist or sexist slur. Racist graffiti appeared on bathroom walls, pop machines, and lockers throughout the plant. As did the other African American women, Hawkins turned to her black co-workers for support.

David Conley hired into Staley in 1963 and, with Lavana Robinson, was one of a handful of blacks in the plant at that time. As other African American men were hired in the mid- and late-1960s, and then women in the mid-1970s, Conley and Robinson, along with Joe Slaw and Robert Slaw, welcomed them and gave them guidance. Conley echoed Hawkins's observations: "If you would go into those rest rooms, they always had marks on the walls about me or others. A lot of times I would go and get soap and we would wash some of that stuff off, but it kept appearing. That went on for years before it actually ceased."

Some union members regularly chanted at Hawkins, "Nigger, nigger, go home, you don't belong here," and once she faced a life-threatening assault. While she was precariously positioned four stories above a concrete floor, hanging on to nothing but a rope, a group of white workers assembled above and poured buckets of water down on her. One slip and Hawkins could easily have fallen to her death. She went to the company first aid station and then to her department manager. The white workers denied everything, and the union took no action. The brutal insults, the assault, and the union's indifference took their toll, and Hawkins took six months off to recover.

Through the 1970s and into the 1980s, the black workers were alienated from the "white union." "The benefits, the good retirement, we were just on the bandwagon," said Hawkins. "We got whatever [the whites] got." "The union," said David Conley, "was two-folded": "They fought for the whites; they voted for arbitration [to save a white worker's job]. But when it came to the blacks, the vote wasn't there. A lot of times there was no arbitration, and the black just lost his job. The union did some good things, and they did some bad things. Overall, as far as wages, benefits, pensions, I think those things were good. But a lot of times, when it came to black issues, like trying to hire more minority women, they turned their face on that."

Mike Odeneal, an African American mechanic with a perfect attendance record since his hire in 1967, expanded: "The one thing the union did provide you was the set of rules you had to go through if they tried to fire you. They could not fire you by word of mouth. It wasn't much but it was something. You had your seniority and you had certain rights."

So most African Americans did not look to the union for help in dealing with the company. Many never wrote a grievance. Those who did often wrote and fought the grievance without the union's help. "I wrote my own grievance; I spoke for myself," stated Conley. Frankie Travis, who was hired in 1970, worked second shift in Five and Ten Building, the department and shift comprising the largest number of black workers. "We had to take care of ourselves," said Travis, "and try to take care of each other. . . . I wanted no part of the union. I didn't want to deal with these people. For years, I thought they were sold."

"I don't think any of the blacks were antiunion," said Al Hawkins, Jeanette's second husband, a seventeen-year Staley veteran who courted and married Jeanette after her divorce. "They just felt they weren't wanted," so they didn't have anything to do with it. "I wasn't talking against the union," echoed Frankie Travis, "but I didn't want no part of it . . . because of all they put us through."

The experience of the black workers varied, depending on the department and steward involved. Stewards who fought aggressively for the black workers won their respect. Rosie Brown came to work in 1976 and faced harassment, but her white steward, Mike Griffin, stood up for her, so Brown never soured on the union: "I always have been a firm believer in the union, always have and always will. They were always there for me. . . . When I had a complaint, they did their best to solve the problem. If there wasn't a union, I probably wouldn't have been there as long as I was, because I'm black and I'm a lady."

Lois Oldham had the opposite experience, and hers was more typical. "I filed [sexual harassment] grievances left and right, but I got laughed at. The union wouldn't do anything at all. The steward said, 'Well, when you took this job, you knew there would be a lot of men here.' They tried to play it off like I was a big crybaby." Oldham wrote over thirty grievances but finally gave up when the supervisors began to punish her for speaking out. "After a while you would quit writing them because you know that you are going to get reprimanded, or demoted off a good job, or whatever. So you suck it in and you endure. I never had one grievance settled by the union. They weren't there when I needed them. So I always looked at our union at a distance."

In 1973 David Conley and Lavana Robinson, two of the black workers with the most seniority, formed a group called "Respect" to advocate for equal rights. The group asked the union leadership to appoint a black worker to a union office such as sergeant-at-arms. When they were rebuffed, they approached the AIW international. Both the local and the international said that the bylaws required an election to all union offices and that they could not circumvent the process.

The group met with management, but the harassment continued. Supervisors regularly used racist language and refused to act when white workers wrote racist graffiti. Black workers would be hired and then unfairly fired before they made it through their probation periods, so that management could claim they were trying to hire blacks but couldn't find good workers.

A group of African American workers eventually filed a class-action suit in the late 1970s, charging the company with systematically denying promotions to blacks. Conley, one of the initiators, held a bachelor's degree in business administration and had twenty years on the job, but white workers with only a high-school diploma and half his experience were repeatedly promoted over him for managerial jobs. To squelch his complaint the company offered Conley a management job, but it was out of town. Not wanting to leave town, he rejected it. Later, when Conley took a test to become a mechanic, the highest-paid union position in the plant, the company refused to show him the test results. Staley fought the class-action suit for seven years, after which the black workers ran out of money to pay a lawyer and had to drop it.

Mike Odeneal experienced discrimination in job assignments and in qualifying for overtime. His supervisor ignored the contract's seniority provisions, and Odeneal was not on the supervisor's list of friends. If there was a task no white worker wanted, however, then the supervisor would order Odeneal to work the overtime. Odeneal described what happened when he was the only African American training with a group of white workers for a more skilled job: "A supervisor told me that I was not to train on Sunday because Sunday was a premium [higher-paid] day. But when I got to work on Monday, I found out that everyone else trained on Sunday. I told them I want to get paid just like everyone else. . . . The building supervisor saw it my way and he approved the extra money for me to get paid."

Several black workers reported that if an African American was the only one to bid on an opening, management would postpone the bidding process. When Al Hawkins sought to qualify for advanced electronic work, he took the test with eleven white workers. Ten of the twelve flunked. Even though Al received the highest score, however, the one white worker who passed was promoted over him.

Eugene Robinson, with four years in the navy and twenty years of Staley experience, quickly learned how to protect himself. If a supervisor told him it was okay to go home early, he would say, "'Go get somebody else.' Because if I left, they could just say that I went home and they could fire me." Robinson recounted his strategy for taking a break, "When the whites took a break, that's when I took a break. That way no one could single me out as being on breaks too often or too long."

A sense of protective, cautious isolation permeated the black workers' approach to the white workers. Dennis Houston, a quiet man with nineteen years on the job at the time of the lockout, summarized his approach, "They never messed with me. I just went out there, did my job. I didn't say too much to anybody, and nobody would say too much to me. I stayed out of the way. I had a job to do, and I did my job."

The greatest gain won by the Respect group was an end to Staley's blatantly illegal refusal to hire black women. Other women soon followed in Jeanette Hawkins's footsteps.

Sexual Harassment

The African American women suffered double harassment. Jeanette Hawkins recalled: "So many guys would proposition you. All the time I would tell them, 'I hired on to work at Staley, not to be a prostitute.'" When she complained to union officials, she was told, "Well, we can't control the men." Once a supervisor got physical: "The supervisor put me out in 101 Building, scooping corn all by myself. He comes up there and offered me a breath mint. I said, 'No, thank you.' Well, I'm scooping corn and he tries to grab me and kiss me. So I stepped back and I slapped him. When I picked up the shovel, he turned around and walked off."

The black women were harassed only by the white men, not the black men. Rosie Brown related that once when she was working alone with a male worker, he pulled his pants down in front of her and began to masturbate. The men constantly ogled her breasts and taunted her to lift her shirt. "One time they were above me, and they threw a bag of flour on me. They'd bump into me, feel my [rear]."

"I can't think of any [woman] who didn't go through a lot," said Lois Oldham, who, like Brown, started in 1976. "Anita Hill didn't have nothing on us!" White workers called her "Ms. Spade" and accused her of taking away a job from their family members. They further degraded her with comments such as "Ms. Spade, you should be at home taking care of babies." For Oldham, among the most aggravating insults was regularly being called "Jezebel."

One guy, said Oldham, "hated my guts for no reason at all. He made my life a living hell for two years. Everything I would do, he would undo. The foreman would come through, and it would look like I hadn't done anything." When Oldham confronted him, the man remained silent. Finally, after two years of torture, he said that "he'd never been next to a 'colored lady' before. I was the first black person he'd ever seen in person. I said, 'I'm not colored! You got color in you, too!' He thought working with me would taint him. And they made me work with him."

Oldham, who never returned to Staley after being locked out, said that it took a long time for the white men to accept her even minimally. "How long did it take for my heart to stop beating every time I got in the parking lot? How long did it take for me when I got off work and I wasn't so upset about something" vicious that someone had said? "I'm going to say six years. The first time I came home and nothing had happened was after six years."

While this chapter discusses the experience of African Americans, it should be noted that the white women also suffered sexual harassment and sex discrimination. Both the male supervisors and many of the male union members gave the women workers, black or white, cold treatment. Every woman in the plant was repeatedly accosted and accused of having taken a job from a man who needed it to take care of his family.

Nancy Hanna was a prominent white unionist. "Nancy went through a lot— she really did," said Lois Oldham. "She had a really sweet personality, but guys associate kindness with weakness," so they harassed her even more. Hanna was hired in 1977, when the government forced Staley to end its sex discrimination. Her father and her grandfather had been Kentucky coal miners.

Hanna described the men's hostile responses to white women working in the plant: "One night someone took acid and sprayed it all over a woman's shoes. Another time they got into the women's bathroom and plugged our sink up and put our shoes in there with the water running. Another time they came into the women's bathroom and peed into our trash can." There was a two-inch space beneath the door to the women's bathroom and shower area, and men would lie on the floor to peek into the bathroom. "I don't know how many grievances we wrote" trying to get management to cover the space, said Hanna.

Hanna's supervisor constantly complained about her being hired, calling her a "stupid bitch." One supervisor regularly exposed himself to her. Hanna complained, but management did nothing. When she told the supervisor she would write a grievance, he laughed: "They're not going to believe you. You're just a woman working out here in the men's plant, listening to all their dirty jokes and everything. *I'm* a night superintendent. You're a nobody, just a peon working out here in the plant."

Although the union only weakly responded to Hanna's complaints, for years she attended the monthly meetings, where she was the only woman present. Through her persistence, she was eventually elected her department's steward.

New Hires

After over a decade of a near hiring freeze, Lorell Patterson, an African American woman in her late twenties, was among the eighty-six workers hired in 1990 and 1991. In January 1990 Patterson was working a low-wage job at a Steak n Shake restaurant when she heard that Staley was hiring. In her interview, management illegally tried to find out whether she had union sympathies. She did, but she gave them the answers they wanted to hear and later got the call that she had been hired. "I was so happy to get a job that actually paid enough to pay the bills," Patterson said.

By 1990 racism and sexism were still present but usually more masked. Nonetheless, Patterson recalled that one of her supervisors was open about his bigotry: "One manager thought it was his job to get as many blacks and women fired as he possibly could before their probation period was up. So he would go around and make these little comments about how he wouldn't have his daughter working out here or his wife, because women are supposed to be at home having babies. . . . He was trying to intimidate people."

Patterson knew that Hawkins and the other black women hired in the 1970s had paved the way:

> By the time we got there the [bigots] had learned to curb their appetite, so to speak. They knew that there were certain laws and certain rules that the company had, and they could probably have charges filed against them. They could get fired. So they were a little more covert about it. At a safety meeting, one of the white guys said that he didn't like the way that they were hiring. What he was really saying was, they used to hire the sons and daughters, nieces and nephews, of the white workers who worked there. But this time they hired through a job service. . . . He was saying to me and a couple of other people that we weren't qualified to be out there.

Patterson had sisters who were union members at other jobs, and she knew the union would provide job protection and a higher wage and benefits. She was pleased to finally have a union job. She "thought unions were a pretty great institution to be in." But she didn't have high expectations:

> I knew I was going into a white man's world. I went in sort of laid back: see who the good guys were, who the assholes were. There were some guys out there who would help you no matter who you were. . . . Most of them didn't really have a problem. One guy was complaining about how they hired us, and another guy just said, 'Look, I don't care how they hired them. I just got tired of working all the damn overtime. I'm glad they got somebody in here. They want to work— what's your problem?' Some were good guys; some, no matter what you did, they wouldn't accept you.

Taken on in the same 1990–91 hiring wave was Tamra "Tammy" McCartney, who is white. Her father, uncle, brother, and brother-in-law all worked at Staley. One night at the end of her shift, after McCartney had showered and was heading downstairs, she heard a man laughingly yell a disparaging comment from the floor above. She realized from his comment that he had been spying on her in the shower.

The next day she went to Nancy Hanna. "I don't know what I would have done without Nancy," recalled McCartney. "She was like my best friend and a mother figure in there. She knew the ropes." The two women investigated and found that someone had been sitting in a utility room, "who knows how many times or how long," and had opened an unlocked door to watch the women showering. If they'd known who it was and that it was a union member, said McCartney, she would have handled it within the union. They didn't, however, so they went to the company, which responded by ordering all the workers to attend sexual harassment workshops.

While she welcomed the company's finally taking a stand against harassment, Jeanette Hawkins recalled laughing with disgust when she heard about the workshops. For years white workers and supervisors had been openly racist, and management had ignored it. For years men had sexually harassed black women, and nothing was done. When a white woman was harassed, however, the company took it seriously. "When they started having these talks on sexual harassment," said Hawkins, "I thought, 'What about us? You never brought anybody in to educate about not discriminating against us!'"

As time went on and many of the men got used to women in the plant (the number of women grew to about fifty by 1991), and with the men now threatened with discipline if they harassed women, the sexual harassment lessened, although it never disappeared. Now when the harassment turned into grabbing and physical threats, some union members would speak forcefully to the offending worker. But management never disciplined or terminated a single male supervisor for sexual harassment.

Work-to-Rule

Black and white workers alike were angry when Tate & Lyle began to impose harsh working conditions, but many of the black workers felt that the white workers were now receiving nothing worse than the kind of treatment that black workers had always endured. When Tate & Lyle imposed "skill blocks," a management maneuver requiring workers to demonstrate aptitude in a variety of jobs, Frankie Travis reflected, "It didn't affect me because I did it all anyway." Jeanette Hawkins elaborated: "The company told us many times that if you couldn't pass those skill block tests, you are going to be on the street. [As was true for a lot of the] young blacks out there, every building I went in, I had to operate. But the older white workers didn't have to operate—they had seniority. . . . So when [skill blocks] happened, the mechanics go, 'Whoa, whoa, whoa. It is time to fight because it came to my door. So I got to fight now.'"

In the spring and summer of 1992 some of the black workers attended the union meetings as members discussed how to respond to Tate & Lyle's attack, but they sat as a group in the back of the hall. Some of the white workers were concerned that the local was racially divided and tried to build relationships with the black workers and draw them into the union. Dan Lane recalled that he "had some very frank discussions with a couple of black workers" in Five and Ten Building. "Betty Walker, Bob Stokes, and I were talking about Martin Luther King around the time of his birthday, and my son's birthday is Dr. King's birthday. Betty said, 'You ought to read this book, *The Color Purple*.' So I read it, and I came back to them saying, 'Oh man, it's a great book!' Bob Stokes and a couple of guys were sitting around—they turned me on to another book. So there was my own awakening to some issues. I had heard about them, but there was an awakening to a deeper issue."

When the workers voted down the contract and began the work-to-rule in October 1992, many of the African Americans were not interested. Frankie Travis, who was divorced, had just gotten custody of his teenage son when the campaign began. He wanted to work as much overtime as he could get and earn a good paycheck. Travis described his futile resistance to work-to-rule: "I didn't want to participate. It just came. There wasn't nothing I could do about it. I'd come to work on my shift and a lot of things would already be done."

Others, such as Jeanette Hawkins and Lorell Patterson, got involved in the in-plant campaign. There were black workers, recalled Patterson, "who didn't trust the union to represent them and didn't trust the company either, so they weren't going to do much of anything." Patterson, however, began attending union meetings, listened to Jerry Tucker describe the campaign, liked what she heard, and began working to rule.

Some black workers called those who worked to rule "Uncle Toms" who were "sucking up" to the white unionists, but the activists persisted in their support for the union's campaign. "At one point," said Patterson, "you have to put aside how you *were* being treated and start standing up for how you *want* to be treated. That's the way I looked at it. I'm never going to erase racism in my life. I would like to, but it's just not going to go away. It's embedded in our society. That's part of life that you have to deal with."

Many of the African American activists, then, worked to rule not so much in solidarity with the union but as a stand against the company *in spite of* the union. Dan Lane recalled that many of the white workers recognized that the union's racism weakened its ability to confront Staley: "The one thing I saw as a barrier was [the racial divisions.] So . . . a lot of what we pushed was to try to open doors, to get people to think in a more tolerant and a broader way than they were, in order for the survival of the group. This was mostly one-on-one conversations. We were challenging everybody to stop and think: 'Here's the corporation, and here we are. If we continue to go different ways, we're never going to win this thing.'"

When Lane was fired in April 1993 for union activity, his African American supervisor falsely accused him of making a racist comment. The supervisor spread the accusation around the plant, and many of the black workers didn't know whom to believe. In response, Betty Walker and several other African Americans who worked with Lane in the Five and Ten Building stood up at the next union meeting and said that they had known Dan Lane for a long time and that he wasn't a racist. The company's effort failed to further divide the local by race.

In spring 1993, when the union began to use the company radios to educate and unify the membership, some black workers participated. An African American worker and minister known as "the preacher" frequently went on the radio to call on the company to repent and ask for forgiveness from the workforce. White and black workers would take to the air to talk about racial unity. The workers would talk about Frederick Douglass or Dr. King, recalled Dan Lane, and "what their role had been in society, and [remind] people what their real message was and how it applied to [the workers] in that plant."

At the time of the safety stand-down in June 1993, many African Americans had mixed feelings and consulted one another before taking action. Jeanette Hawkins, holding the most seniority among the African American women, received many phone calls in her building. When she told her co-workers that she and her husband, Al, were walking out, most joined her.

Hawkins was supportive of the union's actions because seniority was the issue that mattered most to her. After building up her seniority, she had earned Sundays off and could comfortably slip into her favorite pew at church. When the company gutted seniority in 1992 and instead played favorites for days off, Hawkins was outraged. Moreover, the twelve-hour rotating shifts deeply damaged Hawkins's family life. Tate & Lyle "set it up so that husband and wife could not have the same day off without taking a vacation," Hawkins reflected. Al and Jeanette Hawkins were among the twelve married couples in the plant, none of whom were assigned to the same shift. The disruption to family life was unbearable. "It was designed to break up friendships, homes, and families," said Hawkins.

When Lorell Patterson heard that workers were walking out during the safety stand-down, she checked with other members to make sure it wasn't a hoax but had no hesitation about walking out:

> After what I had been through with my supervisors—here's a contract where they define insubordination; it can be if you talk back to one of the supervisors. Why would I agree to something like that? This was just setting up the black people and the females to be fired! You had these racist supervisors and these bigots—they're going to have a field day if they get this contract. So what's the worst that can happen? If they get this contract, they can fire me. And if I walk out, I walk out on my own terms.

But many black workers opposed the walkout. Frankie Travis was furious over it: "I live close to the plant, and I was walking to work. They told me, 'You can't go to work because the union [walked out].' I was mad at the union for walking out. I wasn't a part of it. I didn't feel like I was a part of the union."

Locked Out

After the June 1993 lockout, most African American unionists remained uninvolved in the union. (Jeanette Hawkins and Lorell Patterson were the exceptions.) They continued to sit in the back of the hall during union meetings, and they didn't speak.

When C. J. Hawking began making regular trips to Decatur to help organize support in the religious community, she worried about the racial division she witnessed at union meetings. Watts assented when Hawking asked to call a meeting of the black workers in late November 1993. Frankie Travis was skeptical when he got the call: "There wasn't any trust in the plant. When C. J. called my house and asked me to come out to a meeting, the only reason I came was because Reuben [Thomas] was involved in it. . . . [But also], somebody cared about us and cared about what we think. That's when I started. Each day I learned a little bit more." One reason she attended the meeting, said Jeanette Hawkins, laughing, was that "when they called me and said C. J. Hawking is down here, I said to myself, 'She's got to be black.'"

Sixteen black workers went to the union hall, where Hawking explained that she had volunteered to assist the local with community outreach. She touched on her personal background, which included experience in the African American communities of Chicago, and said her instincts told her that the lockout was different for blacks than it was for whites.

The group was extremely suspicious of Hawking, since she was both a white person and an outsider. Travis spoke the words that many were thinking: "Why should we tell you anything? You are just some white person the union sent here to spy on us. You're going to tell [the union leadership] everything we say here. I don't trust you." When Hawking explained that she was a pastor, some of the suspicions dissipated and tensions eased, and the workers began to open up. Story upon story poured forth, tales about white workers subjecting blacks to humiliating racial epithets and harassment. The sentiment was that the lockout was a white man's fight because this was a white man's union.

As the group talked further, they identified two dynamics that had occurred since the workers had been locked out five months earlier. First, many of the white workers were quickly able to find jobs through their friendships with owners of local small businesses, such as hardware stores or gas stations. The wages were low and the hours part-time, but many white workers were earning something besides their sixty dollars a week picket pay. The town contained only a handful of black-owned small businesses, however. Getting hired by an acquaintance was just not possible for the African American workers. Eugene Robinson, who was caring for a sick wife at home, found the situation unbearable at times. "The whites had a job from their families or friends about two or three days after [the lockout]. Most of us didn't have a job. It took me a year and a half."

Second, the black workers discussed the confusion in the black community. Since lockouts were not commonplace, many people in town mistook the lockout for a strike and assumed that the workers could return to work whenever they wanted. Moreover, as is typical in labor disputes, the public wrongly assumed that the conflict centered on wages. Much of the Decatur black community was unsympathetic to the African American Staley workers for "giving up" their good salaries and steady jobs while so many others were working minimum-wage jobs or were unemployed.

Sharing their lockout experiences and venting about being in a white-led union solidified the group. Several people said that they felt better after talking candidly about the hardships of the lockout and realizing that others were having similar experiences. The group decided to meet again. Willie Newbon, an African American pastor who had previously worked at Staley, offered his church basement as a meeting place. Hawking joined them each week.

By the second meeting the group had grown to twenty-nine. As they talked, a sense of power began to emerge. "By having that meeting at the church, I was taught a lot of things," explained Frankie Travis. "We were sharing things, getting involved in things. I wasn't going to the union hall, no way. . . . I still felt separated. But I didn't feel that way at that church." Travis reflected on what Lavana Robinson had repeatedly told him and other African Americans after Travis had started working at Staley: "You've got to fight, because I won't be here too much longer. So you got to fight."

But some black workers opposed the meetings. "I had several calls that this wasn't going to do no good," said Jeanette Hawkins. "They would say, 'The white folks don't want you in it anyway.'" Hawkins responded, "I have my own plan, I am my own woman, and I am going to do what I have to do." Travis, too, felt the pressure. "We had blacks come down there and try to break it up," he recalled.

The black workers could have walked away from the fight. Certainly each one had endured enough bad experiences to justify doing so. Instead, the group determined to organize as a caucus, throw themselves into the fight, and educate Decatur's black community. Some workers, such as Lorell Patterson and Jeanette Hawkins, had already made that decision during the in-plant campaign. Recalled Hawkins,

> A lot of the blacks that I used to talk to would say about the white unionists, "You know they don't want us there, Jeanette." That's the way a lot of them felt, and in the beginning I felt that way, too. And then I started thinking, I want to be a part of the fight myself because I'm fighting for *my* family. . . . I got into it because I wanted to make a difference for my kids and my grandkids. . . . That's when I really started participating, and we just pulled together as a team. And more and more black people started getting involved.

Others decided that since they had never walked away from a fight before, they weren't going to start now. Most resolved that, however bitter they were toward the union, they hated the company more.

Black Community Awareness

Calling itself the Black Community Awareness Committee, this group of African American workers immediately elected officers and began discussing how to educate Decatur's black community. Travis explained their goals: "In the struggle, the community plays a big part. We started to inform the black community exactly what was going on at Staley's and what we were fighting for. They were not aware; the majority thought we were out to get more money. Some said we should go back, take what the company is offering. Our outreach to the community is that you have to look at the overall situation of what's going on around you. People are just looking at one small part of the picture. Education is the key."[5]

Mike Odeneal was recruited to draft a letter that appeared as a full-page ad in the January 5, 1994, issue of *The Voice*, an African American weekly newspaper in Decatur, and the Local 837 executive board approved the expenditure. The ad outlined the Staley workers' grievances against the company and concluded, "We feel that it is not necessary to have to sacrifice our families, communities, morals, and health, just for huge corporate profits. We also appreciate all the support that our Black Community can give in our on-going struggle."

A few weeks later Mike Odeneal and John Cook drafted a second ad, this one titled "Chemicals Affect Us All." The scabs now performing their jobs posed a safety and environmental threat to the entire community, the workers warned. Referring to the company's illegal practices, the ad declared that charges should be brought "when a major company buries toxic waste in an illegal area." When the white members were handed copies of the ads at the weekly meetings, the response was overwhelmingly positive.

The group quickly decided to organize a labor contingent in Decatur's annual Martin Luther King Day parade on January 17. Watts wrote to the locals in Decatur asking them to join the Staley contingent in the parade. The African Americans began to make announcements at the weekly union meetings. They used the union's Kandy Lane office to make phone calls and to prepare mailings and signs.

But the black Staley workers soon faced a pivotal decision. City officials told the African Americans not to carry any signs about the labor struggle because, they said, "Dr. King had nothing to do with labor." The group knew better. Shortly after forming their black caucus, the workers had watched the documentary *At the River I Stand*. The film chronicles the two-month strike of 1,300 Memphis sanitation workers, all of whom were black, for a living wage and safe working conditions. Dr. King came to Memphis to support these members of the American Federation of State, County, and Municipal Employees (AFSCME). On April 3, 1968, Dr. King gave his final, "I have been to the mountain top" speech to the sanitation workers; the next day he was killed by an assassin's bullet.

After lengthy discussions in the church basement, the Black Community Awareness Committee chose to defy the city's order banning union signs and banners. On a brutally cold Monday, January 17, scores of workers, including an equal number of white and black Staley workers, showed up to march through Decatur. "We carried our [union] signs anyway," said Reuben Thomas, "and we vowed to educate Decatur about King's commitment to labor."[6]

"The [city] had told the union that they wanted it to be a Martin Luther King march, and they didn't want it to turn into a union gathering," recalled Jeanette Hawkins proudly. "But we had our own songs, and we passed out sheets, and we had our banner, and we were *loud!*" The Staley contingent was the largest in the parade that day. Lorell Patterson remembered the day vividly. "A black lady, one of the march organizers, was trying to take our [union] signs. They were not happy that we were there. I said to her, 'Do you know anything about Martin Luther King and what he stood for?' I just went off on her. I had to remind her what Dr. King was fighting for: the sanitation workers that joined a union! They only want to remember the "I have a dream" Martin Luther King. They didn't want to remember the whole man. . . . It's like disgracing the man."

The committee members were jubilant with their success at their first effort. "We showed them we can force our opinion, because that's what [Dr. King] was about," said Frankie Travis. "They didn't want us to show our union colors. They didn't want the union to do anything with [the parade], and they tried to put us in the back. I was proud because we stood up."

The African American workers were determined to escalate their efforts. The group decided to call their own march to educate the entire community about Dr. King's advocacy for workers' rights. The group chose Saturday, April 9, five days after the twenty-sixth anniversary of King's death, for the protest. Jeanette Hawkins, who was chosen to chair the planning committee, explained their purpose: "Some in the black community don't understand the importance of unions. So many of our people are unemployed, so there's pressure on those of us who have jobs to just accept whatever comes. We need to educate folks that unions are the way to get what's fair. Dr. King knew that. We want everyone to know that."[7]

The group opened up the planning meetings to black unionists from other Decatur locals. C. J. Hawking, AFSCME Council 31 regional director Buddy Maupin, and AFSCME union rep Debby Lippincott, all white, played an active role. The plans for the event, dubbed the "Solidarity March for Social and Economic Justice," were extensive. The flyer was carefully designed to be an educational tool. It quoted King's 1961 "If the Negro Wins, Labor Wins" speech to the AFL-CIO, which stated, "We are both confronted by powerful forces telling us to rely on the good will and understanding of those who profit by exploiting us. They deplore our discontent, they resent our will to organize so that we may guarantee humanity will prevail and equity will be exacted." The flyer, with a hand-drawn image of Dr. King, also referred to King's dream of "a land where men will not take the necessities from the many to give luxuries to the few."

The black Staley workers' activities increased exponentially. A black worker gave a report on the march at each Tuesday-night union meeting. The committee members worked out of the Kandy Lane office to build the march, making calls to churches and African American unionists in other locals, putting out mailings, and organizing the logistics. A camaraderie thus grew between the white and black activists at Kandy Lane.

On April 9 over 750 people turned out for Decatur's largest interracial civil-rights march. After speeches and songs at Decatur's Central Park, unionists and their supporters marched behind a twenty-foot-long, hand-painted banner that had taken Bob Durley, a white worker, two weeks to produce. The banner proclaimed "Labor Rights = Civil Rights" and included Dr. King's words. During the march the protesters chanted, "black and white, united we fight." Children and adults poured out of their homes and apartments to watch the parade through the black neighborhoods, and many joined it.

A spirited two-hour rally began at the Northside Baptist Church, with songs by the church's Now Generation Singers and an inspiring invocation by Father Mangan. Norman Hill, director of the A. Philip Randolph Institute (a national organization of black workers affiliated with the AFL-CIO), and Fred McKinney, president of the Decatur NAACP, declared that the fights for civil rights and workers' rights and against union-busting were all the same struggle. The Reverend Ben Cox, from Champaign, Illinois, who had been a 1960s Freedom Rider with Martin Luther King, made the keynote address. Cox called on local churches to give 1 percent of their Sunday collections to the families of locked-out workers.

Days later, to celebrate their success, the black workers organized a picnic in a local park and invited the local's leadership. Watts and other white officers happily attended the barbecue. The workers thought it a nice addition to their celebration that the park was adjacent to Staley spokesperson J. Patrick Mohan's house. About twenty-five people, including Staley workers in their signature red T-shirts, their spouses, and supporters, were present.

Soon, however, the appearance of four squad cars interrupted the celebration. The picnickers were told they weren't allowed to gather in the park. The day after the picnic, the Decatur Park District posted signs reading "Tree Nursery, No Trespassing." Jeanette Hawkins had gone to the park for years without incident. "When Al and I first got married," recalled Hawkins, "and we needed to discuss something [privately], we would go there and we never got arrested. . . . They changed it to a nursery overnight." "The whole park board knew that [the signs] had been changed," said a furious Pat Watts, "and they kept their mouths shut."

A few weeks later, after Mohan and Staley officials interceded with their friends in city government, thirteen workers were arrested and charged with "residential picketing" for holding a picnic on park district property. The union said that the charges were fraudulent and politically motivated, as evidenced by the fact that only the locked-out workers were charged. "If it was illegal for the Staley workers," asked Judy Dulaney, "why wasn't it illegal for everybody else?" Charges against four workers were dropped when they proved that they hadn't attended the picnic.

The Mohan family testified at the trial and admitted that they had not witnessed any picket signs, placards, bullhorns, or microphones. Nevertheless, eight unionists were convicted of trespassing on September 23, 1994.[8]

Later on, when Local 837 invited the Eighth Day Center for Justice to conduct training in nonviolent civil disobedience, the group's instruction centered on the teachings of Dr. King and Mahatma Gandhi. The training further expanded the white members' appreciation for King and the civil rights movement. On June 4, 1994, when forty-eight supporters staged a nonviolent demonstration that blocked the gates to the Staley plant, Dave Watts carried a poignant sign, left over from the April 9 march, reading "King's Dream Lives."

By July 1994 both the Caterpillar and Firestone workers had walked out on strike. Now nearly four thousand blue-collar workers were walking the picket lines, and the three locals were working closely in common cause. In fall 1994 the Decatur Workers Solidarity and Education Coalition, initiated by the three union locals, began publishing a newspaper, the *Decatur Free Press,* to explain the workers' issues to the community. The paper also challenged racism and police brutality in town. The October 22, 1994, issue reprinted a lengthy article from the black paper *The Voice* about the all-too-typical experience of African Americans in Decatur. Reuben Thomas's son Quinten was picked up and detained overnight because he "fit the description of an alleged attacker"—that is, he was a black youth. "This article shows," said the editors, "[that] young African American males can be targeted for unfair treatment by the police."

By this time white and African American unionists were joining in efforts to bring labor education into the Decatur schools, participating in antidrug marches throughout the neighborhoods, and volunteering with local youth organizations.

In early 1994 the Road Warriors began to invite African American workers to join them on their trips. Sometimes they would travel as part of an interracial delegation; other times, when they were speaking to an all-black audience, several black workers would travel together. For Frankie Travis, Eugene Robinson, Jeanette Hawkins, Lorell Patterson, and other black workers, this was their first opportunity to interact with other local unions, many with fully integrated leadership bodies. "A lot of the places I went to," related Travis, "it surprised me to see so many black people in charge, presidents of all these big unions, like the Longshoremen. Twenty or thirty thousand he was in charge of. It was something to see out there. . . . It changed me."[9]

As did many of the white workers, Travis relished traveling the country as a Road Warrior. "It's been rewarding," he said. "People have been very support-ive—the warmth of the reception, the warm smiles we get, the 'I'm proud of what you're doing,' it carries a long way. We are carrying our message: what's going on with us can happen to you . . . if we don't come together as one and try to help each other. We're getting a good response. Unionists know that it's coming sooner or later."[10]

Jeanette Hawkins enjoyed speaking for the union. One of her most memorable presentations was made to Chicago's Operation PUSH, inviting the large black audience and thousands of radio listeners to come to Decatur for the April 9 march. Another time she spoke at an economic forum in the Roosevelt Room of the White House. "President Clinton was supposed to be there," recounted Hawkins, but instead he sent several top aides. "[They] told me his plane was delayed—but I think he didn't want to hear me speak." Hawkins "got so mad at him" for not attending that she wrote the president a strongly worded letter, but her husband convinced her "to tone it down."

Lorell Patterson traveled to many states as a Road Warrior. She was scared at first—"shaking like a leaf"—but steadily developed into one of the local's most powerful speakers. She enjoyed being on the road and traveled constantly. "Me and Frankie were always there," recalled Patterson, "like peas in a pod." Occa-sionally a white worker wouldn't want to travel with her because she was black, but she didn't let it get to her.

In late 1994 an opening on the bargaining committee was announced, with the election to be held in December. Now, eighteen months into the lockout, the activists were aware of the damage wrought by decades of racism and sex-ism within the union. A handful of white workers who were among the local's leading activists and Road Warriors were interested in the bargaining committee position, but when they heard that Jeanette Hawkins was willing to run, they withdrew from the race and threw their support behind her. Many whites lob-bied for Hawkins, citing her outstanding leadership in the April 9 march, her ability to rally other blacks to activism, and her dedication as a Road Warrior. AIW 837 history was made when Hawkins became the first African American and the second woman elected to the local's leadership.[11]

12

Civil Disobedience

In early 1994 Local 7837 members began a spirited discussion about mass nonviolent civil disobedience at the Staley gates. Many of the unionists believed that if the local was to build greater national solidarity and pressure an intransigent management, they must escalate their tactics and stop production. In early March the local decided to call a national mobilization for June 25, 1994, the one-year anniversary of the lockout. As the date for the rally approached, its character was debated. Should the local escalate the fight by marching thousands of protesters to sit down in front of the Staley gates?

Picking up the Pace

Immediately after the lockout the union established pickets at every entrance to the plant, hoping to deter unionized delivery and service workers from crossing the picket line. Since the pickets were too few to deter scabs from entering, Tate & Lyle was able to continue production unhindered.

At 2:30 A.M. on December 17, 1993, some frustrated members decided to move their pickets onto the rail tracks and block an incoming train. The engineer of the Illinois Central locomotive was shocked to see workers standing on the tracks holding picket signs. Since his speed was slow, he saw the picketers in time and stopped the train. He reported the incident to the Staley yardmaster, who quickly called the police. By the time the police arrived, the workers were gone, but the police issued a warning to the union that any workers blocking the tracks would be arrested. The union defiantly declared that it would maintain a regular presence on the railroad line but then backed off, fearing legal repercussions.[1]

Shortly thereafter a small group of workers began meeting secretly to discuss shutting down production by occupying a strategic building in the plant. Their detailed knowledge of plant operations allowed them to identify a building whose incapacitation would bring all production to a grinding halt. Their plan involved remaining in the building until the union's demand for a fair contract was met.

This plan was never put into effect. The workers decided that the logistics of illegally entering the plant and maintaining an occupation were too difficult. Unlike, for example, the situation in the 1937 Flint auto plant occupation or the 1990 Pittston mine occupation, in this case the workers had targeted a building deep within company property, far from a public road. This meant that other workers and supporters could not rally nearby to express their solidarity, and supplies could not easily be delivered to the occupiers. The workers also feared that other members would not support such a militant action, a concern made more pressing because it would not be possible to discuss the tactic first at union meetings, since the element of surprise was essential.

In February 1994 members of the local's newly formed Women's Support Group were inspired by reading about the wives' support group for the striking Pittston mine workers. The miners' wives had taken over company headquarters during the 1989–90 strike and occupied it until they were arrested. Some Decatur women were willing to risk arrest and began planning a similar action for the Staley office building.

Many of these women, however, were the spouses of Staley workers who opposed this plan, preferring to fight their own battle. Consequently, the women instead planned a "women's and children's rally"; they held the event on the front lawn of Staley headquarters in March 1994. Apparently the police got word of the women's original plan, because large numbers arrived in riot gear to confront the peaceful protesters. Staley worker Nancy Hanna "was dumbfounded when the police came up there with their clubs." Hanna yelled, "Why are you guys here? We're just a bunch of grandmothers and mothers and little children. What a waste of our taxpayer money!"

In late February Local 7837 organized mass pickets at the two main Staley gates, and the protest turned into civil disobedience. The action stemmed from the workers' outrage at the lies Tate & Lyle CEO Neil Shaw had told at the company's January 1994 stockholders meeting. A delegation of workers had flown to London to demand an end to the lockout. Shaw, attempting to silence the angry union members, declared that the company would negotiate a fair contract and that the chief negotiator from the union-busting Seyfarth, Shaw law firm would vacate the bargaining table.

When the union returned to the table two weeks later, however, both the company's dismal contract proposal and the Seyfarth attorney were still present. UPIU Region 9 assistant director Danny Wirges wrote union president Wayne Glenn about the frustrating session: "The tone was set by the company in a very negative manner. . . . [The union] went the extra mile but to no avail.

I am firmly convinced now more than ever that this company is clearly out to destroy our local."[2]

The Staley workers were incensed and Dave Watts, who had felt hope when he heard Shaw's words, was furious. The executive board called for a rally in front of the corporate office, halfway between the two main gates on Eldorado Street, at 4:30 P.M. on February 22. "We decided to pick up the pace and show the company we are damn sick of them not negotiating," declared Watts. "There is a high level of frustration because of the lying by the company and attempts to starve people out. It is not going to work."[3]

When forty unionists who had volunteered to be demonstration monitors arrived at the union hall at 2:30 that afternoon, Watts informed them that they would lead the crowd in blocking the west and east plant gates, making it impossible for employees or trucks to enter or leave. The monitors, whom the Staley workers called "chaplains," were quickly assigned to teams, briefly instructed, and outfitted in orange vests. Five minutes after the chaplains had exited the hall, detailed information about the plan was blaring over the police scanner. Either the police had a mole within the union or a bug had been placed in the union hall.[4]

Battling cold, sleeting rain, and thirty-mile-per hour winds, hundreds of members and their supporters, including dozens of workers from the Caterpillar and Firestone unions, rallied in front of the corporate office. Several workers held up a huge new banner reading, "Lies, Lies, and More Lies. No Honor, No Contract, No Peace." Twenty minutes into the rally, the crowd split in half and marched to the two main gates, blocking the driveways.

Upon a signal from the Decatur police chief, city police officers and state troopers, ominously dressed in riot gear, rushed off a waiting bus and charged into the crowd. Using their three-foot batons, they pushed the demonstrators to the sides of the driveway, allowing plant traffic to flow once again. The police maintained a loose human barricade to keep the protesters at bay. At the east gate, however, some determined workers walked through gaps in the police line and were joined by others to again block the driveways. Hundreds of workers walked in a large circle, all the while chanting union slogans at the tops of their voices. After a half-hour the crowd dispersed peacefully.

The Local 7837 activists who had been pushing for such demonstrations and an end to passive rallies were jubilant. Recalling the resistance that he and others continually got from some members of the executive board, Dan Lane said: "I wasn't going to argue anymore. I said, 'Just get people out there!' . . . People were just saying, 'Screw it, we're blocking the gate.' It was just a miserable day; you couldn't pick a worse day. But it was very invigorating. People felt, 'Okay, we're back into it.' [It showed that] people were wanting to fight, wanting to get their jobs, but under the terms that *they* were involved in negotiating, not being dictated to, and they were willing to take the chance of getting arrested or fired."[5]

Later that night at Local 7837's weekly solidarity meeting, the sense of power and elation was evident on members' faces. A hoarse but euphoric Dave Watts declared, "This was a resurgence of our grassroots efforts. This is labor history! This is just the beginning—we have taken the first step towards our Spring Offensive!" After congratulating the workers, Jerry Tucker added, "Don't think that one demonstration will get the job done. It's a process. You need to escalate the fight. It's like hitting the company with water torture—drop after drop. Take the fight forward!"[6]

No arrests were made the day of the rally. Instead, the police videotaped it and returned to the police station to view the tapes. With identification and addresses provided to them by Staley and Caterpillar managers, police singled out three people for arrest. Five days after the rally, on a Saturday morning, locked-out workers Dee Scott, Lorell Patterson, and Don Davis awoke to flashing squad-car lights and police pounding on their doors. Jarred out of bed, they were told they were under arrest for "obstructing the police."[7]

Learning from History

Two weeks after the February 22 protest the local authorized a sixty-thousand-piece national mailing, produced by Corporate Campaign, calling for a June 25 demonstration in Decatur. The headline of the flyer shouted: "CALL IN THE TROOPS . . . It's War! National Mobilization for the Locked-out Staley Workers." At the bottom the union declared, "On the one year anniversary of the Staley lock-out . . . Let the Power of Labor Come Down on Staley!" In smaller print, however, after describing the workers' issues, the flyer captured the fluid state of the Staley workers' discussions about civil disobedience: "The specific activities at the plant are still being planned. But we can tell you this: when thousands of workers descend on Decatur to vent their anger at one of the greediest anti-worker companies in the country, it will send shock waves around the boardrooms of corporate America." Despite the language, the leadership was undecided about engaging in civil disobedience at the plant gates on June 25.

The central problem the workers faced was determining how they could win against an intransigent company that refused to negotiate its demands. Many of the local's activists began to read, deliberate, and discuss the tactic of mass nonviolent civil disobedience and its use by unions in American history. Solidarity committee members shared books, and many workers checked out labor history texts from the Kandy Lane library.

The American economy grew astronomically in the decades after the Civil War, and workers responded by attempting to form unions. Until 1935, when Congress passed the Wagner Act, giving workers the right to form unions and bargain collectively, every strike was in a sense an act of civil disobedience.

From the 1870s through the 1930s, when workers demonstrated or went on strike, they were almost inevitably assaulted by the local police, company-hired "security guards" from the notorious Pinkerton or Baldwin-Felts agencies, the state militia or national guard, or the U.S. Army. Often the unionists defended themselves, usually with fists and sticks. Striking mineworkers frequently armed themselves on the picket line and shot back when fired upon, but they were the exception. Usually, when government forces attacked, the strike collapsed.

In the 1930s, with a surge in labor organizing led by the militant Congress of Industrial Organizations, the pattern of repression was repeated. On December 31, 1936, however, the autoworkers in Flint, Michigan, used a strike tactic that limited picket line violence and kept scabs out of the plant. The workers escorted foremen out of the plant, blockaded the entrances, and occupied the plant for forty-four days. The autoworkers' successful "sit-down" strike was the pivotal moment in U.S. labor history, not only winning the autoworkers a contract but inspiring workers across the country to fight for better treatment. Through 1937 a half-million workers engaged in 477 sit-down strikes. The sit-downs were labor's first large-scale use of nonviolent civil disobedience, though no one called it that at the time.

The 1946 strike wave, when 4.5 million workers walked off the job, was the first time in U.S. history that a national labor upheaval did not result in massive picket-line violence. For the next three decades most major strikes remained relatively peaceful. The tactic of nonviolent mass protests was taken up instead in the struggle to guarantee civil rights for African Americans. In the 1950s and 1960s, greatly influenced by Mohandas Gandhi's use of such protests to gain India's independence from Britain, Dr. Martin Luther King Jr. espoused nonviolent civil disobedience as an unassailable principle of the civil rights movement. Hundreds of thousands of African Americans participated in protests, and tens of thousands were arrested. In 1963 alone almost one thousand demonstrations were mounted in over one hundred Southern cities, resulting in over twenty thousand arrests. In 1968, while in Memphis to support striking sanitation workers, Dr. King defied the government-issued injunction that sought to overturn the workers' constitutionally recognized right to march. In what became his last speech, King exclaimed, "Just as I say we aren't going to let any fire hoses or police dogs turn us around, we aren't going to let any injunctions turn us around."[8]

In the early 1960s farmworkers union leader Cesar Chavez studied the lives and writing of King and Gandhi and adopted their nonviolent stance. In his admonitions to farmworkers struggling to win union recognition, Chavez emphasized two essential precepts. First, nonviolent protest was the only method the United Farm Workers could justifiably undertake, because ends and means are inextricably linked. Peace and justice, argued Chavez, cannot be sought through violence and hatred. "If we're full of hatred, we can't really do our work," Chavez further asserted. "Hatred saps all that strength and energy we need to plan."[9]

Second, Chavez asserted, nonviolent civil disobedience was the most *effective* tactic. When the workers used force to defend themselves against the violence of the police or the growers' hired thugs, the union lost public support. Instead of acting violently, then, the farmworkers "took every case of violence and publicized what [the police and growers] were doing," said Chavez. "Every time [our] opposition commits an unjust act against our hopes and aspirations, we get paid back tenfold in benefits."[10]

After President Reagan broke the air-traffic controllers' strike in 1981, many corporations returned to the historically established strategy for breaking strikes: calling on the police to escort scabs into their plants so that they could permanently replace striking unionists. Strike after strike was defeated as union leaders were unwilling to return to the tactics of the 1930s. One of the principal reasons that unions lost strikes, therefore, was their inability to stop production. As long as a company is able to import replacement workers, maintain production, and keep making a hefty profit, the striking union loses its economic leverage. During the 1980s organized labor became paralyzed as its numbers, influence, and support declined.

Nevertheless, a few unions began to use mass civil disobedience as a strike tactic, often in opposition to their national union leaders. UFCW Local P-9 members used the tactic in their 1985–86 strike against Hormel in Austin, Minnesota. On several occasions hundreds of Hormel workers blocked the plant entrance with a slow-moving car caravan. Strike supporters in the Twin Cities sat in at the governor's office to protest his sending the Minnesota National Guard to break the strike. Over 150 workers and supporters were arrested in several mass demonstrations at the plant gates.[11] These few actions only briefly hindered production, but the union had hoped that their protests would galvanize supporters to join an escalating campaign.

In 1989–90 UMWA president Rich Trumka led the mineworkers in a civil-disobedience strategy to win the Pittston strike. Trained by peace activists, the Virginia miners repeatedly blocked the roads into the mines, and spouses occupied the Pittston headquarters. Through the course of the fifteen-month strike, three thousand workers, spouses, and supporters were arrested, some multiple times, for a total of over five thousand arrests. Finally, ninety-nine workers and one pastor occupied a Pittston coal-processing plant for four days, calling their action "Operation Flintstone" in homage to the 1937 autoworkers' sit-down.[12] During the strike Trumka declared, "Labor law is formulated for labor to lose. If you play by every one of those rules, you lose every time. So what it forces you to do, is to change the way you've operated."[13] UMWA vice president Cecil Roberts noted that observers were surprised to see the mineworkers turn to a nonviolent strategy: "They didn't think that a predominately white, mountain, rural workforce would ever follow the teachings of Dr. King. But they did. Dr. King says there is nothing more invigorating than being in jail for a cause that you believe in. And I think that's absolutely right. There's nothing wrong with going to jail when you're trying to change an unjust system or an unjust law."[14]

The courts fined the UMWA $64 million for refusing to stop its disobedience campaign, but the union counted on winning a settlement with terms requiring the company to ask the government to drop the fines—the scenario that did in fact unfold. Trumka courageously put the entire union treasury at risk to win the strike—a stance no other union international president has taken in recent history.

Educating the Membership

Local 7837 leaders approached the idea of mass civil disobedience the same way they had approached the fight with Tate & Lyle in 1992: by thoroughly educating the membership.

After the success of the February 22 picket line, the activists were pressuring to escalate the struggle. Watts and the activists, however, were determined that all protests be nonviolent; as Chavez and King had argued, picket-line violence was, they believed, both morally wrong and tactically foolhardy. While no one was advocating violence, the principle of nonviolence was repeatedly enforced. Tucker and Rogers reinforced Watts's stance, as did Father Mangan, who told the union, "If this struggle turns violent, I will withdraw." Within three weeks of the lockout, Watts had told the press, "Violence on the picket line would only play into the company's hands. . . . We are not going to let them portray us as thugs."[15] The hostile editors of the *Decatur Herald and Review* had run a photo in their November 6, 1993, edition—the day of the local's first postlockout demonstration—and again on December 26, of a lone Staley worker holding a picket sign reading, "The only good scab is a dead scab." The paper's action reaffirmed to Watts that the media would do everything it could to turn the community against the union and portray the members as gangsters. At union meeting after union meeting Watts declared his opposition to violence: "This local union will be responsible for many, many years if there is mass violence on the picket line—not only in injunctions and fines, but dues will be paid to pay this thing off for many years to come. . . . We have major support because our position has been nonviolence. If we change our position, we lose [support-ers]. . . . Violence is a sure beginning to a quick end, but not in our favor, but in Staley's favor."[16]

At C. J. Hawking's recommendation, Watts agreed to invite religious activists from Chicago's Eighth Day Center for Justice to train the workers in the theory and practice of civil disobedience. As was discussed in chapter 10, activists from Eighth Day—Kathleen Desautels, Mary Kay Flanigan, Jean Hughes, Dolores Brooks, and Bob Bossie—held training sessions at the union hall in April and May 1994, where they taught workers and spouses about nonviolent civil disobedience. They answered questions and conducted role-playing exercises with an eager but cautious audience.

This is nonviolent resistance, not "passive" resistance, the Eighth Day activists told the workers. There is nothing *passive* about risking arrest; civil disobedience is *action*. It's not easy to remain nonviolent, they said. Often a person's natural reaction when assaulted is to fight back. You should know, they told the Staley workers, that the police will wear riot gear, carry billy clubs, march in step, and push and hit you with their batons. Even if the police instigate violence, however, no one is to fight back. If you do, they pointed out, it will give the police another excuse to arrest you and the media the opportunity to smear your cause.

Many workers wondered whether they could subdue their instinctive reaction to defend themselves. Admitted one worker, "There's no way that somebody can put their hands on me, that I'm not going to react in a violent way. I'm sure there are other people that feel the same way. Passive resistance is okay, but my basic makeup is, I just *can't* do that."[17] After thanking the worker for his honesty, the trainers stated unequivocally that anyone who believed that he or she might possibly react violently to a police provocation should not participate in the action. The Eighth Dayers emphasized that there were other tasks for volunteers, such as rallying nearby in support of the action, helping with publicity and media work, going to the jail to support those arrested, and raising funds for legal defense.

During the two training sessions and in private conversations through the spring of 1994, the workers discussed the risks they faced if they blocked the gates. Under U.S. labor law, a striking or locked-out worker who engages in what the company and the courts label aggressive activities on the picket line can be legally fired. Assaulting scabs as they pass the picket line, as well as physically or even verbally intimidating them, may result in legal discharge. In addition, blocking a plant entrance is not protected under the law; the only way to guarantee that workers who do so will retain their jobs is by decisively winning the labor conflict. If a striking or locked-out union is forced to sign a weak contract, workers discharged for picket-line activity generally lose their jobs and any severance benefits. As was discussed previously, during the 1970 strike seven Staley workers were fired for dumping corn from a delivery truck at the picket line, and when the membership was forced to accept the company's demands, the contract did not include amnesty for the seven. In 1992, when the local had launched the work-to-rule campaign, workers had unanimously vowed not to "leave any worker behind," but for many, the memory of those seven workers loomed.

Some workers feared that if they blocked the gates, Tate & Lyle would strip them of their pensions. Some of the local's conservative leaders—encouraged by the UPIU International staff—incessantly repeated this fear and made it a mainstay of their arguments. As a result, many workers were dissuaded from participating in the civil disobedience. Tucker and other longtime activists repeatedly disputed the notion that workers could lose their pensions for picket-line actions. A check with Eddie Burke, a Mine Workers strike leader at Pittston, revealed that the claim was completely unfounded. Said Burke, "I have never heard of a company going after workers' pensions, never heard of workers losing their pensions due to any labor conflict action. Even if they discharge people, I never heard of anyone losing a vested pension. I've been through some pretty rough and tough strike actions, too. Lawyers will always give you arguments why you shouldn't do something. We faced fines of $500,000 a day before we sat down in the mines. But we did what we had to do."[18]

The Chicago-based labor lawyer Michael Holland echoed Burke, saying that "pension rights are vested rights, guaranteed in the contract," using the example of former UMWA president Tony Boyle, who was convicted of murdering a rival, reform candidate Jock Yablonski, in 1970. "Even a *convicted murderer* did not lose his pension!" said Holland.[19]

Some workers also feared that an arrest record might hinder them from finding future jobs. Some worried that even a misdemeanor trespassing charge might be used against them.

Local 7837 leaders were told by the UPIU International staff that they could be held personally liable for any infraction of the law. Watts was told that Staley might sue him and that he stood to lose his home and savings. This was a highly dubious interpretation of the law. Although labor law is complex, and the National Labor Relations Board and federal courts sometimes interpret the law in unpredictable ways, no union official in recent memory has ever had his or her personal assets liquidated because of union activity during a strike or lockout.

Watts had his fears about personal and even criminal liability repeatedly reinforced by the Decatur Police Department. Gary Lamb recalled meetings when the police threatened Watts, saying, "If anything goes wrong, *you're* going to jail. You understand? *You* are the elected leader of the local, and *you* are going to jail." Local 7837 officers were not unique in their fears. International Paper strikers at Jay, Maine, in 1987–88 had decided against civil disobedience at the plant gates. "I was scared," said UPIU Local 14 secretary-treasurer Randy Berry. "I didn't want to lose my house, and as a union officer that could be just the thing to shut us down."[20]

Beyond worrying about financial repercussions, the vast majority of Staley workers found the concept of civil disobedience to be completely foreign, and they viewed an arrest record as a mark of shame. Decent people, thought many Staley unionists, do not break the law. Moreover, the union had fostered and enjoyed a collegial relationship with the Decatur police force. With the exception of the February 22 rally, members of the Local 7837 executive board met regularly with the police to discuss issues concerning upcoming rallies, including plans to close off streets and schedule police escorts to move marchers safely through the city. As is the case in most smaller cities and towns, many union members knew police officers as friends and neighbors. As stated, in August 1993, less than two months after the lockout, the police union had even donated fifteen hundred dollars to the Staley workers.[21]

The workers might have overcome their fears more easily if they had received strong support from their international union, the United Paperworkers, but that was far from the case. U.S. labor law is designed to pressure union leaders, from the internationals down to the locals, to obey the law or face harsh financial penalties. There are two areas where a union's treasury is put at risk for engaging in plant-gate protests. First, corporations can sue a union for financial losses allegedly resulting from lost production. Second, courts are quick to levy fines against unions that violate injunctions limiting the number of picketers and their activity. (Surprisingly, such an injunction did not exist at Staley; the company did not request one until a year after the lockout. When it did, the court promptly granted an injunction in July 1994.)

With only a few exceptions, such as the leadership of the Mine Workers, Service Employees, United Electrical Workers, and Communication Workers, leaders of nearly every international union oppose plant-gate protests that risk arrest. The Paperworkers under Wayne Glenn were no different. The UPIU strongly opposed any demonstrations that might lead to arrests. The staff "will not participate in the civil disobedience," international staff rep Bill Coleman told an April 1994 union meeting: "I've been told that there is potential liability upon the international if I participate in that. I've been instructed not to participate. I've been told that if I choose to do that, I will be disciplined [by president Wayne Glenn]."[22]

June 4

As the discussion accelerated after the union's April and May civil-disobedience training sessions, Watts remained unsure what to do, and the executive board and bargaining committee were deeply divided. Meanwhile, the Kandy Lane activists and Road Warriors were hearing from the local solidarity committees that they were concerned about their ability to turn people out for the upcoming June 25 national mobilization. The Road Warriors were pounding the pavement to build support, but a sense that the workers' resolve was waning seemed to be emerging. Some workers began to argue that a signal of the local's commitment to the struggle had to be sent to supporters across the nation before June 25.

In early May Watts authorized C. J. Hawking to coordinate a "tactical team" of workers and spouses to explore options and make proposals for possible nonviolent civil disobedience. On May 24 the tactical team, which had grown to thirty people, recommended to the executive board that the union call a civil-disobedience protest at the Staley plant gate the next week. After a two-hour debate, the leadership agreed to bring the proposal to that night's union meeting.

That evening, after several officers gave reports, Watts called on Ray Rogers; taking the microphone, Rogers spoke excitedly and at length about marching in J. Patrick Mohan's neighborhood, and the membership ratified the idea. Despite the board's decision just hours before, the planned discussion about an action at the plant gates did not occur. Rogers had given Watts and other leaders who were fearful of civil disobedience a much easier, law-abiding option. Many tactical team members were furious with Rogers and confused and demoralized by Watts's failure to allow discussion of their proposal. One team member told Hawking that night, "We're beating our heads against the wall. They don't want to do it. Dave Watts just scrubbed it."[23]

Over the next two days the elected leaders, the Kandy Lane activists, the union's advisers, and the thirty members of the tactical team had long, intense, and often heated discussions. Finally, on May 26, Watts and the board approved a nonviolent civil disobedience protest at the plant gates for June 4, just three weeks before the June 25 rally marking the one-year anniversary of the lockout. Only supporters and spouses would risk arrest, however, for Watts ordered union members not to participate. The character of the June 25 national demonstration would remain under discussion and be evaluated after June 4. The compromise—an action involving civil disobedience but not including Staley workers—did not satisfy the local's more ardent activists, but they felt it was a step forward.

Watts assigned Hawking to coordinate the June 4 protest, and with only eight days to go, she feverishly called up the most active people in the Staley support groups in nearby cities—St. Louis, Chicago, Springfield, and Champaign-Urbana. Word quickly spread to Staley spouses and to Caterpillar workers, too.

The following Saturday morning over forty union supporters met behind the union hall because of fears that the hall might be bugged. While some had received civil-disobedience training, most had not. The group was alive with nervous excitement, since for most people this was to be their first time risking arrest. Those who were seasoned in civil disobedience—such as the Eighth Day Center activists—were assigned to be team captains and given walkie-talkies for communication with Hawking.

After the leaders discussed the basic tenets of nonviolent civil disobedience and displayed a map detailing the location of each team, they required those risking arrest to sign a form pledging strict adherence to nonviolence. Protesters were also asked to complete a second form listing current medications and a family contact. Each person was asked to give one hundred dollars in cash to the union as bail money; to remove sharp objects, such as jewelry, pocket-knives, or pens, from their pockets; and to carry only their driver's licenses for identification and change for a phone call.

At noon more than five hundred Staley workers, spouses, and supporters rallied in front of the Staley office building and then moved down the street to the west gate. The local had issued a press release about the action the previous day, but surprisingly, the police were nowhere in sight. The first team walked past the yellow property line, which the company had painted on the asphalt the day of the lockout, turned to face the cheering crowd, and sat down. The crowd roared its support at this act of defiance. With an eye toward choosing spokespersons for the media, leaders had formed the first group to include UAW Local 751 president Larry Solomon; Father Mangan; Rev. Darren Cushman-Wood, of Indianapolis; and spouse Sandy Schable.

The next team went even farther onto plant property, holding their fists in the air and shouting "Solidarity!" The crowd again roared support. Within minutes a truck pulling a large semitrailer emerged from the Staley compound, turned a corner, and approached the protesters. They stretched out their arms to hold one another's hands as the onlooking supporters held their breaths. The truck slowed and then stopped within a few yards of the protesters' backs. The crowd erupted with a roar of relief and elation.

Soon another group of supporters shored up the line, and then another team of mostly Staley spouses joined them. A fifth team of nine Caterpillar workers spread out across the four lanes of Eldorado Street, completely shutting down traffic on the highly traveled boulevard. All the protesters repeatedly grasped one another's hands and lifted them high above their heads in a sign of unity and solidarity. The sixth team, consisting of the event's planners, sat down once it became obvious that all aspects of the plan had been successfully carried out and there were no signs of police violence.

Dave Watts, carrying a placard reading "King's Dream Lives," walked among the participants in the sit-down, shaking hands and thanking them for their solidarity. The media arrived and interviewed the first team. Considering the police department's increasingly confrontational posture at demonstrations over the previous few months, the protesters and the workers rallying nearby were puzzled why the police were not present at the beginning of the rally. Thirty minutes into the action, when the police finally arrived, the commanding officer asked Watts to order the protesters to leave. Watts deflected the request, responding: "The position today is justice for workers everywhere. I'm so proud of what those people out there on the line are doing."[24]

The police approached each protester one by one and asked, "Is there anything I can do or say to get you to leave this property?" Each shook his or her head and answered "No." Some added statements such as, "Tell the company to end the lockout, then I'll leave." For some protesters, the moment the police came to them took on profound dimensions. Mike Sacco, a Catholic and a Chicago-based IBEW Local 336 activist, was deeply moved by witnessing the arrest of Father Mangan. In preparation for his own arrest Sacco moved to a kneeling position, made the sign of the cross, and offered a prayer. About half the protesters decided they could not cooperate with the police in any way and went limp. Three officers partially lifted Sandy Schable and dragged her to the police bus. John Keating, an SEIU Local 73 member from Springfield, lay down on the pavement, flustering the police as they determined how to carry him off. As he was carted away Keating shouted "Union! Union!" at the top of his lungs.

The forty-eight arrested protesters came from seven cities and represented ten unions. Seven clergy members and five Staley spouses were arrested. Each person was photographed, handcuffed, and led onto the police bus. When they arrived at the station, the arrestees were fingerprinted and issued a notice to appear stating that they were charged with criminal trespass, obstructing police, mob action, and conspiracy to commit mob action. No bail was requested and no one spent time in a jail cell. As the protesters were released one by one, they were greeted outside the station with hugs and loud cheers from scores of Staley workers and spouses. Although they did not sit down, Watts and Rogers were later charged; hence the workers dubbed the June 4 protesters the "Decatur Fifty."

"I've never seen anything like it before," said Mike Griffin. "Seeing those people out there—it was the best day of the whole Staley fight." "A year ago nobody had ever heard of our local union," said another Staley worker, "and we didn't know any of these people. It's incredible. It's the most beautiful thing I've ever seen."[25] Added sit-down participant and CCI staffer Kip Voytek, "With the exception of the safety stand-down, June 4 was the biggest high the union had had."

The *Decatur Herald and Review,* local radio stations, and television newscasts from Decatur, Champaign, and Springfield covered the event as their top news story. National Public Radio, the Associated Press, the *Chicago Tribune, Chicago Sun-Times,* and several Chicago television stations also covered the story.

"June 4th was a powerful demonstration of solidarity," Watts wrote to the sit-down participants a few days later:

> For our members to see the main gate of the Staley plant shut down for two-and-a-half hours was thrilling and inspiring. One of the arrestees, Donna Sperry, the wife of one of our members, called her action a "wake-up call to the community," and the community is certainly awake. The local media have been talking about the Staley situation, the Mayor made a powerful statement about the pain of the lock-out, and throughout the town we hear the people of Decatur talking about Staley with renewed energy. Our members have seized on this opportunity to communicate directly with the community. Now that our neighbors and friends have been awakened, we have begun hand-billing the town and promoting the

rally on June 25th. We have had many triumphs and many great moments during the last two years, but . . . June 4th is something we'll never, ever forget.[26]

A week later copies of the union's *War Zone* newsletter, its front page featuring a story on the June 4 protest, were mailed to thousands of supporters. The newsletter beckoned them to come to Decatur prepared to engage in mass nonviolent civil disobedience at the Staley gates. Despite the tone of the newsletter and the overwhelming success of the June 4 action, however, the local leaders remained undecided about the character of the June 25 protest. At issue was whether the workers themselves would lead a sit-down and risk arrest.

Debating Civil Disobedience

The leadership had "talked and talked and talked" about the civil disobedience strategy, said Watts, but still had not reached a decision. Everything came to a head at the June 21 union meeting. Watts's main concern remained amnesty for those who risked arrest: "Whether we do civil disobedience or not, we already have seven discharged members, and this fight is not over until they are made whole. Whether that number increases to seventeen or seventy or seven hundred, is our position the same?—there will be no settlement, no signing of a contract, no giving up until *all* are made whole. Those that have paid the ultimate price of discharge, those that face it, and those of us in the future—is our position still the same?"[27]

Many members applauded and yelled their affirmation. But Watts was highly ambivalent and kept returning to the issue. Finally Dee Scott responded with exasperation: "Isn't it 'an injury to one is injury to all'? I just don't understand—why is it even being put on the floor for people to worry about, because we're all in this together. If we're not all in this together, let's just all go home now. [Speaking directly to Watts:] You're putting more doubts in people's minds, and my God, we've got enough to worry about. Let's not start throwing more mud."

Watts responded that there were only about two hundred workers present that night and asked, "Where are the others? What's their vote? Because *all* will vote on the contract. If amnesty is not part of the program, then those [who engage in civil disobedience] will pay the price." When unemployment benefits ended in March 1994, most workers had to find jobs, and attendance at the weekly solidarity meetings fell. Ted Taylor, the local's president during the failed 1970 strike, echoed Watts, reminding all present that the membership then had voted for a contract that didn't give the seven fired workers amnesty.

Watts asked for members only—not supporters or spouses—to stand if they were willing to risk arrest, and about fifty workers stood. Watts shook his head; not enough had stood, he thought to himself. For others, however, it was more than enough, and the debate continued.

The activists spoke out strongly in support of taking action. Dick Schable, whose wife had been arrested on June 4, said, "There's never a better time than right now. All these other people have shown us that they can do this for us. It's time for *us* to be standing up for *us!*" Ron VanScyoc spoke of his conversations with supporters: "Having talked to quite a few people on a regular basis, the support we have from out of town is all looking for a day of action. Even though they have not said it in so many words, they leave the feeling that if we do not have a day of action, our support will dwindle tremendously. We'll probably be standing out here alone all by ourselves if we don't have the intestinal fortitude to stand up and give that company two black eyes and a bloody nose."

"It's time we moved forward," declared Dan Lane. "Whether you participate in civil disobedience or not, the commitment to support anybody that would be involved is very important. You don't have to be the person sitting down."

"The time is right," echoed another worker: "By God, we have to start leading into the battle, rather than having people come up and fight for us. . . . It's time for us to say, you come up and *join* us; *we're* going to do it, as a union. I don't want my brothers coming up here and fighting my battle. I've been at Staley for twenty years. Everything I got, our forefathers got for us. We haven't sacrificed a goddamn thing. It's time to put our lives on the line!"

Another worker expressed reluctance to participate in civil disobedience because he had a felony record: "I can't be involved. [But] I think it's long past overdue. We've shown everybody we want to be passive and all this bull, and it's past that. Take it to the streets; take it inside the plant if necessary."

In an unusual move, Pat Watts, Dave's wife, addressed the meeting and urged caution:

> I understand all your anger and frustration, and I've had it too, but look around you—we don't have half the people. If we can't get them, [then] twenty, thirty, or fifty of you won't make any point but to lose the only thing you'll ever get out of that company, your severance. . . . How can you lead when we can't get the majority? I don't think that there's one person coming to town that would expect our people to lose everything that they're fighting for. . . . You're not the majority. When it comes to a vote, you definitely will be voted out and forgotten.

Mike Griffin quickly stood up to respond to Pat. "Many labor struggles in this country have been won by less than one-fourth of the membership," said Griffin, who had taken to reading much labor history since the lockout. "You're never going to have a majority out there. It doesn't matter if we have the majority, so long as some Local 7837 members are in that street. That's all it takes."

The hour was late and everyone was exhausted. Emotions ran from anxiety and fear to impatience and determination. "We will not be able to resolve this tonight," said a tired Dave Watts. He ended the meeting by stating that the elected leadership would continue to discuss the issue in the three days left before the June 25 rally.

By Friday, June 24, Local 7837 still had not decided what would transpire the next day. At noon the divided executive board and bargaining committee again met to passionately debate the issue. A slim majority opposed the action, but no vote was taken. The group adjourned, with the final decision in Watts's hands.

That night Watts, vice president Bob Hull, Ray Rogers, Jerry Tucker, C. J. Hawking, and Chicago solidarity committee cochair Steven Ashby met in the Decatur apartment that the union rented for its advisers. The group reviewed logistics for the demonstration. The day would begin with supporters assembling in the field adjacent to the UAW 751 union hall, where they would listen to local and national speakers. Then the protesters would march one mile to the front of the Staley headquarters, on Eldorado Street, and hear more speeches. The questions on the table were two: At the end of the second rally, would there be a call to march one block to Staley's west gate and engage in mass civil disobedience? And would Staley workers lead the march to the gates?

All the arguments for and against civil disobedience were rehashed late into the evening. It seemed as if there would be no resolution. Watts had been anxious about the decision for weeks. If he authorized civil disobedience, would it divide the local? Would the union, and he personally, get sued? Should the union be defeated, would he forever regret a decision that led workers to be permanently discharged? But if he did not authorize civil disobedience, might it mean the collapse of support and the end of the struggle, with supporters viewing the local as unwilling to escalate the fight? In the end, Watts agreed to add a speaker at the second rally in front of the Staley headquarters who would call for a sit-down at the west gate. The group determined that Ashby would give the speech. Each Staley worker, said Watts, would make the individual decision whether to block the plant gates. Watts would be close to the action but would not himself risk arrest, for he had already been twice charged by the police.[28]

All assumed that the day would proceed much as June 4 had, but on a far larger scale. After marching and listening to speeches, the protesters would mass in front of Staley's west gate and sit down. The police, it was expected, would move in and begin arrests. After the arrests—some estimated that up to one thousand would come to the protest willing to risk arrest—several thousand supporters would follow the arrestees to the jail as they were hauled away in police buses and continue the protest outside the police station until all were released.

The previous day Watts had authorized the printing of hundreds of placards emphasizing the union's nonviolent stance. Based on advice from Francis Boyle, a professor of international law at the University of Illinois in nearby Champaign-Urbana and author of the 1987 book *Defending Civil Resistance under International Law,* half the placards read, "This is Nonviolent Civil Resistance," and the other half cited five pro-union tenets from the United Nations' Universal Declaration of Human Rights. By wearing these torso-sized placards, Boyle advised, the union would signal to the police its stance of nonviolence. Further, if those arrested were brought to trial, their lawyer could introduce Staley's violation of international law, a legal move that would otherwise be excluded from court proceedings.

Watts had also authorized the printing of two fliers to be distributed to the crowd. One side of the first flier outlined the UN's Declaration of Human Rights; the flipside welcomed the protesters to Decatur and explained that nonviolent civil disobedience was planned. The second flier laid down eight rules for participants willing to risk arrest. The rules advised demonstrators how to conduct themselves while being arrested, booked, and released, including the suggestion that all exercise "bail solidarity"—that "no one goes free until we all go free. We will not leave anyone sitting in jail."[29]

The meeting finally adjourned late that evening, and everyone went home to a fitful night of sleep.

The Courage to Risk It All

The next morning five thousand people assembled outside UAW Local 751's meeting hall. The day was blisteringly hot, but a boisterous spirit permeated the crowd. Staley workers and supporters distributed the flyers and placards, and some of those interested in the nonviolent action met briefly in Grant Park, across the street. After organizers briefed those willing to risk arrest, they made sure each protester received a "Nonviolent Civil Resistance" placard, affixed with a string around the neck. It appeared that everyone present respected the union's position on nonviolence and would follow its lead.

At noon the fiery speeches began. The crowd was particularly attentive to the UAW's Larry Solomon and to Local 876 president Jerry Brown, representing the Decatur and Peoria Caterpillar workers. The UAW had launched a second national strike against Caterpillar just four days before, and thirteen thousand workers had walked off the job. The "Illinois is a War Zone!" slogan was taking on new meaning, since most of the Cat strikers were Illinois workers—including 1,870 in Decatur. The audience gave rousing applause to United Mine Workers vice president Cecil Roberts; Rev. Robert White, of Decatur's Mt. Zion Baptist; and many labor leaders.

When the mile-long march to the plant began, it was launched with the roar of over one hundred motorcycles, mostly Harley-Davidsons, leading the way. American flags, placards, huge union banners from local unions across the country, and bright union T-shirts all added to the crowd's exuberant mood. Decatur's chief of police had formally notified Watts on June 23 that the police would block two lanes of Twenty-second Street and part of Eldorado Street for the march—but not the section in front of A. E. Staley's west gate.[30]

Meanwhile, at the west gate a long row of the police department's emergency response team (ERT) members held their batons tightly in readiness. Two big buses parked behind the police lines contained eighty officers from the Decatur Police Department, the Macon County Sheriff's Department, and the Illinois State Police. At a Decatur firehouse six blocks away sat dozens more police on buses, waiting to be dispatched.

Unbeknownst to the marchers, the Decatur Police Department, the Macon County states' attorney, and Decatur's city manager (the town's highest-ranking official) had met and agreed not to arrest the protesters for trespassing, as was done on June 4.[31] Instead of planning for mass arrests, the police had purchased oleoresin capsicum (OC) and trained all their officers in its use. Commonly known as pepper spray, OC is an oil made from hot peppers that sticks to the skin and other tissue. When dispersed, OC causes an immediate burning sensation, temporary blindness, and constricted bronchial tubes. Gagging, choking, disorientation, and loss of strength and coordination are common responses to being pepper-sprayed.[32] According to literature from the makers of OC, a verbal warning should be issued before use, spraying should last only one second, subjects with contact lenses should be instructed to remove them immediately, and medical treatment should be offered to all subjects.[33]

The police had purchased a great many four-ounce canisters of OC for its officers and one-pound OC "foggers" for the ERT squad leaders. Before the rally, the police and Staley management had met three times to discuss the police plans for June 25. Police officials later reported that they "didn't get any resistance" from the company when they outlined their intention not to arrest the protesters and to arm their officers with pepper spray.[34]

The police department made these arrangements despite the union's unwavering commitment to nonviolence. As Commander Richard Ryan later admitted, "[The union] officially had informed us that they intended to have a peaceful, nonviolent rally and by and large, except for a few minor incidents, they had done a very good job through the course of the labor dispute in maintaining that atmosphere."[35]

When the marchers arrived in front of Staley's fourteen-story headquarters, they were inspired by speeches from Teamsters vice president Diana Kilmury, Communication Workers of America vice president Jan Pierce, locked-out Staley workers Jeanette Hawkins and Dave Watts, and the songs of labor singer Anne Feeney. Ashby spoke on the history of nonviolent civil disobedience in the United States. "Sometimes you have to cross that line," he shouted, referring both to Staley's yellow property line and the line of legality in the fight against injustice. The crowd was ready and eager to march to the plant gate.

"Cross that line! Cross that line," five thousand people roared as dozens of red-shirted Staley workers led the huge crowd down Eldorado Street and toward the west gate. As the workers turned into the driveway, they saw a long row of police roughly fifteen yards behind the yellow property line. The first workers stepped across the line. Gary Lamb recalled: "Dike [Ferris] was first, and I was second, and I had no idea who was behind me because I was looking at the police ahead of me. That's a feeling I'll have forever, when I walked across the Staley west gate, turned around, and saw all the people coming over. It was a feeling of, 'My gosh, I am not alone! We do have friends!' Not only our own members, but a lot of other friends who realized our situation, and were there to help."

Lamb, Ferris, and the other Staley workers stopped three feet short of the police line and turned to face the cheering crowds. They held their arms in the air, linked hands, and joined the crowd in chanting "We Are Union!"

For most of the workers, it had not been an easy decision. "To tell you the truth," said Dick Schable, "I think people were afraid."

For Gary Lamb, a father of three who had twenty-seven years in the plant, the idea of blocking Staley's gates had previously been unimaginable. "I liked working at Staley. We cared about the plant. We felt we had ownership in that plant. That was my life."[36] During the year of the lockout, Lamb thoughtfully considered how he had benefited from the struggles of the previous century's labor activists—good wages and benefits, better working conditions, and a decent life for his family. Lamb reflected on his decision to risk arrest on June 25:

> Once we got into it, I couldn't stop. I was committed to what I did because I thought it was a worthy struggle. The more you learn about labor history—people *died* fighting for the eight-hour day. *We* didn't *earn* those benefits. Others who came before me earned them through struggle. It was payback time. I had to stand up and be counted. And that feeling went through the whole rank-and-file, not just me. . . . On June 4 the people walked across the line and sat down on my behalf. Dave Watts had told us right before that, "You don't go. None of us [Staley workers] go." I watched that and I felt like *I* should be there. It's *my* job. They're getting arrested *for me*.

Lamb described how the solidarity with his union brothers and sisters bolstered his courage that day, despite the enormous financial risk:

> I took a lot of direction off Dike Ferris. I knew him the best of anybody because we worked in the tin shop together, and Dike said he was going to do it. Dan Lane said he was going to do it. So, on that day, I saw Dike and asked him, "Are you still going?" Dike said, "Yup." As we walked [across Twenty-second Street], Dike said to me, "You know, we could get fired for this." I said, "Believe me, I know it! It could be the end of the benefits and everything. But we got this going. We might as well not stop now."

The lockout had also been a transforming experience for African American workers such as Frankie Travis, who joined his fellow union members in leading the marchers across the line. Asked about the risk he was taking, Travis quickly responded, "I don't what you mean by 'risk.' I don't have a job. I've been locked out for a year. Somewhere in life you have to make a stand. Today's a good day to make a stand. Through solidarity, I'm here."[37]

When Dick Schable decided to cross onto Staley property, he was influenced by the memory of his daughter Beth, who had died from cancer three months before the lockout, at age twelve. Schable described how Beth's eight-year battle with cancer had influenced his and Sandy's union activism:

> We found [the cancer] right before she went into kindergarten. She had her leg amputated when she was five. . . . She fought for everything. . . . [It had] a lot to do with the reason I stood up so much and fought so hard for the union. . . . [Beth] taught [her mother and me] how to live, I guess you could say. She probably set a standard for us, just by the way she lived her life and died. . . . I'm sure the fact that she was never willing to give up . . . and believed that you should stand up for the right things . . . had an impact [on us.]

Tammy McCartney was nineteen years old when she was hired in 1990, joining four family members, including her father. Two months after the lockout, Staley notified her that it was downsizing and that she and 195 other low-seniority workers had been laid off. So when McCartney decided to sit down on June 25, she understood that she wasn't risking arrest for herself: "I did it because there are men that have been there twenty and thirty years that deserve to go back into that plant and get their jobs! I did it because there are people who went in there and went through hell so that others could come in there and get a good job, with good benefits. They don't deserve rotating shifts, with their benefits cut after twenty years. . . . If you give your life to that company and that plant, they owe you something back! . . . It was the principle of the thing."

"All Hell Broke Loose"

By 2:30 P.M. over four hundred people had crossed A. E. Staley's yellow line, until there was no more room in the driveway. Thousands more rallied on Eldorado Street. Joining the Staley workers on the front lines were large contingents from Flint, Michigan's, UAW Local 599; steelworkers from Pittsburgh; and Peoria UAW workers, many of whom wore T-shirts that read "Illegally Terminated by Cat." The crowd repeatedly roared "Scabs Out! Union In!" American flags and union banners rose high in the air. The mood was electrifying.

The protesters on the front line, whose backs remained to the police, maintained a three-foot corridor between themselves and the police line, such that several camera operators easily and repeatedly walked through the space. While the crowd was standing shoulder to shoulder, the police left gaps in their line, often four and five feet wide. Clearly, if protesters had wanted to break through the police line, they could have done so, but none did.

With so many people crowded into the driveway, protesters were bumping into one another. "The crowd was moving around. I was pushed many times," said Gary Lamb, but he managed to maintain his balance.[38] When Dan Lane was pushed in the back by a police baton, he responded by sitting down, legs crossed, with his back to the police. Others on the front line followed suit, maintaining their backs to the police and keeping the three-foot corridor. "I was standing there chanting with the rest of the people," recounted Dick Schable. "The police had drawn their line; we were in as far as we could go through the plant gates, so people started to sit down." As Schable was bending to sit down he was bumped, and he and four others tumbled to the ground. As he fell, Schable recalled, "the police let go of the pepper gas and all hell broke loose. . . . The police came *toward us*. Nobody tried to break through the [police] line."

Just three minutes after the protesters had arrived at the Staley gate, Commander Richard Ryan and several other officers unleashed blasts of pepper spray on the five people who were innocently tumbling to the ground. Other officers immediately opened up on the rest of the crowd. Despite their training, the police did not issue an advance warning, and the blasts of spray lasted far beyond the recommended one second. In fact, the one-pound foggers were emptied onto the crowd.[39] In some cases several officers simultaneously directed their canisters of pepper spray at the same worker. Many leaned in to direct the OC at protesters' faces and eyes.

"I got sprayed right in the face," recalled Schable. "I could hardly breathe, let alone see anything. I was totally incapacitated. I was shaking uncontrollably. Sandy said she thought I was having a heart attack." "I couldn't get any air," recounted Lamb. "The back of my neck was burning like it was on fire. . . . I remember wondering if I going to get hit in the head with a club, but I had to get up because I had no air."[40]

Staley worker Danny Rhodes said that after being sprayed, he immediately tried to cover up: "I couldn't breathe. My neck and eyes were on fire. I was afraid. It finally got to the point where I thought I was going to throw up. So I got up and walked away. And then I got mad, outraged, and went back and sat down."[41] Staley worker Jerry Frazier told the Labor Vision video crew, "I feel like I'm on fire. . . . They've got a lot of appreciation. . . . A locked-out vet. But I've been through it before, in Vietnam. . . . It won't turn me around."[42]

"I can't open my eyes and it's a searing pain," said Dan Lane, "but we're not moving. We've lost cars, homes, everything, but we're not giving up."[43] With his face stinging from the pepper spray, Frankie Travis said, "The cops are just doing their job—whatever corporate greed tells them to do."[44]

Jerry Tucker was standing with his arms at his sides when he was sprayed directly in the face. "I didn't do anything," said Tucker. "I was just standing there and a policeman began pushing me with his stick. And then another one came running up, reached over and shot me right in the face."[45] Observers thought that officers had singled out Tucker and other leading activists.

A spontaneous emergency brigade formed as the noninjured cared for those writhing in pain. People ran across Eldorado Street to the union's drinking-water stand, rushed back with cups of water in hand, and gently saturated the workers' burning eyes and skin. Some grabbed T-shirts off the union's literature table and created makeshift compresses. The police neither offered first aid nor advised protesters what they had learned in their training: applying water worsens the effects of OC.

Staley worker Vic Pickle fell down in agony and remained crouched on his knees with his face in his hands. Blinded and disoriented, he fell a couple of feet behind the police line. One officer turned Pickle on his back and leaned in to blast pepper spray directly into his eyes. Several officers then hoisted Pickle, handcuffed him, and placed him on the police bus with no offer of medical treatment. Pickle sat, sweltering in the heat, for two hours; the temperature was eighty-five degrees outside and far hotter inside the bus. Pickle was the only protester arrested that day.

Several journalists and at least four children were sprayed. When Galen and Debbie Garrett walked with their three children—ages five, seven, and ten—to the west gate, they did not realize they had crossed onto Staley property. They were simply following the crowd to continue the peaceful protest. After his family was sprayed, Galen Garrett, a Decatur resident and IBEW member, took his five-year-old daughter, Jennifer, to the hospital. Before he left, Garrett told Mike Griffin, one of several people videotaping the events that day, "This demonstration was nonviolent. It was stressed to be nonviolent, but the police just moved in and started gassing us. Our front line never moved. . . . The police moved in but our line stayed the same. . . . What kind of public servants gas children?"[46]

After the OC canisters were emptied onto the demonstrators, a military-style replacement of the troops ensued, with three dozen Illinois State Police officers emerging from their buses. Dressed in riot gear and wearing gas masks, the state troopers angled their batons across their chests and stood stiffly, forming a shoulder-to-shoulder human barricade. Meanwhile, the Decatur police restocked their canisters.

After regaining the ability to breathe, many Staley workers returned to the front line and continued their sit-down. The workers were horrified by what the police had done to their peaceful demonstration and summoned their nonviolence training to help manage their response. Many channeled their anger into shouts of "Scabs out, union in" and exclamations of "Tax dollars at work!" About thirty minutes after the first attack, the police unleashed another torturous spray on the crowd. After the second spraying a large number of demonstrators left, fearing further police violence.

While many of those sitting down wanted to keep the protest going, Watts and Rogers wanted to end it. Rogers went behind police lines and asked Commander Ryan to allow Watts, who had remained on public property throughout, to give a speech to end the rally. When permission was granted, Watts walked to the wall of police, turned around, and told the protesters over a bullhorn, "It's time to call this to an end. I am walking out of here now, and I ask all of you to follow me. We have a success here. Let's leave it at that and let's move on."[47]

Most of the sit-down participants, by now numbering about a hundred, with several hundred more protesters standing nearby, did not budge. They looked for direction to the Staley workers who had been pepper-sprayed in the face. Among the Staley workers, options were informally and quickly explored. Although some wanted to hold their protest through the night, an overwhelming majority feared further police violence, especially with night approaching and their numbers dwindling.

Dan Lane arose and gave a powerful speech about the history of the struggle, including the story of Jim Beals's death, and urged supporters to carry on the fight. Chicago solidarity committee activist Jack Spiegel gave an impassioned speech about the need for all to redouble their efforts in support of the Staley workers. "I've been involved in (campaigns) like this since 1930," said the eighty-nine-year-old Spiegel, "and this is one of the most inspiring. Go back to your union, your church. Raise money to help them survive the struggle. When they win, we all win."[48] The demonstration came to an end when Lane again took the bullhorn, led the crowd in a union chant, and marched off Staley property with the crowd following him.

The Decatur police returned to their headquarters to design their response to the media's questions about their actions. They planned to keep secret their pre-rally decision to pepper-spray the demonstrators instead of arresting them, and they would not reveal that the three most powerful government officials in the city, together with Staley management, had fully endorsed their plan. The department's official statement falsely charged that the protesters had "rushed police lines," forcing the officers to spray the crowd. That evening Staley spokesperson J. Patrick Mohan told the press that the "police did an outstanding job."[49]

The attempt to spin the attack as a defensive action immediately met a serious problem. A local TV newscaster had been sprayed and went on television to accurately report what had happened. During her live spot for the 6:00 P.M. newscast, she said that the protesters, including young children, had been sprayed without provocation. The spot included footage of the spraying. "On the six o'clock news, she's still got the runny nose, watery eyes, and the whole bit," recalled Art Dhermy, "and she reports about children being sprayed." These facts were left out of the 10:00 P.M. newscast, however, which stated that the police "used pepper spray only when some of the demonstrators tried to break through the police line."

Reevaluating the Role of the Police

Until the June 25 rally, most Staley workers viewed the police as respected public servants who risk their lives to protect citizens from criminals. "This is a town where we've always been friendly with the police," noted Gary Lamb. "They were the good guys! They're our neighbors, cousins, fellow churchgoers. Heck, we even went to high school with some of those guys."[50]

After the pepper-spraying, however, workers from Staley and elsewhere in Decatur found themselves radically reevaluating. "You know, a lot of [the police] say that they are just doing their job," said Lamb. "Well, that's what they said at the Nuremberg trials. And that's what the Selma police said when they used dogs and water hoses [on civil rights protesters]. It's a poor crutch to use. It's as if their jobs are more important than our rights. . . . [Now] I have no respect for the police. I can feel my ire come up when I see a squad car go by."

"I wouldn't trust the police ever again for much of anything," echoed Dick Schable. "I don't like to be around them. They make me leery. I'm always expecting something to happen. They were supposed to be your friend and look out for you and all that. Well, [June 25] sure changed my perception of police and what their role is in the community."

For many African Americans, however, the assault was simply an extension of the abuse of power that their community had long endured. As is true of every U.S. city, Decatur's black and white citizens experienced the police and courts in radically different ways. As a result of the pepper-spraying, though, many of the white Staley workers developed a new sensitivity to issues of police brutality.

The union's response to the attack was decided at a union meeting ten days later. The local would henceforth cease all meetings with the police to inform them about plans for upcoming rallies. Still, for some workers, including Watts, the idea that the police had attacked a peaceful protest without provocation was difficult to accept. For several days Watts and other union officers watched and rewatched nine different videotapes, including two provided by the police. They looked closely to see whether any protester had assaulted the police and precipitated the attack. But it was clear that the protesters, many with their backs to the police, had not provoked the violence.

After several weeks of intense discussions, the union published its official position in the July 17, 1994, *Decatur Herald and Review.* The statement criticized the police actions but was more temperate than the pepper-sprayed workers would have liked:

> The union has no problems with individual police officers, many of whom have supported our struggle. We have attempted to maintain a working relationship with the police throughout the struggle. . . . Nevertheless . . . we condemn the blanket pepper spraying of demonstrators who were sitting down at the police's feet. . . . We completely object to the fact that Vic Pickle, after being soaked in pepper spray and being arrested, was forced to sit in the back of the police bus, hands cuffed behind him, with no water or relief from the pepper spray, for two hours. . . . Our union did not, and does not, advocate crossing police lines. Our commitment to nonviolent civil resistance as one of the many tactics in our corporate campaign is firm and inviolate among our members and officers.[51]

The Illinois AFL-CIO called on Decatur's mayor to investigate the attack, citing a "serious question about whether the police overreacted."[52]

Within days of the rally, St. Louis–based supporters Rose Feurer, Dave Rathke, and their Labor Vision team set to work producing a film for their weekly cable show. Feurer and Rathke, who had produced Local 837's *Deadly Corn* video in July 1993, had both been arrested during the June 4 sit-down and had been among the hundreds that crossed Staley's line on June 25. By mid-July Labor Vision had produced a twenty-eight-minute video, *Struggle in the Heartland,* that reported on both June sit-downs. After riveting testimonies from June 4 demonstrators, the video showed their arrests against a soundtrack of Billy Bragg's pulsating rock-and-roll song "There Is Power in the Union." The film then showed the June 25 rally, depicting the pepper-spraying in slow motion from many angles. The video made use of multiple recordings, including, ironically, the police tapes. At the request of Watts, Rathke's voiceover used the phrase "the police overreacted" to describe the assault.

If the Decatur city officials who authorized the pepper-spraying intended to defeat the Staley workers' morale and support, their efforts backfired. Road Warriors fanned out across the country and found a heightened interest in their fight. Their presentations now included a showing of the new video, and they sold thousands of copies for five dollars each. Solidarity committees widely distributed the tape, which helped propel the Staley fight into the forefront of labor activists' consciousness.

With the UAW Caterpillar workers on strike as of June 21, and the United Rubber Workers at Bridgestone/Firestone walking out July 12, Decatur was quickly becoming the emblem for an embattled labor movement. Solidarity among unionists in Decatur, along with national solidarity efforts and national media coverage, sharply escalated.

13

Strike City, USA

The "War Zone" slogan was first raised by Illinois workers in 1991 when members of the United Auto Workers struck Caterpillar. By the summer of 1994, when workers at three of the largest companies in Decatur—Staley, Caterpillar, and Bridgestone/Firestone—walked the picket lines, it took on renewed meaning. As the workers found common cause, however, they came up against a city government and a police force that were allied with the companies. The Staley workers challenged the corporate-government alliance by attacking Staley's harmful environmental practices and its tax subsidies, and the three locals initiated a nascent labor political party to support union president Dave Watts's campaign for a city council seat.

Caterpillar and Bridgestone/Firestone on Strike

In December 1991 the United Auto Workers had launched a strike against Caterpillar, the largest earthmoving equipment producer in the world (see chapter 3). By early 1992, 13,400 Cat workers in seven plants were walking picket lines; over 12,000 were in the Illinois towns of Decatur, Aurora, and Peoria, site of the main plant.[1] On April 19, 1992, after the company had hired hundreds of scabs and declared that strikers would be permanently replaced unless they returned, and after 600 strikers had crossed their union's picket line, an alarmed UAW leadership declared an end to the strike and sent its members back to work without a contract. The UAW International had miscalculated and suffered a huge defeat.

Although the strike was lost, the battle was not over. The union formed "contract action teams" in the Cat plants to organize shop-floor unity and job actions, and in spring 1992 the UAW initiated a work-to-rule campaign. It started more slowly than did the one Staley workers would launch that fall, however, and it had been ordered from the top rather than discussed and voted on by the rank-and-file. Ironically, the union movement's leading expert on work-to-rule campaigns, Jerry Tucker, was not called on to assist the Cat workers; he was a UAW dissident and thus a pariah to the international's leadership.[2]

Nevertheless, the Caterpillar workers steadily got more involved in working to rule. One day steward Ken Meyers pinned an angry slogan on the T-shirt he wore to work: "Permanently Replace Fites," referring to the Caterpillar CEO Don Fites. The slogan caught on, and soon hundreds of workers in every Caterpillar plant were wearing that and other rebellious slogans on union T-shirts and buttons. Management responded by illegally harassing, suspending, and firing scores of workers. The union answered by stepping up its in-plant campaign and by filing scores of charges with the National Labor Relations Board. "Caterpillar's attitude is that it is easier to pay fines than obey the law," said UAW Local 751 president Larry Solomon.[3]

As more workers were fired for wearing union T-shirts and buttons, the workforce became more angry and determined. Activists said privately that the company had actually saved the union. When the strike was defeated in 1992, morale hit bottom, but Caterpillar's subsequent tactics of treating the workers brutally and firing large numbers of activists backfired, and the in-plant struggle intensified.

Then, on June 22, 1994, after working over two years without a contract, the UAW International called its workers out on strike again. This time the strike had a different legal twist. Under the law, when a union strikes over charges of "unfair labor practices" (rather than for economic goals), the workers cannot be permanently replaced, which gives the union an edge. They can, however, be temporarily replaced, so once again Cat management determined to run the plant without the workers to force the union to buckle to management's demands.

On July 12, 1994, the United Rubber Workers (URW) top leadership called a national strike of four thousand workers in five plants against Bridgestone/ Firestone, a huge multinational with eighty-five plants in nineteen countries. (Bridgestone and Firestone had merged in 1988, forming the largest rubber company and the second largest-tire company in the world.)

The strike came four months after the contract expired. The issue, as at Caterpillar, was pattern bargaining. The union insisted that the company follow its decades-long practice by signing a contract patterned on the one recently signed by Goodyear Tire and Rubber. Bridgestone/Firestone refused and demanded radical changes: twelve-hour rotating shifts, a two-tier wage system, elimination of seniority rights, increased use of outside contractors, reductions in health-care benefits, slashed holidays and reduced vacation time, and drastic alterations to work rules. "There is no end to what they are trying to take away," said Decatur URW Local 713 president Roger Gates.[4] As was the case at Caterpillar and Staley, the corporation's harsh demands came after the union had participated for years in a labor-management cooperation program to increase productivity and profits. Workers had not received a general wage increase since 1985.

In Decatur 1,270 Bridgestone/Firestone workers joined the Cat and Staley workers on the picket line. Now workers at the largest (Caterpillar) and third-largest (Bridgestone/Firestone) manufacturers in town were on strike. "We never thought we'd end up in the same place as other unions," said Gates, "but that's exactly where we are. And you know what? It's right. We're all in the same place fighting together. That's the way it should be."[5] By July 1994 nearly four thousand Decatur workers—7 percent of the city's entire workforce and 25 percent of the blue-collar workforce—were united in battle. "You couldn't go two yards over without running into somebody who was directly affected," said Gary Lamb.[6]

The rubber workers were the slowest of the three Decatur locals to understand what they were facing and to try to organize national solidarity. "You could see what was going on with the labor movement," said rubber worker Dave Frasier, "that they were doing their best to break us. And our people did not respond; [UPIU 7837] did."

Tyna McDuffie was hired by Staley in July 1991 and locked out two years later. In May 1994 she was hired at the Bridgestone/Firestone plant, but in July 1994 she had the dubious distinction of being the only worker in the country simultaneously locked out and on strike. And her husband Brian, whom she married four days after the URW went out, was on strike against Caterpillar. McDuffie noted that when the Bridgestone/Firestone strike began, many of the URW workers took trips for a couple of weeks, as if they were on vacation. "Most rubber workers thought it was going to be a traditional strike, where the workers would be out for a while, both sides would compromise, and they'd go back in. When that didn't happened, the workers were stunned."[7]

In addition, the Rubber Workers' actions tended to limit their ability to build global solidarity. Responding to the fact that the Firestone factories' new owners, Bridgestone, were headquartered in Japan, Local 713 put up a banner at the plant gate: "1941, Japan Attacks Pearl Harbor. July 12, 1994, Bridgestone/Firestone Attacks American Workers." The union regularly called the company's assault on the union a "second Pearl Harbor," and URW national leaders railed against "foreign owners." Headlines on flyers emphasized that the workers were on strike against a "Japanese owned" company.[8]

The problem, however, wasn't the location of the company's home office—Caterpillar, based in the United States but with factories worldwide, and Tate & Lyle, based in England, were carrying out identical policies. (Later, when the URW ended the strike without a contract and merged with the United Steelworkers, the USWA launched a dynamic global solidarity campaign, jettisoned the racist rhetoric, and traveled to Japan to march with Japanese unionists.)

Decatur Workers Solidarity and Education Coalition

Staley, Caterpillar, and Bridgestone/Firestone workers faced markedly similar issues—so similar, in fact, that the town's unionists firmly believed the three corporations to be working together to bust the three unions. During the past year the three locals had been strengthening their relationships. In June 1993, the UAW and AIW locals sponsored a 2.6-mile human chain between the Staley and Cat plants; both UAW 751 and URW 713 made sizable donations to the Staley workers after the lockout; and in late 1993 and early 1994, large numbers of UAW and URW members turned out for Staley workers' activities and rallies.

So in February 1994—five months before Cat and Bridgestone workers hit the picket lines—the three locals joined forces to form the Decatur Workers Solidarity and Education Coalition. "The group has two primary goals," said Lamb. "To have a strong, city-wide labor coalition, and to educate the community about the benefits it gains from organized labor." "Caterpillar and Firestone workers have watched the union-busting tactics of Staley/Tate & Lyle with great concern," said URW 713 president Roger Gates in early 1994. "We know that if workers don't support each other and learn from each other, our locals could be next"—as, indeed, they were.[9]

The coalition's first activities were to organize unionists to give presentations in area high schools describing what America would look like without unions and to distribute blue ribbons to the Decatur community. "The wives of the locked-out Staley workers started wearing blue lapel ribbons to show they're 'true-blue' in their loyalty," said URW member Jack Lamont. "We wanted to take it another step and say, 'We're proud to be blue-collar workers.'"[10]

The coalition's first public protest, on March 9, 1994, brought one hundred workers to the major intersection of Highway 36 and Twenty-second Street (known as "Five Points"), where they held signs and received a steady stream of supportive horn-honking from passing motorists. The coalition publicized the April 9 march initiated by the African American Staley activists, and nine Caterpillar workers, including Larry Solomon, were arrested in the June 4 blockade of Staley's west gate. In October 1994, aided by volunteer Doug Kandt, the coalition launched a newspaper, the *Decatur Free Press*, which workers distributed throughout the city.[11]

Larry Solomon was a strong advocate of a close working relationship among the locals. This "horizontal unionism" involved getting rank-and-file unionists and local unions to build ties across occupations and industries without asking for permission from their internationals. Recalled Solomon,

> I got to feeling like when I was in the Firestone union hall, this is *my* union hall, too. Or when I was at the Staley union hall, I felt like, it's part of the union struggle, and I just feel at home. And the workers, when they would come in, there'd be some Firestone workers, and some Cat workers, and some Staley workers sitting at a table and talking, and maybe some of them would have their kids with them, and you could watch that and see the closeness, and it was just a great feeling. It was a closeness that I'll always remember.

But this new horizontal unionism in Decatur caused apprehension at the three internationals' headquarters. Recalled Solomon, "The UAW International leadership said, 'We'll take care of our business; you take care of yours.' That's what they told me, when we first started getting together with the other unions in town. We said, 'We've got to stick together. This is going to be a big fight.' But all the international unions said, 'Well, we've got our own issues to worry about here. We ought to concentrate on our problems and let them work on their problems over there. We really shouldn't get tied up, get to mingling our issues.'"

Officers of the Decatur central labor council—called the Decatur Trades and Labor Assembly—were no less hostile to the three locals' grassroots solidarity efforts. By rights, the assembly should have stood at the forefront of solidarity efforts for the three embattled locals, yet its president, William "Skip" Dempsey, repeatedly downplayed the three conflicts, suggested that in each case both sides should compromise, and recommended that the unions end their struggles. Dempsey decried the national media attention to Decatur's labor battles: "There is more cooperation between labor and management in Decatur than there is strife, but cooperation doesn't make news," he said.[12] He criticized the militancy of the unions and blamed their "tunnel vision" for the work stoppages.[13]

Thus the three locals were forced to form the solidarity coalition. An exasperated Dave Watts wrote to the coalition, asking, "Where are they [the Trades and Labor Council]? Meeting after meeting [of the coalition] they are not here! We are duplicating a lot of efforts that the Decatur Trades & Labor fail at doing."[14]

The Decatur Workers Solidarity and Education Coalition had modest success in its first few months, but by July 1994, with all three locals on the lines, triunion solidarity was stepped up. Workers felt that they were part of something much larger than their individual conflicts. The *New York Times* declared Decatur "Strike City, USA," and other newspapers repeated the phrase as attention on Decatur escalated. Some workers began to echo the words of Royal Plankenhorn:

> We have to get back to the concept of the IWW [Industrial Workers of the World, an early 1900s radical union]. One big union. Because we built these walls of internationals and locals, and it has worked against us. It's been, "Well, that's his fight. Don't bother me. He's the one going through that. I've got a job." We can't

do that anymore. The fact is, we have to break down the walls that divide us, because his battle is my battle, my battle is his battle, and your battle is my battle. We can't succeed any other way.[15]

UAW 751 activist Randy Morrell, with twenty-eight years at the Cat plant, celebrated the workers' new found unity: "We've developed whole new families here. Folks who didn't know each other and belong to different unions are now working on projects together."[16]

The Staley workers continued their Road Warrior trips, but they were now often joined by striking Cat and Firestone workers. Brian and Tyna McDuffie were among the first to join the team. "Part of [why I do it] is because I've read history—and understand why I have what I have," said Tyna. "Part of it is my kids: I want a good job for me, but mostly I'm fighting for my kids and the people who fought and died for what I have."[17] Brian McDuffie "was very unselfish, very special," recalled Gary Lamb. "He would make phone calls and strong-arm the UAW locals. He would flat-out tell them, 'We need to do a bucket drop at the gate; you ought to be able to get a thousand dollars out of the treasury to give to [Local 7837], and get somebody selling T-shirts.'"

Since his local's members were receiving far higher strike pay—three hundred dollars a week plus health insurance, while the Firestone workers received one hundred dollars a week, and the Staley workers a meager sixty—Solomon declared that his local would not take a share of the funds raised by the Road Warriors.[18] Recalled Plankenhorn, "Larry Solomon told his people, 'Any money we get is theirs. They need the money—we don't. Go out and tell the story and give them the limelight.'" Because the UAW was one of the country's larger, more important unions, the Cat workers opened some new doors for speaking engagements, and the Staley workers volunteered their extensive list of contacts and solidarity committees for use by all three locals.

Following the lockout Decatur labor demonstrations had been initiated solely by the Staley workers, but from the autumn of 1994 through the summer of 1995 all three local unions sponsored every major demonstration.

The October 15 Rally

Through the summer the Road Warriors fanned out across the country. At each speaking engagement they showed the union's *Struggle in the Heartland* video depicting the police pepper-spraying on June 25 and asked the enraged audiences to come to Decatur on October 15 to show the three companies that the workers would not be intimidated by police violence.

On that day seven thousand people converged on Decatur for the third national mobilization in eleven months. Large numbers wore red union T-shirts, now sported not just by the Staley workers, who had started the practice, but by the striking Cat and Bridgestone/Firestone workers, too. They brought union banners, handmade signs, and American flags. "If they bust the unions here, it'll be everywhere," said Billie Coffee, who had driven 850 miles from Texas. "It will be like a chain reaction."[19]

Throughout the day, hundreds of protesters rode on twenty chartered school-buses for tours of the three plants' picket lines. Worker "tour guides" shared their stories. Expecting that the bus tours would end in unannounced civil disobedience, the police diligently followed the protesters across town all day. Management also anticipated action at the plant gates; the Caterpillar, Bridge-stone, and Staley plants were all closed.

Meanwhile, the bulk of the crowd assembled in the field outside the UAW hall and listened to fiery speeches from labor leaders and rank-and-file workers. Prominent among the speakers were URW International president Ken Coss; Teamsters International vice president Dennis Skelton; and the Democratic candidate for lieutenant governor of Illinois, Penny Severns. Simultaneously, smaller rallies were held outside the three plants. The four contingents then marched toward the Staley plant, taking over two lanes and eventually all four lanes of Twenty-second Street, one of Decatur's main thoroughfares. Through-out the march, police helicopters buzzed overhead. Decatur police, reported the *Chicago Tribune*, "were deployed throughout the city, in buses and garbage trucks, some ready with riot gear."[20]

At the four-lane overpass connecting two parts of the Staley complex, work-ers stopped for Father Mangan to dedicate it as the "Workers Memorial Via-duct" in memory of Jim Beals.[21] Protesters then marched away from the Staley plant, past the Bridgestone/Firestone plant, and on to the intersection of state highways 48 and 121. At that point several hundred workers and supporters sat down, blocking the intersection and tying up traffic for over an hour. The Decatur police, Macon County sheriffs, and Illinois State Police, who were out in force, made no arrests.

"I'm doing this for my grandkids," said Cat worker Donald Long as he sat down on the highway. "I don't want them to look back and say, 'Maybe if my grandfather had done something, it might be better.'" "It was a big plus for us when Caterpillar and Firestone went out," said Mike Griffin. "This was the ultimate ignorance of management, because when you've got a town out on strike, you've got an army. You could see that at the October 15 rally." "We're all union, all family," said Ed Hemrich, a worker at Decatur's Mueller Company plant. "A lot of our friends work at Cat, Staley and Firestone. It's them now, but it may be us next."[22]

Nonetheless, a number of Local 7837's most active members and most of the activists in the solidarity committees were disappointed that no mass civil disobedience occurred at any of the three plants. The union had emerged from the June 25 rally even more divided over the tactic of civil disobedience. The police pepper-spray attack had badly shaken the union. Both its officers and many members feared that another plant-gate rally would again result in a police attack, this time perhaps even more violent. Some leaders believed, after watching the videotapes, that one of the union's supporters might have pushed a worker, resulting in several people falling on top of one another, which the police seized as an excuse to assault the entire crowd. For that matter, they asked, how could the union prevent a supporter from provoking an attack?

Most important, Staley had secured an injunction prohibiting more than ten workers from picketing at each gate. Another plant-gate rally, let alone one involving civil disobedience, could bring down sizable fines on the local and the international—something UPIU president Wayne Glenn was determined to avoid. The international's staff, along with the police, continued to tell Dave Watts that, should he violate the injunction, he could face imprisonment and personal fines that would bankrupt his family.

At the same time, the solidarity committees were lobbying to escalate the struggle. Only a sustained effort to block the gates could cut the company's production and bring national publicity, they argued. One proposal from some members of the Chicago solidarity committee was to conduct an ongoing civil-disobedience effort modeled on the June 4 protest. Once or twice a week a group of supporters would block the gates and be arrested. Unions could be encouraged to sign up for their turn—the teachers' unions one week, AFSCME government workers the next, USWA members after that. College campuses could take a date and bring carloads of students to Decatur. Religious denominations could take a turn. But Watts and some on the executive board feared that such a strategy would result in huge fines.

Most of the seven thousand people who came to Decatur on October 15 had viewed the *Struggle in the Heartland* video, which depicted participants in the June 4 and June 25 sit-downs as heroes. They had been inspired and came to Decatur expecting either to participate in nonviolent civil disobedience or to rally nearby, expressing their solidarity while hundreds of workers and supporters risked arrest. They were stunned to find that they were to march away from the Staley plant to a highway intersection. They had not come to Decatur to sit in a street in the middle of nowhere, surrounded by grass-covered vacant lots, an action so unthreatening that the police didn't deem it necessary even to warn the crowd that they risked arrest. When the folksinger Anne Feeney marched off to another intersection to lie down and be carted away, prompting the day's sole arrest, she was not alone in her disappointment at the demonstration's passivity.[23]

Company Town

Throughout Local 7837's 3½-year struggle for a contract, the unionists felt they were being attacked from two sides: the company and Decatur's city government. "A concerted effort to intimidate and harass the locked-out Staley workers and their supporters grows daily in Decatur," said the *War Zone* newsletter in June 1994, "bearing much evidence that A. E. Staley Company and corporate greed dictates the actions of city officials."

Unionists and community supporters often called Decatur a modern-day "company town," that is, one where a company completely dominates a town's economy and its politics. The three companies' demands to roll back work rules and set up twelve-hour shifts were antifamily and anticommunity, declared Father Mangan. "It's like going back to the company town. It's an insidious form of control over people's lives."[24]

A major topic of discussion among the unionists was the lack of justice that Decatur workers received from police, the state's attorney, and the courts. The police and the justice system were, they said furiously, puppets of the major corporations in town. Workers frequently wrote letters to the *Decatur Herald and Review* expressing their dismay and disgust at their treatment. Workers were particularly angry that scabs far exceeded the speed limit as they entered or exited the plants but were never ticketed. When scabs drove at picketers and swerved at the last minute, the police would come and make a report but never file charges. When scabs in their cars raised handguns to threaten picketers, again the police did nothing.

Over the course of the lockout, more than one hundred workers were arrested. When they went to court, they found no justice. Invariably, the state's attorney would weed from the jury pool anyone who was in a union, had a relative or friend or neighbor in a union, had any sympathy for unions, or had even kept up on the news about Decatur's labor conflicts. In a trial of some members of the Decatur Fifty, who had been charged with criminal trespass, obstructing police, mob action, and conspiracy to commit mob action, the state's attorney managed to find a jury whose nearly sole reading material consisted of romance novels (see chapter 16).

In one case, the company went beyond utilizing the city government and police to harass a union activist. In the spring of 1994 Mike Griffin opened his door to find two FBI agents. His wife, Jan, recalled the ensuing year as "a very scary and stressful time. I was afraid Mike would be framed and sent to prison." A Staley executive had received a threatening letter. The company, with no evidence, pointed the finger at Griffin. In fact, the letter had been written by a right-handed person, and Griffin is left-handed. When he refused to talk with the agents, he was subpoenaed to appear before a grand jury. When he received a court order, he traveled to Springfield on June 8 to give the FBI his fingerprints and a handwriting sample. Two dozen union members and spouses picketed outside while inside a defiant Griffin refused to testify, invoking his Fifth Amendment right. The FBI subsequently dropped him as a suspect—although without bothering to notify him that they had done so.[25]

As discussed earlier, the editors of the *Decatur Herald and Review* made no secret of their sympathies with management. In a typical editorial written shortly after the lockout, the newspaper accepted Staley's claims that the contract had to be gutted in the name of "competitiveness." The editors lectured the union, belligerently insisting that it fire Ray Rogers and accept twelve-hour shifts, drastic cuts in jobs, and unlimited subcontracting.[26] In the first of several protests, on November 18, 1993, 130 unionists and spouses picketed the *Herald and Review* offices in downtown Decatur while passing motorists honked loudly in approval. The paper, the workers declared, covered union events poorly, undercounted the turnout at union rallies, consistently expressed a procorporate bias in its news reports, and printed editorials that could have been written by management. A few days later the *Herald and Review*'s editor, George Althoff, berated the workers in a mean-spirited opinion piece, declaring that their "struggle is over."[27]

The newspaper did, however, print many workers' letters, and throughout the fight workers used this forum.

In September 1994 the newspaper challenged union and management to open negotiating sessions to observers from the press and the public. The union quickly agreed, but when management refused, the paper dropped the matter and did not criticize Staley. "Perhaps the best way to find out what is really going on is to stop reading the *Herald & Review* and see for yourself," declared the October 1994 *Decatur Free Press*. "Come to a union meeting; come to a rally; talk to the striking family on your street. Maybe then, if you don't know already, you'll understand what a union is all about—sticking together to benefit everyone."

"We're Being Lawyered to Death"

Decatur mayor Eric Brechnitz quickly drew the enmity of the town's unionists. The workers noted that Brechnitz, a senior vice president of Kemper Securities and manager of its Decatur office, flaunted his wealth by driving his red, twelve-cylinder Jaguar convertible around town. The mayor repeatedly refused to meet with the Staley workers and made it clear that he sided with management: his own son was a scab at Staley.[28] Some city council members were also retired corporate managers with strong ties to Staley, Caterpillar, ADM, and Bridgestone/Firestone.

Local 7837's leaders spent literally thousands of hours wrangling with with the city over one issue: the right to put up shelters to provide picketers warmth and protection from the wind and rain. The wooden shacks—about six feet high, eight feet wide, and four feet deep—are commonly put up by unions during strikes and lockouts.[29] When Staley filed complaints with the city in the winter of 1993–94, the mayor promptly took the union to court to force it to take down the makeshift shelters, charging that the law prohibited such structures on city property. The chief of police and the county sheriff admitted that the shelters presented no safety hazard to the public, but the city nevertheless pursued the litigation.

Congressman Glenn Poshard intervened to get the city and Staley to drop the issue, but to no avail. "To deny somebody shelter during a winter—that should never have been an issue," recalled the congressman. "When it's zero degrees and the wind is blowing thirty miles per hour, it just cuts into you!"

In March 1994, a judge found in favor of the city and fined the union $2,300. The city removed the picket shelters in front of the Staley gates. The city council could have passed a special ordinance allowing picket shelters, but such motions could not reach the floor without being forwarded by at least two of the council's seven members, and only one was willing to do so.

In May the union put up temporary, lighter shelters on wheels and argued that they were no longer violating the ordinance since they regularly moved the huts a few feet. In July, however, the city charged that these structures, too, violated city building and zoning laws and that the union signs on the shacks violated an ordinance against erecting signs on a public right-of-way. In August a judge ruled that the shelters on wheels must be removed. Even the *Decatur Herald and Review* viewed this as beyond the pale, defending the huts in a May 13, 1994, editorial: "Of course the huts break a city ordinance. So what? Who do they injure? What public interest is served by forcing their removal?"

Throughout 1994 members of the three locals regularly showed up at city council meetings to demand action on the shelters, and regularly they were rebuffed. In August 1994 they marched to the opening ceremonies of the Decatur Celebration festival behind a banner asking, "What's Decatur Got to Celebrate?" As Brechnitz spoke, twelve hundred workers, chanting "The mayor's son is a scab!" stood, turned their backs on the mayor, and walked away as he spoke, protesting his refusal to allow them to have picket shelters and his general hostility to the worker's plight. Brechnitz continued with his speech detailing what a wonderful town Decatur was and made no mention of the town's workers.

In September 1994 Decatur city manager Jim Bacon proposed an ordinance that would require permits fifteen days in advance for all public assemblies. Three hundred unionists turned out at the council meeting to protest. While Bacon said he made the proposal in reaction to a small Ku Klux Klan rally held in February, unionists were convinced he was attacking their right to peacefully assemble, guaranteed under the Constitution. As a result of the protest, the ordinance was withdrawn.

The three unions pointed out they had not been able to locate a single other city in Illinois—or anywhere in the country—that refused shelters for union pickets. The City of Decatur required pet-owners to provide shelters for their dogs, said the unionists, but would not allow picketers shelter from rain and snow. Solomon summarized the workers' view: "Removing the shelters was an anti-union tactic. The city went out and picked up an ordinance designed for residential areas to keep sheds off property lines, and used it" to attack the unions.[30] Mike Griffin expressed a common sentiment when he said in October 1994, "There's a court injunction against about anything you do to express your freedom of speech and your freedom of assembly rights in this town."[31]

Finally, when 250 angry workers showed up at an October 24 council meeting, the council voted to consider granting unions special ordinances to erect picket shelters on public property. The city, however, then drew up eight pages of "guidelines" that in effect continued the prohibition on picket shelters, including a demand that the unions pay for a $1 million liability insurance policy. At the next council meeting Ethel Fargusson blew up: "The city dumps on us in any way they possibly can; the companies dump on us. What are we to do? I'm asking our mayor and our city government and our city officials to *quit dumping on the workers!* You've taken away our picket shacks. We couldn't have them on city property! Couldn't you have given us a variance? No! You wanted to dump on us!"[32]

"This is a bunch of bureaucracy, red tape, and bullshit," said Dave Watts. "We're being lawyered to death," declared Larry Solomon.[33] The mayor finally met with the unions to work out a compromise on the picket shacks and brought it to the three companies, but they all rejected the proposal, declaring it unacceptable for "safety reasons."

March to Springfield

Recognizing after the October 15 action that they could not win the leadership's endorsement of civil disobedience at the plant gates, and furious over city hall's stripping them of their picket shacks, the union's activists directed their attention away from Decatur to Republican governor Jim Edgar. On November 29 over fifty workers and spouses from the three locals met at Decatur City Hall to begin a two-day, forty-mile march to the state capitol in Springfield. "They've taken away our rights in the factory," said UAW member Tom Meir. "Now they're taking them away on the streets."[34]

Others joined the march midway, including UAW International secretary-treasurer Bill Casstevens, the union's lead negotiator with Caterpillar. The marchers erected a huge tent and spent the night near the small town of Illiopolis. It was a cold night, but "the brotherhood among us kept us warm," said URW member Roger Walker.[35] By the time they reached the state capitol, the marchers' numbers had grown to four hundred, and they were joined by the three local union presidents. The raucous crowd marched into the building and up the stairs to the governor's office. When an aide told them Edgar was not available—he had left for his mansion several blocks away—the protesters marched into the auditorium where the Illinois House of Representatives was in session, chanting "Solidarity," "Justice," and "You represent us."

When the governor's aide offered to discuss the issues privately, but only with two of their leaders, the workers began chanting, "We are all leaders!" Later, as they sat to occupy the hall outside the governor's office, Art Dhermy talked about the meaning of the chant. "You are a leader. I am a leader. Be a leader. What they're trying to do is deny that, and what we need to do is to show them that they can't do this to us any more."[36]

Jesse Jackson Jr., the son of the civil rights leader and soon to be a U.S. congressman from Chicago, flew in from Washington, D.C., to join the protest. "For more than a year," roared Jackson, "the people of Decatur and Peoria have struggled to fight for the right to organize. We should not let our elected officials, we should not let this governor, we should not let corporate America, turn back the hands [of the clock] for what we fought for."[37]

When the building closed at 6:00 P.M. and the governor had not appeared, the workers were told to leave or face arrest. They refused, and thirty-one people were arrested, including workers from the three Decatur locals and UAW 974 in Peoria. Modeling the June 4 protesters, many went limp and were carried away by police officers. "I was scared to death at first," said URW member Thom Welsh. "But then we started singing songs, and pretty soon we were like a family. We were proud that we did it." "It was a great day," said Sharon Fischer, spouse of a UAW 974 member. "The camaraderie of being with union people means more than anything the police or companies can do to us."[38]

A week later the governor finally met with the three local presidents at his Springfield office but made no offer of help.

In December 1994 Governor Edgar pressured Decatur to construct city bus shelters—funded by the federal government—outside the Caterpillar and Bridgestone/Firestone plants; the structures would also function as picket shelters. Bus shelters were not erected at Staley, however, until early September 1995. The mayor said the city had delayed in the hopes that the lockout would be settled, but union pressure forced him finally to build the shelters.

After two years of fighting city hall—after writing a huge volume of letters to the editor, making hundreds of phone calls to council members and the mayor, enduring endless negotiations, and packing many city council meetings—the

Staley workers finally got their picket shelters. The battle with the city, however, had wasted enormous union resources and exhausted the unionists—which undoubtedly, said the three unions, was exactly the intention of the three corporations and the city government.

Challenging Environmental and Tax Abuses

Local 7837's corporate campaign sought to attack Tate & Lyle in many ways besides targeting its financial backers and customers. In particular, the union pursued Tate & Lyle for its atrocious environmental record and challenged the company's tax abatements, thus building pressure campaigns to force city and state governments to hold the company accountable.

Workers repeatedly demanded that the mayor and city council take a stand for the environment, but their calls for action were ignored. For decades Staley workers, in a practice common in factories across the country, were ordered to allow dangerous chemicals to be flushed down the plant's drains, and workers were told to dump toxins in the Staley landfill. The workers knew that they and their families would be the victims of a degraded environment, but they chose their jobs over their health. "Staley has admitted to the Environmental Protection Agency that it dumps huge amounts of toxic substances into the air and water of Decatur," declared the union's 1992 "Crisis in Decatur" brochure. The union publicized the fact that, according to Tate & Lyle's own records, in 1990 the company released 337,500 pounds of ethylene glycol, 11,400 pounds of hydrochloric acid, and 12,700 pounds of sulfuric acid into the air and water. "Just think what has gone unreported!" declared the union.

The plant, the union declared in the 1993 "Deadly Corn" brochure, was not simply a food-processing plant but a chemical plant that regularly used "deadly carcinogens like propylene oxide and ethylene oxide as well as other hazardous substances like chlorine and hexane." The "huge chemical complex can be as dangerous as those run by DuPont or Union Carbide." By "cutting too many corners in recent years," they said, the company had endangered not just the workers in the plant but also "residents of the surrounding community." If proper safety measures were not taken, "huge reactors . . . can explode and spew their contents over a wide area." The brochure added that "large quantities of toxic substances are released into the air, water and land" on a regular basis. In January 1994 black workers wrote a piece focusing on the dangers the plant posed to the community and published the text as an ad in the African American weekly *The Voice*.

"Are You Being Poisoned?" headlined an issue of the triunion coalition's *Decatur Free Press*. Reporting on Local 7837's July 1994 press conference, the paper announced that the union intended to sue Staley over toxins buried in the company's forty-acre landfill east of the plant. The union had previously asked the Illinois Environmental Protection Agency and the federal EPA to investigate, but the EPA claimed there were no problems. The workers said that the chemicals could be leaching out into the soil and groundwater and into a creek that flowed into Lake Decatur, a source for the city's drinking water. The lake was just a quarter-mile from the landfill.

Union vice president Bob Hull said that the workers knew that the landfill contained toxic chemicals "because we dumped them ourselves under company orders." "We picked up whatever they gave us to take to the landfill—paint thinner, old paint from the paint shop, chemicals from the control lab," said Tom Roberts, who drove a scrap truck. "They had plant security dump other things which they didn't want us to see." "I know there were toxins out there," said Gary Lamb. "They'd come out with one or two drums and make me bury them away from the other stuff, and they'd tell me to be especially careful not to break them." The *Free Press* reported that when workers challenged orders to contaminate Decatur's air, ground soil, or water, supervisors told them to shut up and follow orders, warning them, "You got a job, don't you?"

The newspaper revealed that studies by environmental groups had already called into question the safety of the city's drinking water; for example, farm chemicals in Decatur's water were nineteen times higher than the EPA's cancer-risk standard. Keith Romig, the UPIU International's environmental expert, collected testimony from thirty Staley workers about toxic chemicals they had been ordered to move to the dump. Unfortunately, the UPIU International, after originally promising it would support the local's litigation, decided that the lawsuit was too costly. The local was forced to back off the suit but continued to hammer the company on its environmental record and to challenge city officials to ensure Decatur citizens had clean air, water, and soil.

The three unions were also incensed that their companies were waging a war on Decatur's workers and simultaneously receiving city and state tax cuts and subsidies funded by Decatur's working-class taxpayers. Most corporations receive sizable "corporate-welfare" subsidies. Tax abatements are reductions in property taxes, on average 50 percent over ten years, that city and state governments offer to corporations to induce them to build or expand facilities or not to shut down and move their operations elsewhere. Water, sewage, utility, sales, and other taxes may be reduced or waived. The expectation is that in return for tax cuts, the corporation will provide good-paying jobs.

Challenging a corporation's tax cuts and subsidies is an effective corporate-campaign tactic. Unions can appeal to home owners and small-business owners who are subsidizing the corporation's tax breaks through their own higher property taxes. Shortly after the lockout Art Dhermy started thinking about all the tax abatements he had heard A. E. Staley received, and he determined to challenge them. Dhermy spent countless tedious hours studying tax abatement law and researching Staley's abatements, with the assistance of UPIU special projects staffer and lawyer Mark Brooks. At one point Dhermy went to discuss the tax abatements with the Decatur city attorney, who told him, "We can't give the information to you." Dhermy, who had done his homework, said, "The Freedom of Information Act says you have to." The city attorney pulled a law book off a shelf, pointed to it, and said, "See, we don't have to do it." Dhermy pulled a copy of the Freedom of Information Act out of his pocket and said, "Yes, you do!"

The city attorney spoke at length, trying to intimidate Dhermy by quoting legal cases. "You don't need to use all those three-foot-long words," Dhermy told him. "I'm just an old country boy. Explain it in English why you claim you're not violating the Freedom of Information Act." Dhermy persevered and eventually got the documentation. He found that in many of the previous dozen years, Staley had received exemptions from state utility taxes and retailers' occupation taxes totaling hundreds of thousands of dollars. Dhermy found that Staley was given tax breaks for being in a Decatur enterprise zone. The tax breaks included a 100 percent tax exemption on its $1 million-a-month utility bill granted in 1992 and an exemption from paying sales tax on new equipment granted in 1994. Both deals were to run for five years and would save the company more than $5.5 million. In return, Staley had promised to retain 1,620 full-time jobs in Decatur.

In August 1995 Local 7837 filed suit against Staley, charging the company was taking tax subsidies in violation of the law. The union held a press conference in front of the Staley office building. "We said they were feeding at the public trough and gobbling up goodies as fast as they could," Dhermy said, pointing to two pigs eating at a trough. "To drive our point home, we brought a couple of pigs with us."[39] Dhermy told the press:

> They don't come even close to employing 1,000 people. The way they do it is they include those of us who are locked-out as employees. Talk about voting the dead! . . . Enterprise zones and tax abatements are supposed to help companies create jobs and improve a community's economy. Staley has cut jobs and shifted the tax burden to the individual taxpayer even as public services are cut for lack of funds. . . . It's the community which is stuck with higher tax bills to make up for Staley's free ride.[40]

On August 22, 1995, the Illinois Department of Commerce and Community Affairs announced it would disqualify Staley from two major tax exemptions that it should not have received, retroactive to July 1993. Staley had received tax cuts that were not legally warranted because of the reduction of its workforce and had committed fraud by applying for a renewal of the tax cut in October 1994 using the prelockout employment figures. The union's lawsuit resulted in the State of Illinois forcing the company to repay over $3 million in tax breaks plus interest and penalties.[41]

"Watts for City Council"

In the fall of 1994, as an outgrowth of the Decatur Workers Solidarity and Education Coalition, "Friends of Labor" was formed as an embryonic citywide labor party. "The community as a whole is fed up with the kind of government we've got, and we're going to change it," said Dan Kashefska, spokesperson for Friends of Labor. "In the long run, if we cannot get what we need from the Republican or Democratic parties, it leaves us no alternative but to set up another political party."[42]

Dave Watts decided to run for city council. He was joined by Michael Carrigan, the business agent for International Brotherhood of Electrical Workers Local 146. Friends of Labor quickly gathered enough signatures to put the two on the ballot. "A labor party of our own is the only way working people are going to get any justice in this country," Watts said repeatedly.[43] In the February 1995 primary twelve candidates ran for city council, with the six highest vote-getters to face one another for the three council seats in the April election. This was the first time in the city's history that labor had put two unionists on the ballot.

Friends of Labor focused its energies on Watts's campaign, because he ran on a clear platform supporting workers' rights and unions. "Bringing the voice of working-class people to city government" was Watts's campaign slogan. Carrigan had a separate campaign committee, and his candidacy was not uniformly supported by Staley and Caterpillar activists, for some of Carrigan's union members were employed by outside contractors who regularly crossed the Staley and Caterpillar picket lines.

The corporations took an extra interest in the campaign and made sure their supervisors were talking up the need to defeat the labor candidates. Staley and Caterpillar management made a special effort to tell scabs working in their plants to register and vote.

In the February 28 primary Carrigan and Watts placed third and fourth, respectively, and made it to the April runoff. "Labor leaders make history!" declared an ecstatic Friends of Labor.[44] Thirty percent of registered voters turned out, much higher than the usual rate of twelve percent. "This is a record since they've been keeping track of the city elections," said Dan Kashefska. "Labor did its job and got the vote out."[45] The group stepped up efforts to publicize the campaign among unions and solidarity committees nationally. The group raised twenty thousand dollars from Decatur unionists and supporters across the country, most of the money in five- and ten-dollar donations.

Friends of Labor did not endorse a candidate in the mayoral primary. Initially it appeared that Brechnitz would run for reelection, but tired of being denounced by the city's working people, he decided to step down. The decision wasn't made for lack of campaign funds. When he took a new job as a stockbroker with Dean Witter in October 1994, he told his new bosses he was thinking of running for a second term. Said Brechnitz, they "asked how much it took, how much of a campaign fund. I gave them a reasonable figure, and they were ready to cut me a check."[46] When Brechnitz announced on November 10, 1994, that he would not run, five individuals quickly filed for candidacy.

For the general election, Friends of Labor again focused on Watts's campaign, although members also campaigned for Carrigan and endorsed Terry Howley for mayor. Howley, a liberal Democrat running against a Republican, did not forcefully speak for workers' rights but pledged to listen to both management and labor. Howley was also a stockbroker, a vice president with the brokerage firm of Smith, Barney.

Turnout for the April 1995 general election was the highest in thirty-five years. Howley became mayor, winning about 11,000 votes, but Watts failed to win the city council seat. The three winners each received over 9,500 votes, far more than normal, and Watts came in fifth with 7,073. Carrigan was elected with 9,993 votes. Councilman Randy Van Alstine blamed labor for his defeat in the mayoral race, asserting that Howley "got the labor vote out in force. It didn't help me that the Council has been perceived as against the labor unions recently."[47]

Although disappointed that Watts had lost, Friends of Labor rightly viewed the campaign as a success in its effort to educate the public on workers' rights. "Dave Watts raised issues that even the other candidates began to address," said Kashefska. "Watts was the first to point out that Decatur lost 4,600 jobs between 1980 and 1990, and that the average wage is $6,000 below the state level. And he showed that we need good-paying jobs, not hamburger-flipper jobs. . . . Decatur needs programs for the youth. Because he talked about these things, the other candidates began to talk about them."[48]

Although the electoral defeat was disappointing, Watts turned his full attention back to his union. The internal chasm between the local's conservatives and activists was widening, while the Paperworkers International was clamping down on the local union.

14

The Paperworkers

By late 1994 the Staley workers had organized widespread national support, and the fact that three unions were now walking picket lines in Decatur had attracted national media coverage. The Staley workers were hopeful that their multipronged campaign would pressure Tate & Lyle to negotiate a fair contract. In January 1994, however, the Allied Industrial Workers had merged with the much larger Paperworkers union, and the Staley workers came to believe that their new international was an obstacle to winning a decent contract.

The AIW-UPIU Merger

In June 1993, when the members of Allied Industrial Workers Local 837 were locked out of their plant, the United Paperworkers International Union (UPIU) was in the midst of a full-fledged courtship of the AIW International. A few days later, when the local demonstrated for unemployment benefits at the state capitol, UPIU vice president Glenn Goss added to their numbers by bringing two hundred Paperworkers who happened to be in Springfield attending a union education seminar. Goss, who had attended the "Hands across Decatur" rally the day before the lockout, said of the Staley workers, "These folks need and deserve our support. They're being dished a raw deal by their employer, and they're currently on the front lines of the labor movement in trying to fend off contract concessions."[1]

Putting on its best face for AIW delegates, who would vote on the merger at their September 1993 convention, the UPIU's monthly newspaper carried articles and photos describing the UPIU as leading the way in building solidarity with the embattled Decatur union. "Eighty UPIU locals across America's heartland were preparing to host traveling Staley workers and to conduct plant-gate collections at their plants and mills," declared *The Paperworker*. The UPIU Executive Board authorized a ten thousand–dollar donation to Local 837. Union president Wayne Glenn lobbied the AFL-CIO Executive Council to pass a resolution in August 1993 calling on affiliated unions to give the Staley workers "all appropriate assistance."[2]

During the previous two decades the Milwaukee-based AIW International had lost half its members, falling to just 48,000 by 1993. With dwindling income, the union was forced to lay off large numbers of staff. AIW leaders announced that dues would have to increase by four or five dollars per worker per month, but when local officers balked, they escalated their efforts to merge with another union. Such fusions had become common; in the previous two decades there had been forty-six mergers of international unions. The AIW had "been talking [merger] since 1975," the leadership said in its magazine, and now "it was time for action."[3]

Several internationals were interested in acquiring the Allied Industrial Workers, including the union from which they had split in 1939, the United Auto Workers, but the AIW chose the Nashville-based UPIU, with 230,000 members. AIW president Nick Serraglio said that leaders had found the UPIU most similar "in structure, program, and emphasis on services to the membership" and that the unions shared "a strong tradition of local autonomy." Combining the AIW's $8.6 million strike fund with the UPIU's $13 million, said Serraglio, the merged union would be better prepared to assist striking or locked-out locals. The UPIU had substantial other resources to offer as well, including a large national office building in Nashville, training, research, and corporate-campaign support. Serraglio, an AIW member for fifty years and its president for two, reported "having mixed feelings about the merger" but saw it as "the only realistic course of action." The AIW's executive board unanimously supported the move.[4]

In September 1993, as delegates arrived in Minneapolis for the last convention in AIW history, many were nostalgic but resigned. With the UPIU's resources and promises spread out before them, one promerger AIW delegate shared his perception: "This week you are being asked to abandon a steamship that has served us well for years and years, and now we are being asked to climb aboard a nuclear-powered ship, alias UPIU. And I think this ship is going to take us onto a bigger, brighter and better future for all of us as one union."[5] By a vote of 302 to 35 the delegates voted to approve the merger. Serraglio was greeted with a standing ovation and declared, "The UPIU has been a great union, and from this day forward, with the addition of the AIW, it is going to be the greatest union in the world."[6]

Dave Watts spoke to the delegates about the local's work-to-rule campaign and the lockout and showed the *Deadly Corn* video. A collection of $2,730 was matched by the UPIU International. Watts later characterized Glenn and other UPIU officers as "wining and dining" the AIW delegates. "All the way up to the vote, Glenn was in there doing his organizing, patting backs and shaking hands, and passing out promises like they were candy. . . . Glenn said, 'The merger has got to happen; it's got to happen. We can provide this. We can do that. There will be more money, more special projects, and all of those things.'"[7]

The Paperworkers and President Wayne Glenn

With roots running back to 1884, the UPIU was formed out of a 1957 merger of two paperworkers unions—AFL and CIO counterparts—followed by a 1972 merger with the Pulp and Sulphite Workers. Membership reached 389,000 in the early 1970s but then steadily declined, both because of mill closings and severe downsizing in the paper industry and because the Paperworkers, like most U.S. unions in the 1970s and 1980s, did not make a serious effort to organize new members. Still, in 1993 the UPIU's 230,000 members made it the thirteenth-largest union in the AFL-CIO, and its president sat on the AFL-CIO Executive Council. While paper-mill locals dominated the union, about one-third of its members worked in other types of manufacturing.

Serraglio's assertion that the UPIU and AIW shared a history of local union autonomy was not accurate. The UPIU structure was light on union democracy. As in most internationals, members did not vote directly for their top officers; instead, delegates at conventions held every four years voted for the president and executive board. (The UPIU held conventions in August 1992 and August 1996, so no convention took place during the forty-month Staley fight.) Any local strikes had to be approved by the UPIU International president as well as by two-thirds of the local membership. The UPIU president could unilaterally call off a strike and order members to vote on a management contract offer. Strike benefits were a meager sixty dollars a week, an incentive to forgo strikes and accept concessions.

In the 1960s and 1970s the union had experienced both a rebellion and corruption. In 1964, twenty-two thousand West Coast unionists split to form the Association of Western Pulp and Paper Workers when they were unable to move the leadership to enact democratic reforms. In 1978, a federal grand jury indicted UPIU president Joseph Tonelli on charges of embezzling $360,000; Tonelli pleaded guilty and was sentenced to three years in prison.[8] To replace Tonelli, the board appointed Wayne Glenn, who then won election at the 1980 convention and served as president until his retirement in 1996. Glenn, a native of Ft. Smith, Arkansas, and the son of a union mineworker, was initially seen as a reformer who could be trusted to reinstate a clean reputation for the international.

In 1988 and again in 1992 union vice president Glenn Goss challenged Glenn for the presidency but was defeated both times. The mutual dislike between Glenn and Goss was palpable, and each had a loyal caucus among the board members and convention delegates. The 1992 convention, when the two publicly squared off, provided a rare glimpse into the international's abuse of members' dues. Goss accused Glenn of using union funds for personal vacations. Glenn's caucus countered that Goss and his executive board caucus members had taken an all-expenses-paid vacation with their wives to Europe, including Russia. One of the accused vice presidents didn't deny that his trip had been paid for by the union but countered that this was business as usual for *both* factions. Vice president Cliff King said, "If we're going to talk about the trip to Russia, then I want to talk about trips to Sweden. I want to talk about the trips to Brazil. I want to talk about the trips everywhere."[9]

Glenn's greatest passion was convincing Congress to pass proworker legislation. He persistently urged the AFL-CIO Executive Council to organize in support of a "Striker Replacement Bill" designed to ban companies from permanently replacing striking workers. Since the United States is the only industrialized country that lacks such a law, Glenn felt that its chances were strong. In 1992, after three years of lobbying, the bill was approved by the House but failed in the Senate when Republicans threatened a filibuster.

Glenn's zealous focus on a legislative solution to labor's problems illustrated his paternalistic philosophy of the way unions should operate: the officers take care of the members rather than educate and mobilize them. This approach, common among international union presidents, is called "business unionism": the union is seen as a business, with decisions made at the top, rather than as a democratic, grassroots organization driven by its members. Paid union staff at the national and regional level are the full-time experts whose job is to service the membership, much as an insurance company or a law firm services its clients.

Unaware of this history, Local 837's delegates supported the merger, hoping that the UPIU's resources could help bring them victory. They were aware that the UPIU had suffered a big defeat at Jay, Maine, but many internationals had experienced major defeats since the early 1980s. After the merger, as the Staley workers began to question the depth of UPIU leaders' support, they researched the Maine strike more closely. In 1987–88, UPIU Local 14's 1,250 members at International Paper's Jay plant had struck against concessions for seventeen months. Local 14, joined by three other IP locals on strike or locked out, "were solely responsible for creating the solidarity around the strike," said Peter Kellman, a Maine AFL-CIO staffer brought in to help coordinate solidarity efforts.[10]

However, as Julius Getman describes in *The Betrayal of Local 14,* the UPIU International quietly opposed Local 14's efforts and worked behind the scenes to undermine the strikers. When the local proposed that other IP locals join the strike when their contracts expired, the international nixed the idea. Local 14 then asked for funds to launch a Road Warrior–type program, but Glenn rejected that proposal, too, stating, "I don't think it is necessary to have groups traveling around the country. I think it would be much less expensive if we let our trained staff work on this problem in each location."[11] Getman wrote that the UPIU "had no experience conducting a nationwide strike against a determined multinational company that no longer felt itself bound by the standard conventions of U.S. industrial relations."[12]

Dissident Children

After the AIW's September 1993 convention, Glenn Goss returned to Indianapolis to resume his duties as Region 9 director, responsible for locals in Illinois, Indiana, and Michigan. Goss was a skilled negotiator who had bargained hundreds of contracts, working long hours on behalf of the members (he retired in 2000). Nonetheless, he epitomized traditional business unionism, in which collective bargaining comes down to one thing: the skill of the union representatives who bargain with management. During strikes and lockouts, in this view, the members' role is simply to walk the picket line and to hold out one day longer than the company. Goss thus had little interest in the transformation of Local 837 (soon to be Local 7837) into a member-driven, activist unit. He derided the weekly meetings that drew hundreds of workers and supporters as "rah-rah meetings." Along with Glenn and most other UPIU leaders, he had no enthusiasm for the work-to-rule campaign, the Road Warriors, the dozens of solidarity committees, or the outreach to Decatur's African American and religious communities. They had no interest in waging, or knowledge about building, a national battle that would turn a labor-management conflict into a social movement.[13]

Glenn and Goss also viewed Local 7837's officers as unwilling to compromise, leading them to echo the company's assertion that the local "had no leadership." Goss described negotiations as "gang warfare." They told Dave Watts and the executive board that they would have to accept concessions just as other UPIU locals had been forced to do. What was needed, believed the UPIU national leaders, was for the UPIU to take over negotiations and make the necessary compromises to get the Staley workers back in the plant. From their perspective, experienced labor leaders could always get a settlement, and it was better to negotiate a terrible contract than to launch a fight that risked losing the local altogether.

Once Goss began attending bargaining sessions in spring 1994, he quickly became convinced that the union would have to stop insisting on negotiating from the old contract. The union would have to acquiesce to the company's insistence on its much shorter proposal as the basis for bargaining, and it would have to accept substantial concessions. Goss was prepared to work methodically to get the bargaining committee to see things his way.[14] He did not have to worry about Wayne Glenn trying to usurp his role: Glenn told Goss to take charge of the situation.

The Staley workers came to believe that Glenn and Goss just wanted the Decatur struggle to go away. The UPIU had inherited a democratic, mobilized, fighting local union—and, believed the Staley activists, they didn't like it. "To Wayne Glenn, we were dissident children," said Gary Lamb. "They didn't want us to move forward," said Dave Watts. "They don't want anyone that's brazen or bold."

"One time we went down to Nashville for some bucket drops at the paper mills," said Royal Plankenhorn. "The UPIU [staffer] taking us around says, 'You're the guys that never paid any union dues.' That's how we were perceived by the UPIU leadership. . . . They never wanted us to do any of this. I think we were an embarrassment to them." The Staley workers felt that the UPIU leaders looked down on them because they drew picket pay from the UPIU treasury but had never contributed to it.

Like most rank-and-file union members, the Staley workers resented the officers' high salaries, lavish perks, and misuse of members' dues money. Gary Lamb described his perception of the way the UPIU built loyalty from its international reps:

> He's got a cell phone, a union-paid car; he's making sixty-five thousand dollars a year. And that is the finest way to get a paid puppet for you, from the international's point of view. You've got a rep there, you can pull that string anytime. That guys knows, "There's nowhere I can go and duplicate what I've got here. I've got to play ball. When the guys on top say 'go!,' I better go. Because I'm a high-school graduate. I'm used to the sixty-five thousand dollars a year. I'll lose that car, those benefits, that paycheck." And that buys homage. I've watched it.

Watts reported a conversation with Bill Coleman, a former AIW industrial worker in Decatur's Mueller factory who had gotten used to life on the union payroll: "I considered Bill a good union man. But he told me, 'David, I will do absolutely anything not to go back into that plant.' It became clear that he would sell us short. He would feather his own bed. He would take care of himself."

A Different Kind of Leadership

Dave Watts came to believe that UPIU leaders "either did not know how to fight and to win, or they did not want to win. . . . They did assist us, but they damn sure never led."[15] Wayne Glenn did assign UPIU special projects coordinator Mark Brooks to work on the corporate campaign, and the *The Paperworker*, edited by Dick Blinn, gave some positive coverage.[16]

The Staley workers, however, wanted the UPIU to make the lockout a top priority by putting significant resources, both money and staff, into their fight. They wanted leadership of the sort that Mine Workers president Richard Trumka had exerted in the successful 1989–90 Pittston strike. They wanted the level of resources that the Steelworkers had put into the Ravenswood lockout in 1990–91. The Staley workers wanted the 16 regional directors and assistant directors and the 140 international reps to devote time to building solidarity among the 1,400 UPIU locals.[17] Local 7837 knew that real grassroots solidarity would come only if UPIU staffers took a personal interest and aggressively encouraged their locals to get involved in the Staley fight. "When we were AIW," wrote Watts to Glenn, "there was some active participation in our fight by [International] Representatives. . . . Since the merger with the UPIU, that participation is noticeably no longer visible. We need to see this change."[18]

Given the UPIU's 270,000 members, the local wondered why the UPIU couldn't turn out thousands of its own members for the Decatur rallies. The UPIU was strongest in the Northeast and South but had thousands of members in the Midwest. But the staff made no effort to mobilize for the national rallies. *The Paperworker* refused to publicize the June 25 and October 14, 1994, national mobilizations and gave only brief coverage after the fact. Neither did the paper report on the Road Warriors or the solidarity committees or explain how workers could join the corporate campaign against Miller (or later, Pepsi). As Watts wrote to Glenn in January 1995 the local repeatedly asked for but never received "an 'all out effort' public endorsement of the corporate campaign . . . by [Glenn] and the UPIU Executive Committee."[19]

Members' morale would have been boosted if Wayne Glenn had visited them in Decatur. Over and over they asked, "Where is Wayne Glenn? Why won't he come to Decatur?" The workers wanted Glenn to attend a Tuesday-night solidarity meeting, to talk with workers on the picket line, to speak at the national demonstrations. Coming to Decatur would show, said local leaders, that Glenn was not just giving "lip service"—a phrase they repeatedly used—but was personally involved in their fight. By the end of 1994, however, a year after the merger and eighteen months after the lockout, Glenn had never visited Decatur. "The very minute the vote came down" for the merger at the September 1993 AIW convention, said Watts, "Wayne Glenn disappeared. He was not at the convention another second and was hell and hard to find from that point forward."

Local leaders also wanted Glenn to convince AFL-CIO leaders to visit Decatur—"an AFL-CIO presence in Decatur would send a message of strength," declared Watts—but how, they asked themselves, could Glenn do that when he himself had never been there? The reason AFL-CIO leaders were providing only limited support, the Staley activists believed, was that Glenn was telling them it was not a top priority. "There was so much more [the other international unions] could actually do," explained Gary Lamb. "The stumbling part was Wayne Glenn. He was not giving the signal. It was, 'Give them token service, but don't throw everything in.' I would hate to think that was all the international unions could do for a struggling local."

Local 7837's leaders worried that mounting debts would enable Tate & Lyle to break the workers' will. Over four hundred families had no health insurance, and all struggled to survive on the $60 weekly check from the now $21 million strike fund. Local officers pleaded unsuccessfully with Glenn to raise picket pay by authorizing a special assessment of one dollar per member per month, which would generate $270,000 a month. Glenn also refused their request to call a special convention where delegates could authorize such a special fund. In response to appeals in *The Paperworker*, thirty-three locals adopted Staley worker families, contributing up to $600 a month. But if the international's staff had aggressively advocated for the adopt-a-family program, many more of the UPIU's nearly 1,400 locals would have helped sustain the Staley workers' fight.[20]

Local 7837 knew it would strengthen their fight if the UPIU launched successful organizing drives at the two nonunion Staley corn-processing plants in Lafayette, Indiana, and Loudon, Tennessee. In early 1994 the local sent members to talk to workers in the two plants but didn't have the resources to sustain a campaign, and the UPIU provided no help.

Finally, Local 7837 repeatedly asked the UPIU to help deal with other unions whose members crossed their picket lines to work inside the plant. Teamsters were driving trucks across Local 7837 picket lines. Members of the Brotherhood of Locomotive Engineers were driving trains loaded with corn syrup in and out. Members of the Boilermakers, International Brotherhood of Electrical Workers, and Laborers, employed by outside contractors, were crossing the lines every day. "By crossing our picket lines, you are aiding and abetting A. E. Staley Company," Watts repeatedly wrote to presidents of the Decatur locals and to their internationals' presidents. The locals either ignored Watts or responded that in their interpretation of the law, their members would not be protected from disciplinary action by their employers if they refused to cross. Watts regularly asked Glenn to convince the internationals to pressure their Decatur locals to stop crossing the lines. "We have yet to receive any response to our letters regarding the IBEW, IBT, Boilermakers, and Laborers crossing our picket lines," a frustrated Watts wrote Glenn.[21]

Business Unionism in Britain

The Staley workers met still more bureaucracy and inaction when they reached across the Atlantic. Each January from 1993 through 1995 a delegation traveled to London to spotlight their cause at the Tate & Lyle stockholders' meeting. While some positive publicity was attained, the corporate campaign never really took on international dimensions. The conservative leadership at the top of the British labor movement, beleaguered by their own decade of losses suffered at the hands of Margaret Thatcher and her Tory government, never seriously took up the Staley fight. In fact, several British labor leaders worked behind the scenes to pressure the UPIU and Local 7837 to accede to Tate & Lyle's demands; the list included top officers of the General Municipal and Boilermakers (GMB), which represented Tate & Lyle workers; the International Union of Food Workers (IUF), an international coordinating body of unions in the food industry; and the Trades Union Congress (TUC), the British counterpart to the AFL-CIO. While some British leaders participated with the Staley workers at the shareholder meetings, other key leaders blamed the workers for the impasse in negotiations and demanded that the UPIU pressure the local to fire Ray Rogers and Jerry Tucker.

When Mark Brooks tried to use his contacts with British unionists to bring pressure on Tate & Lyle, he found a web of resistance. British union leaders "were very hostile to the campaign; they had a very negative reaction," recalled Brooks. Some leaders were irate that a mass mailing of Staley literature had gone out to British unions without their permission. "I sent a letter and a tape" to British local unions, recalled Rogers, "and we got a lot of donations. But man, we got the unions pissed off, [especially] the General Municipal and Boilermakers union, who had the Tate & Lyle local in Silvertown, England. . . . I got letters telling me, 'You can't be sending stuff overseas like that. Only the AFL-CIO can do that. You have to work through the UPIU International and the AFL-CIO.' . . . That's what ticked them off: 'You're not going through channels.'"

The British unionists were also angry that the mailing called for a boycott of Tate & Lyle's Domino subsidiary when they had not endorsed the call. Local 7837 had always expected that unions representing Domino workers would express some opposition to the boycott, but the local hoped the unions would see that it was in their interests to help the Staley workers beat back concessions.[22]

"The General Municipal and Boilermakers union and the International Union of Food Workers really got very upset," recalled Brooks, "and told the local that they were not going to cooperate with them any more." The GMB leaders, noted Brooks, "had a really good relationship with Tate & Lyle." In early 1992, when AIW 837 had sought information about Tate & Lyle's track record with unions, the inquiry was forwarded to GMB general secretary David Williams, who wrote to Tate & Lyle asking about the situation at Staley. The company's personnel director, R. Anderton, assured Williams that the company wanted to work with the union and sought only to "improve its business performance" by "making the Decatur plant more competitive." "The situation has a familiar ring to it!" Anderton wrote jovially to Williams. "Such necessary business objectives often meet employee resistance, as we both know!"[23]

Before the lockout Williams wrote to the IUF, which forwarded the information to the UPIU and Local 837, saying that labor relations with Tate & Lyle were "reasonable." Williams endorsed the company's demands for concessions from its British workers, arguing that "costs are continually having to be examined and indeed pruned, to maintain competitiveness." Tate & Lyle, Williams assured the American unionists, is "not an anti-union company."[24] Needless to say, Local 837's leaders were shocked.

In May 1994 Williams again wrote to IUF general secretary Dan Gallin that the company's demands were reasonable, that "Tate & Lyle wants to negotiate an honourable settlement to the dispute," and that the UPIU "should advise the local to dispense with the services of Ray Rogers and Jerry Tucker."[25] Top UPIU officials affirm that Williams deeply resented the Staley workers' leadership and thought their militant attitude was "improper." In addition, Williams was a personal friend of Tate & Lyle CEO Neil Shaw and owned a restaurant where Shaw sometimes dined.

Williams next took his campaign against Rogers and Tucker to the top of the British labor movement. After talking with Williams in November 1994, TUC general secretary John Monks wrote to his U.S. counterpart, AFL-CIO president Lane Kirkland (who passed the letter to Wayne Glenn), that British labor leaders were "recommending that the negotiating team should be changed, with the UPIU leadership exerting greater influence, and that the local should dispense with the services of the paid outside consultants Mr. Ray Rogers and Mr. Jerry Tucker." Monks made it clear that he thought the Staley workers should accept the company's terms and that a quick settlement could be reached if the UPIU had Rogers and Tucker fired and took control over negotiations. "Some of the working practices sought by the Staley management," wrote Monks, "are already widely adopted in the UK and many of our workers work them."[26] Gallin told the UPIU that the IUF would cease working with the Staley workers unless Rogers was fired.[27]

Since the UPIU International had long desired to rein in Local 7837, the British unionists' arguments simply reinforced Wayne Glenn's own predisposition to remove Rogers and Tucker.

Jerry Tucker Is Pushed Aside

In mid-November 1994 Wayne Glenn ordered Local 7837 to remove Tucker from the bargaining table. Both Glenn and Goss viewed Tucker as an outsider who was "meddling" in negotiations by advising the workers to resist concessions and as a major obstacle to ending the lockout. Glenn was also getting heat from United Auto Workers national leaders, who sought to isolate Tucker because he led the reform caucus in their own union. The impetus for Tucker's removal wasn't pressure from British or UAW union leaders, however; their arguments simply reinforced the UPIU national leaders' inclination to force Tucker out of negotiations.

Local 7837's leaders were outraged. "We're paying the bills and we'll decide who our advisers will be," said Watts. "Early in this fight our membership developed a strategy that utilized the expertise of Mr. Tucker," Watts and bargaining committee chair Dike Ferris wrote to Glenn. "For the international union to mandate Mr. Tucker's removal over the wishes of the 'highest tribunal,' the membership, is unconscionable. It is the position of our leadership (without dissent) and of our membership, that Mr. Tucker's presence and strategy is necessary at negotiations. It is strongly felt that deviating from this strategy could be detrimental to a favorable resolution."[28]

"It is time we tried new people and new tactics," Glenn angrily retorted. "What we need is for the officers of the local to cooperate." Glenn said that he was exercising his power under article 15 of the UPIU constitution: "Negotiations for collective bargaining agreements shall be subject to supervision by, and their terms, conditions and termination shall be subject to the approval of, the International President."[29] It would not be the last time that Glenn invoked the union's constitution to demand obedience.

Excluding Tucker was the result of an "agreement between the company and the UPIU," said Dike Ferris. "The company realized that Tucker was a little too strong for them. They wanted somebody who would start being conciliatory, somebody who would start really giving up stuff." "Clearly the international was trying to find ways to bring this thing to an end," said Tucker. "They were applying a lot of pressure; pushing me out of negotiations was the first installment of that." When the UPIU staff condescendingly told Tucker he could wait in the hall during bargaining sessions, he rejected the offer.

Although banned from the bargaining table, Tucker continued his weekly trips to Decatur, because the union had asked him to continue meeting with the executive board to plan strategy, attend the weekly solidarity meetings, and edit the *War Zone.*[30]

UNIVERSITY OF ILLINOIS PRESS

1325 South Oak Street • Champaign, IL 61820-6903
www.press.uillinois.edu • (800) 621-2736

Receipt

Customer Name _____

Number of books purchased ___2___

Author last name ___Cohen,___

___Ashby + Hawley___

_____

_____

Paid $___25.50___   By ☐cash ☐check ☐credit card

☐Visa ☐MasterCard ☐AmEx ☐Discover

Last four digits _____

Credit card statements will read "Chicago Distribution Center."

UIP staff initials ___ ___ Date ___4-22-12___

Meeting ___OAH___

Ray Rogers Is Fired

In early October, a month before Tucker's dismissal from the negotiating table, Glenn called Watts to Nashville to order him to fire Ray Rogers. Watts brought executive board members Dike Ferris, Bob Hull, and Gary Lamb for support. Glenn hadn't invited Rogers to the meeting, but surprisingly Rogers showed up to argue his case.

As they walked into Glenn's private office, the workers recoiled. "It was as big as my house," said Gary Lamb. The workers were stunned to see the most ostentatious display of privilege in the palatial office: a hot tub. Even a top-ranking UPIU official called the hot tub "a disgrace." (Word of the hot tub spread like wildfire when the workers returned to Decatur.)

The local officers were livid over the demand to fire Rogers. Watts argued that Rogers and his CCI staff had "been a great resource and organizational help . . . with strategies and methods of survival" and that they had helped "when no one else came forward."[31] In any event, the local was covering Rogers's services, so why should it matter to the international? Moreover, the local did not want marching orders from a president who had offered them minimal assistance thus far.

Wayne Glenn and Ray Rogers knew each other; the UPIU International, at the insistence of UPIU Local 14 in Jay, Maine, had hired Rogers to direct a corporate campaign during the 1987–88 International Paper strike.[32] Now Rogers pleaded his case. "Tell me what you are going to do," said Rogers, "if you want us out." Glenn responded, "We're going to do everything that needs to be done." Rogers replied, "What is it? Be specific. We're very specific about what we do." Glenn wouldn't answer, however, except to declare as Rogers left the room, "I don't have to take this. I'm an international president."

"They promised us the moon and stars," recalled Gary Lamb, but the Staley workers weren't buying it. That night "they took us out to a fancy dinner club and said, 'Order anything you want.' Glenn Goss was wining and dining us. Wayne Glenn had enough of us." The local officers were told that UPIU special projects director Mark Brooks could do everything Rogers was doing. "But Brooks would only do what Glenn told him to do," said Lamb. Firing Rogers meant that henceforth the UPIU would run the local's campaign—which meant sapping the momentum. Watts told the UPIU officials that he would not and could not override the members' decision to hire Rogers. "Rogers was hired by the floor," said Watts, "and only the floor could fire him. I won't do it."

At the January 10, 1995, union meeting, workers were deeply divided about Rogers. On the one hand, they were virtually unanimous in the opinion that Rogers had put their struggle on the map. Rogers had been with the local from the beginning, and his energy and commitment were contagious. Distribution of the CCI literature had made a deep impact both in Decatur and across the country. The series of national mailings to the sixty thousand union supporters on the CCI list had helped publicize the struggle and brought in much needed funds.

On the other hand, thought many members, the choice of State Farm as a corporate-campaign target had been a mistake. Only when the campaign switched to Miller beer, under Jerry Tucker's direction and over the objections of Rogers, had momentum picked up. "Timing is everything, and our timing was off," said Barrie Williams, in sentiments expressed by many members. Miller should have been targeted "from the get-go." Since the lockout Rogers had ceased coming regularly to Decatur; sometimes many months passed between his visits. Lorell Patterson said, "After a while, if he ain't doing nothing new, then why is he coming to the meeting? I haven't heard nothing new. I haven't heard nothing different."

"The screws were being tightened on us financially by the UPIU," said Mike Griffin, a Rogers supporter. If the UPIU withdrew support, the already tepid support from other internationals would dry up completely. "The price for the key to that door was getting rid of Rogers. The UPIU was pulling our strings."

After a lengthy debate, 60 percent of the workers voted to sever their relationship with Rogers. They were assured that the UPIU would commit its full resources until a fair contract was won. But few workers in the hall that night believed the UPIU's promises.

That month the presidents of the three Decatur locals decided that it was time to put the heat on the top leaders of the AFL-CIO to radically step up solidarity for the four thousand workers on the front lines of the corporate war on unions. Watts, Gates, and Solomon wrote to their three international presidents, asking them to kick off a "month-long vigil of solidarity" involving every AFL-CIO union. "Each union president could notify the appropriate people throughout their union who would spread the word that all members were welcome to tour the picket lines and bolster the fight for the 'American Dream' here in Decatur," wrote the three.[33] When they got no response, the Decatur unionists decided that, as the old saying goes, if the mountain won't come to Muhammad, then Muhammad must go to the mountain.

15

Mission to Bal Harbour

On a cold winter morning in February 1995, dozens of Road Warriors crammed onto a big old yellow schoolbus for a thousand-mile trip to sunny Florida. Although the workers were headed to a resort, this was no vacation. Taking their struggle up a notch, seventy Staley, Caterpillar, and Bridgestone/Firestone workers were on a mission to Bal Harbour, Florida, to confront their leaders at the annual winter meeting of the AFL-CIO's executive council. The workers were no longer battling just the corporations; they were now intent on challenging the top leadership of the labor movement.

Signs of Crisis

Over the preceding year and a half the Road Warriors had spoken in hundreds of union halls across the nation. Solidarity committees were organizing support in dozens of cities. Local unions and sympathetic individuals had donated huge sums of money—by the start of the year the figure for the Staley workers alone was more than $1.5 million. Scores of families had been adopted. The Miller beer campaign had been a success, and attention had turned to a national campaign to pressure PepsiCo to switch corn-sweetener companies. Over one hundred Staley workers and supporters had been arrested for nonviolent protests. One national mobilization had drawn five thousand people; the next, seven thousand.

The "Illinois Is a War Zone" slogan that the workers had adopted in 1992 seemed more on point than ever, with the Caterpillar and Bridgestone/Firestone workers on strike since June and July 1994, respectively. Close to four thousand workers in Decatur, a quarter of the blue-collar workforce, were walking picket lines.

But there were growing signs of crisis. In January the United Rubber Workers national strike fund was depleted and the union ceased paying its one hundred dollars a week in strike benefits. The URW was making no progress in negotiations but was nevertheless stunned when, on January 4, management announced it had hired 2,300 scabs to replace its 4,000 strikers in five plants. Between the scabs, strikers crossing their own lines, and management personnel doing assembly work, the company was reportedly maintaining production at the struck plants. Under U.S. law, the union workers could be permanently replaced with no hope of ever getting their jobs back unless a contract was negotiated by July 12, 1995 (one year after the strike began), or the union agreed to return to work without a contract.

The United Auto Workers, too, were facing stalled negotiations with Caterpillar. To keep their 12,000 members united, the UAW was paying three hundred dollars a week in strike benefits and funding the strikers' health insurance. As happened at Bridgestone/Firestone, however, management, scabs, and hundreds of unionists who crossed the lines were keeping production going.

While the URW and UAW locals had to endure the betrayal of having some of their own members cross the union picket line, this was not the case for the Staley workers. Local 7837 members were locked out and could not return to work, so there was no ready gauge of the number of workers who still stood strongly behind their union. But there were signs that support among the Staley workers was weakening. Large numbers had found other work and were dropping away from active participation in the struggle. Attendance at the weekly solidarity meetings was declining. The emotional and financial stress of eighteen months without a paycheck was bearing down on the workers and their families.

"Where the Hell Is the AFL-CIO?"

When they launched their struggle against Tate & Lyle, the workers had fervently believed that organized labor would come to their side. Thirty months later, Local 7837 was furious and bewildered by the AFL-CIO's inaction. "We were willing to lay *everything* on the line," said Gary Lamb. "I laid my twenty-seven years right on the line to fight this fight. [The locked-out workers] had centuries of seniority on the line because we felt *that* strongly about what we were fighting for. Yet the other internationals would not come to our aid in a *serious* manner."[1]

The backbone of Local 7837's support was coming not from the AFL-CIO Executive Council or from most of the federation's 72 international unions, 50 state federations, or 600 central labor councils but from local unions and solidarity committees. With hundreds of thousands of unionists living within a three-hour drive of Decatur, workers asked, "Why hasn't there been a national mobilization of tens of thousands?" Anger at the lack of support from AFL-CIO leaders was reaching volcanic proportions among the activists. In unionists' homes across Decatur, and in the Staley workers' Kandy Lane office and the union hall, day after day, week after week, workers would pound the table and exclaim, "Where the hell is the AFL-CIO?"

In the seven decades between the Civil War and World War II, working people repeatedly rose up in mass upheavals to assert their rights. Time and again, workers would strike and demonstrate for fair wages and working conditions, only to find the forces of the state arrayed against them. Strikes were crushed, with leaders arrested, activists beaten and shot in the streets, and union halls raided and demolished. Finally, with the massive labor uprising of the 1930s, unionism became a stable feature of American society. By the 1950s, 35 percent of the U.S. workforce was organized. In the 1950s and 1960s, millions of unionized workers, particularly in manufacturing, won steady improvements with each succeeding contract. Unprecedented benefits were achieved for millions of workers: pensions, health insurance, dental and vision coverage, cost-of-living increases to match inflation, profit-sharing bonuses, and supplemental unemployment benefits during periodic layoffs.

In the context of this postwar labor peace and these steady gains for unionized workers, the labor movement gradually changed. Although the process was uneven, in the 1950s, 1960s, and 1970s most national unions gradually became businesslike institutions. It would be too easy to blame either the rank-and-file union members or AFL-CIO leaders for this change, but both contributed to the rise of this hierarchical business unionism.

Thus most members began to disengage from their unions. With unions no longer battling for their very existence, most members didn't feel it necessary to be active. Most remained strongly pro-union, and large numbers would turn out at union meetings when contract negotiations were in progress. When necessary, workers reluctantly struck and stayed out as long as it took to defend their rights and win better wages and benefits. Still, the majority came to the union only when they had a grievance against the company, and attendance at monthly meetings dropped steadily.[2]

In the 1980s, Allied Industrial Workers Local 837 typified labor's evolution. As in most locals its size, monthly meetings drew only two dozen workers, a small fraction of the membership. Most who attended were union officers or stewards. Workers supported the union, but not enough to regularly attend meetings. The local did not involve itself in local social issues, such as civil rights, police brutality, or homelessness. So in the mid-1990s, when the Staley workers reached out for support from the fifty thousand local unions across the country, often they found locals much like their own had been in the 1980s— willing to send a small donation but uninterested in doing more or unable to mobilize their members to participate in Local 7837's corporate campaign or to come to Decatur for demonstrations.

As the members disengaged from their unions, most national leaders accepted and even welcomed the process. "At one point labor really had clout," recalled Larry Solomon. "They had people in there who came up through the ranks, had the knowledge, had the scars, knew exactly what to do to get the job done. Then we started losing those people, and people got [staff jobs] by appointments and politics, and it wasn't people who had ever fought in the plants . . . but were good old boys. . . . And the unions were really headed for trouble."

By the early 1990s labor had been in a free fall for over a decade, while its top leaders stood back and watched. Union density had fallen from 35 percent in 1955 to just 16 percent in 1990. The percentage of unionized manufacturing workers fell from a peak of 52 percent in 1958 to only 19 percent in 1993. The AFL-CIO had no strategy to deal with the rampant plant closings that devastated industrial cities across the United States in the 1980s and early 1990s, as corporations moved their plants first to southern states and then to Mexico and the Third World.

Organized labor remained tied to the Democratic party even as labor won few legislative gains and mostly fought a rearguard battle to defend what was already the weakest labor and social legislation in the industrialized world with the exception of apartheid South Africa. Opinion polls showed that the public viewed organized labor as corrupt, greedy, and out of touch with the average worker. A 1995 AFL-CIO–funded survey found that 65 percent of Americans felt unions were concerned only with their own members.[3]

Meanwhile, AFL-CIO president Kirkland and most top federation leaders bemoaned the loss of what they had viewed as a labor-management partnership in the 1950s and 1960s. In 1978, in a much publicized statement, UAW president Douglas Fraser decried the assault on American workers, declaring that "the leaders of the business community, with few exceptions, have chosen to wage a one-sided class war in this country—a war against working people, the unemployed, the poor, the minorities, the very young and the very old, and even many in the middle class of our society. . . . The leaders of industry, commerce and finance have broken and discarded the fragile, unwritten compact previously existing during a past period of growth and progress."[4]

Labor progressives agreed with Fraser that labor was under attack but responded by asking why the UAW president and other top AFL-CIO leaders had allowed the class war to be one-sided. Why, they asked, wasn't labor fighting back?[5] "Under Lane Kirkland," said Solomon, "labor was really being hit hard, and there was no strategy. In a word, the AFL-CIO under Lane Kirkland's leadership was decrepit." Instead of calling for workers to take to the streets in the tradition of the 1930s, AFL-CIO leaders advocated that unions accept

concessions and work closely with management in labor-management cooperation programs.

"My impression of Lane," said former Oil, Chemical and Atomic Workers
president Bob Wages, "was that he was a sincere person who didn't have a clue.
Leadership is not a word that springs to mind as a descriptive word of Lane's
tenure as president of the Federation." The labor movement under Kirkland,
echoed Service Employees International Union president John Sweeney, was
fast becoming irrelevant to its own members and was already "irrelevant to the
vast majority of unorganized workers in our country."[6]

Instead of welcoming the Staley fight as a model for the labor movement, Kirkland and other AFL-CIO leaders viewed Local 7837 as a threat to their passive,
accommodationist strategy and top-down leadership. Only a handful of national
labor leaders saw the fight as a crucial moment in labor history. The Staley fight,
declared Communication Workers of America vice president Jan Pierce, was a
"rank-and-file fight that really did have the potential of revitalizing the union
movement. Which just *scared the hell* out of national union leaders."

In a 1995 letter to UPIU and AFL-CIO leaders, Dave Watts eloquently summarized labor's crisis:

> All of us in the movement must take the responsibility that we have allowed
> big business and big government to take the teeth out of our organization. The
> AFL-CIO has always had the resources, talent and the ability to do the neces-
> sary things for workers everywhere. However, when some deny that politics and
> bureaucracy within this system don't exist, they are hiding behind denial. The
> AFL-CIO and most Internationals have failed to be a force to be reckoned with
> at the bargaining table and political arena. . . .
>
> There are too many extravagances and too many limousines that carry labor
> representatives around town with the rich and powerful, and we even do it with
> some people in politics that we in the working world would not even allow in
> our homes. The house of labor must decide which side it is really on, and do
> it soon. I know you have heard what we here in Decatur have adopted as our
> battle theme—"If not now, when? If not here, where? If not us, then who?" We
> also believe that if it is too hot in the kitchen for some, then get out and make
> room for the revitalized spirit that it is going to take to get the labor reform that
> workers worldwide so desperately deserve and need.[7]

On the Road Again

In January 1995, no top AFL-CIO officer had ever attended any of the national
demonstrations organized by the Staley workers or visited the local's picket lines.
Only one national union president had come to Decatur to express solidarity
with the workers, the URW's Ken Coss, who spoke at the rally on October 15,

1994.[8] The Staley workers were particularly incensed that Wayne Glenn, based just a few hundred miles away in Nashville, had not once visited Decatur in the nineteen months since A. E. Staley had locked out its workforce.

So the Decatur workers felt that, as Barrie Williams argued, "If they are unwilling to come to the War Zone and support us, then we are more than willing and able to move the War Zone to them."[9] The idea for the trip to the AFL-CIO Executive Council meeting in Bal Harbour, just north of Miami, sprang from a meeting of the Decatur Workers Solidarity and Education Coalition, and the three local presidents quickly embraced the idea. (The thirty-five member executive council, which sets policy for the AFL-CIO between its biennial conventions, consisted of the presidents of the largest unions in the United States.) The three local union presidents wrote a collective letter to their internationals' presidents, explaining that "the consequences are too great for us *not* to seek the solidarity of our sisters and brothers in Miami. . . . Our sole interest is to encourage open discussion about winning."[10] UAW president Owen Bieber wrote back urging the workers to stay home. Coming to Bal Harbour "serves no useful purpose," said Bieber.[11] Glenn echoed this sentiment: "You already have the support of the Executive Council. . . . The members would be better served if [only] the three local presidents came and used the funds that you would expend transporting the [others] to feed and clothe the needy families there at home."[12]

The unionists were undeterred. Gary Lamb rented the cheapest bus he could find, a "90-inch-wide bus because it was a big difference [in price] from the 110-inch bus." The workers crammed into the bus for the twenty-seven-hour drive to Miami. Since smoking wasn't allowed, "we had to stop every hour and a half," recalled Lamb. "Tensions were running high because people needed to smoke. . . . If I had the money, I would have gotten off and got me a plane back. . . . That's the closest I've ever come to going nuts." "We weren't sure where we were going to sleep," recalled Williams. So, as had become their custom, the Road Warriors brought sleeping bags in case they ended up sleeping "on the beach chasing sand fleas for lunch."

After the arduous trip, the group was rewarded with a pleasant climate but scanty accommodations. "We found this flophouse motel, the cheapest we could find," recalled Watts. "It had broken windows, tattered and torn drapes. We packed people into rooms—three, four, five people per room" for forty-nine dollars a night. Lamb said he "slept on the floor with the cockroaches—and Florida's got big cockroaches."

In a rare moment of comic relief, the workers discovered that, unbeknownst to the three union presidents, the motel had a topless swimming pool. "We checked all these people in and we were having a strategy meeting," recounted Watts. "A few folks were looking out the window and said, 'Hey, that gal's topless!' So everybody crowded over to the window. On top of that, it turned out that either side of the motel was a nude beach. Some of us hadn't ever even seen the ocean, let alone a nude beach. I had no idea!"

Across town, the thirty-five members of the AFL-CIO Executive Council and their aides were checking into the Bal Harbour Sheraton, one of the plushest beach resorts in the United States. As they checked into their rooms, which went for up to $325 a night, and suites (for twice that amount), they could look down from their balconies to the lagoon-style pool, replete with waterfalls, that snaked for hundreds of yards through ten acres of tropical gardens and palm trees and to the glistening Atlantic.

"That Was Opulence!"

When the Decatur unionists first arrived at the Sheraton, it was a watershed moment. "I was aghast," said Lamb. "You didn't see Fords and Chevies on the strip. You saw Mercedes and Jaguars—and new ones. That was opulence! The wages of union leaders are being paid by people who can't afford that kind of vacation."

At the close of each day's council session, the Sheraton's driveway would be packed with stretch limousines for the international union presidents. "There were more limos circling the meeting area than at the Academy Awards," noted Watts.[13]

> Each international president had their own limo—they didn't even put three or four of them in one limo. We're standing there, just in awe of all this, and here comes UPIU president Wayne Glenn. A group of us just happened to be standing near his limo, and we're looking right into his eyes. We're watching him get into that stretch limo, and he's doing everything he can to crawl down into his shirt. It's disgusting. The elaborate fanfare that takes place, the steak and lobster meals, drinks, clothing—it's not your five hundred–dollar suits, it's your five thousand–dollar suits—all of those things that are pure outright disgusting. And here we are trying to catch a city bus to get back to our flophouse.

While not prepared for the luxury, the Decatur contingent kept to its strategy for approaching the council. The meetings were closed to rank-and-file workers, so the seventy red T-shirted, blue-jeaned workers sporting union caps lined the hallways outside the meeting room. "We were good soldiers," Lamb recalled. "We did only what we were supposed to do. We mingled, were pleasant. Dave gave us direction before we went. . . . 'Grip and grin' and always wear red. Everyone else had suits on so we stood out like a sore thumb." Day after day, when council members took breaks, the Decatur folks were there to shake hands, talk with them, and hand them a leaflet. One flyer read: "We have come here from the picket lines in Illinois to appeal to you for support in our grim battles with three giant, worldwide corporations that are determined to slash the workforce, reduce our wages and benefits, and impose intolerable working conditions such as 12-hour shifts and weekend work. . . . Don't let the battle in Illinois become another PATCO. . . . We have earned the right to the full support of the AFL-CIO."[14]

Watts recalled standing in the hallway, trying to get into a conversation with the nation's top labor leaders: "They'd see us in the hall every time they'd take a break . . . and they knew we weren't going away. . . . It's been a long, long time since a lot of those folks have been by a burn barrel [on a picket line] . . . and some have never been by one, except to say, 'Hey, we're here to support you.' But they've never really had their ass on the line. [Our goal] was to bring that reality of the real grassroots movement to the highest authority."[15]

Even the most seasoned Road Warriors were apprehensive as they leafleted the labor leaders. "None of us knew what was going to take place," said Lamb. "Were they going to call the police on us and get us out of there?" To their relief, however, "mostly we were well received," said Lamb, although some officials criticized them for coming to Bal Harbour.[16] "Illinois AFL-CIO president Don Johnson flat-out told us," remembered Watts, "'You guys are an embarrassment to the labor movement.' We didn't follow protocols, we showed up at their big party, we're trying to get the AFL-CIO to do something, so Johnson says we're an 'embarrassment.' . . . At one point, Wayne Glenn confronted us in the hallway, yelling at us. He poked me right in the chest, saying 'I thought I told you people you couldn't do this!' I poked him right back in the chest, saying, 'Wayne, if this is the only way we can get anything done, then we're going to do it!'"

The Honor Roll of Solidarity

As they talked to union leaders and their aides in the hallways, the Decatur unionists appealed for aggressive leadership. Watts summarized their specific requests: "We needed more money and we needed support and we needed visibility. . . . We wanted a Solidarity Bank to support us as well as other strikes and lock-outs, so that the labor movement can actually come alive."[17] Solomon told the New York Times, "The AFL-CIO has the organization and national standing to raise money better than we can."[18]

The three locals requested that their presidents be allowed to speak to the council, but Glenn said it was out of the question. He told Watts that the executive council wasn't interested in hearing from an "upstart" local union president. Watts was unswayed and thought, "How can Wayne Glenn claim he can speak for us when he's never even been to Decatur?"

Eventually the council, mindful of the national media's extensive coverage of the Decatur workers, allowed the three Decatur presidents to attend a session but not to speak. Their three international presidents presented the request for a national strike fund, which was immediately turned down. "Theoretically, it is the dream of the labor movement to have a national strike fund," UMWA president Rich Trumka told the *New York Times* later that day. "But you have all the logistical problems. Some people, government workers, for example, don't [have the legal right to] strike and they say, 'Why should we participate?' Some unions are strapped and could not contribute to a fund, while others who could participate already have adequate strike funds."[19]

The council unanimously agreed to the Decatur unionists' second request—that all present sign an "Honor Roll of Solidarity," pledging to come to Decatur and to increase support. Solomon recalled that Watts again asked to speak: "Dave made the request and Lane Kirkland said, 'My understanding was that the international presidents were going to speak for you.' As Kirkland [rose and] turned, everyone rose out of their chairs and got in line to sign. . . . It was just like a dance class. . . . While they were doing that, no one was looking at us. It was theatrical. It was done so they wouldn't have to look at us."[20]

Later, when the three local presidents met with their international presidents, they raised a third issue. As is often the case, all three companies had hired unionized contractors—such as electricians, pipefitters, carpenters, and boiler-makers—during the lockout and strikes. The three local unions were furious that union workers were crossing their picket lines and thus helping the companies' efforts to break the unions. Said Watts, "We told them the situation, and they all said, 'By God, we're going to stop this.' They went straight into the executive council. Later they came out, heads bowed, and said, 'There isn't anything we can do.' The skilled trades' union presidents on the council blocked any action. They had no solidarity amongst themselves to help common workers' needs."

Although the rank-and-file workers were not permitted to speak, the council did welcome Vice President Al Gore and Secretary of Labor Robert Reich to make lengthy presentations. And the top Republican legislators in Illinois—including Governor Jim Edgar and Illinois House Speaker Lee Daniels—were wined and dined by their state's delegation to the AFL-CIO meeting. Although Edgar and Daniels were outspoken opponents of the labor movement, Chicago Federation of Labor president Michael Burton said that embracing them was the hallmark of "a new breed of labor leader today."[21]

Much to the frustration of the nonsmokers, the ride back to Decatur was again broken up every ninety minutes by smoke stops. Nevertheless, the atmosphere on the bus was buoyant. The seventy Road Warriors felt that they had achieved their purpose. They had confronted the AFL-CIO Executive Council and they had received promises that support would be escalated. The workers felt the trip to Bal Harbour, recalled Lamb, was "quite an event unto its own. The one thing that will linger in [the council members'] minds is that they are still accountable to the rank-and-file, and we can go anywhere they are." "We made labor history," Watts asserted. Although the leaders wouldn't let the rank-and-file workers speak, "unfortunately for the labor movement, no other unions have ever even gotten in the door!"[22]

On March 3 the fruits of the Bal Harbour solidarity pledge began to be reaped as UAW president Bieber and AFSCME president Gerald McEntee became the first AFL-CIO leaders other than Coss to make the pilgrimage to Decatur. On March 22, UMWA president Richard Trumka arrived, followed on March 27 by Kirkland, Coss (for his second trip), AFL-CIO secretary-treasurer Tom Donahue, SEIU president John Sweeney, USWA president George Becker, Machinists president George Kourpias, and Graphic Communications president James Norton. The March 27 delegation donated $40,000 to the URW and UPIU for their members. According to Watts, about half the international presidents who had signed the "Honor Roll of Solidarity" at Bal Harbour fulfilled their promise and came to Decatur.[23]

And on April 3—645 days after the Staley lockout and 560 days after the UPIU and AIW voted to merge—Wayne Glenn finally found his way to Decatur. He stopped by the picket line to have his picture taken for *The Paperworker*, shook hands with workers in the union hall, met briefly with Local 7837's officers, and left.

Palace Revolt

The Decatur workers' lobbying of the executive council added to an already tense session. At least ten of the thirty-five international union presidents argued that it was time for Kirkland to retire. The labor movement had suffered one defeat after another since he had become president in 1979, they argued. Its numbers were steadily declining, and new leadership was necessary to turn things around. Some suggested that Kirkland's second in command, Thomas Donahue, should take over. "The discussion of Lane Kirkland's future," argued John Sweeney in February 1995, "has really turned into a discussion of how we address all our difficulties."[24] Although shaken by the criticism and the size of the opposition faction, Kirkland refused to step down.

So the Decatur workers' confrontation with their top leaders had an unexpected result—it provided an additional inducement for the forces opposed to Kirkland to embark on the road to the first contested election in the AFL-CIO's history. The three labor conflicts "in Decatur contributed mightily to an atmosphere of a labor movement desperately needing change," said AFL-CIO staffer Joe Uehlein. "That whole dynamic contributed to the 'Where's Lane?' phenomenon. He was not there on the ground during these fights." The Kirkland foes "saw a labor movement that was on its final legs and that was amplified in Decatur. And something had to be done."

In its 108-year history, the AFL/AFL-CIO had seen just four presidents. By unspoken agreement of international union heads, presidents held the position for life. Beginning in 1886, Samuel Gompers served for thirty-eight years; William Green, for twenty-eight; and George Meany, for twenty-seven years, until he became terminally ill. In 1979 obedient convention delegates unanimously elected Meany's chosen successor, Kirkland, to lead the federation. Kirkland fully expected to serve until he died.

For fifty years, said longtime labor educator Harry Kelber, the AFL-CIO Executive Council "was conducted like a private club. No disagreement among its members was ever aired publicly."[25] After February 1995, however, that was no longer the case; the opposition forces coalesced around a slate to challenge Kirkland. The New Voices slate ran John Sweeney for president, Rich Trumka for secretary-treasurer, and AFSCME's Linda Chavez-Thompson for a proposed new position of executive vice president.

Each side lashed out at the other in the press. "To those leaders who've made careers out of urging caution and patience when action is required," Trumka declared, "we have only one message: Either lead or follow. Just get the hell out of the way!"[26] Kirkland responded by charging his opponents with a campaign of "mendacity and falsehood," and his supporters accused the dissidents of "dividing and diverting" the labor movement and of giving ammunition to antiunion employers.[27]

The AFL-CIO president is elected by convention delegates, not by membership vote. Nevertheless, Kirkland and Sweeney barnstormed the country in the spring of 1995, speaking at union gatherings in an attempt to build momentum for their campaigns. Speaking at a regional AFL-CIO meeting in Boston on June 2, Kirkland claimed that the AFL-CIO was doing everything it could to assist the Decatur unions. He blamed the "disaster" on the internationals and urged affiliates "who are locked in a struggle with an employer to come to the federation in a timely fashion and not when they've got a loser on their hands." When the crowd protested, Kirkland responded, "Boo if you like; that's the truth. If you can't take it, that's the way it is."[28]

Staley workers got an audiotape of the speech, and henceforth wherever Kirkland spoke, Staley workers or their supporters would chastise him for calling the struggle a "loser." Why, they demanded to know, had he provided ammunition to the companies? "Everywhere Kirkland went, the Staley struggle haunted him," said Mike Griffin, who organized many of the confrontations.[29] When the

AFL-CIO president denied making the statement, supporters would hold the tape in the air and shout challenges: "Then let's play this tape so everyone can hear whether you really said it or not."

On June 12, the seventy-three-year-old Kirkland buckled under the pressure and announced that he would step down at the executive council's August 1 session and name Tom Donahue as his successor. The opposition slate already had its campaign in full gear, however, and refused to back down and accept Donahue. "The train has left the station," said AFSCME spokesperson Bob Harmon.[30]

For the embattled Decatur workers, the internal debates within the AFL-CIO held promise. Could the federation transform itself and deliver tangible support for workers on labor's battlefields?

16

Still in the Fight

As the triumphant Road Warriors returned from Bal Harbour, they faced another challenge. Former bargaining committee chair Jim Shinall and his supporters reasserted their push for an end to the lockout on the company's terms. Two years into the lockout, as thousands of supporters converged on Decatur for a rally to mark its second anniversary, members prepared to vote again on the company's contract.

The Surrender Crowd Emerges

When the workers were locked out in June 1993, none of them imagined that their fight would last so long. When unemployment benefits ran out in March 1994, many were able to subsist on a combination of part-time jobs, savings, the union's food bank, sixty dollars a week in picket pay, and their spouse's paycheck. As discussed earlier, many were "adopted" by supporters and received monthly checks for six hundred dollars.

But some workers had to find full-time jobs to pay their bills. Jim Shinall was one of them. A few months after the tumultuous January 1994 union meeting that pitted him against Dan Lane, Shinall opted to resign as bargaining committee chairperson and take a job driving trucks for a firm that crossed the Staley picket lines, although Shinall himself never crossed. Denton Larrimore, who shared Shinall's view that the union should accept the company's terms, also resigned from the bargaining committee. "We knew some people had to get jobs," said an angry Dave Watts. "But getting a job didn't mean leaving the fight. We never asked people to leave the fight. . . . When you take a job, that doesn't relieve you of your responsibilities and obligations to your union brothers and sisters still in the fight. [Shinall] resigned not only from his union position but from this fight as well."[1]

Shinall soon devised a plan that would bring the conflict to a halt. At a November 1994 union meeting he and his supporters raised a motion mandating that the leadership bring back a contract, regardless of its content, for a membership vote. The motion contravened the conventional strategy, which gave a local's bargaining committee the authority to decide whether a proposal was worthy of a membership vote. When the members rejected the motion, Shinall sought advice from Danny Wirges, now the UPIU Region 9 assistant director. Wirges advised Shinall and others on a strategy for ending the fight. "My phone rang off the hook," recounted Wirges. "Jim Shinall and other folks were the ones who said, 'Hey, the battle's over. It's time to get the best we can and move on and save the jobs we can.' I characterize them as the ones who had common sense. Dave Watts and the Kandy Lane people lost touch with reality. . . . You could see the handwriting on the wall. They needed new leadership. They needed somebody who could pull the membership together. I'm glad Jim Shinall had the guts enough to do what he did."

Through the early months of 1995 Shinall and his supporters worked feverishly to build support for their faction. They told workers in the union hall and at the picket lines that the fight had been lost and it was time to sign the company's contract. By March 1995 Shinall and his followers gauged that it was time to raise the motion again. They argued that the membership had a democratic right to see the company's best offer; there had been no contract vote since October 6, 1992, and it was necessary to see where the membership stood. Let those who wanted to take a negotiated severance payment get their money and move on with their lives, they asserted; let those who wanted to return to work at Staley go back under the company's terms.

With the December 1994 union elections the activists had won a majority on the nine-member executive board and controlled all five bargaining committee seats. Now a large majority of the elected leaders angrily opposed Shinall's motion.[2] Week after week they had reported honestly and in great detail about every bargaining session, they argued, and the company had refused to budge on a single important issue. Passing the motion would send a signal to the company that the union was weak and divided. The union would win a fair contract only by standing united and keeping the pressure on Staley's customers, such as Pepsi.

The bargaining committee distributed a passionate two-page statement calling for the membership to reject the motion:

> [The company's contract] represents a surrender by the local. . . . Most of the pressure to [pass the motion] is coming from members who have no intention of ever going back to work at Staley, and many have admitted that they just want "their" [severance] money. This is unfair to those of us who will return to Staley under the harsh working conditions. . . . The company is encouraged by this

type of divisive action on the floor. They want us fighting among ourselves for the "crumbs." . . . Our fight is one of principle. We are fighting for dignity and respect as much as money for a selected few. Millions of workers in this country and around the world have contributed to this struggle. They know that our fight is their fight. They have seen too many surrenders to corporate aggression. They know it is tough on us here. That's why their support is growing. We can't let them down. . . . Our membership should reject efforts to "turn tail" and run from a fight we have waged so valiantly and well.

The Women's Support Group discussed the union's crisis, and twenty-nine wives signed a letter that was read at the members-only meeting on March 14, 1995:

> We feel that we are as much a part of this union and this fight as you and there-fore, we want everyone to know that we are not ready to give up. . . . We are not ready to see our lives centered around 12-hour rotating shifts where we no longer have a family or community life. We want our children to know their fathers and mothers as part of an active family, not just as a paycheck. We want healthy partners in our marriages—not ones who have been destroyed by long hours and unsafe working conditions. . . . We have watched you suffer from depression, anger, frustration, and heartache. . . . We stand by you now and will continue to do so, even if it takes many more months to reach a fair and just contract. . . . We do not want you to cave in and give in to such underhanded tactics that are being forced down your throats by disgruntled members, some of whom won't be returning to the plant anyway. We want you to hold your heads up high and continue fighting for what is right. . . . With the multitude of people and other unions across the country helping us, how can we face them and the entire labor movement if we give up now?[3]

By a vote of 259 to 115, however, the workers mandated the leadership to bring back a contract for a vote. Shinall and his surrender faction had won their first victory.

The activists were deeply dejected. Some hoped that a visit from Lane Kirk-land and six international presidents scheduled for March 27—fulfilling the promise they had made in Bal Harbour—would inspire the workers to stay in the fight, but few were optimistic.

On June 12 the local's leadership called key Midwest solidarity activists to come to Decatur for a strategy session. Once again Father Mangan opened the St. James rectory basement. Now that Miller had broken with Staley, the meeting was called to make plans to escalate the Pepsi campaign. (As will be discussed in the next chapter, PepsiCo, one of Staley's main customers, was the union's next corporate-campaign target, and its contract with the company expired December 31, 1995.)

The session began with a discussion on the situation in Decatur, however, and the workers expressed their anguish. "I'm looking at the floor," said Gary Lamb, referring to the membership, "and they've almost quit."[4] Whereas six to eight hundred regularly attended union meetings in 1993 and 1994, now just two or three hundred workers attended. Seventy-eight had retired, and many more had taken other jobs to support their families. Families were getting desperate as their credit-card bills skyrocketed and hospital bills mounted, and too many were falling into severe debt. "The floor is more hostile since last winter," echoed Dike Ferris. "They blame the bargaining committee. The floor is ready to accept the company's package. We need to figure out how to get a majority of the floor back on our agenda—winning a contract that's fair for all."

"Some members are still solid," argued Mike Griffin. "We need to organize this membership." "We won't last six months," replied Dan Lane. "We need a thirty- to forty-five-day plan on how we can win a contract we can live with." "The company is stalling in negotiations," said Dave Watts. "Pepsi is waiting to see how the floor votes when we bring a contract back."

Adding to the activists' demoralization was the May announcement that the Rubber Workers were ending their ten-month strike. Under U.S. law, if a contract cannot be negotiated within one year of a strike, then the company has the right to permanently replace its workforce, so the union felt compelled to accede. The company announced that only a small number of union workers were needed, however, and the rest would be put on a waiting list and get their jobs back only as scabs quit.

At this juncture the Staley activists were fighting on multiple fronts besides their battle with the company. They were fighting the Shinall-led surrender crowd within the local. They were fighting UPIU president Wayne Glenn, who had pushed Jerry Tucker out of negotiations and pressured the local to fire Ray Rogers. They were fighting a complacent AFL-CIO leadership that had not come forward with any substantial support. They were fighting the members of other unions who were crossing their picket lines. They were fighting the city of Decatur for the right to have picket shacks and picket lines. And they were fighting against horrendous labor laws that placed them at a constant disadvantage.

Despite the many fronts of opposition, however, it was time for the local to build for another national rally to mark the two-year anniversary of the lockout.

The June 25 Rally

Watts once again wrote to the dozens of solidarity committees, asking the union's most active supporters to pull out all the stops. "Two days before the rally," wrote Watts, "we return to the bargaining table in search of a negotiated solution to this conflict." A large turnout at the protest and an escalation of pressure on Pepsi would "send a powerful message" to management at the bargaining session.[5]

Watts had hoped to precede the national rally with a debate between the two candidates for the AFL-CIO presidency, John Sweeney and Tom Donahue—why not have them debate their respective programs for revitalizing the labor movement in the heart of the Illinois war zone?[6] Sweeney's New Voices slate had promised an aggressive solidarity effort for striking or locked-out unions. Rich Trumka had agreed to be the rally's keynote speaker, and Donahue had also asked to speak. But when Wayne Glenn got wind of the proposed debate, he squashed it. "This type of invite detracts totally from our effort to provide unity of support for our fight against Staley," declared Glenn.[7]

Instead, on June 24 the three Decatur local presidents convened a "War Zone labor conference" to discuss Decatur's labor battles and to pass resolutions to present at the upcoming AFL-CIO convention.[8] Watts kicked off the rally, attended by 170 activists from twenty-two states, by declaring, "With a global economy, multinational corporations have a solidarity of their own—greed and extortion of workers is giving the corporations more profits. Workers have to follow that example. They've got the money. We've got the *numbers.*"[9]

On Sunday, June 25, supporters from across the country arrived in Decatur for the city's fourth national protest against union-busting in two years. Seven thousand activists assembled at the three union halls and converged to walk through town to the Decatur Civic Center. In blistering ninety-four-degree heat, the workers marched along the four-mile route past the Caterpillar, Bridgestone/Firestone, and Staley plants.

When they passed the Staley gates where the police had pepper-sprayed hundreds of workers exactly a year before, the crowd's chants and shouts rose to a fever pitch. Many paused at the Staley gate to scream their anger at the company, but then the demonstrators marched on. As with the October 1994 march and rally, the three unions planned no civil disobedience. Facing injunctions, the threat of huge fines, and false threats from the police that union leaders could be personally bankrupted if they organized illegal demonstrations, and with Glenn and his staff continuing to pressure Watts against further plant-gate rallies, the unionists felt they had no recourse but to keep their protest legal.

From a distance the marchers were a sea of scarlet, with thousands wearing red shirts symbolizing their solidarity with the three embattled unions. Scores of unions brought huge banners declaring their unity. A spirit of militancy was in the air as the activists chanted, "We Are. . . . Un-ion!" and "Scabs Out, Union In!" and repeatedly shouted "Solidarity!" "It's rejuvenating; it's exciting; it makes me proud to be in a union to come to something like this," asserted a Madison unionist. "When you see this sort of solidarity," declared another, "this sort of commitment, it makes you feel like—despite all the negative news—there's a real future for the labor movement."[10]

At the end of the march the protesters listened to AFL-CIO leaders denounce the aggression of the three multinationals. The 3½-hour rally, occurring four months before the AFL-CIO convention, rapidly took on the character of a campaign debate. Trumka gave the most thunderous speech of the day and, unlike AFL-CIO secretary-treasurer Donahue, received repeated standing ovations.[11] Trumka called for a "new kind of labor movement. . . . We can't afford to think of ourselves as rubber workers, or auto workers, or chemical workers. What we are is union. What we are is family. What we are is brothers and sisters fighting to protect our way of life!"[12]

The passionate, tear-inducing speeches by children of the striking and locked-out workers were another highlight. Ten-year-old Bailey Elliott, the daughter of a Bridgestone/Firestone striker, told the audience, "The reason my mom helps with the unions is because she says, 'You're nobody unless you help the guy next to you up the same hill.'" Staley worker Ron VanScyoc's ten-year-old son, Joey, said, "When you decide to be a worker, the bosses will try to steal your job, your dignity, and your life. . . . I will have to be strong of mind and strong of body because I will have to fight for the right to be a human person. . . . Tate & Lyle has stolen my childhood and I won't let them steal the rest of my life." Mary Ferriell, whose dad worked at Caterpillar, said, "It's going to affect everyone, and some people fail to realize this. Young people are going to be made to work for substandard wages in unsafe working conditions. That's if the unions give up the fight, but you haven't and don't plan to, and for that I thank you."[13]

The Reverend Jesse Jackson's forty-minute speech galvanized the crowd. "It's not about black and white; it's about wrong and right," roared Jackson. "Don't let them divide us by race. They use my skin color and put it over your problem and shoot both of us with one bullet. The American dream is under assault. We who march are its defenders. . . . As Calvary was the defining place for Christians, as Selma was the defining place for the civil rights movement, let Decatur be the defining place for economic justice!" Jackson hit a nerve when he called for direct action. "It's not enough to march in Decatur," he declared. "We should be marching in Detroit and Chicago" and, he said, in twenty-five other American cities, every night for a week, "marching over bridges at rush hour," not on Sunday with a police permit.

As the rally progressed, national and local union leaders presented checks to the Decatur unionists for more than fifty thousand dollars. Yet the event left the Staley workers simultaneously uplifted and dispirited. One national labor leader after another called for more and bigger labor mobilizations, yet none brought more than a few dozen of his own workers with him. Mike Griffin commented that "the demonstration was about the same size as the one in 1994, but it should have been—and could have been—three times bigger. The problem is that the AFL-CIO leadership did not build the march."[14] Each national labor figure called for greater militancy, but none presented a plan for winning the three battles. In particular, none pledged resources to stop production through mass plant-gate protests. Many called for building labor-community coalitions, but none had thrown their unions' resources into the corporate campaign targeting PepsiCo.

An exasperated Dave Watts spoke to the crowd as the rally came to an end. "I welcome and honor all these international presidents," said Watts. "But it's got to go further than dog and pony shows. I am here asking . . . all these people that are here, the secretary-treasurer of the AFL-CIO, the different internationals that are here and those that *should* be here—we need a plan that works. Workers need to stand up, but they can't stand up alone, and the help that we are getting is not enough."[15] Wayne Glenn later admonished Watts for publicly "berating leaders of the labor movement. . . . If you want to get people's help and assistance, you cannot jump on them because they are not doing more."[16] But Watts's patience had been exhausted. Decorum had resulted in only meager support from the AFL-CIO's top leaders. The local was staring defeat in the face, and this was no time for politeness.

The Trial of the Decatur Fifty

The day after the rally, seven members of the Decatur Fifty went on trial. The union supporters, the reader will recall, had been arrested on June 4, 1994, for nonviolently blocking the Staley west gate. Most of the fifty had determined to stand trial rather than plead guilty, using their testimony to educate the public: they would put Tate & Lyle and the lockout on trial.[17]

The state's attorney decided to break the fifty into four groups. A year after the sit-down, the first group—spouse Mona Williams, the nuns Kathleen Desautels and Mary Kay Flanigan, Chicago solidarity activists C. J. Hawking and Steven Ashby, Kandy Lane volunteer organizer Doug Kandt, and Decatur AFSCME member Mark Daley—finally came to trial. Throughout the three-day trial the small courtroom was packed with over forty union members and spouses in their signature red shirts. Jury selection took up most of the first day; the state's attorney, Jay Scott, eliminated potential jurors who were in a union, had been in a union, had a relative in a union, knew anyone in a union, or had regularly read about the labor conflicts in the newspaper.

On the second day, after opening statements, Scott moved for a mistrial because the defendants' attorney, Melinda Power, from Chicago's West Town Community Law Office, had made "prejudicial remarks in her opening statement." Scott was referring to Power's description of the lockout as unjust and illegal.

The judge denied the motion. The third day the judge rejected a second motion for a mistrial, this one because, the prosecutor complained, the defendants and their attorney had spoken to local media and received sympathetic coverage. "The lockout is the real crime, and the company is the criminal," Power had told the media, including the three regional television stations, which carried her comments on the nightly news. "Staley/Tate & Lyle should be on trial for the injustice they have inflicted on these workers, their families, and the Decatur community."

As the seven defendants testified, each was able to weave in the hardships of the lockout and the political and spiritual convictions that had brought them to the demonstration. Mark Daley testified that he felt compelled to join the sit-down out of his conviction for workers' rights and to support his stepfather, a Staley worker. Sister Kathleen Desautels proclaimed that her faith required her to take a stand in solidarity with the workers. When Steven Ashby testified, the judge threatened him with contempt of court three times for "making speeches" about Local 7837's broad national support and for refusing to answer yes or no to the prosecutor's questions.

Mona Williams gave heartfelt testimony about the the lockout's harm to her family, especially her teenage daughter, who had extensive medical problems. She read a statement of remarkable honesty and poignancy:

> Twenty-three years ago I stood in the Macon County Court House as a rape victim. I stand here today as the accused. I will tell you the feelings of being violated then are not a lot different from the violations I feel from Tate & Lyle today. The main difference is that this violation has affected all of the workers and their families and this entire community. Being thrown out on the street by this company with no warning or explanation has taken away our right to work, our paychecks, our health insurance, and our basic lifestyles as we knew them. It makes us feel like we are the criminals, when in fact we are the victims. We may lose our home, our car, and everything else we own, but the two things I refuse to give to this company are my family and our dignity.[18]

After deliberating for two hours, the jury returned a not guilty verdict on three of the four charges: obstructing a police officer, mob action, and conspiracy to commit mob action. These charges carried a maximum penalty of a $1,000 fine and 364 days in jail. On the least serious charge, criminal trespass, the defendants were ordered to pay a $205 fine. Upon hearing the verdict, supporters filled the courtroom with shouts of "Solidarity!" The seven defendants and dozens of supporters poured into the hallway, linked arms, and joyously sang "Solidarity Forever" while reporters surrounded them. Television and newspaper coverage uncharacteristically echoed the defendants' declaration of victory, much to the chagrin of the state's attorney.

"For anyone who is familiar with the previous trials which have taken place in Decatur, this trial is a historic event," said a jubilant Sister Kathleen Desautels. "Each time the Staley workers have come to trial in Decatur, they've been found guilty. We hope this victory will give union members courage to keep fighting for justice." The remaining defendants never went to trial; charges were dismissed after the labor conflict ended in December 1995.

The Union Votes

A few days after the June 25 rally, the bargaining committee received a contract proposal from Tate & Lyle and scheduled a vote for July 9 and 10. The only changes from the October 1992 proposal were worsened conditions. Management would have unlimited rights to subcontract, leaving only 349 union jobs in the plant, with a further reduction in two years to 210. The twelve-hour shifts would rotate every six days, worse than the thirty-day rotation in the rejected 1992 contract. Long-standing seniority, health and safety, grievance, and arbitration provisions would be gutted.

All on the bargaining committee and nearly all on the executive board recommended rejection. Surprisingly, even Glenn Goss advised that the workers could do better. The activists handed out a flyer summarizing and attacking the contract: "Although we sometimes disagree, we are all fighting for the same fair, just contract with integrity. Let's not let our own individual needs overshadow those of the membership as a whole and lead us to play into Staley's waiting game—where the company gets what it's wanted from the beginning, to watch us divide and self-destruct. So keep the faith and continue with our greatest strength—our *unity*."[19]

"With that kind of a rotation you wouldn't know if you were working or sleeping," said Robert Traughbel as he voted to reject the contract. "They'd take all your human rights away when you walked in that gate. . . . They could take your job away at any time and farm it out."[20] "They really didn't want us back with a contract like that," added Art Dhermy. "If you unwrap it, it smells like an outhouse in summertime."[21]

Managers assumed that they could "get the people who were close to retirement . . . to sign on," said Dike Ferris. Support in the community was waning, and this fact was bound to affect the vote. "The longer it went," noted Congressman Glenn Poshard, "especially with other companies in town experiencing similar types of situations, I think the community started feeling shell-shocked. And after a time, they just wanted it over with."

As the ballots were counted late on the evening of July 10, more than fifty workers nervously stood in the union's hallway waiting for the results. Dave Watts smiled as he announced that, with 93 percent of the members voting, the contract had been rejected by 57 percent, 318 to 241.[22] The workers screamed with delight, roared "Solidarity!" cried, and hugged one another. "Our members have demonstrated that they are committed to this fight," Watts told the press, "and that we will not allow Staley to starve us into submission. The union's members have spoken, and they clearly aren't ready to give up this struggle."[23] That night the union faxed solidarity committees across the country that they were still in the fight, and asked for an escalation against PepsiCo. Now "the focus has to be on Pepsi," said Lamb. "[The pressure] must come down like it never has before."[24]

17

In the Fast Lane

After Miller Brewing Company dropped Staley as a supplier, Local 7837 focused its corporate campaign on another Staley customer, PepsiCo. The union knew that Staley was vulnerable; management could not afford to keep losing major customers. In the fall of 1995, however, Dan Lane, feeling the struggle was faltering, launched a sixty-five-day hunger strike to galvanize supporters.

Taking on Pepsi

The unionists were ecstatic when Miller announced in October 1994, after a six-month pressure campaign, that it would no longer purchase corn sweetener from Staley. Jerry Tucker, who continued to make weekly trips to Decatur even though UPIU president Glenn had pushed him off the bargaining committee, initially recommended a dual campaign against two other customers, Pepsi and Coca-Cola, with hopes of whipsawing one against the other. Pepsi accounted for 30 percent of Staley sales of high-fructose corn syrup, and Coca-Cola, for another 15–20 percent. In March 1995, however, when neither company had budged, the local narrowed its focus to Pepsi alone. "Staley can continue this lockout only if its customers continue subsidizing this outrageous conduct," declared Dave Watts. "We want Pepsi to understand that its reputation and the image of its restaurant subsidiaries will be tarnished if it continues to aid Staley's attack on our members."[1]

The local also engaged the one consistent support offered by the UPIU International—the special projects department, headed by attorney Mark Brooks, who embraced the anti-Pepsi campaign. "Pepsi accounts for a giant share of Staley's business," Brooks explained. "It has a generally poor relationship with unions and with other activist groups. And it owns three restaurant chains which depend on the goodwill of their customers and are vulnerable to customer leafleting."[2]

The local knew that Pepsi's annual contract with Staley expired December 31, 1995. The Road Warriors flooded their supporters with requests to call Pepsi's toll-free number and ask the company to end the contract, and the solidarity groups made Pepsi their highest priority. As they had done during the Miller campaign, supporters perused newspapers for advertisements of festivals, art fairs, parades, and other community events, looking for Pepsi sponsorship. In the spring and summer months in particular, large numbers of outdoor events drawing huge crowds are held in cities across the country. Posing as a college student researching a paper, Rose Feurer, a solidarity coordinator in St. Louis, talked to a Pepsi spokesperson to cull information on the community sponsorships. In April 1995 Feurer informed the local:

> Pepsi places great value on the community involvement programs. [Their spokesperson] talked at length about how this sort of strategy has brought Pepsi up to a 47% share in St. Louis, compared to 28% for Coke. (Nationwide that market share is about 38% for Coke versus around 35% for Pepsi.) He called sponsorship a "key strength" in their marketing. He gave several examples of how sponsorship of events was meant to reinforce images of Pepsi in commercials. . . . He emphasized that the Midwest's market share for Pepsi in general is much better than Coke's, in part because of this "involvement" strategy. . . . His comments about the extreme value they place on "involvement in the African-American community" are important to [the union's] strategy.[3]

Solidarity activists found that PepsiCo sponsored events and organizations in cities across the United States, including outdoor jazz, blues, and gospel concerts; food festivals; African American cultural fairs; county and state fairs; boys and girls clubs; the Boy Scouts, Cub Scouts, and Girl Scouts; boat races; kite festivals; and sporting events. In the summer and fall of 1995, they handed out many thousands of flyers at scores of events. A flyer headlined "Pepsi-Cola: Stop Staley's War on Workers" featured a photo of police pepper-spraying Staley workers. Often these solidarity activists were themselves harassed. At a kite festival in St. Louis, for example, committee members were photographed, harassed, ordered to leave, and threatened with arrest by Pepsi officials. The activists stood their ground, insisting on their First Amendment rights to operate on public property, and after consulting with the police, the Pepsi officials backed off.

Local 7837 sent lists of local Pepsi bottlers to each solidarity committee, asking them to urge the bottlers to pressure Pepsi to drop Staley. Some committees organized delegations of community, religious, and union activists to meet with bottlers. In Chicago, for example, a delegation of clergy led by Rev. Jesse DeWitt, a retired United Methodist bishop and the president of the Chicago Interfaith

Committee on Worker Issues, met with bottlers. The solidarity committees periodically wrote to the bottlers and to CEO Wayne Callaway detailing every action they had taken in the escalating campaign.

Committees asked local unions to organize their members to write, fax, or call Pepsi headquarters, threatening to stop drinking Pepsi products if the company continued to support Staley financially. Union leaders pressuring PepsiCo included Henry Bayer, director of AFSCME Council 31, based in Chicago, who wrote to Callaway: "If I have not received an affirmative response from you by Friday, August 4 [1995], it is my intention to ask each of our 225 local unions in Illinois to refrain from serving Pepsi products at picnics and other union-sponsored functions, and to ask our 80,000 members and their families to stop buying Pepsi products."[4]

The Kandy Lane center sent the support groups a template that could be copied onto sheets of labels and used as stickers. The two-by-four-inch stickers reproduced labor cartoonists Huck and Konopacki's rendition of the 1994 pepper-spraying: the Staley workers being assaulted by a Pepsi can emitting pepper spray. Often supporters put the stickers on Pepsi machines in service stations, on college campuses, and in high schools. The stickers found their way onto every Pepsi vending machine in the rest stops on the highways leading into Decatur.

The Pepsi campaign became a major activity of the Student Labor Action Coalition groups that were quickly being organized on campuses across the country. When Local 7837 called for a weekend of anti-Pepsi leafleting on April 14–15, 1995, the SLAC network organized significant student participation. Student groups also built ties with other groups who were angry at Pepsi. In Madison, Wisconsin, SLAC teamed up with the Free Burma Coalition, which was protesting Pepsi's ties to the repressive Burmese government, to pressure the University of Wisconsin's food service to ban Pepsi. The protesters dumped Pepsi on the pavement to express outrage at the company's antiworker and anti–human rights actions.

Three targets overseen by Mark Brooks were PepsiCo's Kentucky Fried Chicken, Taco Bell, and Pizza Hut subsidiaries.[5] Larger cities often had dozens of the three franchises. Brooks researched the franchises, including records of their health infractions, and designed flyers for national distribution. By March 1995 supporters in seventy cities were leafleting customers—and local franchise owners were calling Pepsi headquarters with complaints. For example, a Taco Bell flyer was headlined "Hepatitis and Food Poisoning Linked to Taco Bell" and cited recent outbreaks in five cities. Taco Bell unleashed its lawyers on the UPIU, repeatedly threatening a lawsuit, but the flyer was factually correct, so the union was on safe ground.

In April 1995 the AFL-CIO endorsed April actions against Pepsi, sending a mailing to its sixty-five largest central labor councils, and in August 1995 endorsed a week of action. But the endorsements brought little in the way of grassroots activism. Though it found support from a handful of activist CLCs, the local's corporate campaign continued to rely principally on the solidarity committees, student groups, and newly formed Jobs with Justice chapters. Over the previous two years, Jobs with Justice had grown significantly as a national grassroots network of labor and community activists. In late March 1995 Staley workers had addressed the JwJ convention in Cleveland, speaking to activists from fifty cities and receiving substantial commitments to work on the Pepsi campaign.

Corporate Campaigns and the Law

Throughout the Miller and especially the Pepsi campaigns, the Kandy Lane organizers and some of the solidarity committees had an ongoing disagreement with Mark Brooks. Brooks, trained as a labor lawyer, was adamant that the committees not call for a secondary boycott of the customers. In 1947 big business had succeeded in getting Congress to pass the Taft-Hartley Act, which amended the 1935 Wagner Act with severe restrictions on unions. As discussed in chapter 8, Taft-Hartley mandates that a union boycott only the products of a company directly involved in a labor dispute. Unions are still able to launch campaigns targeting a company's customers or clients, so long as they do not call for boycotts.

As with the Miller campaign, the Staley workers did not technically call for people to boycott PepsiCo. Rather, Local 7837 asserted that it was simply educating the public about Pepsi's complicity in Staley's union-busting and asking people to tell Pepsi to drop Staley as a supplier. Brooks repeatedly mailed the support groups instructions for their volunteers. He asked that all volunteers sign a statement agreeing to the instructions and mail the statement back to the UPIU. The instructions told the volunteers not to use signs, banners, sandwich boards, or balloons with a printed message while handing out Miller or Pepsi flyers. They must not organize rallies, informational picket lines, marches, or demonstrations. Supporters could not engage in conversations while leafleting. "In particular," wrote Brooks to the solidarity committees, "we request that if you are asked why we are distributing the leaflets, please respond only 'please read the leaflet' or 'as a public service.' *Please do not give any other response.*"[6]

Brooks recalled that he spent an "enormous amount of time" debating tactics with leaders of the solidarity groups and with the Kandy Lane organizers. "To me, it's a no-brainer," said Brooks. "The question is, do you hand your enemies a weapon that they can use against you for no good reason? Rather than spend enormous time and money defending a lawsuit that we are going to lose, I would rather take that energy and [focus] on inflicting damage on our enemies."[7]

The Staley workers and the solidarity activists found Brooks's assertion that activists handing out flyers could not even explain the issues to people to be an overly strict interpretation of the law. Further, they felt that time was not on their side; the union could not hold out indefinitely. Visible actions against Staley customers had a benefit, they felt, that outweighed the legal risks. Nonviolent direct actions, they further argued, galvanized supporters by making it clear that this was a not an ordinary labor-management conflict. Such actions were far more likely to garner media publicity and to provoke concern in the boardrooms of Staley's corporate customers.

Many of the solidarity committee members were longtime labor activists and had experience with the inherent conservatism of labor lawyers. Many of them agreed with a coal miner whom Tom Geoghegan quotes in his book *Which Side Are You On?* Describing a miners' wildcat strike, Geoghegan explained that in his role as a Mine Workers lawyer, he had to tell the workers to obey the law, however unjust. "We whispered to the men, politely: *Please,* go back to work. . . . We just wanted them to behave." But a miner set the lawyer straight: "Boy, your job as the union lawyer is not to keep us out of jail. Your job as the union lawyer is to get us *out* of jail."[8]

On the weekend of July 15–16, forty-five Chicago activists distributed ten thousand flyers at the grand reopening of Navy Pier. The revitalization of the pier as a mall and entertainment center was a large-scale joint municipal-business effort to increase tourism. Pepsi was a major sponsor and had exclusive rights to sell its soft drinks at the site. While the supporters leafleted, a plane chartered by the UPIU flew overhead pulling a huge banner addressed to Pepsi: "Stop Corporate Greed: Dump Staley." (UPIU attorneys said that unlike ones on the ground, banners in the air did not violate the Taft-Hartley Act.) A team of actors from the Second City comedy troupe made an appearance at the end of Navy Pier, lampooning Pepsi for its role in the Staley conflict. The crowd assumed the skits were part of the pier's grand opening activities.

In August the Chicago committee returned to Navy Pier to take direct action against Pepsi. UPIU attorney Lynn Agee wrote to the committee, reiterating that "the union does not support the use of pickets, banners, or mass demonstrations targeting Staley customers. These activities threaten to jeopardize the entire Pepsi campaign by embroiling the union and its supporters in completely unnecessary litigation." "Our committee understands and respects your position," the committee wrote back to Agee. "Nevertheless, after lengthy discussion, we did vote to engage" in nonviolent civil disobedience targeting Pepsi. The committee pledged to hand out only its own flyers, not UPIU Local 7837 leaflets, and promised to explain to the press that it was acting on its own initiative, that the action was not endorsed by the UPIU, and that no Staley workers were involved.[9]

So, on August 27, as part of an AFL-CIO–endorsed national week of action against Pepsi, nine members of the Chicago solidarity committee occupied the roof of the pier, draping a two-hundred-square-foot banner over the main entrance, for more than two hours. Nearly one hundred supporters stood below at the entrance to the pier, handing out thousands of flyers and cheering on those engaged in civil disobedience above. The protesters wore T-shirts made for the occasion, declaring, "Pepsi Destroys Decatur Families." The protesters were eventually detained by the police, but to avoid further publicity, Navy Pier declined to press trespassing charges. News of the action and the reasons behind it aired on four of the five major Chicago television stations that night and were the hourly headline on WMAQ Newsradio throughout the night. The next day the Chicago committee enthusiastically faxed the local, "*Great* reception by big crowds at Pier. Action was seen as a *great success* by all our people."[10]

Six weeks later, on October 8, supporters again raised their huge banner over the pier's entrance, while six protesters chained themselves to the main gate and activists handed out thousands of flyers. After an hour, two hundred protesters took their demonstration onto the pier itself. Security personnel formed a wall to block protesters from entering but couldn't do so without also blocking the public. Protesters linked arms to emphasize that they meant no injury to the guards and edged their way through. The activists then marched triumphantly down the half-mile pier, chanting "Tell Pepsi: dump Staley" and handing out flyers along the way. Activity came to a halt as surprised Chicagoans and tourists watched the marchers go by. Pepsi was then ceremonially dumped into Lake Michigan, and a "Pepsi Dump Staley" banner was hung from the supportive Greenpeace ship docked at the pier.

The UPIU was incensed at the Chicago committee's August and October events. Brooks insisted that Watts tell the Chicago committee to halt their actions. He also demanded that the local cease publicizing the actions, pointing to the August–September *War Zone,* which included an article and photograph on the Navy Pier action. "If the Chicago Support Committee cannot follow the union's suggestions," said Brooks, "I recommend the local union stop sending information or having any other contact with these Chicago supporters." Feeling he was legally bound to do so, Watts wrote the committee asking supporters to engage only in corporate-campaign actions that did not violate the UPIU guidelines. But Watts refused to break contact with his flagship support group.[11]

"We Are Down on One Knee"

When the three locals were walking picket lines, Local 7837 continued to get far more media coverage than it had during the first year of the lockout. By August 1995, for example, Michael Moore, already renowned for his first documentary

Roger and Me, brought his *TV Nation* show to Decatur, and "Crackers, the corporate crime-fighting chicken," walked the picket line and interviewed locked-out workers.[12] The national media were further drawn to Decatur's labor battles when FBI agents raided Archer Daniels Midland's corporate headquarters on July 27 and 28, searching for documents in a price-fixing probe.

Both Tate & Lyle and the local's leaders had been surprised when the membership turned down the contract proposal in July. The union had determined to fight on, but both the company and Jim Shinall's surrender faction knew that convincing only a few dozen workers to change their votes could end the conflict. The Kandy Lane activists resumed the battle, but like the rest of the membership, they were tired. They were having trouble finding enough volunteers to fill all the requests for Road Warriors. The local was weakening, and no one expected that it could continue fighting for another year. How could the pressure on Pepsi be stepped up to ensure that it wouldn't renew its contract at the end of the year?

Dan Lane decided that he had to take extraordinary action to force Pepsi to stop buying Staley's corn sweetener and to convince the labor movement to escalate its support for the besieged workers. Lane was one of many activists who found themselves deep in thought through the summer of 1995. The June 25 rally and the contract rejection in July had lifted their spirits, but their anxiety soon returned. "We just can't lose this thing," they kept saying to themselves and to one another. Lane had been fully committed to the union's fight since Jim Beals's death in 1990. But now, he decided, he had to do even more. Lane was greatly influenced by fellow Road Warrior Dave Hays. That spring Hays had returned from a Kansas City road trip to enter a Decatur hospital and passed away on July 25, at the age of fifty. "When I was reading about Dr. King and Gandhi and people in the civil rights movement," recalled Lane, "in my mind Dave Hays was a very similar type of person. He had lung cancer and yet he was dragging himself out all across the country. And Dave even said, 'I'm not going to benefit directly by the results of this fight. But it is important enough that I get out and work as hard as I can.'"[13]

When Hays was hospitalized, Lane was deeply grieved, as were all other members who knew the man. Although he was not Catholic, Lane turned to Father Mangan. With tears in his eyes, Lane said, "Father, we have to do more." He feared that the fight was wavering: "It's more than wobbling—we are down on one knee trying to clear our head. We are basically pretty close to having the knockout punch put on us."

Inspired by the example Hays had set, Lane confided in the priest that he was contemplating a hunger strike to escalate the publicity and pressure on Pepsi. Mangan was stunned, but he listened intently as Lane unfolded his plan. Mangan knew that fasting had a long history associated with both political and spiritual activity. Short fasts are a time-honored spiritual discipline in all major faith traditions. But a prolonged fast, as Lane was contemplating, can end in death. A fasting body consumes itself to sustain its organs. At some unpredictable but inevitable point, the organs fail and death comes quickly. A hunger strike entails a willingness to risk one's life for one's beliefs. Gandhi repeatedly fasted, and farmworkers' leader Cesar Chavez launched a fast to convince his members to retain a nonviolent stance in the face of the growers' physical attacks.

"I know your intentions are good," Mangan responded. "But you're also a father and a husband. You need to weigh out, how is this going to affect other people? What if something would happen to you during the fast?" Lane was about to leave on a Road Warrior trip to Kansas. Mangan told him to make a list of pros and cons and to call him while on the trip. Lane stopped at a rest stop between St. Louis and Kansas City and found a picnic table. "I started writing it out [and did] a lot of personal soul searching," recalled Lane. When he returned to Decatur, he met with Mangan several more times.

Father Mangan never told Lane that he should undertake the fast. "If anything," recalled Lane, "it was just the opposite. He tried to do everything he could to try to sway me the other way." "How will you take care of your family?" Mangan asked. Lane explained that his wife, Donna, had increased her hours to full-time at a Decatur store. The Lanes had been "adopted" and were receiving six hundred dollars each month from Chicago's SEIU Local 73. Lane also rose every morning before sunrise to do a paper route, which his wife and children took over when he was away on trips. Lane took the job for additional income and because it allowed him to be free in the daylight hours for his bargaining committee and organizing tasks.

Finally one day Lane came to the St. James rectory and told the priest, "I'm going to do it. It's something that needs to be done." Father Mangan asked, "Dan, are you planning to take it all the way, indefinitely? Are you willing to risk death?" Lane answered that he was. "You've given this serious thought?" asked Mangan. "Yes, I have," answered Lane. "All right, then," said Mangan. The priest promised to be there for him whenever he needed to talk, but he went one step further. In order to protect Lane's family from intrusive media and to provide physical and spiritual support, Mangan invited Lane to live in the rectory while he fasted.

"A Million Calls to Pepsi"

Now Lane had to tell his loved ones of his decision. He went home and gathered his family for the hardest conversation they had ever had. "It's no different than when I went as a soldier to Vietnam," Lane told Donna, his wife of twenty-four years, and their five kids, ages thirteen to twenty-one. "During the war I risked my life when my country called upon me. Now I have to risk my life for my union and for the labor movement. This is the biggest decision I have ever struggled with. There are times in your life where you have to put your life on the line for what you believe in." Looking at his children, he said, "That's what I believe, and that's what I've taught you kids." His family was horrified at the news. Reluctantly, they accepted his decision.

When Lane told his close friends, he did not find much support. "In particular," he recalled, "Jack Spiegel, Earl Silbar, and Rusty Gilbert of the Chicago solidarity committee, who I had become close to since the struggle started, were really upset." They pleaded with Lane not to do it. But Lane had made up his mind.

Lane got a similar reception from members of his local. "I don't support an all-out fast," said Dave Watts. "I'm worried about his health and his family." "I'd rather go back and work 12-hour rotating shifts for Staley's than you take on this fast," Jerry Fargusson told Lane.[14] Some felt that the union's tactics should be chosen by the membership, not by one person. Lane's reputation as one of the union's most radical members also affected others' reactions. "There are those who say, 'Well, it's a good thing. It may get us somewhere,'" explained executive board member Ron VanSycoc. But there were others who said "it is crazy."

"I deeply appreciate your concern," Lane responded when unionists and supporters pleaded with him not to fast. "But I'm not asking for your permission. This is just something I have to do." On September 1 Lane brought a duffel bag of clothes and several books, including his Bible, to the St. James rectory. He took a bedroom on the second floor, which Father Mangan now dubbed "the Fast Lane," down the hall from the priest. From that day he abstained from solid food, drinking only water, juice, and broth.

Nuns from the Eighth Day Center for Justice provided Lane with books and articles on fasting. These nuns, who had come to Decatur the year before to train the workers in civil disobedience and had been arrested on June 4, insisted that he get a physical exam before starting and that he see a doctor at least weekly for the duration.

In an open letter to Pepsi CEO Callaway, Lane declared his purpose. "There is no doubt in my mind that if PepsiCo would withdraw its business, Staley would come to realize the serious consequences of terrorizing our community," wrote Lane. "It is my family's and my hope that you, sir, will sever all ties with A. E. Staley. Until that time, I will fast. . . . The lives of 750 families, including my own, are in your hands."[15] In the union's *War Zone* newsletter, which was mailed to over twenty thousand supporters, Lane said that he hoped to galvanize people to push harder on Pepsi. "My hope is that the fast will raise the consciousness of the Decatur community and working people everywhere," Lane explained. "I'm no Gandhi or Dr. King, but I believe we're fighting for our lives here, just like they were."[16]

The first week of the fast was difficult for Lane. He grew light-headed, frequently nauseated, and physically exhausted. His muscles ached more with each passing day. In spite of this, he did his newspaper route each morning and visited with his family each day.

Laura Kurre, a solidarity activist in nearby Champaign-Urbana, volunteered to coordinate the organizing activities of the fast. Kurre worked feverishly out of the rectory and the Kandy Lane office. Together with Jerry Tucker, she faxed frequent bulletins to supporters and media across the country.

Shortly after the fast began, Father Mangan saw a newscast about the upcoming "Million Man March," a demonstration of black men to take place in Washington, D.C. Mangan said to Lane, "Why don't we have a million calls to Pepsi? Why don't we get people to think on that order? We can have our march, but through the phone." Kurre contacted the solidarity committees, suggesting that people "get up in the morning, brush your teeth, wash your face, and call Pepsi." The committees stepped up their efforts against Pepsi, linking it to the fast. The company's phone lines were soon flooded. "I would call," recalled Lane, "and you couldn't get through after a while. They had hired a contractor and were sending all the phone calls through there, but it was still too busy."

As the days turned to weeks, Lane's body adjusted somewhat to the fast. He was no longer so light-headed, but he was weaker. Soon his wife and children took over the paper route. In the first thirty days, he lost thirty pounds.[17]

Chain Gang

Three days after Lane began his fast, Local 7837's activists began another public campaign to draw attention to their struggle. On Labor Day, after thousands of unionists marched through downtown Decatur in the union parade, 150 workers climbed into forty pickup trucks and convoyed to the Staley plant. After a short rally, several individuals were ceremoniously chained to the fence at Staley's west gate: Dick Schable; his wife, Sandy; Father Mangan; and Bob Naiman, a member of the Champaign County Board and an avid supporter.

Dubbing themselves the "Chain Gang," the four declared that they intended to stay chained to the fence for twelve hours to dramatize the brutality of the twelve-hour rotating shifts demanded by Tate & Lyle. "The chaining is symbolic of what the company is asking of workers," declared Mangan. "Twelve-hour shifts are immoral. Rotating every six days is immoral. We are here to dramatize the immorality."[18]

Gary Lamb was saddled with the task of chaining Mangan. "I asked Father Mangan, 'Will God get me for this?'" recalled Lamb. "I didn't mean it as a joke. This guy is a priest and I am chaining him up. This is something like you read out of the Bible." But Mangan looked back at Lamb and grinned. "No, Gary," he said, "you'll be all right." Meanwhile the others were telling Lamb, "Hurry up! The police will be coming!" "Clicking that lock on there was pretty hard to do," reflected Lamb.

The four were not certain whether the company would call the police. Fearing bad publicity, however, Staley vice president J. Patrick Mohan told the press that although the protesters were on company property, they would not be arrested. When they had completed their twelve-hour shift, four more protesters replaced them. The next day Art Dhermy and Rev. Bob Wiedrich, a Decatur United Methodist pastor, were chained. "There has been a steady stream of people who came by to bring food and offer support," reported Wiedrich. "Many people in Decatur realize that the company is destroying the lives of working people."[19]

From August 22 to October 1 a group of workers, spouses, and supporters participated in fasts. Throughout these forty days, at least one person was always on a three-day fast. "My fasting," Sister Glenda Bourgeois told the *Decatur Herald and Review,* "is Gospel activity to change the hearts of those driven by the demon of corporate greed."[20] During this period eighty-six workers, spouses, and supporters chained themselves to the Staley gate. Some even volunteered for several shifts. They felt buoyed by the three-day fasts that they and others were undertaking, as well as by Dan Lane's fast. The Women's Support Group held weekly candlelight vigils at dusk, next to the "Links of Solidarity" protesters and in support of all who were fasting. On October 1, marking three years since the expiration of the Staley contract, the chaining protests and the three-day fasting ended.

Lane had planned to go to London to chain himself to the headquarters of Tate & Lyle, but thirty-four days without food had left him too weak. In his stead, Rev. Bob Wiedrich made the trip. On October 4, surrounded by supporters, Wiedrich chained himself to the portico of Tate & Lyle's global headquarters.[21]

In response to Lane's sacrifice, the solidarity committees escalated their campaign against Pepsi. They put Lane's picture and story on tens of thousands of fliers that were handed out across the country. With thriving committees in Chicago, Boston, Champaign, Milwaukee, Madison, San Francisco, New York, and Los Angeles, heightened media and public attention was brought to the Staley workers' plight. By early October, National Public Radio, *The Christian Science Monitor, Time* magazine, *The Nation* magazine, the *AFL-CIO News,* NBC and CBS news, many radio stations, and major labor publications had covered the story.

The average healthy person can fast for about thirty days without suffering permanent damage. After that point, a fast becomes increasingly risky to the faster's vital organs. As Lane's health deteriorated, Laura Kurre faxed daily bulletins about his condition to the media and supporters. "My pulse is weaker and numbness in my legs is occurring," said Lane on day 44 (Oct. 14).[22] "I feel like I'm aging very quickly," he said on day 53 (Oct. 23).[23] In October Lane's doctor ordered that the trips for a medical exam and blood tests be increased to twice a week.

While at the rectory, Lane often lay in bed reading the Bible. He also read and reflected on the works of John Locke, Ralph Waldo Emerson, and Henry David Thoreau and spent much time studying the lives of Gandhi and King. Lane experienced a profound spiritual dimension to the fast. "I've spent a large percentage of every day in prayer," Lane explained to a reporter. "There has to be a social conscience in America. . . . I pray for courage to do the right thing. I pray for understanding. I pray for the anger and bitterness to go away. . . . and for the strength to accept whatever happens."[24]

The AFL-CIO Convention

Meanwhile, as Lane fasted through September and October, the contest for AFL-CIO president reached a fever pitch. The Staley workers watched the campaign closely and planned to send a large delegation to the October 23–26 convention in New York.

At the convention, the New Voices slate was victorious with 56 percent of the vote. SEIU president John Sweeney's election was assured when the largest unions threw him their support. "We saw that most of our unions were losing membership strength and bargaining power," Sweeney told the convention. "We had become too much of a movement of agonizers rather than organizers. Organized labor had declined from a political powerhouse to a political patsy." Referring to a recent militant action by janitors in Washington, D.C., Sweeney had promised to "block bridges" to defend workers' rights. This endorsement of nonviolent civil disobedience came to be a catchphrase of the campaign, contrasted to Donahue's call to "build bridges" to employers. Sweeney pledged to devote massive resources to organizing new members and to grassroots political action to elect prolabor candidates to Congress. And he promised to announce a new program to help the besieged workers in Decatur.[25]

The 1995 AFL-CIO convention was the largest ever held—more than 3,000 people attended, including 488 delegates (only 186 attended in 1993) and hundreds of invited observers and reporters. For the first time in decades, the convention hall was filled not only with high-level, mostly white, male AFL-CIO officials in suits and ties but also with hundreds of working unionists. Striking and locked-out workers were invited. Thirty Decatur workers attended, including twelve from Staley. But while the Decatur unionists were glad to see the Kirkland-Donahue days end, they were focused on concrete actions of solidarity. "Sweeney versus Donahue isn't the point for us," said Watts. "I don't care who's at the helm, as long as it's somebody who's a hell of a lot more progressive than who's been there the past twenty years. We cannot take another complacent decade and expect workers to have any confidence whatsoever in the labor movement. The workers out on the picket lines and at the burn barrels, they don't feel connected to the top of the house. If you pay dues for twenty-five years, and then all of a sudden you've got a labor dispute that nobody can help you with, it makes you wonder."[26]

The convention's final day featured strikes and lockouts, and rank-and-file workers were invited to speak, including Dan Lane. Pale and weak after fifty-six days without food, Lane slowly stood to speak. He began by reading the words to the union anthem, "Solidarity Forever": "When the union's inspiration through the workers' blood shall run," he began quietly. "There shall be no power greater, anywhere beneath the sun," he continued, as the crowd went silent, straining to hear. "For what force on earth is weaker than the feeble strength of one. . . . But the union makes us . . . strong." Then, raising his voice so that it rang throughout the hall, he shouted, "Brothers and sisters, Solidarity!" Three thousand people leapt to their feet and applauded.[27]

Then Lane put aside his typed speech and spoke straight from the heart. "Every one of you sitting here," he declared, "you're responsible for my children, you're responsible for your children, you are responsible for the person next to you's children, and for the children to come."[28] The three thousand unionists stood and stayed standing for the duration of his speech as Lane electrified the crowd:

> Now, I've heard this week and I've heard for the last three years that we're going to put a new movement back in the labor movement. . . . Well, I challenge you to get on board. And getting on board isn't simply walking out of here today and forgetting. . . . Getting on board is going back and writing a letter to Pepsi. Getting on board is going back and . . . reaching out to other workers and giving them the same message. Because 750 workers at Staley cannot win this battle by themselves! . . . We never thought we could. It is only through solidarity, it is only through workers standing up together, that we can survive! We have always trusted you! We have always depended on you! You need to be there, to commit to a higher calling! We can't do it by ourselves.

Lane called on the AFL-CIO to organize a national mobilization against Pepsi and its three fast-food chains. As the unionists chanted at the tops of their lungs "Boycott! Boycott!" Lane shouted to be heard. "By God, if I can do without food for sixty days, then you can do without Pepsi! If I can do without food for sixty days, you can do without Frito snacks! If I can do without food for sixty days, you can do without Taco Bell, Pizza Hut, and Kentucky Fried Chicken!" When Lane finished his speech, the crowded roared its approval.

Not all the labor leaders present were pleased. "They paraded Lane around like a Kewpie doll," a national UPIU leader said derisively. *The Paperworker* did not mention Lane's fast and ignored his speech to the convention.

Lane flew home to Decatur and returned to his room at the rectory. The trip to New York had taken its toll. On November 2, with Lane's weight down to less than 170 from his prefast 216 pounds, his doctor came to his bedside and warned that he risked permanent damage to his system or even death if he did not immediately end the fast. "His blood pressure is low, his heart is weak, [and] he is declining rapidly," Dr. David Gill told the press. "Dan is, without question, in great danger. I think Dan has hit his own personal wall. He is risking his life. I have recommended that he stop his fast."[29]

When news of Lane's declining health was faxed across the country, he was flooded with phone calls from sympathizers and union leaders. Congressmen Glenn Poshard and Dick Durbin called, as did SEIU Local 73 president Tom Balanoff (whose local had adopted the Lane family), to plead with Lane to call off the fast. The Associated Press sent the story over the wires, and the *Chicago Tribune* and *New York Times* ran stories. C. J. Hawking drove to Decatur to respond to the barrage of media requests. The outpouring of support, she said, is "very impassioned, very emotional, and caring. It's incredible."[30]

On November 4, sixty-five days into his fast, Lane received a momentous phone call. John Sweeney urged Lane to end the fast, telling him that the labor movement needed him "strong and vital." Sweeney told Lane, "Your courage has been an inspiration to [us], and your strength gives us all strength."[31] Most important, Sweeney said that the AFL-CIO would devote extraordinary resources to help the Staley workers win. He reported that, just the day before, he had appointed a special Staley task force to escalate the workers' fight and had put winning Local 7837's battle on "the top of our priority list." The task force would involve forty AFL-CIO organizers, twelve full-time and twenty-eight part-time, Sweeney pledged.[32]

With Sweeney on the speaker phone and reporters present, Dan Lane announced the end of the fast. "I'm elated," said Lane as he gingerly ate a small portion of a reporter's cookie to break the fast and then shared it with those present. "The massive resources of the AFL-CIO will kick our campaign into high gear. With workers across the country mobilizing against Pepsi, Pepsi will fall," and Staley will be forced to negotiate a fair contract.[33] It appeared that the AFL-CIO would finally bring to bear its full resources to help the workers achieve their long-awaited victory.

Showdown

In the fall of 1995 the local's internal struggle reached a crescendo over control of the union. The activists, who controlled the executive board and bargaining committee, battled the conservatives, who had the open support of the UPIU staff. In November UPIU vice president Glenn Goss declared that the international was taking over negotiations. In the December 1995 election, the conservative Jim Shinall and his supporters challenged Dave Watts and the activists for leadership of the union. And a few days before Christmas, the members again voted on the company's odious contract.

"I Want My Money!"

As discussed earlier, in March 1995 Jim Shinall and his supporters had managed to pass a motion forcing the bargaining committee to bring the company's latest proposal, however loathsome, to the membership for a vote. Members had debated the June 1995 proposal, found it little changed from the one that they had rejected in October 1992, and voted it down by 57 percent. Shinall's group was dejected but not defeated. The close vote told them that if they persisted, they might soon have a majority behind them.

In late August union member Dewey "Monty" Henderson wrote to Wayne Glenn, asking how the international could take over negotiations from Local 7837's elected officers. The letter was signed by six other members of the conservative faction. On September 6 Glenn responded that Henderson would need to organize the members to vote for the international to take negotiations out of the hands of their bargaining committee.

When he saw copies of the exchange, Dave Watts was furious that Glenn was assisting dissident members and had written to Henderson without first talking to Watts—a violation of the labor movement's treasured protocol if ever there was one. Glenn's letter was an "insult" that made a "mockery of our union," wrote Watts to Glenn, and showed why there was such widespread "distrust, dissatisfaction, and low opinion" of the UPIU leadership. "*Never* has the UPIU International ever told this union's leadership or Bargaining Committee," declared Watts, "that we were not negotiating in good faith, as you have implied with your response to Dewey Henderson's letter. I realize you wish for this 'thorn' in your lifestyle to end and go away," but, he said, the local would persevere even though UPIU leaders were "running from this fight."

Glenn indignantly responded that he would communicate with any UPIU member he chose and paternalistically instructed Watts, "You do not take advice very well and the members would be better served if you would listen to your leadership."[1]

At the September 14 union meeting the Shinall group moved that the UPIU International take over bargaining. The group had distributed a flyer on the picket lines that read, "The time has come for our membership to take whatever steps are necessary to end this dispute with the A. E. Staley company. The reality of our situation must be faced regardless of how unpleasant or disappointing the truth may be." The executive board and bargaining committee opposed the motion, and the members—three hundred were present—voted it down.

Shinall's supporters were surprised at the vote but deepened their resolve to organize more fervently. They began to talk more forcefully on the picket lines and to spread lies about Dave Watts and the activist wing. "You only get adopted if you're a union militant," they told whoever would listen. "Dave Watts only wants a staff job with the UPIU." "The way this leadership hates the company, and the company hates them right back, we'll never get a contract with this leadership. There'll never be an end to this thing."

Road Warriors were a particular object of the conservatives' lies. "They're raising huge sums of money on the road—who's to say they're not stealing some of it?" they asked. "The Road Warriors aren't suffering like the rest of us. Some of them are adopted four or five times; they're getting rich off this struggle—no wonder they won't bargain a fair contract. They're more interested in their idealistic visions than in the members who want this thing to end so they can get on with their lives. They love the limelight and they don't want to see it end."

In an unsigned letter that captured the conservative faction's hostility, a worker wrote to Watts: "Most of us want to get on with our lives and end this once and for all. Many families are 'adopted,' go on trips as road warriors, and are all in all, having a good ole time. The rest of us are working and earning a living at new jobs. . . . We need to get what we can from this (severance) and get on with our lives. The union is broken."[2]

Week after week the Shinall group talked of surrendering. Often members would accuse them of spreading discord and division, but a growing number of weary workers would listen and wonder whether the rumors might be true. When *would* the lockout end? Shinall's group found their most receptive audience among older workers and those with the most seniority. At the time of the lockout 93 workers had more than thirty years in the plant, and another 160 had over twenty-five. "This fight is lost," Shinall's group told these workers. "We need to negotiate the best pension plan we can get and end this thing." Shinall, who had twenty-nine years, said that he was planning to retire as soon as a contract was signed. "I want my money!" he told the older workers.[3]

Shinall's group also talked to workers who had found other jobs and had no intention of returning to Staley. Eighty-seven workers had less than five years' seniority, and with the announced downsizing, they assumed that their jobs were gone. "Why not negotiate the best severance package we can?" asked Shinall's group. "You won't have to work under whatever contract is voted in. You'll get several thousand dollars if you give in."

The activists who wanted to fight until an acceptable contract was won found their greatest support among the four hundred workers who had fifteen to twenty-five years in the plant. Mostly in their forties and fifties, these workers were too young to retire. If a draconian contract was signed, they would be the ones working under it.

The activists labeled the Shinall group the "sideliners," "bar crowd," "sell-out crowd," and "boo-birds." "Shinall had a plantation mentality," said Mike Griffin. His attitude, according to Griffin, was "they're the boss and there's nothing we can do about it." The activists were furious that Shinall's faction attacked the Road Warriors, who had worked so tirelessly to raise money and support for the union. Above all, the activists were particularly indignant that Shinall was organizing workers to accept an odious contract under which he, personally, would never have to work. Mike Dulaney wrote to the Chicago solidarity committee, "He keeps saying that he has traveled all over the country (he's driving a truck) and there is no reason why 'you guys' can't work twelve hour shifts like 'everyone' else."[4]

The ranks of the Road Warriors were thinning, however, and as a result the union's most active members were forced to spend more time on the road and less time talking to workers on the picket line. "We just didn't watch our backs close enough," reflected Art Dhermy.[5] With rare exceptions, it had been many months since the Tuesday-night solidarity meetings had drawn over two hundred people. "Our membership was being chewed at," said Watts. "They were losing their homes, were dying without health insurance, were seeing divorce rates skyrocket. A membership that was once so strong became divided and lost its will and determination."[6] Kandy Lane activist Bill Winter described the situation in late 1995:

For many months now, our Executive Board and Bargaining Committee have been forced to divide their efforts between Tate & Lyle and those within our membership who seek to end our struggle for a fair contract for everyone. There are forces within our own ranks . . . , self-centered, greedy, uncaring, traitorous members . . . , who continue to come up with motion after motion, all of which are self-serving methods of ending our struggle and lining their own pockets with a few dollars, enabling them to go about their lives, while selling everyone who desires to go back to work under a fair and just contract down the river. The future of our kids and grandkids is much more important than the few dollars to be gained by selling out to Staley's.[7]

"A Controlled Democracy"

Meanwhile, the relationship between Watts and UPIU president Wayne Glenn continued to deteriorate. In September they battled over the role the Staley workers would play at the AFL-CIO convention. Glenn informed the local that he was appointing Mark Brooks to speak for the workers there. In late September Watts wrote Glenn a sharp letter of protest. "We are the ones who have stood on the line," said Watts. "It is the workers involved in these disputes in Decatur that have earned the right to address that great assembly."[8] After appealing directly to Tom Donahue and John Sweeney, the local got its way, and Dan Lane spoke after being introduced by Brooks.

Throughout October Watts and Glenn exchanged sharp letters over an audit of the local's books. On October 18 Watts wrote that the local welcomed an audit but decried the accusatory tone of Glenn's letters. The two of them, said Watts, had "spent far too much time and energy back-biting and battling each other" when they should instead be focused on "anti-labor corporations like Staley/ Tate & Lyle, who are the true culprits." But Watts's bitterness nevertheless came out: "I respect your duties as International President, but have little compassion for those that live the good life very comfortably under much better conditions than any of my members and their families will ever see. So pardon our rudeness and brashness if we seem to push too hard, but it is all we have left, and you can count on a lot more of it until justice is served or we too have become another labor history statistic."[9]

Events began to move quickly when, at the November 14 union meeting, UPIU vice president Glenn Goss declared that he was taking over negotiations. "Wayne Glenn asked me where things stood with negotiations," Goss informed the packed hall. "I told him that nothing happened at the last negotiations. Wayne Glenn and I had a lengthy discussion about what it would take to get something going. When Wayne Glenn quizzes me, I'm not about to say to him, 'Hang in there; I think we're gaining on them.' I don't believe that."[10]

"We've got to find a way out, an honorable way out," Goss told the Staley workers. He reminded them that the Bridgestone/Firestone workers had ended their strike the previous May; the Caterpillar workers were rumored to be about to do the same. "I don't want us out there by ourselves," said Goss. He assured the workers that he would not have the workers again vote the same contract they had twice rejected, promising to bring them "the best damn thing we can get."

The Pepsi campaign wouldn't get a settlement, declared Goss, disavowing the local's strategy. "What's going to get us a contract is an examination by us of where the hell we stand. We have to face up to where we stand, and get ourselves a contract as soon as we can." The Pepsi contract would be up for renewal on December 31. The activists argued that a huge push by the entire UPIU with the full resources of the new AFL-CIO leadership would force Pepsi to dump Staley, and the loss of Pepsi's business on top of Miller's would compel Staley to negotiate a fair contract. Goss completely rejected that strategy. "It is in our favor to get a contract before Pepsi does or does not sign," said Goss. "Staley doesn't know what will happen with Pepsi."

For three years Local 7837's bargaining committee had argued with Staley officials across the table. For three years the local had insisted that negotiations begin with the union's previous contract, and for three years the company had demanded that the old contract be tossed aside. Since August 1992 neither side had budged. Now Goss told the workers that the company had won. "When Staley took away your contract, they took away everything. Now it's a question of what we can get back."

Goss's meaning was clear: it was time to end the fight. When Shinall went to the microphone and asked Goss, "What happens if you and the bargaining committee disagree?" Goss declared, "This is a controlled democracy." The UPIU was taking control. Goss was going to bring back a contract and the international was going to do everything in its power to get members to accept it.

"Glenn Goss wanted me out of office," bargaining committee chair Dike Ferris commented. "He got to the point he wanted this over, and we weren't going to do it, [so he was] going to do it Jim Shinall's way—take whatever the company wanted to get it over." Ferris became convinced that deals were being reached behind the backs of the local leadership after UPIU assistant regional director Danny Wirges advised Ferris to propose to the company that it not outsource all the mechanic work, keeping fifty mechanics. When the union then met with management, the company made just that proposal. "I'm sure from the evidence I saw that they were doing a sidebar," said Ferris. "You could see in bargaining sessions," agreed Art Dhermy, "that the company and the upper echelon of the [international] had talked among themselves before the meetings, just by the way things went across."

"Wayne Glenn did not want to win on the militants' terms," said Jerry Tucker. "He would then have had [other UPIU locals] say to him, 'Wayne, we want to do what the Staley workers did.'" By the time of Sweeney's election in late October 1995, said Tucker, Glenn's "position toward surrender was fairly clear."

All Hopes on the Pepsi Campaign

Meanwhile the Pepsi campaign was in high gear. The activists placed their hopes on a big, final push, led by Sweeney, that would convince Pepsi to stop purchasing Staley corn sweetener when its contract expired. As discussed in the previous chapter, on November 4 Sweeney had promised Lane that he would assign forty organizers to the struggle and that winning the Staley fight would be a "top priority." The solidarity committees were fervently flyering Pepsi-sponsored city festivals and Pepsi-owned fast-food franchises through the summer and fall. "A lot of the best activity happened in the last year," said Brooks.

Immediately after the AFL-CIO convention, a delegation of twenty Staley workers and supporters traveled from New York City to nearby Purchase, New York, to talk to Pepsi officials at corporate headquarters. After demonstrating outside, recalled CWA vice president Jan Pierce, the protesters "went right in the front door and sat down. Pepsi officials came down and took a representative group up. . . . We went to the board room and made our case. But we were just stroked by the [public relations] person."

The union's activists and its supporters in the Northeast were eager to mark a dramatic escalation of the campaign with a mass demonstration at Pepsi headquarters on December 8. In mid-November the local's Kandy Lane organizers, together with unions and Jobs with Justice chapters in New York, New Jersey, and Massachusetts, began organizing for a demonstration that would involve significant nonviolent civil disobedience. Such an action would attract media attention and alert Pepsi that the already strong national campaign was now going to be sharply escalated with the full resources of the AFL-CIO. "Pepsi had given A. E. Staley until December 31 to get this settled," said Mike Griffin. "The AFL-CIO's New Jersey Industrial Union Council was working on the Purchase rally in early December. All of our support groups were tied into it. We were going to engage in civil disobedience, whatever it took."[11]

The UPIU International intervened, however, telling New England union officials and AFL-CIO leaders that there would be no rallies at Pepsi headquarters and no civil disobedience. Union supporters sorrowfully called Kandy Lane to tell the Staley activists that their international unions wouldn't allow them to proceed without the UPIU's endorsement. "According to sources inside the AFL-CIO, Wayne Glenn ordered the AFL-CIO to withhold its support [because]

Glenn wanted to put the struggle to bed," the local's *War Zone* newsletter later declared.[12] Mark Brooks was one of the UPIU staffers with orders to stop the demonstration. Brooks defended his actions as necessary to ensure that the union did not violate the Taft-Hartley Act's prohibition of secondary boycotts: "I kept hearing about this demonstration that Jobs with Justice was going to do. I got with somebody in JwJ and told them, as I always do, that the UPIU does not support civil disobedience or pickets or demonstrations at secondary targets. The company can bring a giant lawsuit against you."

"We were working on logistics and getting local support" for the Pepsi rally, recalled Jan Pierce, "and then it was called off. The CWA has a real militant local, CWA Local 1103, in the Purchase area. . . . With the Paperworkers' blessing, we were going to have more involvement by other national unions. [Purchase] being just a bus ride from a million union members in New York City, it could have been quite impressive."

The activists were furious. Ferris dejectedly reported at the December 5 union meeting that while "supporters in New Jersey and New York are chomping at the bit to be there," the UPIU had called off the action. "Instead we're sending a 'delegation'—the international wants us to use that word"—to quietly meet with Pepsi officials.[13]

Labor lawyers give advice because "that's lawyers doing their job," argued Pierce. "But union leaders have to do *their* job."

> If that's ignoring unfair labor laws, that occasionally has to be done. Let them sue us. There has to be a spark somewhere. So the union movement gets sued by Pepsi. So leaders are carted off to jail. And they're told "no bail." And you have international union leaders rotting in jail, and going on a hunger strike. By God, then you're going to bring the spotlight on the unfair nature of labor laws! You gotta take those risks! That takes risk-takers, and there ain't no damned risk-takers.

The final blow came when the new AFL-CIO leaders backed off from their promise to make the Staley fight a priority. The only action that Sweeney took was to meet briefly on December 5 with Tate & Lyle CEO Neil Shaw while in England on other business. Local 7837's leaders were not invited, even though they had been promised they would be included should such a meeting occur. Wayne Glenn later praised Sweeney's meeting with Shaw as "the key break in the struggle" and credited Sweeney with "helping to persuade [the company] to bring a new offer to the table."[14] Shaw knew that there was dissension within Local 7837, however, and that Glenn had ordered Goss to take over negotiations. Shaw saw no need to retreat from the company's original October 1992 proposal. Sweeney's meeting with Shaw had no significant effect.

Election of Union Officers

At the November 14 union meeting, after Goss announced the international's takeover of bargaining, Dave Watts opened the floor for the local's annual leadership nominations. The regularly scheduled election of officers would occur four weeks later, on December 12. Terms ran two years, and each December the membership voted for half the offices. This year the presidency and several slots on the executive board and bargaining committee were up.

Watts, exhausted from the long struggle and the opposition's personal attacks, had declared at the October 10 union meeting that he did not want to lead a union that was unwilling to fight. "It may be time for those complaining the loudest to have a try," said Watts.[15] His supporters, however, told Watts that the fight would collapse without him. Watts reluctantly agreed to stand for reelection.

At the November 14 meeting, Watts and former vice president Bob Hull called on Shinall and his supporters to either quit complaining or run for office. "Don't blame the bargaining committee," said Hull. "They're working night and day for this local. If you ain't got the guts to take one of those nominations tonight, shame on you. Quit sitting on your ass and bitching. Get off your ass and do something."[16] Watts likewise lambasted the "sideliners" for constantly criticizing while others did the fighting, and to emphasize his point he read a list of nine names, including Jim Shinall's. Three months earlier, seven of the nine had signed a letter to Wayne Glenn asking the international to take over negotiations. Said Watts supporter Walter Maus, "Dave goaded several of the 'let's give up' negative do-nothings into running for office. He challenged them to do some good, instead of just finding fault with our current leadership, who are doing all they can to fight tyranny."[17]

The conservative faction nominated Shinall for president and several others for board positions. For the next four weeks, the opposition group focused its attention on ousting Watts and the activist board. Shinall's ticket promised to "end this within one week of taking office." On December 3 the *Decatur Herald and Review* featured a long, highly favorable front-page article and interview with Shinall. The obstacle to a settlement was the mutual hatred between Staley management and Dave Watts, Shinall told the paper. "You can't go around making derogatory statements about the company when you're trying to negotiate," he said, although he had done just that many times as bargaining committee chair. It was time, Shinall insisted, for the workers to get the best contract that could be achieved and move on with their lives. The UPIU International must be given power to end the conflict, and a contract shouldn't be held up with demands that the seven workers fired for union activity during the in-plant campaign get their jobs back.

Watts declined to campaign and refused the *Herald and Review*'s offer of an interview. "After three years of struggle, the members should know where I stand. Let the members decide," said Watts.[18] While his supporters on the board and bargaining committee did campaign, the absence of Watts's voice seriously weakened their effort.

On December 2 the Local 7837 activists received another blow when the UAW International called off the Caterpillar strike. On December 3 the twelve thousand strikers began voting on a new contract, but the international declared that the strike would end even if the agreement was rejected. Nearly 80 percent of the UAW members voted no, but the Cat workers returned to work without a contract. Once again the Staley workers were walking the picket lines alone in Decatur. The UAW's defeat gave added ammunition to Shinall. Speaking to workers on the picket line, the conservatives asked how their small local could beat a multinational corporation when even the mighty UAW, through two long strikes, was beaten by Cat.

On December 11 the Decatur newspaper predicted Shinall's victory, as did a local television station. On December 12, election day, workers woke up to find the lead editorial in the *Decatur Herald and Review* endorsing Jim Shinall. Echoing Shinall's platform, the editors argued that "people need to get on with their lives, especially those near retirement age."

UPIU leaders Glenn Goss and Danny Wirges were forthright about their roles in the election. Wirges regularly received calls from members of the Shinall group asking for advice on how to end the fight, and he happily counseled them. "We hit a point where we knew the battle wasn't winnable," said Wirges, "and then it was time to work off the [company's] proposal . . . , get the best we could get out of the situation, and get the heck out of there."

Jim Shinall was elected president by a vote of 249 to 200. His slate won a majority on the bargaining committee but not on the executive board. While 93 percent of the membership had come out for the vote that rejected the contract in July 1995, only 75 percent voted on the union's officers five months later.[19] According to the union's bylaws, however, the newly elected officers would not take office until January 10.

"Get That Son of a Bitch off the Air!"

On December 6, six days before the election, the bargaining committee had met with the company. Goss instructed the committee to submit to the company's demand that negotiating begin with management's seventeen-page contract proposal. The next day, negotiations ended with a proposal that differed only slightly from those that members had rejected in October 1992 and July 1995.

There would still be twelve-hour rotating shifts, although rotating every thirty days instead of every six. The company would be allowed unlimited subcontracting. The health and safety committee would be substantially weakened, with no right to inspect safety violations. The arbitration and grievance process would be eviscerated. Workers could be forced to work sixteen-hour days (four hours of mandatory overtime per shift). The company would be free to change insurance carriers, health coverage, and employee co-pays at any time. The union could no longer bargain for retirees. There would be no amnesty for the seven fired workers. All prelockout National Labor Relations Board charges, grievances, and arbitrations would be dropped.

Further, the plant would now employ just 350 union workers, to be slashed to 220 within two years. The proposed contract allowed for over one hundred union jobs to be contracted out to nonunion firms, including most of the jobs for the higher-paid maintenance workers. To add further insult, returning workers would be forced to endure "training" by scabs for three months. The proposal offered modest wage increases over the previous proposal—$1.80 over the first three years, up from the July offer of $0.90 over two years—and modest increases in company contribution to workers' 401K accounts. The company agreed to return standard contract language requiring "just cause" to discipline workers, instead of the much weaker "reasonable cause" language from July. Staley also dropped its demand that union officers be prohibited from taking time off the job for union business.

The severance package remained unchanged from the rejected July offer. Workers with less than ten years of service would get an $8,000 severance check; those with ten to fifteen years would receive $20,000; those with fifteen to twenty years, $25,000; and those with more than twenty years, $30,000 plus $1,000 for each year of service over thirty years. The retirement package offered just $22 per month per year worked; a worker who retired with twenty-five years, for example, would receive a pension of just $550 a month. Workers over fifty-five years of age with more than ten years' service could choose either the severance check or an enhanced retirement package with a monthly pension of $29 per year of service.

A change from the July proposal was that forty-four workers who had been laid off and taken a small severance package two months after the lockout would now be offered the enhanced severance package and would be eligible to vote on the contract—a move that Watts charged was designed solely to give these members the chance to vote. Workers who were unlikely ever to be offered their jobs back could now vote for a contract that would bring them severance checks. Watts filed charges with the National Labor Relations Board, but to no avail.[20]

Watts had insisted that the leadership not reveal the December 7 proposal to the membership, so that the December 12 officers' election would be about candidates and their programs, not the contract. Since they were in office for another twenty-nine days, Watts and the other officers who were determined to salvage the fight were still in control. The day after the election they made the company's offer public. The committee and board discussed it at length and "rejected the proposal unanimously for a clear lack of any substantial changes from the June 30 proposal," they said in a December 14 press statement. "We saw only minor improvements on grievance and arbitration steps. Health and safety issues are still of the utmost concern. The company has refused to move on amnesty and on 12-hour rotating shifts. And they still have *unlimited* sub-contracting at-will." The officers voted eleven to two against sending a virtually identical contract to the members for a vote.

Within a few hours after receiving Local 7837's press release and after consulting with Goss, Wayne Glenn overrode the decision of the bargaining committee and executive board and ordered the local to vote on the contract. In a fax to Watts, Glenn argued that this proposal differed from the rejected July offer in "many . . . substantial" ways. "Under the power invested in me by the International Constitution," declared Glenn, "I am hereby directing that the offer be brought before the membership of Local 7837."[21] The contract might not be perfect, said Glenn, but "we don't get many perfect proposals from companies these days. It has a lot of good things in it."[22]

To Glenn's consternation, Watts immediately released Glenn's letter to the press along with the executive board's own press release. The activists' attitude toward the UPIU International, said Dike Ferris, was that "if you want to stick something down the throats of our people, then you just gotta do it without our participation." Goss claimed that "there was no way he could recommend the contract," but the activists weren't impressed with Goss's supposed opposition.[23] Goss's goal all along, said Ferris, was to "get a few of the sharp edges out of the proposal, to make it a little more easy for the members to swallow the package. And that's all they did, is take some of the things out that might be construed as punitive."

That day UPIU staffers began campaigning for the contract. Decatur's popular WSOY radio interviewed Gordon Brehm, Glenn's executive assistant, by phone.[24] Brehm promoted the contract and implicitly threatened the workers:

> [BREHM:] There are substantial changes—improvements, in our
>   mind—from the company's offer of last June. . . . It is one of the
>   most generous severance agreements I've ever seen. . . . The local
>   knew long before the lock-out began, we've known from the start,
>   that a large number of jobs were going to be eliminated. Certainly,
>   it's not any surprise to us. . . . We've grown used to twelve-hour shifts
>   in the Paperworkers Union. Most of the major paper mills in the

United States have gone to twelve-hour shifts in the last five to ten years. At first, many of our members were very opposed to them. After they got used to them, they like them now. . . .

[INTERVIEWER:] What if they vote the contract down?

[BREHM:] I hate to even *think* about that. But I don't see any end to this dispute in the foreseeable future if that should happen. The people are going to be told that this is their last opportunity in the foreseeable future to get this matter resolved. If we don't get it settled now, on this basis, I think we would be back to square one, we'd have to start all over. And whether or not any of our people ever go back to work is a question.[25]

In the midst of the broadcast, Watts called UPIU headquarters and screamed, "Get that son of a bitch off the air!" But the damage was done. Staley workers and their spouses across the city had heard the broadcast and understood that the international union was telling them to surrender. In response to a letter that Mike Griffin wrote to Brehm the next day, Brehm declared, "Thank you for saying Wayne Glenn and I are 'cut from the same cloth.' I have never had a finer compliment."[26]

Given the international's message that its support would dry up should the members reject the contract, said Dike Ferris, "it would take a monumental effort for the [members] to muster the courage to reject this offer and carry on the fight."[27] "It was a death blow," said Royal Plankenhorn. On December 19, seven enraged Staley workers drove 350 miles to Nashville to picket UPIU headquarters, carrying signs and using bullhorns to denounce the union's betrayal.

Meanwhile, for the third year in a row solidarity caravans arrived in Decatur to help workers' families through the difficult holiday season. On December 11 St. Louis supporters brought checks for thirty thousand dollars, a semitrailer full of food valued at twenty-four thousand dollars, and trucks loaded with toys. On December 15 more packages arrived from Columbus, Ohio. And on December 19 a caravan of thirty-five supporters from Chicago, Madison, Milwaukee, Gary, South Bend, Terre Haute, and other cities brought more than seventy thousand dollars, along with toys and food that filled two semitrailers. The Staley workers again hosted a dinner to thank their friends. With the contract vote just two days away, it was a bittersweet moment for both workers and supporters. The hall was filled with people from across the Midwest, embracing and shedding tears of appreciation.

On December 21 the *Decatur Herald and Review*'s front-page headline quoted Jim Shinall: "We Lost This War." The article repeatedly quoted J. Patrick Mohan, twice quoted Shinall, but only once quoted from the executive board's press release critiquing the contract. At the union meeting that evening bargaining chair

Dike Ferris spent an hour meticulously going through the proposal and taking questions and comments. Speaking for the board and the committee, Watts urged a no vote. Responding to Brehm's endorsement of twelve-hour shifts, Watts read a statement that Glenn had sent to UPIU locals just four years before:

> The International Executive Board has discussed at length the growing trend of younger workers in our industry pursuing 12-hour work days. This flies directly in the face of a fifty-year fight by the labor movement to seek 8-hour work days. The Executive Board is not asking you to undo any agreements that have already been reached but they have taken an official position of stating, and I quote, "That it shall be the policy of the International Union to discourage this trend whenever and wherever possible."[28]

But on December 21 and 22, the members voted by a 56 percent majority—286 to 226—to accept the company's offer. Three and one-half years after it began, the Staley workers' fight was over.

The Light Just Went Out

Watts, the executive board, the bargaining committee, and the Kandy Lane activists denounced the settlement as a complete defeat. Even Jim Shinall admitted the union had been defeated.[29] But the UPIU's press release and the January 1996 *Paperworker* praised the contract, as did the *AFL-CIO News*. "We eased many of the harsh work rule changes," declared Glenn. "I want to thank you," wrote Goss in a letter to supporters, "for helping us to defeat some of the worst of Staley's concessionary demands."[30]

The defeat hit the Staley workers like a punch in the gut. "I am devastated," said Mike Dulaney. "We were so close to winning, but we just quit."[31] Many people were furious with Shinall, often referring to him as "Judas." Bill Hanna echoed many members' feelings when he called Shinall "the son of a bitch that sold us out." "I hope the people realize what they have done," said Ron VanScyoc. "I think they are going to find the horrors of hell inside those gates." The vast majority of Staley workers will refuse "to return to work in a police state atmosphere," said members of the executive board in a statement to the press.[32]

The sellout was all about money, said many workers. "It was costing [UPIU] too much money," said spouse Susan Hull. Local 7837 "had to be disposed of." Dick Schable echoed this sentiment, arguing that the UPIU's "big interest was getting money back into their coffers." "We were sold out on both sides," declared Lorell Patterson, "from the local union officials and from the international union. They all got together and decided 'we want this thing over with.'" As for the resolve of the members, Patterson reflected that "it seemed like the light just went out of people in the end."

Underneath the next day's front-page headline in the *Decatur Herald and Review*—"Staley Lockout Ends"—another headline seemed to portend the future facing Decatur workers: "Third Worker Dies at ADM in a Month." One worker had fallen fifty feet from a platform, and a second had been scalded to death. The third died while rescuing a foreman who had collapsed from toxic fumes inside a tank. Although the company did not call the police or the fire department, ADM was not charged with any criminal offense. Two weeks later, on January 6, three more ADM workers nearly died from carbon monoxide poisoning, and four others were injured.

On December 27 Dave Watts stood at the podium in the packed union hall, as he had done hundreds of times before, and talked to his fellow unionists for the last time. Watts read a poem from an anonymous worker, "I'm Proud to Be Union":

> It's obvious now that times are hard;
> Our nation's image is deeply scarred.
> The government gives the unions blame,
> And too many of us accept the shame.
> Instead of applying the things we've learned,
> We take for granted what our forefathers earned.
> Our newest enemy is our sister or brother;
> Ignorance says we fight each other.
> These back-stabbing people are so confused;
> They're not union members, they just pay their dues.
> Members don't tell on their brother, man,
> Or refuse to help when they know they can!
> It's easy to talk, to complain, and to cuss,
> But our union's future depends on us!!
> We can put dignity back in our label;
> It won't be easy, but I know we're able.
> Being strong takes more than a few;
> It takes everyone, and that includes you!
> Let's all be proud to be union.

Watts spoke solemnly and with great dignity. The workers listened intently and with great respect as he declared that he would not return to work under the degrading contract. "They'll not get another moment of my life," Watts declared.

> I don't think we'll ever know how close we came to winning this thing. But I think we can all recognize the fact that if we'd had as many fighting to win as we had [seeking] to close it at the end, the outcome might have been different. . . . Many of you and your families, I've worked side by side with and I hope we can

be friends forever, and I wish you nothing but the best. Some I'm glad to separate myself from. For some, it's okay to leave members behind in such a war as we have faced. Some find it acceptable to send people back into the plant under these terms. Some have earned their thirty pieces of silver. . . .

Many of us vowed to stay with this fight, and see it through. . . . We didn't always have the answers, but we did try. We weren't always able to stop the pain, but we shared it with you. We weren't able to win this labor battle, and there is more fighting ahead for us all. We did do our best, and no one can ask more. This union has the utmost respect nationwide . . . , and this union and its families can forever hold our heads very high. The respect that this union has acquired will not die with this battle. Your courage and determination is evident everywhere and inspirational to more than you will know. I'm extremely proud to have been part of it with you all. . . . We may all be poorer and have less monetary things, but we are all much richer in the true values, and in the morals, and in what life really is all about. God bless us all.[33]

After Watts spoke, he turned the gavel over to Dike Ferris and left the hall. In his remaining two weeks as president, he refused to sign the contract. Instead, the UPIU International had to provide the official signature that sealed the terms of Local 7837's surrender.

"A Tortured Silence"

On January 9, 1996, as their last act, the outgoing officers sent a final *War Zone* newsletter to the twenty-four thousand local unions and individuals who had contributed to the union's three-year campaign. They worked all day at the Kandy Lane office to get the newsletter addressed, stamped, and bundled, all the while looking out the window to see whether Shinall and his group would attempt to stop them. For several of the board and bargaining committee members working to get the newsletter to the post office, this would be their last day as union officials; the new officers would be sworn in at that night's meeting.

This *War Zone* was like no other. The bitter headline read, "Corporate Greed and Wimpy Labor Leaders Team Up to Defeat Staley Workers." The first sentences spoke of the workers' immense pain at their defeat:

Here, in the heart of the Central Illinois War Zone, there's a tortured silence, like someone choking for air after a heavy punch to the stomach. The pickets are gone from all the plant gates now. You can still smell the thick air of the corn grind from the Staley and ADM plants, where workers die in industrial accidents on a regular basis. The Cat and Bridgestone plants hum along, still manned by more scabs than union workers. The Staley lock-out, the flagship of the tri-union Decatur labor struggles, is over. Corporate greed has won another round in America.

The newsletter detailed the workers' valiant three-year fight against the largest sugar conglomerate in the world and thanked the tens of thousands of people who had supported them. The issue's theme, though, was the need for a fighting leadership to halt labor's endless series of defeats.[34] "Sadly, all of the problems faced by the locked-out Staley families weren't across the bargaining table and the picket line from them," said the *War Zone*.

"We did everything we could do to win this struggle," Lorell Patterson was quoted as saying. "We took our message everywhere and workers and unions responded. They knew it was their fight, too. We raised several million dollars to support our fight for justice. In the end, we were betrayed by national union leaders." The *War Zone* concluded:

> For the embattled workers, the price of resistance has been very high. Homes and livelihoods have been destroyed, and previously held values forever altered. Decatur families, like so many everywhere, have been the victims of America's dirty "big" secret, that a one-sided class war is being waged by the rich and powerful against the rest of us. Important battles have been lost. Battles which, with consistent strategies and unfailing solidarity, could have been won. But the workers in Decatur have not lost these battles. It took *yesterday's* labor movement to do that! Out of the courage and lessons of the warriors in the War Zone, let's build *tomorrow's* labor movement.

Infuriated by this last issue of the *War Zone,* the UPIU filed charges against five of the executive board members, claiming that printing and mailing the newsletter violated the union's constitution. On January 12 Shinall appeared at the Kandy Lane office with a locksmith in tow. Just as the Staley management had done before him, he ordered those workers present to leave. Shinall then had the locks changed and the office closed—a second lockout as heartbreaking as the first.[35] Members and supporters who had donated computer equipment and other furnishings were never able to recover them. The remaining union T-shirts, literature, and campaign materials were destroyed.

On January 16 some of the members who had taken their severance attended the union's morning meeting, held for workers who worked the night shift. A motion was passed at the beginning of the 3½-hour meeting that recently severed members could attend and have voice but no vote. But under Shinall's command, no spouses or supporters would ever again be allowed into the meetings. A second heavily attended union meeting was held that evening. Beforehand, Shinall called the police and asked them to stand by. Watts and the activists, many of whom had signed papers to sever their employment, came to the union hall to insist that the remaining $140,000 raised by the Road Warriors should be distributed to the local's members and not be left in the treasury. It was unfathomable to them that Shinall and his faction, together with the scabs, who were soon to be union members, would be in charge of that money.

Shinall tried to silence Watts and the other activists, but he was reminded that severed members were able to attend and speak. Shinall responded by calling the police. Eleven cars were waiting a block away. When the police arrived, Shinall ordered them to remove the severed members from the hall. Despite a chorus of protest from the floor, Danny Wirges adjourned the meeting just twenty minutes after it had been called to order. At Shinall's request, Glenn then declared that all union meetings were canceled until February 13 and that henceforth severed members would be blocked from entering the hall.

"The police pepper gassed us and harassed us throughout this struggle," said Jim Roarick. "Now they've called on the same police to keep us out of the union hall."[36] "For three long years we fought corporate greed," said the majority of the former executive board in a January 22, 1996, press release. "Now we're being treated like criminals by our own union."

Even though Shinall had announced his retirement, he and Staley had made a separate deal, outside the contract, allowing him to stay on as union president. All the other retiring workers were given a January deadline to file their papers, but under the side agreement Shinall would remain on the company payroll until April without working in the plant. At the company's request, Shinall would now orchestrate the return to the plant.

19

Aftermath

On the day the lockout ended, Mary Brummett went out to her front yard, on Decatur's heavily traveled Main Street, where she had posted a yard sign tracking the number of days Local 7837 had been locked out. "Every day I went out and changed it," she said, so that the town would not be able to forget the workers' hardship. On the day the members voted the contract in, Mary's sign read, "Locked out by A. E. Staley—908 days." On December 22, 1995, Mary took down her sign.[1]

"When the lockout ended," recalled Susan Hull, "I took every single thing that had the Staley name, anything that had to do with Staley, and put it away. Every trinket, gift, ornament, it is all boxed up and in the attic, including the red T-shirts."

At the end of the lockout the Road Warriors and their spouses were overwhelmed with emotions. With help from Father Martin Mangan, Sister Glenda Bourgeois, and Eighth Day Sisters Jean Hughes, Kathleen Desautels, and Mary Kay Flanigan, C. J. Hawking organized a retreat that would allow the most dedicated activists to process the defeat but also to acknowledge all they had accomplished.

"I Feel Like a Part of Me Has Died"

Over thirty of the most active workers and spouses gathered in the St. James rectory basement on the last weekend of January 1996. They openly discussed the emotional turmoil of the defeat—their intense "angry sadness," as one worker put it. They talked about their feelings of emptiness, of a deep heaviness, of short tempers, and of depression.[2]

"I feel like a part of me has died," said one worker. "Nothing means anything to me anymore," said another. Still other workers added: "We were so close to winning, and that's what makes it hurt so much." "This is the most painful time in my whole life, and I don't know if this pain will ever go away." "I can't sleep, I'm just so angry." "I'm angry at Staley management. I'm angry at the workers who only cared for themselves, took their severance, and left everyone else hanging. And I'm angry at the UPIU for betraying us and the AFL-CIO for abandoning us."

Despite the pain, most workers were also able to remember their own personal highlights of the struggle: How liberating the work-to-rule had been. How deeply touched they were by the support from rank-and-file workers across the nation. How invigorating it had been to be a Road Warrior. How meaningful had become the lifelong friendships they had formed. How they had been personally transformed.

They laughed as they recounted humorous stories from nearly four years of struggle. After a closing banquet on Saturday evening, they hugged one another, promising that they would stay in touch and that the friendships forged would not be forgotten. They vowed to hold an annual picnic, and the women decided to continue to meet biweekly, which they do to this day.

Returning to the Plant

The Staley plant had reduced its 850 union jobs in 1992 to 762 at the time of the lockout and finally to 350. The workers' numbers had fallen to 600 since the lockout, but most members expected that all 350 jobs would be filled and that those with the lowest seniority would be placed on a waiting list. Instead, only 181 unionists decided to return to the plant. On January 22 the first group of about 90 reported to work, and a second group entered on February 5. Each time workers returned to the plant, a group of their fellow union members and spouses stood silently across the street wearing black armbands, to signify mourning for their union.

Some of the remaining unionists had found other jobs or had moved away and were eager to get their severance checks. Some were set to take early retirement. Most workers, however, would not return to the plant because they refused to work for a company that was so openly hostile to its workforce, and they believed that life in the plant under the company's contract would be horrific. The bitter feelings toward the company were too harsh to set aside. Most of the activists interviewed for this book chose not to return to the plant.

Some workers who considered themselves too young to retire and too old to be hired elsewhere were badly in need of a good-paying job; they talked at length with their families about whether to go back to Staley. Returning was perilous, especially for those who were the most visible activists. In a letter, Tate & Lyle clearly articulated the conditions under which the locked-out workers would return. Each would have a three-week orientation period. The union members, who averaged twenty-one years in the plant, would be trained by the scabs who had taken their jobs for two and one-half years. At the first sign of insubordination or disrespect toward scabs or managers, the union member would be disciplined or fired. Discipline would be "aggressive, swift and decisive."[3] The contract, with its twelve-hour rotating shifts and gutted seniority, health and safety, and grievance procedures, would be strictly enforced.

His first day back, recalled Bill Winter, was "weird." Because of the extensive restructuring during the lockout, he had to learn "a whole new process." The company had instituted massive changes to the corn-processing plant. Many of the previously manual jobs were now performed by operators sitting at computer consoles. "I think that was part of the reason they locked us out," said Winter. "They didn't have to negotiate any of these things with the union. They had a lot of ideas on downsizing, and they didn't want to have to go through all the hoops. . . . They would just toss everybody out and then do it, and then maybe let them back in. . . . It was a very cold-hearted way to go about whatever they wanted to accomplish."

Even with all the new technology and the downsized workforce, the workers' greater adjustment came when surveying their new co-workers. "I was returning to a department with twenty-four people and it was half of the old union and half [scabs]," said Winter. "You had to be careful of what you said" so as not to get fired. The company had made it clear that the scabs must be called "replacements," under threat of discipline. Since the scabs were now to become members of the union, the activists immediately dubbed them "half-brothers" and "half-sisters," a term still in use today.

All the returning union members had to decide how to work with people who had done the most unconscionable act—crossing the picket line. Working side-by-side with the scabs, along with the company's new ban on smoking, led Art Dhermy to take up chewing tobacco, which he artfully used when he had to speak to the scabs. "They would get together in a group and call one another 'scab,'" recalled Dhermy. "Then they'd turn around and laugh and look at me and say, 'Isn't that what you called us?'" Dhermy knew that they were trying to bait him into using the word so that he would get fired. Dhermy would reply, "No, I didn't call you anything that good." The scabs would continue talking and laughing about the lockout. Then, said Dhermy, "I'd start spitting tobacco juice on their shoes. They didn't like it, but I told them every time they'd talk that way, you're going to get spit on."

Bill Winter made an effort to understand his new co-workers and former enemies. "As you worked with them and eventually got to know some of these people," said Winter, "you discovered that a lot of them were in difficult straits themselves. They didn't have anything against me or anyone locked out. They just looked at them as job opportunities and they took them. That didn't necessarily make them bad people. . . . Most of them are younger. Many of them didn't have a sense of a union and a lot of them still don't."

For many of the activists, however, working alongside the scabs and being subjected to the company's constant intimidation was too much to bear. Of the 181 locked-out workers who returned to the plant, within a month only 140 remained.

State of the Union

When Jim Shinall ran for local president, he pledged that he would settle the contract and then retire, but the company kept Shinall on the payroll to keep someone they trusted in charge of the union while the locked-out workers returned to the plant. When Art Dhermy filed a grievance that forced the company to end its sweetheart deal with Shinall, thus forcing him to retire on February 13, the presidency stood vacant. Dike Ferris decided to run, but he "didn't campaign to any scab. I didn't want their votes." Ferris was "soundly defeated," and he jokingly stated that he could "probably name the people who voted for" him.

Steve Haseley, who did get the scab votes, became president, a position he holds to this day. Haseley, who was on the executive board at the time of the lockout, had been a Shinall supporter and had worked throughout 1995 to convince workers to accept the company's contract.

Ferris, who rarely missed a union meeting for decades, no longer attends Local 7837 meetings. "I think the union has been reduced to a boys' club," said Ferris. "To my estimation, there's nothing that's done that's grievable because you've got no contract language. I don't see a need to attend." "I have a real hard time going into the union hall," echoed Art Dhermy, "knowing that I might be sitting next to scabs. I have a *real hard* time with that. I used to not miss a one. I used to take a day off to make sure that I got to go to my union meeting."

Bill Winter, however, who served as a steward for nineteen years before the lockout, was asked to fill a vacancy on the bargaining committee. He has since successfully run for and still maintains a position on the executive board as recording secretary. Winter described the current union meetings as having "ten to twelve people present, not counting the union officers who have to be there." Of the members who were locked out, Winter said, "Most of them are burnt-out from two and a half years of meetings once a week. I can understand that. The half-brothers, a lot of them are scared to show up at the union hall." Since the workers returned to the plant, all the positions on the executive board have been held by former locked-out union members. No scab has run for office.

Today, of the roughly three hundred union members in the plant, about a third are former locked-out members, a third are scabs, and a third are new hires.

"What Good Is the AFL-CIO?"

The activists' anger at the AFL-CIO leadership was immeasurable. When Sweeney spoke at the University of Illinois in nearby Champaign-Urbana, workers handed out flyers to the crowd listing pointed questions about the reasons the AFL-CIO had not come to their aid. In April 1996 a contingent drove to Madison, Wisconsin, where Sweeney was speaking at a Workers Memorial Day rally honoring workers who had been killed on their jobs. They carried a black coffin in front of the speakers' stand marked "Staley workers."[4]

In the months after the defeat, some of the Staley workers came to St. James Church to be counseled by Father Mangan. He listened to their anger and sadness and did his best to comfort them, but he wanted to do more. Mangan flew to Washington, D.C., and, with help from AFL-CIO labor-religion coordinator Rev. Michael Szpak, arranged for Rich Trumka to come to Decatur. Trumka knew it would not be a pleasant encounter. "I wasn't going to run away," said Trumka. "They asked me to come, and I went. . . . These were some of the best trade unionists I've ever been around. . . . They probably thought I didn't do some things they thought I should have, and they had a right to tell me that. They had a right to get it off their chest. Did I need to go there and let them strip some bark off of me if that's what they needed to do? Yep. I don't regret it and I'd do it again."

In July 1996 Trumka met with nearly forty workers in the basement of St. James Church. The workers were seething and didn't hold anything back. They had been disgusted with the feeble leadership of Lane Kirkland, but their rage at Trumka was greater. Trumka had led the Pittston workers in a militant battle that resulted in victory. Trumka—who is one of labor's greatest orators—had declared at the three unions' June 1995 rally that labor was drawing a line in the sand and would pull out all stops to win. Trumka had promised the workers that the new AFL-CIO leadership would commit all its resources to the Decatur labor battles. Trumka had brought the Staley workers hope. And Trumka, the workers felt, had sorely let them down.

"We chewed on him, gave him hell," said Royal Plankenhorn. "And I don't care. A lot of people would be so awed. But he's just another guy." Lorell Patterson said to Trumka, "Where is your fight, your gumption? You're supposed to fight for us. The AFL-CIO has all this money, all this power; you could have helped us in a big way, and we're getting a measly sixty dollars a week in picket pay. Tell me face-to-face why you guys didn't pull out the big guns and come help us." But, said Patterson, "I just didn't get a satisfactory answer. I know we pissed him off, but I didn't care."

"You stand up and make a lot of good speeches," Dave Watts thundered, "but you don't walk the walk!" Trumka "got on his high horse," said Watts, "and talked about how many times he'd been arrested. But I said, 'The promises didn't come through for us in Decatur.'"

According to the workers, Trumka told them that the AFL-CIO could not "render services to a local union unless requested by a national union affiliate." The clear implication was that the UPIU International had told the AFL-CIO to back off. Discussing the meeting years later, Trumka elaborated that the AFL-CIO "is not going to presume to tell [an international] what they should do and what they shouldn't do" in a strike or lockout. The AFL-CIO cannot give orders to the international unions and cannot assist a local when the international has not requested it. "We give them our advice, and we'll urge them" to adopt certain strategies, said Trumka. "But ultimately *they're* going to decide on their strategy."

"Then why did you make the promises to us?" a worker shouted at him at the 1996 meeting. "What good is the AFL-CIO if you can't come to the aid of a local union that is willing to fight?" "I want the words 'Remember Decatur' to haunt Sweeney and Trumka," said Gary Lamb. "Not that it will help us, but maybe it will push them to do something" to win future labor battles.[5]

Taking the Cops to Court

Over six years after they were pepper-sprayed, the Staley workers fought one last battle. Their civil action against the City of Decatur and its police department finally came to trial on November 1, 2000, in an Urbana courtroom. The federal civil trial, a class-action suit for seventy plaintiffs led by Gary Lamb, Dan Rhodes, Dick Schable, and Jerry Tucker, was filed by attorneys from the Chicago-based People's Law Office. The suit charged the city and the police with violating their civil rights by spraying them directly in the face without provocation.

The jurors watched videos recorded by the police, WAND-TV, and independent labor film crews. Rhodes and Lamb explained that they were peacefully sitting with their backs to the police when they were sprayed in the face. Tucker said that he was standing on the front line when an officer shoved a canister within inches of his face. Schable testified that he was first sprayed as he fell to the ground after being jostled, and then he was sprayed again as he sat peacefully on the ground. "It burned," Schable recalled. "[My] eyes were watering. I shook uncontrollably because I couldn't catch my breath. I was gasping for air."[6]

The defense told the all-white, eleven-member jury—chosen from among those who stated that they were not in a union, had no family members in unions, and didn't know anyone in a union—that the protesters were attempting to break through police lines. The city's lawyers falsely charged that protesters' chants of "Cross that line!" referring to the Staley yellow property line, demonstrated the workers' intention to attack the police line. The police, the lawyers argued, had used reasonable restraint and acted in self-defense.

The question put to the jurors was to determine whether the police had used excessive and unreasonable force in their use of pepper spray. The jurors met for ninety minutes and came back with a not guilty verdict. The workers were stunned. They had been certain that, finally, they would win a modicum of justice. Unionist Marty Conlisk, who had videotaped the spraying as a member of the Chicago-based Labor Beat film crew, expressed their ire: "The jury deliberated for the length of time it took to eat a ham sandwich and came back and let the cops go completely. The video evidence we helped provide (and risked our necks for) had absolutely no weight in the outcome. Seeing their neighbors getting pepper sprayed three inches from their faces, picking certain people from the crowd for abuse, police causing physical pain and suffering, had no impact on the jurors' lives. It sure did on many of us."[7]

The defense attorney praised what he called "a fine, just decision," but the unionists' attorney, Jan Susler, responded, "The workers got screwed by Tate & Lyle, the Decatur police, and this is number three."[8]

"How could they watch the videotape and come up with that conclusion?" asked a dumbfounded Gary Lamb. Judge Baker had instructed the jury to consider only whether the police used unreasonable force when they "seized" the plaintiffs with pepper spray. "This is certainly a case about 'seizure,'" noted Tucker. "The corporations 'seized' the workers' jobs and livelihoods, the Decatur police 'seized' their rights to peaceful protest, and today, in court, the process 'seized' justice."[9]

Back in a Decatur Courtroom

Six and one-half years after the Decatur Fifty were arrested for the June 4, 1994, sit-down at the Staley gates, two of the participants were again on the front page of the *Decatur Herald and Review.* When the jury had found them guilty of trespassing, five of the seven who had gone to trial in July 1995 paid a $205 fine. But Sisters Kathleen Desautels and Mary Kay Flanigan, from the Eighth Day Center, refused to pay a fine to a system they said was abetting injustice against workers. Their offer to perform community service was ignored.

In January 2001 the two activist nuns were part of a group arrested for staging a peaceful sit-in at U.S. Senator Peter Fitzgerald's Chicago office.[10] They thought they would be arraigned and let out in time for dinner. To their surprise, however, the Decatur police had an outstanding warrant for their refusal to pay their fines. After the two nuns spent the night in a Chicago jail, an Illinois state trooper and a Decatur police officer arrived to extradite the criminals. The two spent the trip downstate explaining their social justice causes.

Halfway to Decatur, the police car pulled in to a rest stop. The state trooper was extremely polite and kept insisting, over the nuns' objections, on buying them a soft drink and something to eat. Finally he said to the two, "Sisters, my father was a locked-out Staley worker, and buying you a Coke is the least I can do for all you and the others did for my Dad and the other workers." He added, "You know, my Dad's going to be really upset." The sisters were taken aback at the providence of it all. *Chicago Tribune* columnist Mary Schmich got wind of the story and described the saga with biting humor in the paper's January 28, 2001, issue.[11]

Father Mangan, with whom the sisters had been arrested in 1994, went to visit them at the Decatur jail. He was shocked to see them dressed in jail-issued orange jumpsuits. The next day the state's attorney, true to form, argued with the judge about releasing the two nuns pending a court date, but the judge released them on personal recognizance. At the trial itself, on February 20, the courtroom was packed with supporters, including a group of Staley and Caterpillar workers and many nuns from throughout the state. Gary Lamb called Sister Glenda Bourgeois and said, "Hey, I can get some people together and we'll pay that fine," she responded, "That's not the point. They'll never pay the fine. That's not their goal in life." Lamb thought to himself, "I'm still learning about this labor fight years later. Will the learning never quit?"[12]

The state's attorney demanded jail time, but the judge sentenced the two nuns to twenty hours of community service—which they could perform at the Eighth Day Center in Chicago doing what they did every day: organizing people to fight for social justice.

Labor Day 2001

The UAW finally signed a contract with Caterpillar in 1998—six and one-half long years after the union first struck the company. The company won almost everything it had first demanded in 1991.[13] When the UAW brought the contract to the members in February 1998, they surprised their national union leaders by rejecting it 58 percent to 42 percent. The workers recognized that they had been defeated but turned the contract down because it would have left on the street 50 of the 160 activists fired during the dispute.

The Decatur Caterpillar workers stood fast to the end. UAW Local 751 members voted the contract down by a ratio of nine to one. A month later, facing the same contract but with all 160 illegally fired workers given amnesty, the Caterpillar unionists as a whole reluctantly voted yes by 54 percent—but the Decatur workers again voted no three to one.

The Caterpillar workers have not given up, but it will be a long, hard road back to regaining the union's former strength and reversing the rollbacks in wages and workers' rights.

The United Rubber Workers merged with the United Steelworkers in June 1995. Their new union committed the resources of the international union to launch an aggressive national and global corporate campaign that won the workers a partial victory in November 1996. The Bridgestone/Firestone workers, alone among the three embattled Decatur unions, emerged with a contract that beat back many of the company's demands.[14]

When Decatur's workers came together on Labor Day 2001, however, it was not to celebrate labor's strength but to mourn its losses. Gone were the union banners, the militant chants, the fiery speeches, the sea of red shirts, and the determination that Decatur was and would remain forever a union town. The grand marshals of the Labor Day Parade were the 1,200 Bridgestone/Firestone workers, all of whom were about to lose their jobs.

In 1998 reports began to emerge that Bridgestone/Firestone tires on Ford Explorers were suddenly blowing up on the highways. Government investigators found that faulty manufacture had led to over one hundred deaths from accidents involving these Explorers. The cause of the crashes was disputed for years as Ford and Bridgestone/Firestone angrily blamed each other. Undoubtedly one factor was the inexperienced scabs who made tires during the 1994–95 strike. In any case, the faulty tires dealt such a blow to the company's sales that it closed its Decatur plant.[15]

Many Labor Day marchers were also shedding tears for a beloved friend who was dying of cancer. Father Martin Mangan had never belonged to a union, but in the eyes of the workers he was among the most dedicated labor activists in Decatur. Surely he was the most beloved. As they assembled, the labor leaders announced that henceforth every Labor Day the "Father Martin Mangan Humanitarian Award" would be awarded to an advocate for the rights of working people. The first award would be given to Father Mangan himself.

Mangan was too ill to attend the ceremony, so Dave Watts, Larry Solomon, USWA Local 713 president Roger Gates, and labor historian Bob Sampson presented Mangan with the award at his bedside. Eleven days later, Father Mangan died quietly in his home. Over five thousand mourners paraded slowly by his coffin in the sanctuary of St. James Church. More than a quarter were unionists saying good-bye to the beloved priest of Decatur's labor wars.

Impact on Race Relations

Through the hard work of the African American Staley workers, Decatur's black community became more aware of the ties between the fights for civil rights and for workers' rights. "We did some good in this town," said Frankie Travis, voicing words echoed by the other locked-out workers. The workers particularly recall the pride and power they felt as they marched through Decatur on the April 9 March for Social and Economic Justice. "I was looking at the kids that were running out onto the porch," recalled Travis. "They didn't know exactly what we were doing. But they knew it was a lot of black people doing something that was good, coming through their neighborhood. That was a positive thing."

Jeanette Hawkins agreed, adding that the children cheered the marchers: "They were saying, 'Solidarity!'"

The African Americans' assessment of their impact on the white workers rac-ism is more complex. While Hawkins knew that her election to the executive board was a historic moment in the life of the local, she had doubts about the reasons behind the white workers' support. She reflected, "I was voted in because they had to have a black in there, because wherever the Road Warriors went, their supporters wanted to know, 'Do you have any blacks on your bargaining committee or holding any office?' . . . I was the token."

Yet, says Hawkins, that isn't the whole story:

> I think some of the whites that had never been around blacks [were changed]. I had a lot of whites tell me that. They would talk prejudice, but after they were around us and they saw that we were nothing like what they had heard, they starting liking us. Some of the people in the union saw that we were smarter than they thought. Some of the Road Warriors, they became friends with one another. They had to travel together, and they sort of bonded. Racism was changed to a certain degree. . . . We had our issues, we had our racism, we had disagreement, but then we all united together.

Frankie Travis agreed with Hawkins's cynical appraisal of her election. The local's white activists, he said, "campaigned for her because they knew what they needed to keep the fight going." Yet Travis views his transformation into a union activist positively. "I came to a point in my life that I had a direction, and nothing could change it," said Travis. "I just loved it!" As one of the most traveled Road Warriors, Travis, too, built friendships with white workers that he never before would have dreamed possible: "Anytime I asked Dave Watts for anything, it was well-received. I think that is due to the fact that we were involved in the fight, and it did make an impact on the whites. They needed help, and so did we. It was a common cause. I think some of the blacks and some of the whites did get close. I did get close to some of the Road Warriors. I learned a lot of things."

It is difficult to assess the degree to which the attitudes of the seven hundred white workers were changed. As with most whites in the country as a whole, most white Staley workers are reluctant to openly admit to their own racist at-titudes, whether past or present. The more involved a white Staley worker was in the fight, however, the greater his or her transformation on issues of race. The Staley workers did not eradicate racism from their union, but they did chip away at it and forged new, lasting relationships among blacks and whites. They further demonstrated an old lesson of labor history: when a group of people are unified for a common goal, their own prejudices can be transformed. The trans-formation happens more quickly in struggle than it does in ordinary times.

When the Staley workers' fight with Tate & Lyle ended, union member Dick Schable, who is white, moved to St. Louis so that his wife, Sandy, could pursue her studies as a chiropractor. During one of their first trips to St. Louis to search for housing, Dick and Sandy passed a group of African Americans demonstrating against police brutality. Without hesitation, Dick and Sandy stopped the car and jumped out to join the group. Within a minute, they, too, were carrying signs and marching, and they came back the next night to protest again. "It kind of shocked them, especially when they found out where we had come from," recalled Schable, who added, "Anytime we can stand with people, we have to do it."

Gary Lamb recounted one of his most profound memories from the fight, one that reflects his personal transformation. Lamb and Art Dhermy, both white, took a Road Warrior trip to New York City and stayed with supporters in Harlem.

> Everyone was black in that neighborhood in northern Manhattan. It was pretty desolate. The people didn't have much. We found the building, and it smelled of urine in the elevator. Two women came to the door, one white and the other black, and they were lesbians. They said, "You're welcome to spend the night on the floor in the living room!" They had five locks on their steel door. The next morning, they gave us a key and they went to work.
>
> We went out for our meetings. It'd been a good day; I had three thousand dollars in my pockets, and Art Dhermy had the same in his. But I got lost. All the buildings looked alike, and we took a wrong exit out of the subway. There were lots of people on the street, and everyone was black. Two fat, middle-aged white guys walking down the street—we were like feathers on a fish. And some said to us, "Good evening!" I thought to myself, if it were two black guys walking by thirty white guys, would the white folks say, "Good evening!" No, they wouldn't. Finally, I didn't know where I was. I pulled out the map from my back pocket.
>
> I was studying the map when a guy walked up to us and said, "Can I help you, brother?" I said, "To tell you the truth, I'm lost." I didn't even have an address. [When we described the building], he gave us directions: "A block down, a block over, you'll be right there." I said, "Thanks!" He said, "That's all right, brother. We're all in this together."

Black and white, "we're all in this together"—that was the powerful lesson of the struggle for many of the Staley workers.

"In a Heartbeat"

Despite their defeat, the Staley activists remain proud of what they accomplished, and they leave the labor movement valuable lessons. While history will judge the impact of their struggle, it remains clear that everyone who was committed to it, both workers and supporters, drew great strength from the depth of solidarity. Of the dozens of union activists interviewed for this book, not one person has regrets about taking on the company. "I'd do it all over again, in a heartbeat," said Royal Plankenhorn. "It had to be done." Working as a Local 7837 organizer "was the best job I ever had," agreed Mike Griffin. Dike Ferris quips that his only regret is that he "would have loved to vote twice" to reject the contract. "If I had to do it over again, it wouldn't take me a minute to decide. . . . You either give up and die, or do what you think is right, and I still think what we did was right." The activists are bitter over the UPIU's and AFL-CIO's lack of solidarity, but they all expressed sentiments similar to those of Dave Watts, who said, "Knowing what we knew at the time, I would do it all the same."

The Staley workers expressed immense gratitude to their supporters. "We are very thankful," said Mona Williams, uttering words echoed by all the activists, "to the many wonderful people who put a lot of their time, energy, and heart into our cause . . . , who shared our laughter, our tears, fears, and our sweat and blood."[16] But their supporters reported that they received more than they gave. The solidarity activists who devoted their energies to the Staley struggle have no regrets. "The Staley workers were a breath of fresh air," said San Francisco Bay area UAW member Caroline Lund. It was exciting to "see average workers coming out and speaking out, and standing up for themselves." The Staley workers gave labor activists across the country renewed energy to keep struggling to rebuild the labor movement.

Hundreds of local unions were grateful to the Staley workers for passing on their passion and their spirit of solidarity. "As our people picked up on the Staley workers' solidarity, their willingness to sacrifice, their commitment to making change," said Milwaukee CLC president Bruce Colburn, "it helped develop our own people's commitment and leadership." Organizing solidarity with the Staley workers brought new people into the labor movement, developed many activists' organizing skills, launched a student movement for workers' rights, and profoundly affected supporters on a personal level. "The Staley struggle opened people's eyes to class struggle," said David Klein of Chicago. "It was an awakening for me," echoed Chicago IBEW member Mike Sacco. "There were hallmarks there of class struggle. . . . I came into this a trade unionist, and I left as a socialist."

"The fight forever changed me," reflected Gary Lamb. "I will never be the person I was before." "I don't have any regrets," concluded Art Dhermy. "It's my history, and it makes me stronger. We put a building block down. Even though we didn't win, we did a lot of things right. You take the things we did right and build on that."

20

A Winnable Fight

While Jerry Tucker was editing an issue of the *War Zone,* a phrase stuck in his mind, and he made it the front-page headline: "Messengers of Struggle."[1] And messengers the Staley workers surely were. Decatur could have been a rousing victory, a rallying cry for a resurgent labor movement. Instead Decatur is yet another reminder that for the labor movement to survive, let alone thrive, it must jettison its failed strategies and the union leaders who still adhere to them.

A clear lesson of Decatur is that corporations are becoming more aggressive in crippling and destroying unions and that U.S. labor law—the weakest in the industrialized world—makes a mockery of workers' rights. Nevertheless, the Staley workers did not have to lose. If ever there was a struggle that should have been won, this was it. The Staley workers lost because of the weakness of the American labor movement. Theirs was always a dual struggle: to resist Tate & Lyle's union-busting and to challenge labor's bureaucracy and lethargy. The Staley workers were fighting for a new American labor movement.

The defeat at Staley wasn't caused by the local union's tactics. It was caused by the fact that those groundbreaking tactics are the exception, not the rule. Rich Trumka was right when he said, "Sometimes a generation forgets how to fight and they have to relearn it."[2] The Staley workers weren't fighting just for themselves—they were fighting to help the labor movement relearn how to win.

Power at Work

The labor movement is only as strong as its members' commitment, but that commitment has weakened over the decades. History demonstrates that unions cannot resist employers' attacks and advance workers' rights without an educated and involved membership. As Mike Griffin put it, however, the labor movement "went to sleep in the 1960s and '70s."[3] Even after nearly three decades of stepped-up employer hostility, too many of the country's fifty thousand local unions are still, as Dave Watts described AIW 837 before 1992, "living in a cloud." Another major problem arises, as AFL-CIO staffer Joe Uehlein commented, from the fact that most central labor councils are "not mobilized and active."[4]

Despite three and one-half years of outreach, the Decatur labor struggles only drew seven thousand workers to a national mobilization—even though Illinois and its six bordering states were home to 3.5 million unionists in 1995.[5]

Yet the Staley workers demonstrated that apathy can be overcome. In 1991 AIW Local 837 was a typical, inward-looking local, with minimal attendance at meetings or participation in union affairs. The local was divided by skill, race, gender, and age, yet it transformed itself into a fighting force with a mobilized membership capable of taking on a multinational corporation.[6] It was this element, more than any other, that drew so many people to go all-out for the Staley workers. "How did these guys in the middle of nowhere do things that no one else was doing?" asked Machinist Jon Baker of the Chicago solidarity committee. According to Baker, it was the Staley workers' successful internal organizing that got him interested. Many supporters felt as did SEIU member Joe Iosbaker, also with the Chicago committee, who said straightforwardly, "I was looking for a fight like the Staley workers. Since P-9 lost at Hormel, I was waiting for the next chapter. And there they were, in my home state!"

Five ingredients were critical to Local 837's internal transformation. First, leaders invited labor educators to teach the membership about the lucrative corn-processing industry, corporate America's successful assault on unions since the 1980s, and creative strategies to resist concessions.

Second, when the union opened its meetings to spouses and other workers, it went from monthly union meetings of two dozen members to weekly meetings with often seven or eight hundred in attendance. The local determined that an informed membership together with their spouses would decide how to respond to the company's attacks. "The floor rules this union" was the guiding principle.

Third, the workers pulled off one of the most successful work-to-rule campaigns in recent history. Jerry Tucker understood that his goal was not just to teach the workers how to organize the in-plant campaign but also to draw on their creativity, help them develop a sense of their own power, and transform them into rank-and-file leaders. "You could see the evolution of the workers, . . . see them emerge, and develop, and take responsibility, and take charge," recounted Tucker. "They went from being relatively good, docile, following-orders" employees to unionists who were "going to find a way to resist." The cohesiveness and power created by this strategy culminated when the vast majority of the workers walked off the job in June 1993. After they were locked out, the solidarity built during the in-plant campaign became the foundation for all their subsequent work.

Fourth, the local had a strong leader at the helm: Dave Watts, who as president helped transform Local 837 into a membership-driven union. Royal Planken-horn reflected, "Dave wanted everybody to be involved; he wanted everybody's voice to be heard; he wanted everything to be done by the vote of the membership." One of the keys to the union's transformation was the philosophy of inclusion held by Watts and the other activists, the idea that every worker was a leader. A great example came in November 1994 when workers staged a sit-in and demanded to see Governor Jim Edgar. When his aide responded that he would meet only with two of their leaders, the workers began chanting, "We are all leaders!" Further, Watts worked skillfully to overcome divisions about strategy and to hold the union together as long as he could.

Fifth, the leaders who emerged from among the rank-and-file discovered qualities they hadn't known they possessed. Lorell Patterson said, "The fight educated me. . . . Come to find out, the only ones that are going to fight for you are the rank-and-file. If you have a strong rank-and-file, you have a strong union. If you don't have a strong rank-and-file, you've got a weak union." Gary Lamb expanded, "We really did, as a small group of people and terribly inexperienced, stand up and give a good account of ourselves. And if this formerly laid-back, nonactive local union could do it, then anybody could do it." Confrontations with authority figures—from the AFL-CIO at Bal Harbour to the governor of Illinois to the Decatur city council, the police, and the courts—awakened a deep sense of citizenship and unionism in most of the rank-and-file.

A Social Movement

The Staley fight was far more than a labor conflict; the workers turned it into a social movement.

The Staley workers went door-to-door four times distributing literature that explained the union's stance. Large numbers of Decatur residents were sympathetic, and when the workers were locked out, hundreds posted pro-union signs on their lawns. Literature from Corporate Campaign, Inc., was mailed to tens of thousands of activists across the country, putting the Staley struggle on the map. To counter the media's antiunion stance, the local wrote and published several issues of the *Decatur Free Press,* distributing it widely in working-class neighborhoods.

The Staley workers were determined to reach out to workers across the country. While Local 7837 welcomed the endorsements of official labor bodies—international unions, state federations, and central labor councils—it did not rely on them to build a solidarity movement. The Road Warriors established strong ties with thousands of locals. No other union has put so many rank-and-filers on the road, speaking to hundreds of thousands of people, over such a prolonged period, and garnered such strong support. The adopt-a-family program personalized their struggle, and the $3.5 million in donations helped to sustain it, but worker-to-worker solidarity was the foundation of the Staley fight.

In addition, Local 7837 cultivated supporters. Dozens of solidarity committees across the country set up trips for the Road Warriors, raised money, mobilized in the corporate campaigns, and brought large numbers to Decatur demonstrations. Committees held rallies, fundraisers, and direct actions in their own cities and showed the videos that captured the Staley workers' resistance. The local welcomed five full-time volunteer organizers from nearby cities into the Kandy Lane organizing center, further strengthening their ties to the solidarity committees. As the local designed its strategy, moreover, key leaders from nearby cities were invited to participate and advise.

The combined forces of the Road Warrior program and the solidarity committees created a worker-to-worker network that convinced Miller Brewing Company to stop purchasing Staley product, a feat that would very likely have been repeated at PepsiCo had the struggle not been shut down. The union put out more than a million pieces of direct mail and corporate-campaign literature, and workers and activists talked with tens of thousands of Americans about not purchasing Miller and Pepsi products.

Although no one would claim that Decatur stands at the cutting edge of improving race relations—in September 1999 the town again made national headlines when school officials expelled seven African American students for fighting—Local 7837 challenged racism in its own ranks and transformed itself. It united blacks and whites in the two marches initiated by its African American members and for the first time in its history elected an African American, Jeanette Hawkins, to its executive board. Local 7837 also welcomed visiting unionists from Mexico, Germany, and Cuba to its union hall, a sign of a broadening global consciousness.

The union built a powerful local religious coalition that drew national and international support. A union with few past ties to community organizations was able to mobilize clergy in solidarity with the workers' fight. Father Martin Mangan and hundreds of religious supporters provided moral strength to the unionists by declaring that theirs was a righteous struggle.

Finally, Local 7837 union debated and then engaged in mass nonviolent civil disobedience. On February 22, June 4, and June 25, 1994, the union sought to shut down production and gain national publicity with a sit-down at the Staley gates, and on November 30, 1994, they held another sit-down at the state capitol.

Twenty-Twenty Hindsight

Although Local 7837 waged a heroic struggle, it was not flawless.

Perhaps the local's most serious mistake was to target State Farm Insurance in its corporate campaign. A. E. Staley's connection to State Farm was obscure and difficult to explain to supporters, and the request to change insurance companies often met a lukewarm response. During the first eight months after the lockout, when union members were most energized and still receiving unemployment benefits, the union lost valuable time focusing on a poor target. "We fell off after we got locked-out," said Art Dhermy. "We needed to do more right after the lockout to keep the membership mobilized." "We were beating their butts all over the place inside the plant," echoed Dan Lane. "We could have beat them on the outside if we had come out swinging with both fists. . . . It took too long to get the Miller campaign off the ground."[7] Once the Miller campaign kicked off in March 1994, unionists and supporters were invigorated with a more explainable and ultimately successful target. The same held true for the Pepsi campaign.

Even after the target was switched, however, the corporate campaign alone was not enough to force the company to negotiate a fair contract. To be most effective, a corporate campaign should be combined with a strategy to stop or hinder production. After the sit-down on June 25, 1994, a number of the activists wanted to continue the civil disobedience campaign. "The whole concept of shutting down the plant," said Dan Lane, "even if you can only sustain it for several hours, is potentially like a spark under kindling which grows into a great flame. . . . Nobody can ever convince me that [our] people weren't willing to go much further than the leadership or Ray Rogers were willing to let them go."[8] Unfortunately, facing opposition from their own international and the AFL-CIO, and threatened with huge fines if they violated injunctions, local leaders called a halt to the civil disobedience.

Nearly every major, successful social movement in U.S. history has involved mass nonviolent civil disobedience—from the American colonists' revolutionary struggle against the British, to the abolitionist movement, to the labor movement's sit-down strikes in the 1930s, to the civil rights movement in the 1950s and 1960s, to the anti–Vietnam War movement, to the thousands of young people who shut down the 1999 World Trade Organization meeting in Seattle.

Rich Trumka, labor's foremost advocate for a civil disobedience strategy, was United Mine Workers president during the 1989–90 Pittston strike, when three thousand workers and supporters participated in civil disobedience that resulted in over five thousand arrests. The Pittston workers created a situation of "no contract, no peace" in southwest Virginia, provoking a social and political crisis for local government, the police, the courts, and the company. "Labor law is formulated for labor to lose," declared Trumka. "If you play by every one of those rules, you lose every time. So what it forces you to do, is to change the way you've operated."[9] As a critical part of an overall strategy, however, a campaign of civil disobedience must be *sustained,* and this was a failing of the Staley effort. "It has to be an ongoing effort that never ceases," said Trumka.

> You can't do it one day and then walk away for six months and do it again. It has to be an integral part of your strategy. And that can only be done by the people that are in the dispute. Others will come and help you, but only if you are willing to do it yourself. And if you're not willing to do that, it's not a strategy you can employ. You have to have buy-in. You have to have training. You have to have determination, and you have to exhibit to everybody there that people are willing to pursue this strategy for as long as it takes to bring justice and fairness back to the workplace.

It would be unfair, however, to overly criticize Local 7837 on this score. It is virtually impossible for one small local to stop production through sustained civil disobedience when its international opposes that action. The labor movement as a whole must adopt mass nonviolent civil disobedience, which must include community supporters, as a strategy to win major labor battles.

A third and final criticism of Local 7837 can be leveled at its inability to sustain its initial high level of membership organization. As the struggle took on national visibility in 1995, the demand for Road Warriors to speak across the country rose dramatically—but at the same time, the number of Road Warriors dwindled and attendance at meetings fell as some members got other jobs and dropped out of the struggle. The union's best activists thus found themselves constantly on the road while Shinall and his faction were working the picket lines, slandering the activists and talking surrender.

International Unions

Rank-and-file members who are prepared to lead a militant fight using bold tactics face a tremendous uphill battle if the leadership of their international is unwilling to back them. The UPIU officers were all too typical of most national union leaders.[10] While tens of thousands of people across the country were enthralled and inspired by the Staley workers' example, Wayne Glenn never was. The international's opposition to Local 7837's militant fight and the measly picket pay (but not health insurance) it provided were crucial factors that convinced a majority of the Staley workers to finally give up after thirty months.

Dave Watts said:

> Our fight was winnable, but Wayne Glenn was never a champion. He threw some crumbs out there . . . but never supplied the resources. . . . The UPIU leadership still to this day don't know that it takes national support and global unity to win

against companies that have all the money in the world. . . . You can't win today on your own. It takes national leadership to pave the way. Labor will not win or lose the battle for America because of the employers. They'll lose it because of a lack of leadership, a lack of direction, and a lack of strategy.[11]

Things were not always this way. In the late 1930s and early 1940s it was rank-and-file workers' aggressive grassroots activism that built the Congress of Industrial Organizations and brought millions of American workers into unions. But those victories also required a fearless leadership.

Today when international unions resolutely support their workers, the union is often victorious. The Pittston strikers won in 1990 when the UMWA staked the future and the treasury of the union on winning their fight. The Pittston fight was "seamless," said Trumka. "It was a seamless operation because it was *our* struggle. It wasn't the local's struggle. It wasn't the district union's struggle. It wasn't the international's struggle. It was *our* struggle. You couldn't tell where one part of the organization stopped. It was all blended together. It wasn't their fight or his fight, it was *our* fight." Similarly, the locked-out Ravenswood workers won in 1992 when the United Steelworkers of America dedicated its resources to their fight. In addition to disbursing picket pay, the union spent over $5 million on the campaign. The Steelworkers won again when they took in the Bridgestone/Firestone workers after their strike collapsed in May 1995 and launched an aggressive, twenty-two-month global corporate campaign. The USWA under the leadership of George Becker again committed tremendous staff time and spent $20 million to win a fair contract. "Defeat is not an option," Becker declared repeatedly. The Teamsters International led by Ron Carey spent a year educating and mobilizing its members at UPS and then led the striking workers to victory in 1997.[12] Finally, the Service Employees International Union has poured tremendous resources into its Justice for Janitors campaigns.

Most national union leaders, however, are incapable of or opposed to such militancy. Until the rank-and-file mobilize to replace their moribund leaders and transform their unions from the bottom up, labor will continue to decline. Trumka expressed this sentiment to the Staley workers when he came to Decatur in March 1995. "The leadership of a lot of unions better pay attention to their members, about members that want to stand up and fight," declared Trumka at a press conference. "Because if you're a leader in America today and you don't want to represent and fight for your members, I can tell you what's going to happen. They're going to put somebody in there that *is* going to fight for them. And you know what? That's what *should* happen."[13]

The AFL-CIO

Although the future of the labor movement ultimately depends on rank-and-file activism, it also depends on the labor movement's willingness to wage a militant fight—and to step beyond protocol.

For most of the Staley workers' fight for a fair contract, the AFL-CIO was led by Lane Kirkland. "There's no question," says AFL-CIO staffer Joe Uehlein, that the Decatur labor wars "contributed mightily to finally pushing leaders" to launch an unprecedented and ultimately successful campaign to unseat Kirkland. In October 1995 the New Voices slate began making changes in the sleepy AFL-CIO.

At the AFL-CIO convention in October 1995, when the New Voices slate swept to power, it seemed "certain that there was going to be a plan to hit the ground running," said Dave Watts early the next year. "The Sweeney-Trumka ticket . . . paraded ten locals that were on strike or locked out, patted us on the back, and said, 'We're proud of you. There's some plans. We're going to work hard. We're going to make some things happen with Pepsi.'"[14] And on November 4 Dan Lane ended his sixty-five-day fast when Sweeney assured him he would make winning the Staley fight a top priority. But the promises failed to materialize. "As long as I live," said Gary Lamb in words that could have been voiced by scores of Staley activists, "there will always be a cold spot in my heart for the AFL-CIO. They left us hanging."[15]

The Staley workers wanted Sweeney and Trumka to come to Decatur soon after their October 25 election, give strength to the battered workers, declare at a national press conference that they were mobilizing the entire labor movement to win the fight, and assign the promised AFL-CIO organizers to the Pepsi campaign. Pepsi had been targeted with protests for nearly a year in dozens of cities across the country, and its contract was up for renewal in two months— more than enough time, the workers felt, for Sweeney to escalate the campaign and give the final push to pressure Pepsi to stop buying Staley corn syrup. "We had contacts within the Pepsi plants from our trip to Purchase," said Art Dhermy. "We got word that Pepsi had given [Staley] an ultimatum, 'Have this thing settled by the end of the year or we're going elsewhere.'" Dick Blinn, editor of *The Paperworker,* agreed that the campaign "had [Staley] customers on the run. Pepsi was close to pulling the plug."[16]

Moreover, if losing Miller and then Pepsi wasn't enough to force Staley to the table, the local had further plans—with the help of the AFL-CIO, it would target the Coca-Cola Company, Staley's other primary customer. The Staley activists were certain that, viewing what had happened to Pepsi and Miller and seeing Sweeney's commitment, Coca-Cola would decide that its best course was to buy corn sweetener elsewhere. "If Pepsi had pulled out," said Mike Griffin, "then

I believe Coke would have followed suit and the company would have had to deal with us."[17] With three of its largest customers lost, Staley would have had no choice but to bargain a fair contract with the union.

The new AFL-CIO leaders said that they concurred with the union's strategy. The Staley workers "have a good strategy and what we want to do is bring more power to it, escalate it, and ratchet up the decibel level very quickly," said AFL-CIO staffer Joe Uehlein, whom Sweeney assigned to head the Staley task force in early November. "It is not a question of new strategic directions but of bringing more resources to an existing strategy."[18] In a November 14 fax to Watts, UPUI special projects coordinator Mark Brooks reported that he had spoken with Uehlein and that "Joe agrees with my suggestion that the AFL-CIO should assign as many AFL-CIO field representatives as possible to help us escalate the Pepsi campaign. The AFL-CIO will also help us to urge all national unions to organize their members to become involved in this campaign."[19]

But suddenly the AFL-CIO's Staley task force folded. "Nothing happened," said Dan Lane. No AFL-CIO leaders "ever came to Decatur, and no one ever asked us to go to Washington."[20] When the buoyant workers returned to Decatur after the AFL-CIO convention, said Watts, they believed Sweeney's promises that the new leadership team would immediately come to their assistance. "But we waited and waited and waited, and the membership finally got fed up."[21]

Why didn't Sweeney and Trumka deliver on their promise to put the full resources of the AFL-CIO behind the Pepsi campaign? There are three possible explanations.

First, Sweeney may never have intended to assign forty organizers and make Staley a "top priority." When Dan Lane's doctor reported to the press in early November that Lane risked death if he continued the fast, Sweeney undoubtedly felt tremendous pressure. Sweeney "was probably feeling desperate to get this guy to stop starving himself to death," said Madison, Wisconsin, CLC president Jim Cavanaugh. Jeremy Brecher suggests this explanation in his classic labor history text *Strike!* Brecher quotes an anonymous top AFL-CIO staffer as saying that Sweeney's promises were "a facade—a smoke-and-mirrors thing."[22] But Uehlein adamantly denies this charge as "absolutely false, ridiculous," and totally contrary to Sweeney's character.[23]

Second, perhaps the new AFL-CIO leaders simply ran out of time. Brooks argues that Sweeney "did not have a lot of time to bring things to bear" between October 25, when he was elected, and December 12, when Jim Shinall was elected Local 7837 president. Brooks speculated, "All Tate & Lyle had to do was [to say to Pepsi], 'Look, this local is about to collapse. So don't worry about it.'" The Staley activists, however, argued that seven weeks was more than enough time for Sweeney to make clear to Staley and Pepsi that the new AFL-CIO leadership was throwing enormous resources into the campaign and would not accept defeat. "If Trumka and Sweeney had come to Decatur and gathered the membership," argued Gary Lamb, "and Trumka had laid out a plan to get Pepsi separated from Staley, I am quite sure the membership would have given him the time"—that is, they would not have voted for Shinall for president or voted for the company's contract.[24]

The third possible explanation is that Wayne Glenn contacted Sweeney and "ordered the AFL-CIO to withhold its support," as the last issue of the *War Zone* reported, and that Sweeney agreed.[25] The AFL-CIO is a federation of unions that voluntarily choose to affiliate. The national union presidents call the shots within their unions, and the AFL-CIO president is supposed to respect the autonomy of its affiliates. "There's this agreement that the federation does not get involved in an affiliate's battles" when they're told not to, said CWA vice president Jan Pierce. "It's damn obvious that the [AFL-CIO] were called off. . . . Sweeney promised he'd give [Local 7837] the organizers. There's only one organization capable of calling that off, the UPIU. There's only one person who could have called it off, Wayne Glenn." Jim Cavanaugh agreed. "I suspect that Wayne Glenn told Sweeney to keep his nose out of it, and Sweeney was embarrassed to admit that."

"What would happen if John Sweeney violates protocol?" wondered AFL-CIO staffer Uehlein. "It's almost a question that we don't even ask. . . . We do what the affiliates want us to do. We'll argue with them. We'll work with them to move in a certain direction that we think is right and give our best advice. . . . But the best we can do at the federation is try to lead, to set an example through some of our best campaigns. . . . We can't run over affiliates in the process. . . . When decisions get made, we go with that decision. We have to—they're paying the freight."

Since taking office in 1995 Sweeney has set aside 30 percent of the AFL-CIO's budget for union organizing drives and has pressured the national unions to follow suit. In 1996 the AFL-CIO launched "Union Summer" to give college students experience as union organizers during their summer breaks, and that endeavor was a strong impetus in the birth of the two-hundred-campus anti-sweatshop movement. The AFL-CIO has built relationships with civil rights and women's rights organizations. It has backed the labor-community grass-roots coalition Jobs with Justice and encouraged local unions and central labor councils to affiliate. It has actively supported the formation of Interfaith Worker Justice, which now boasts over sixty affiliates, some with paid staff, across the nation. The AFL-CIO has championed immigrant rights, supported the 2003 Immigrant Workers Freedom Ride, endorsed the massive 2006 immigrants' rights rallies, and backed workers' centers. It has helped form chapters of Pride at Work, which advocates for gay and lesbian workers' rights.

Yet the experience of the Staley workers prompts nagging questions: Does the AFL-CIO leadership have a plan to win strikes and lockouts when a big corporation has declared all-out war on a union? Does it have the strategy and the will to do whatever is necessary to win a major labor battle? It is abundantly clear that the new AFL-CIO will unleash all its resources in election campaigns. But will it unleash the same resources to win the next national labor battle?

The CWA's Jan Pierce argues that labor misplaces its priorities when every two years it organizes a full-scale mobilization for political campaigns but expends minimal resources to support militant workers' struggles such as the one at Staley. In 2004 labor spent over $100 million, and reportedly "the AFL-CIO and its member unions mobilized 5,000 paid staffers, more than 225,000 volunteers, staffed hundreds of phone banks, knocked on 6 million doors, and distributed 32 million fliers."[26] Labor has pledged to spend $300 million in the 2008 elections.[27] But, says Pierce, "The same sort of mobilization that the union movement is able to do on behalf of phony Democrats could have been done on behalf of legitimate rank-and-file unionists who had already made *tremendous* sacrifices. Look what forces could have been brought to bear on Pepsi. The potential was unlimited. And that would certainly have brought Pepsi at least to the table, brought them to some sort of sensible resolution and [Staley to a] collective bargaining agreement."

Uehlein puts it bluntly: the AFL-CIO's "structure defies strategic action." When will the AFL-CIO leadership, asks Jerry Tucker, "step past the parochial nature of internal relationships," override an affiliated national union if necessary, and pull out all the stops to win?[28] And in 2005 SEIU leader Stephen Lerner echoed this point:

> We all agree that if the labor movement is going to survive, it has to reshape itself, build coalitions with other movements, and offer a new vision. But what are the concrete things that we can do? What are the things that we in organized labor can actually control that might really make a difference? We have to begin taking a hard look at how the labor movement has chosen to structure itself. . . . Right now, we have no way to make decisions as a movement; instead, each individual union does whatever it likes. The AFL-CIO as a whole doesn't have any power. It is basically a bunch of separate fiefdoms, each of which can do anything they want. . . . Because the AFL operates on consensus, you have to get all [the] unions to think something's a good idea or else it's hopeless.[29]

In a final letter to Chicago supporters who had adopted his family during the lockout, Staley worker Walter Maus aptly wrote, "John Sweeney, Rich Trumka and Linda Chavez-Thompson must take firm, decisive control of the AFL-CIO. They must learn by what has happened to us, and use it in the future to never let this happen again. If they don't, this was all for nothing and organized labor is doomed."[30]

Change to Win

After a year of bitter, tumultuous debate among labor leaders, on the eve of the August 2005 AFL-CIO convention two of its largest unions, the Service Employees and Teamsters, announced they were leaving to form a new, competing labor federation. The six-million member Change to Win federation soon included five more unions: United Farm Workers; Laborers; Carpenters; UNITE-HERE, representing hotel, restaurant, and garment workers; and the United Food and Commercial Workers. The AFL-CIO has fifty-three unions with nine million members.[31]

The Change to Win unions argued that the AFL-CIO under John Sweeny had failed to reverse labor's decline. While in 2005 union density fell to 7.9 percent in the private sector, despite Sweeny's efforts, most unions were not putting significant resources into organizing new members. AFL-CIO leaders countered that splitting labor into two federations would weaken and divide unions at a time when unity was essential to defend workers' rights. They suggested that the two factions did not differ substantively.

The AFL-CIO versus Change to Win debate, however, has taken place largely among labor's leaders, not the nearly 16 million rank-and-file unionists. Moreover, the lessons of Decatur have not been central to the discussion. The words of Dan Lane capture the ongoing challenge to both federations: "We lost this battle, but the war against American workers continues. The rest of corporate America was watching Decatur closely. Make no mistake, there'll be no peace for American workers. The question is, when are we going to unite, turn [the labor movement] around, meet fire with fire, and fight until we win?"[32]

Appendix
Sources

We would like to thank the following people, who allowed us access to their materials:

- Prof. Laurie Clements (files)
- Prof. Mark Crouch (files)
- Art Dhermy (files)
- Ethel Fargusson (videotapes of every union meeting, rally, and local television newscast, 1993–95)
- Mike Griffin (files)
- Nancy Hanna (files)
- Labor Beat (videotapes)
- Tamra McCartney (files)
- People's Law Office (pretrial depositions from the November 2000 civil trial against the Decatur police for the June 25, 1994, pepper-spraying)
- Ray Rogers (files)
- Michael Szpak (files)
- Jerry Tucker (files)
- United Paperworkers International Union (files)
- University of Illinois at Urbana-Champaign (Martin Mangan files)
- Dave Watts (files)
- Mona Williams (copies of every *Decatur Herald and Review* article that mentioned Staley or the union, June 1993–January 1996)
- Bill Winter (files)

We would like to thank the following people, who graciously agreed to be interviewed. Without their assistance, this project would not have been possible. In the endnotes we consistently use the wording "interview with authors," but some interviews were done by Hawking, some by Ashby, and some by both authors.

All interviews with Staley workers and spouses were conducted in person in Decatur, Illinois, unless otherwise noted.

Staley Workers and Spouses

Phyllis Beals	7/20/01	Decatur, by phone
Rosie Brown	10/9/02	
Mary Brummett	10/25/01	
Richard Brummett	7/7/93	
David Conley	3/25/01	
John Cook	3/25/01	
Art Dhermy	3/12/01; 10/31/03	
Linda Dhermy	10/31/03	
Judy Dulaney	10/25/01	
Ethel Fargusson	3/16/01; 10/25/01	
Dike Ferris	2/21/01; 10/30/03	
Stephen Fischer	7/7/93	
Sandy Gosnell	10/25/01	
Jan Griffin	10/25/01	
Mike Griffin	2/20/01; 3/12/01	
Nancy Hanna	7/10/02	
Steve Haseley	7/12/01; 9/12/01	
Al Hawkins	2/20/01; 3/25/01	
Jeanette Hawkins	2/20/01; 2/25/01; 3/25/01; 10/25/01	
Barb Henson	7/12/01	
Dennis Houston	3/25/01	
Bob Hull	10/26/01	
Susan Hull	10/25/01; 10/26/01	
Cheryl Lamb	7/10/02	
Gary Lamb	3/26/01; 7/10/02	
Dan Lane	2/20/01; 11/20–21/01	
Tamra McCartney	10/10/02	Monticello, Ill.
Mike Odeneal	3/25/01	
Lois Oldham	10/9/02	
Lorell Patterson	6/17/01	Decatur, by phone
Rhonda Plankenhorn	10/25/01	
Royal Plankenhorn	3/25/01	
Sarah Plankenhorn	10/25/01	
Eugene Robinson	3/25/01	
Dick Schable	2/20/01; 7/17/01	
Michael Stewart	7/7/93	
Bill Strohl	2/20/01; 3/3/01	
Frankie Travis	3/25/01	
Ron VanScyoc	2/20/01	
Tonia VanScyoc	10/25/01	
Betty Walker	10/9/02	
Dave Watts	7/7/93; 7/14/93; 2/20/01; 3/12/01; 7/11/01	

Pat Watts	10/25/01	
Barrie Williams	2/20/01; 3/12/01	
Bill Winter	2/20/01; 10/29/03	
Janet Winter	10/29/03	

Union Advisers

Ray Rogers	4/29/01	New York City
Jerry Tucker	2/20/01; 2/21/01; 4/21/01	Decatur, Ill., and Dearborn, Mich.
Kip Voytek	4/29/01	New York City

AIW/UPIU

Dick Blinn	4/24/03	Nashville, Tenn., by phone
Tom Braun	8/1/01	Fort Wayne, Ind.
Mark Brooks	5/22/01	Nashville, Tenn.
Wayne Glenn	5/22/01	Nashville, Tenn.
Glen Goss	6/28/01	Indianapolis, Ind.
Danny Wirges	8/1/01	Fort Wayne, Ind.

AFL-CIO

Michael Szpak	8/17/01; 8/18/01	Washington, D.C.
Rich Trumka	5/20/03	Washington, D.C.
Joe Uehlein	8/17/01	Washington, D.C.

Supporters

Jon Baker	11/12/01	Elmhurst, Ill.
Kim Bobo	5/17/03	Washington, D.C.
Jim Cavanaugh	3/23/01	Madison, Wis., by phone
Bruce Colburn	3/17/01	Milwaukee, Wis., by phone
Joe Iosbaker	11/12/01	Elmhurst, Ill.
Harry Kelber	4/29/01	New York City
David Klein	11/12/01	Elmhurst, Ill.
Caroline Lund	3/18/01	San Francisco, Calif., by phone
Staughton Lynd	4/21/01	Dearborn, Mich.
Jan Pierce	6/1/01	New York City, by phone
Glenn Poshard	10/25/01	Carbondale, Ill.
Mike Sacco	11/12/01	Elmhurst, Ill.

Simone Sagovac	3/12/03	Detroit, Mich.
Tony Silano	5/19/03	Washington, D.C.
Jane Slaughter	3/12/03	Detroit, Mich.
Larry Solomon	3/12/01	Decatur, Ill.
Bob Wages	3/27/01	Denver, Colo.
		(by phone)

Additionally, we received thirty-eight responses to a survey of Staley workers and spouses; the survey, which we designed, went out to individuals whose names and addresses appeared on a June 1993 AIW 837 mailing list.

Notes

Preface

1. Interview with authors, August 17, 2001.
2. "Afterward," in *A New Labor Movement for the New Century*, ed. Gregory Mantsios (New York: Monthly Review Press, 1998), 329.

Prologue: Jim Beals

1. Interview with authors, July 20, 2001. Unless otherwise indicated, all quotations from Phyllis "P. J." Beals are from this source.
2. Tom Frank and Dave Mulcahey, "This Is War," *Chicago Reader*, January 20, 1995.
3. "Deadly Corn," brochure published by AIW 837, 1993.
4. Masha Alexander, "State of the Union," *N Magazine* (Northwestern University), March 1994.
5. "Deadly Corn."
6. *Allied Industrial Worker*, monthly newsletter, June 1990.
7. "Crisis in Decatur," brochure published by AIW 837, 1992.
8. "Deadly Corn." Unless otherwise indicated, all quotations from Jerry Sumner, Larry Shook, and Walter Maus describing Beals's death are from this source.
9. *Deadly Corn*, video produced by Labor Vision for AIW 837, 1993.
10. Interview with authors, AIW 837 War Zone Command Center, July 7, 1993.
11. *Allied Industrial Worker*, June 1990.
12. Most states allow workers to sue their employers for *intentional* misconduct, but this is extremely hard to prove, and state's attorneys almost never pursue such charges against corporations.
13. "A Dangerous Business," special episode of *Frontline* (PBS), September 30, 2002.
14. *Decatur Herald and Review*, July 22, 1995.
15. *Deadly Corn*.
16. Rose Feurer, "The Staley Lockout: A View from Below," *Impact: The Rank and*

File Newsletter (Youngstown, Ohio), July 1995; Bill Strohl, interviews with the authors, February 20 and March 2, 2001.

Chapter 1: The Company and the Union

1. Becky Bradway, *Pink Houses and Family Taverns* (Bloomington: Indiana University Press, 2002), 8, 36.

2. Dan J. Forrestal, *The Kernel and the Bean: The 75-Year Story of the Staley Company* (New York: Simon and Schuster, 1982), 25. All material in this subsection is drawn from Forrestal's text unless otherwise cited.

3. Forrestal, *Kernel and the Bean*, 45–46.

4. Ibid, 42.

5. Ibid, 73.

6. Letter to the editor, *Decatur Herald and Review*, August 18, 1993.

7. *Decatur Herald and Review*, May 14, 1995.

8. Interview with authors, March 12, 2001.

9. Milton Derber, *Labor in Illinois: The Affluent Years, 1945–1980* (Urbana: University of Illinois Press, 1989), 312.

10. On the rise of the UAW and the split with Martin's faction, see Sidney Fine, *Sit-down: The General Motors Strike of 1936–37* (Ann Arbor: University of Michigan Press, 1969); Nelson Lichtenstein, *The Most Dangerous Man in Detroit: Walter Reuther and the Fate of American Labor* (New York: Basic Books, 1995); Frank Cormier and William J. Eaton, *Reuther* (Englewood Cliffs, N.J.: Prentice-Hall, 1970); Roger Keeran, *The Communist Party and the Auto Workers Unions* (Bloomington: Indiana University Press, 1980); Frank Marquart, *An Auto Worker's Journal: The UAW from Crusade to One-Party Union* (University Park: Pennsylvania State University Press, 1975); Henry Kraus, *Heroes of Unwritten Story: The UAW, 1934–1939* (Urbana: University of Illinois Press, 1993); Irving Howe and B. J. Widick, *The UAW and Walter Reuther* (New York: Random House, 1949; repr., 1973); and C. J. Hawking, "Homer Martin," unpublished paper, Union Leadership and Administration graduate program, University of Massachusetts at Amherst.

11. Widick and Howe, *The UAW and Walter Reuther*, 51.

12. *Allied Industrial Worker*, monthly newsletter, December, 1993, reprinting an article on the history of the AIW in commemoration of the union's fiftieth anniversary, *Allied Industrial Worker*, September 1985.

13. The rightward evolution of the CIO and the AFL-CIO merger are discussed in greater detail in the next chapter.

14. During World War II the UAW-AFL organized a number of Decatur factories, including A. E. Staley, Mueller, Wagner Castings, Chambers-Bearing-Quinlan, A. W. Cash, Houdaille-Hershey, Leader Iron Works, and Ornamental Metalworks. In the late 1940s and early 1950s the UAW-AFL organized General Electric, Mississippi Valley Structural Steel, Archer Daniels Midland, Essex Wire, Hi-Flier Manufacturing, and the Marvel-Schebler-Tillotson Division of Borg Warner. The Congress of Industrial Organizations failed to organize any of Decatur's many manufacturing plants until the UAW-CIO organized the Caterpillar plant in 1955 (*Allied Industrial Worker*, December 1993).

15. Bill Strohl, interview with the authors, March 2, 2001.

16. Quotations without an endnote are drawn from the authors' 2001–3 interviews listed in the appendix.

17. Brewster Kneen, *Invisible Giant: Cargill and Its Transnational Strategies* (East Haven, Conn.: Pluto, 1995), 19–20.

18. *Corn Annual 1993,* report of the Corn Refiners Association (Washington, D.C., 1993).

19. Forrestal, *Kernel and the Bean,* 236.

20. Rita Koselka, "Back to What We Do Best," *Forbes,* June 24, 1991.

21. James Lieber, *Rats in the Grain: The Dirty Tricks and Trials of Archer Daniels Midland* (New York: Four Walls Eight Windows, 2000), 346.

22. Unless otherwise cited, Decatur statistics are drawn from the Economic Development Corporation of Decatur, Illinois, Web site.

23. At the close of the 1970 strike there was a dispute over the discharge of seven strikers who were accused of dumping corn from a delivery truck at a plant gate. The Staley company hired the Chicago-based law firm Seyfarth, Shaw, which was notorious for its antiunion expertise, to fight the union, which was adamantly seeking amnesty for the seven workers. Eventually the union lost, and the seven men were formally discharged.

24. "Corn Refining: The Process, the Products," a pamphlet published by the Corn Refiners Association; *Deadly Corn,* video produced by Labor Vision for AIW 837, 1993.

25. On labor-management cooperation plans, see chapter 6, "Saving Good Jobs" Fighting Lean Production and Outsourcing," in *A Troublemaker's Handbook 2: How to Fight Back Where You Work and Win!* ed. Jane Slaughter, 61–78 (Detroit: Labor Notes, 2005); Mike Parker and Jane Slaughter, *Choosing Sides: Unions and the Team Concept* (Detroit: Labor Notes, 1988); Mike Parker and Jane Slaughter, *Working Smart: A Union Guide to Participation Programs and Reengineering* (Detroit: Labor Notes, 1994); Bruce Nissen, ed., *Unions and Workplace Reorganization* (Detroit: Wayne State University Press, 1997); Kim Moody, *Workers in a Lean World: Unions in the International Economy* (London: Verso, 1997); Steve Babson, ed., *Lean Work: Empowerment and Exploitation in the Global Auto Industry* (Detroit: Wayne State University Press, 1995); Laurie Graham, *On the Line at Subaru-Isuzu: The Japanese Model and the American Worker* (Ithaca, N.Y.: Cornel University Press, 1995); and James Rinehart, Christopher Huxley, and David Robertson, *Just Another Car Factory? Lean Production and Its Discontents* (Ithaca, N.Y.: Cornell University Press, 1997).

26. Forrestal, *Kernel and the Bean,* 257–58.

27. Talk given at the first meeting of the Chicago Staley Workers Solidarity Committee, July 17, 1993, videotaped and transcribed by Steven Ashby.

28. Ben Oertle, *History of the Inter-Union Wet Corn Milling Council, United States and Canada: 25 Years of Progress, 1965–1990* (1990); "The Wet Corn Industry," presentation by Laurie Clements to the Inter-Union Wet/Dry Corn Milling Council, 1994 (in authors' possession).

29. On the corporate assault on unions and subsequent decline of the labor movement since the 1980s, see Kim Moody, *An Injury to All: The Decline of American Unionism* (New

York: Verso, 1988); Mike Davis, *Prisoners of the American Dream: Politics and Economy in the History of the U.S. Working Class* (London: Verso Press, 1986); Michael Goldfield, *The Decline of Organized Labor in the United States* (Chicago: University of Chicago Press, 1987); Nelson Lichtenstein, *State of the Union: A Century of American Labor* (Princeton, N.J.: Princeton University Press, 2002); Tom Geoghegan, *Which Side Are You On? Trying to Be for Labor When It's Flat on Its Back* (New York: Farrar, Straus and Giroux, 1991); Paul Buhle, *Taking Care of Business: Samuel Gompers, George Meany, Lane Kirkland, and the Tragedy of American Labor* (New York: Monthly Review Press, 1999).

Chapter 2: Tate & Lyle Comes to Decatur

1. Milton Derber, *Labor in Illinois: The Affluent Years, 1945–1980* (Urbana: University of Illinois Press, 1989), 309; O. T. Banton, ed., *History of Macon County* (Decatur, Ill.: Macon County Historical Society, 1976), 266–72.

2. *Decatur Herald and Review,* May 17 and 31, 1988.

3. Quotations without an endnote are drawn from the authors' 2001–3 interviews listed in the appendix.

4. "From Love Lane Liverpool to Decatur, Illinois: A Bitter Sweet Story of Our Globalized Times," paper drafted for the Tate & Lyle Workers Council, undated, 32.

5. *Decatur Herald and Review,* April 14, 1988.

6. Philippe Chalmin, *The Making of a Sugar Giant: Tate & Lyle, 1859–1989* (Chur, Switzerland: Harwood, 1990).

7. David C. Ranney and Paul Schwalb, "An Analysis of the A. E. Staley/Tate & Lyle Lockout in Decatur, Illinois," unpublished paper, Center for Urban Economic Development, University of Illinois at Chicago, March 1995.

8. The concentration extended globally; eight firms, Tate & Lyle among them, controlled the world market in corn wet-milling, cane-sugar refining, and beet-sugar production.

9. Sharon Walsh and Jackie Spinner, "Unusual Links Forged by Two Firms Facing Price-Fixing Probe," *Washington Post,* July 22, 1995.

10. Qtd. in Mark Whitacre, as told to Ronald Henkoff, "My Life as a Mole for the FBI," *Fortune,* September 4, 1995.

11. Walsh and Spinner, "Unusual Links."

12. Masha Alexander, "State of the Union," *N Magazine* (Northwestern University), March 1994.

13. Ranney, "An Analysis"; "The Struggle at Staley—A Special Report," *Tate & Lyle Worker News,* undated (summer or fall 1994); "The Wet Corn Industry," presentation by Laurie Clements to the Inter-Union Wet/Dry Corn Milling Council, 1994. See also *Decatur Herald and Review,* July 1, 1993.

14. "The Wet Corn Industry"; Ranney, "An Analysis"; Tom Frank and Dave Mulcahey, "This Is War," *Chicago Reader,* January 20, 1995 (citing Clements's findings on the corn wet-milling industry).

15. Dan Lane, Mike Griffin, Bill Strohl, Barrie Williams, Jeanette Hawkins, Al Hawkins, Ron VanScyoc, Bill Winter, Jerry Tucker, and Dick Schable, group interview with authors, February 20, 2001; Dave Watts, interview with authors, March 12, 2001; Dan Lane, interview with authors, November 20–21, 2001.

16. *Decatur Herald and Review,* April 16, 1993.

17. Ibid., April 7, 1991.

18. Ibid., July 26, 1993.

19. "A Dangerous Business," special episode of *Frontline* (PBS), September 30, 2002.

20. "Safety Statement to Decatur Management," AIW Local 837 Executive Board and Bargaining Committee, undated (first week of February 1992).

21. A. E. Staley director of operations Red Geurts to AIW 837 president Dave Watts, letter, October 2, 1991.

22. Ranney, "An Analysis." However, the union challenged and won the reinstatement of seven of the nine fired workers.

23. Interview with authors, July 7, 1993.

24. *Decatur Herald and Review,* October 1, 1992.

25. A. E. Staley director of operations Red Geurts to Local 837 Bargaining Committee chairperson Jim Shinall, memo, August 13, 1992.

26. "Crisis in Decatur," brochure produced for AIW 837, 1993.

27. David Moberg, "War Zone," *In These Times,* July 24, 1995; Frank and Mulcahey, "This Is War."

28. AIW International representative Ronnie Straw to AIW International president Nick Serraglio, memo, March 24, 1992.

29. Throughout its struggle the union's literature cited a profile of the firm written by Harvard law school students: "The union-busting activities of Seyfarth are national in scope: farmworkers in California lettuce fields, pressmen in Washington, D.C., firemen in Normal, Illinois, and clerical workers at Yale all share the common bond of having confronted Seyfarth" (qtd. in "Crisis in Decatur"). For further information on union-busting consultants and law firms, see Marty Leavitt, *Confessions of a Union Buster* (New York: Crown, 1993). As of 2005, Seyfarth, Shaw reports on their Web site (www.seyfarth.com) that the firm employs 600 lawyers, with 245 devoted to labor law, including "union avoidance."

30. AIW Region 8 director Dan Wirges, AIW union representative Bill Coleman, and AIW Local 837 president Dave Watts were present at the meeting. Slightly different versions of the statement appeared in the union's corporate-campaign literature throughout the fight, including "Crisis in Decatur"; "Clarity Statement to AIW 837 Membership and Families, Community, and Staley Tate & Lyle," internal union document, undated (just before the October 5, 1992, contract vote); and "UPIU 7837 Chronological Listing of the A. E. Staley Dispute," January 26, 1996 (in authors' possession).

Chapter 3: The Union Prepares to Resist

1. Alexander Cockburn, "Beat the Devil" column, *The Nation,* May 17, 1993; *Decatur Herald and Review,* September 29, 1992.

2. Quotations without an endnote are drawn from the authors' 2001–3 interviews listed in the appendix.

3. "AIW Local 837 vs. A. E. Staley: From In-Plant Strategy to Lock-out: An Interview with Staley workers Richard Brummett, Emery Scrimpsher, and David Atteberry," *Impact: The Rank and File Newsletter* (Youngstown, Ohio), November 1993. Alice Lynd transcribed and edited the interview.

4. Dan Lane, Mike Griffin, Bill Strohl, Barrie Williams, Jeanette Hawkins, Al Hawkins, Ron VanScyoc, Bill Winter, Jerry Tucker, and Dick Schable, group interview with authors, February 20, 2001.

5. *Allied Industrial Worker,* monthly newsletter, December 1993.

6. The description of hiring clusters is based on an analysis of AIW Local 837's June 1993 membership list.

7. As southern blacks migrated northward, between 1950 and 1980 Decatur's black population rose from 3,458 (5.2% of the population) to 13,700 (14.6% of the population) (Sundiata Keita Cha-Jua, "Resistance and Self-Development: An Outline History of the Black Community of Decatur, Illinois, 1830–1980," unpublished paper).

8. Frankie Travis, Jeanette Hawkins, Al Hawkins, David Conley, John Cook, Dennis Houston, Mike Odeneal, and Eugene Robinson, group interview with authors, March 25, 2001.

9. Stephen Franklin, *Three Strikes: Labor's Heartland Losses and What They Mean for Working Americans* (New York: Guilford, 2001), 66.

10. Mark Singer, "Town on a String," *New Yorker,* October 30, 2000.

11. James Loewen, *Sundown Towns: A Hidden Dimension of American Racism* (New York: New Press, 2005). Loewen reports that from the late 1800s through the 1960s, across America whites created thousands of "sundown towns," with signs posted at the city limits warning African-Americans to stay away: "N——, Don't Let The Sun Set On You In [This Town]." Loewen, who grew up in Decatur, notes (388) that by 2000 Decatur's African American population had risen to 19.5 percent. Decatur whites fled to nearby towns such as Maroa (0.2% African American in 2000), Niantic (0.0%), and Pana (0.1%).

12. Barry Bearak, "Cat on Strike: The Waning Power of Unions," part 3 of a five-part series, "The Strike at Caterpillar," *Los Angeles Times,* May 16, 1995. For more on the Caterpillar strike, also see Michael H. Cimini, "Caterpillar's Prolonged Dispute Ends," *Compensation and Working Conditions,* Washington, D.C.: Bureau of Labor Statistics/ GPO, 1998); and Isaac Cohen, "The Caterpillar Labor Dispute and the UAW, 1991–1998," *Labor Studies Journal* 27, no. 4 (Winter 2003): 77–99.

13. On the evolution of the CIO in the 1940s and 1950s and the 1955 merger with the AFL, see Nelson Lichtenstein, *State of the Union: A Century of American Labor* (Princeton, N.J.: Princeton University Press, 2002); Martin Halpern, *UAW Politics in the Cold War Era* (Albany: State University of New York Press, 1988); Robert H. Zieger, *The CIO, 1935–1955* (Chapel Hill: University of North Carolina Press, 1995); Art Preis, *Labor's Giant Step: Twenty Years of the CIO* (New York: Pathfinder, 1964); Bert Cochran, *Labor and Communism: The Conflict That Shaped American Unions* (Princeton, N.J.: Princeton University Press, 1977); Kim Moody, *An Injury to All: The Decline of American Unionism* (New York: Verso, 1988); George Lipsitz, *Rainbow at Midnight: Labor and Culture in the 1940s* (Urbana: University of Illinois Press, 1994); Steve Fraser and Gary Gerstle, *The Rise and Fall of the New Deal Order, 1930–1980* (Princeton, N.J.: Princeton University Press, 1989); and Steven Ashby, "The American Working Class and the Coming of the Cold War, 1945–1949," Ph.D. diss., University of Chicago, 1993.

14. Moody, *An Injury to All,* 44.

15. On the PATCO strike see Arthur Shostak, *The Air Controllers Controversy: Lessons*

from the PATCO Strike (New York: Human Sciences, 1986); Michael Round, *Grounded: Reagan and the PATCO Crash* (New York: Garland, 1999); and Rebecca Pels, "The Pressures of PATCO: Strikes and Stress in the 1980s," *Essays in History* 37 (1995).

16. However, when workers engage in a National Labor Relations Board–authorized strike over an employer's illegal labor practices—an "unfair labor practices" strike—they cannot be permanently replaced. For more information on U.S. labor law, see Robert M. Schwartz, "Strike Strategy: Countering Permanent Replacements," *Labor Notes,* February 2003; and Douglas E. Ray, Calvin William Sharpe, and Robert N. Strassfeld, *Understanding Labor Law* (New York: Matthew Bender, 1999).

17. Steve Babson, *The Unfinished Struggle: Turning Points in American Labor, 1877–Present* (Lanham, Md.: Rowan and Littlefield, 1999), 158. Jeremy Brecher, "American Labor on the Eve of the Millennium," *Strike!* updated ed. (Cambridge, Mass.: South End Press, 1997), analyzes a number of labor conflicts in the 1980s, and the Hormel, Phelps Dodge, and International Paper strikes are recounted in Dave Hage and Paul Klauda, *No Retreat, No Surrender: Labor's War at Hormel* (New York: William Morrow, 1989); Hardy Green, *On Strike at Hormel: The Struggle for a Democratic Labor Movement* (Philadelphia: Temple University Press, 1990); Peter Rachleff, *Hard-Pressed in the Heartland: The Hormel Strike and the Future of the American Labor Movement* (Cambridge, Mass.: South End, 1992); Jonathan Rosenblum, *Copper Crucible: How the Arizona Miners' Strike of 1983 Recast Labor-Management Relations in America* (Ithaca, N.Y.: ILR Press, 1995); Barbara Kingsolver, *Holding the Line: Women in the Great Arizona Mine Strike of 1983* (Ithaca, N.Y.: ILR Press, 1989); and Julius Getman, *The Betrayal of Local 14: Paperworkers, Politics, and Permanent Replacements* (Ithaca, N.Y.: Cornell University Press, 1998).

18. Bureau of Labor Statistics, Department of Labor, Web site, www.bls.gov.

19. "The Downsizing of America," eight-part series, *New York Times,* March 3–December 29, 1996.

20. "The Downsizing of America"; United for a Fair Economy Web site, www.faireconomy.org.

21. Bureau of Labor Statistics, Department of Labor, Web page, http://www.bls.gov/news.release/wkstp.t01.htm. The bureau keeps statistics only on work stoppages involving one thousand or more workers, not on all strikes and lockouts that occur in the United States.

22. Stephen Franklin and Sharon Strangenes, "Union Stays on the Job, but Strikes Out at Staley," *Chicago Tribune,* December 12, 1992.

23. "AIW Local 837 vs. A. E. Staley."

24. Mark Crouch and Laurie Clements allowed the authors access to their AIW Local 837 files, including notes on their talks.

25. David Moberg, "Striking Back without Striking," *In These Times,* April 5, 1993. Clements had a great familiarity with the industry because he had previously done research for the corn council. The corn council, officially the Inter-Union Wet/Dry Corn Milling Council, represented the seventeen local unions and seven international unions in the industry. The council held a press conference at the AIW union hall on October 31, 1992, to denounce the company's contract proposal.

26. "AIW Local 837 vs. A. E. Staley."

27. Interview with authors, July 14, 1993.

28. Joe Uehlein, who was the full-time coordinator for the Industrial Union Department within the AFL-CIO—the CIO unions led by UAW president Walter Reuther had formed the IUD shortly after the 1955 merger—traveled to Decatur twice to meet with the local, in November 1992 and January 1993. "In December 1992," read an August 1995 report by the AFL-CIO Strategic Approaches Committee recounting the limited activity in support of the Staley workers, "the AFL-CIO Department of Organization and Field Services assisted with coordinating Staley campaign activities. The AFL-CIO's support focused on the development of an international strategy to pressure Tate & Lyle, which is Staley's London-based parent company." The meetings had the sole purpose of preparing for the local's January 1993 trip to London to confront Tate & Lyle top executives at the annual shareholders meeting. The local wanted, and expected, far more commitment to their struggle from the AFL-CIO.

29. Serraglio's statement recalled by Dave Watts, interview with authors, February 20, 2001.

30. Stephen Franklin, "Leading Labor's Battles," *Chicago Tribune,* July 26, 1993; interview with authors, February 20, 2001.

31. Franklin and Strangenes, "Union Stays on the Job."

32. Wirges's statement recalled by Dave Watts, interviews with authors, July 14, 1993, and February 20, 2001.

33. The authors worked with Ray Rogers during the Staley conflict and interviewed Rogers for this book. In addition, Rogers's work and personal history are discussed in Jarol B. Manheim, *The Death of a Thousand Cuts: Corporate Campaigns and the Attack on the Corporation* (Mahwah, N.J.: Lawrence Erlbaum, 2001)—the book's title comes from a remark by AFL-CIO secretary-treasurer Rich Trumka, who described corporate campaigns as "inflicting upon the employer the death of a thousand cuts"; Getman, *Betrayal of Local 14*; Jeremy Brecher and Tim Costello, eds., *Building Bridges: The Emerging Grassroots Coalition of Labor and Community* (New York: Monthly Review Press, 1990); Hage and Klauda, *No Retreat, No Surrender*; Green, *On Strike at Hormel*; Rachleff, *Hard-Pressed in the Heartland.*

34. The idea of a corporate campaign antedates Rogers's work in the J. P. Stevens's campaign. The first corporate campaign was organized in California in the 1960s by the United Farm Workers (UFW) led by Cesar Chavez. In an effort to get agribusiness to recognize the union and improve the farmworkers' dismal wages and atrocious working conditions, the UFW mobilized rank-and-file members to build a social movement and national boycott campaign against nonunion grapes and Gallo wine. The effort involved tens of thousands of unionists, Latinos, students, and clergy members across the United States. Also see Susan Ferriss and Ricardo Sandoval, *Fight in the Fields: Cesar Chavez and the Farmworkers Movement* (New York: Harcourt, Brace, 1997); Frederick John Dalton, *The Moral Vision of Cesar Chavez* (London: Orbis, 2003); and Peter Matthiessen, *Sal Si Puedes (Escape If You Can): Cesar Chavez and the New American Revolution* (Berkeley: University of California Press, 1969; repr., 2000).

35. Rogers handed out two articles to the Staley workers describing his work: "Rogers'

Tough, Unorthodox Tactics Prevail in Stevens Organizing Fight," *Wall Street Journal*, October 21, 1980; and "Labor's Boardroom Guerrilla: Ray Rogers Leads the Union Fight against International Paper," *Time* magazine, June 20, 1988.

36. Ray Rogers's role in the Hormel and International Paper strikes is discussed in Getman, *Betrayal of Local 14*; Hage and Klauda, *No Retreat, No Surrender*; Green, *On Strike at Hormel*; Rachleff, *Hard-Pressed in the Heartland*.

37. Recalled by Dan Lane, talk at the first meeting of the Chicago Staley Workers Solidarity Committee, July 17, 1993.

38. For an analysis of corporate campaigns, also called "strategic campaigns" or "comprehensive campaigns," see Dan La Botz, *A Troublemaker's Handbook: How to Fight Back Where You Work and Win!* (Detroit: Labor Notes, 1991), ch. 13; and "Corporate Campaigns," in *A Troublemaker's Handbook 2: How to Fight Back Where You Work and Win!* ed. Jane Slaughter (Detroit: Labor Notes, 2005). In 1992 only a handful of international unions endorsed the idea of corporate campaigns, and even fewer had staff members trained in organizing them. Nonetheless, two of labor's greatest victories at that time involved corporate campaigns: the United Mine Workers of America's 1989–90 strike against Pittston and the United Steel Workers of America Local 5668's 1991–92 campaign against Ravenswood Aluminum, which had locked out its union workforce. See Kate Bronfenbrenner and Tom Juravich, *Ravenswood: The Steelworkers' Victory and the Revival of American Labor* (Ithaca, N.Y.: Cornell University Press, 1999); James Green, "Camp Solidarity: The United Mine Workers, the Pittston Strike, and the New 'People's Movement,'" in *Building Bridges: The Emerging Grassroots Coalition of Labor and Community*, ed. Jeremy Brecher and Tim Costello, 15–24 (New York: Monthly Review Press, 1990); "Planting the Seeds of Resurgence: The United Mine Workers Strike Pittston Coal in 1989," in James Green, *Taking History to Heart: The Power of the Past in Building Social Movements* (Boston: University of Massachusetts Press, 2000), 227–54.

39. Ray Rogers, "How Labor Can Fight Back," *USA Today*, July 1984.

40. A. E. Staley operations director Red Geurts to employees, memo, March 5, 1993.

41. "AIW Local 837 vs. A. E. Staley."

42. Interview with authors, March 16, 1994.

43. Mike Griffin to Tate & Lyle CEO Larry Pillard, letter, November 16, 1992.

44. "Union Stays on the Job."

45. *Local 837 News*, October 1992.

46. "Crisis in Decatur."

47. "Clarity Statement."

48. AIW 837 flyer handed out in the plant, undated (late September, 1992). Also see "'Remember Jay' Slogan Adopted by AIW Illinois Local," *The Paperworker* (UPIU), November 1992.

49. *Decatur Herald and Review*, October 1, 1992.

50. Ibid., October 3, 1992.

51. Michael Stewart, letter to the editor, ibid.

52. *Midnight Express*, Local 837's hand-written in-plant newsletter, undated (around October 20, 1992).

53. Interview with authors, July 7, 1993.

54. "A Call to Action," letter to the membership, undated (around November 17, 1992).

55. *Local 837 News*, October 1992.

Chapter 4: Work-to-Rule

1. Quotations without an endnote are drawn from the authors' 2001–3 interviews listed in the appendix.

2. Detailed accounts of these in-plant campaigns were published in the June 1982, December 1983, and August 1985 issues of *Solidarity*, the UAW's monthly magazine, and in Jack Metzgar, "Running the Plant Backwards in UAW Region 5," *Labor Research Review* (Fall 1985): 35–44.

3. Jerry Tucker, interview with authors, February 21, 2001; Kim Moody, *An Injury to All: The Decline of American Unionism* (New York: Verso, 1988), 238–39; Ray Tillman, "Reform Movement in the Teamsters and United Auto Workers," in *The Transformation of U.S. Unions: Voices, Visions, and Strategies from the Grassroots*, ed. Ray Tillman and Michael Cummins, 150–63 (Boulder, Colo.: Lynnee Rienner, 1999).

4. *A Troublemaker's Handbook* is published by *Labor Notes*, a monthly labor magazine that advocates for a more militant and democratic labor movement. The chapter on work-to-rule that Tucker distributed had been reprinted by the UAW New Directions Caucus, which Tucker headed. See Dan La Botz, *A Troublemaker's Handbook: How to Fight Back Where You Work and Win!* (Detroit: Labor Notes, 1991).

5. For a prolabor analysis of work-to-rule see Aaron Brenner, "Inside Strategies," in *A Troublemaker's Handbook 2: How to Fight Back Where You Work and Win!* ed. Jane Slaughter, 127–39 (Detroit: Labor Notes, 2005); Isaac Cohen, "The Caterpillar Labor Dispute and the UAW, 1991–1998," *Labor Studies Journal* 27, no. 4 (Winter 2003): 77–99; and Stephen Franklin, *Three Strikes: Labor's Heartland Losses and What They Mean for Working Americans* (New York: Guilford, 2001). For an excellent journalist's account also see Barry Bearak, "The Inside Strategy: Less Work and More Play at Cat," part 3 of a five-part series, "The Strike at Caterpillar," *Los Angeles Times*, May 16, 1995. For a promanagement analysis of work-to-rule, see Columbus R. Gangemi and Joseph J. Torres, "The Corporate Campaign at Caterpillar," *Journal of Labor Research* 17, no. 3 (Summer 1996): 377–94; Herbert R. Northrup, "Corporate Campaigns: The Perversion of the Regulatory Process," *Journal of Labor Research* 17 (Summer 1996): 345–58; and Herbert R. Northrup, "Union Corporate Campaigns and Inside Games as a Strike Form," *Employee Relations Law Journal* 19 (Spring 1994): 507–38.

6. Joyce L. Kornbluh, ed., *Rebel Voices: An IWW Anthology* (Ann Arbor: University of Michigan Press, 1964), pt. 2; see also Elizabeth Gurley Flynn, *Sabotage: The Conscious Withdrawal of the Workers' Industrial Efficiency* (Cleveland: IWW Publishing Bureau, 1916), available on the Web at http://www.lyalls.net/sabotage/sabotage.html.

7. Tom Frank and Dave Mulcahey, "This Is War," *Chicago Reader*, January 20, 1995.

8. Eric Jarosinski, "Labor War Zone in Illinois," *The Progressive*, February 1994.

9. Interview with authors, February 20, 2001; *Impact: The Rank and File Newsletter*, November 1995.

10. *Midnight Express,* Local 837's hand-written in-plant newsletter, undated (early March 1993).

11. "AIW Local 837 vs. A. E. Staley: From In-Plant Strategy to Lock-out: An Interview with Staley workers Richard Brummett, Emery Scrimpsher, and David Atteberry," *Impact: The Rank and File Newsletter* (Youngstown, Ohio), November 1993.

12. Ibid.

13. Masha Alexander, "State of the Union," *N Magazine* (Northwestern University), March 1994.

14. Interview with authors, March 16, 1994.

15. Frank and Mulcahey, "This Is War."

16. *Deadly Corn,* video produced by Labor Vision for AIW 837, 1993.

17. AIW 837 flyer, undated (around February 20, 1993).

18. Bill Carey, "Staley Workers Are Not Giving Up," *Local 1010 Steelworker,* monthly union newspaper, May 1995.

19. AIW in-plant flyer, undated (around late September 1992); Jane Slaughter, "Productivity Plummets as Staley Imposes Contract at Decatur Plant," *Labor Notes,* April 1993.

20. Interview with authors, March 16, 1994.

21. Interview with authors, March 16, 1994.

22. "AIW Local 837 vs. A. E. Staley."

23. "Workers in Decatur, Illinois Hold the Line with Solidarity Unionism," *Forward Motion,* May–June 1993.

24. *Midnight Express,* undated (early February 1993).

25. David Prosten, ed., *The Union Steward's Complete Guide* (Washington, D.C.: Union Communication Services, 1997).

26. Interview with authors, March 16, 1994.

27. *Deadly Corn.*

28. Laura McClure, interview with Jerry Tucker, *McClure's Labor News,* August 1993.

29. *Midnight Express,* March 1, 1993 (referring to Mohan's statement to the *Decatur Herald and Review*); see also Slaughter, "Productivity Plummets."

30. Talk given at the first meeting of the Chicago Staley Workers Solidarity Committee, July 17, 1993.

31. *The Paperworker* (UPIU), June 1993.

Chapter 5: The Temperature Rises

1. "The Lockout at A. E. Staley: Answers to Questions from the Community," Local 837 flyer, undated (October 1994).

2. Ibid.

3. Ibid.

4. Quotations without an endnote are drawn from the authors' 2001–3 interviews listed in the appendix.

5. *The Paperworker* (UPIU), February 1993.

6. *Midnight Express,* Local 837's hand-written in-plant newsletter, undated (early January 1993).

7. Jane Slaughter, "Productivity Plummets as Staley Imposes Contract at Decatur Plant," *Labor Notes,* April 1993.

8. Jim Gallagher, "Director Quits; Was Protest Target," *St. Louis Post-Dispatch,* May 15, 1993.

9. Staley director of operations Red Geurts to all salaried employees, memo, February 19, 1993.

10. *Deadly Corn,* video produced by Labor Vision for AIW 837, 1993.

11. Interview with authors, July 7, 1993.

12. *Decatur Herald and Review,* June 20, 1993.

13. Masha Alexander, "State of the Union," *N Magazine* (Northwestern University), March 1994.

14. Peter Downs, "Splitting Shifts, Splitting Families," *Commonweal,* June 4, 1993.

15. Ibid.

16. *Decatur Herald and Review,* June 20, 1993 (Jelks); *Deadly Corn* (Griffin).

17. AIW 837 Executive Board and Bargaining Committee to Staley official John Phillips, letter, March 3, 1993.

18. "The Lockout at A. E. Staley."

19. *Midnight Express,* June 8, 1993.

20. Ibid., undated (around April 20, 1993).

21. Jan Griffin, "Locked Out! One Wife's Story of the Staley Struggle," *New Democracy Newsletter* (Boston, Mass.), July–August 1997. Mike Griffin's harassment by management was also discussed in the union's brochure "Deadly Corn" (1993).

22. A description of management's harassment of Griffin appears in a one-page flyer, "The Trash We Serve," January 1993, and a two-page flyer, "Hemmerlein Strikes Again!" February 1993. Both flyers were handed out in the plant.

23. Interview with authors, March 16, 1994.

24. Interview with authors, July 14, 1993.

25. Kip Voytek, "Staley Workers Score a Victory as They Escalate Their Campaign," *Labor Notes,* July 1993.

26. Kenneth Long, letter to the editor, *Decatur Herald and Review,* July 1, 1993; Macon County Red Cross executive director Kerry Onyett, letter to the editor, *Decatur Herald and Review,* July 7, 1993.

27. "Once, Twice: A. E. Staley Locks Out AIW Local 837," *The Paperworker* (UPIU), July 1993.

Chapter 6: Locked Out

1. Quotations without an endnote are drawn from the authors' 2001–3 interviews listed in the appendix.

2. Kip Voytek, "Staley Workers Locked Out," *Labor Notes,* August 1993.

3. L. M. Ballard, letter to the editor, *Decatur Herald and Review,* July 10, 1993.

4. Staley worker and spouse survey conducted by the authors in fall 2001.

5. Lockouts have been more common in sports than other sectors of the economy.

Football owners locked out players in 1968 and 1970; baseball owners locked out players in 1976 and 1990; hockey owners locked out players in 1994–95; and basketball owners locked out referees in 1995 and players in 1998–99. See Paul D. Staudohar, "Baseball Labor Relations: The Lockout of 1990," *Monthly Labor Review* 113 (October 1990): 32–36; Timothy Minchin, *Forging a Common Bond: Labor and Environmental Activism during the BASF Lockout* (Gainesville: University of Florida Press, 2003); Douglas E. Ray, Calvin William Sharpe, and Robert N. Strassfeld, *Understanding Labor Law* (New York: Matthew Bender, 1999), 291–302.

6. *Decatur Herald and Review,* June 28, 1993.

7. Ibid.

8. On March 7, 2005, Illinois governor Rod Blagojevich signed into law an act that amended section 604 of the Illinois Unemployment Insurance Act, providing unemployment benefits to employees who are locked out by their employer. Currently, thirty-four states allow locked-out workers to draw unemployment benefits. Strikers are eligible only in New York (Steve Early, "Strike Lessons from the Last Twenty-Five Years: Walking Out and Winning," *Against the Current,* September–October 2006).

9. *Allied Industrial Worker,* monthly newsletter, August 1993.

10. *Decatur Herald and Review,* October 9, 1993. Although the company claimed to have stopped the practice, it soon resumed videotaping workers at the picket line.

11. *Decatur Herald and Review,* June 30, 1993. The federal Consolidated Omnibus Budget Reconciliation Act (COBRA) of 1985 mandates companies to provide workers who are on strike, locked out, or laid off the opportunity to continue their health insurance for a year and a half, provided the employee pay the entire cost.

12. *New York Times,* June 29, 1993.

13. Letter to the editor, *Decatur Herald and Review,* August 5, 1993.

14. Ibid., July 16, 1993.

15. Letter to the editor, *Decatur Herald and Review,* July 28, 1994.

16. Letters to the editor, *Decatur Herald and Review*: Sharon Tripp, January 8, 1994; Angela Williams, February 2, 1994; and Mona Williams, February 16, 1994.

17. *Decatur Herald and Review,* June 28, 1993.

18. Ibid., July 16, 1993.

19. Voytek, "Staley Workers Locked Out."

20. "AIW Local 837 vs. A. E. Staley: From In-Plant Strategy to Lock-out: An Interview with Staley workers Richard Brummett, Emery Scrimpsher, and David Atteberry," *Impact: The Rank and File Newsletter* (Youngstown, Ohio), November 1993.

21. AIW 837 press release, July 1, 1993.

22. "88 Staley Jobs Lost in Closure," *Decatur Herald and Review,* July 24, 1993; "Staley, AIW Plan Job Cut Meeting," *Decatur Herald and Review,* August 26, 1993.

23. *Decatur Herald and Review,* August 28, 1993.

24. Ibid., August 6, 1993.

25. Ibid., July 17 (UAW) and September 8 (URW), 1993; *Local 837 News,* July 1992 (Grainmillers 103); *Stand Fast in Liberty,* AIW 837 newsletter, September 4, 1993 (Decatur police union).

26. Letter to the editor, *Decatur Herald and Review,* August 31, 1993.

27. *Decatur Herald and Review,* July 26, 1993.

28. Masha Alexander, "The State of the Union," *N Magazine* (Northwestern University), March 1994.

29. Shari Grider, letter to the editor, *Decatur Herald and Review,* July 11, 1993; Gene Wooters, letter to the editor, *Decatur Herald and Review,* July 11, 1993.

30. Karl Brownlee, letter to the editor, *Decatur Herald and Review,* July 13, 1993.

31. Interview with authors, July 14, 1993.

32. Staley worker and spouse survey.

33. "AIW Local 837 vs. A. E. Staley."

34. *Decatur Herald and Review,* August 6, 1994.

35. All quotations from "Women's Support Group" section are drawn from a group interview with authors, October 21, 2001. The group included Rhonda Plankenhorn (husband, Royal); Sarah Plankenhorn (Rhonda and Royal's daughter); Judy Dulaney (husband, Mike); Ethel Fargusson (husband, Jerry); Jan Griffin (husband, Mike); Sandy Gosnell (husband, Tim); Mary Brummett (husband, Rick); Tanya VanScyoc (husband, Ron); Pat Watts (husband, Dave); Susan Hull (husband, Bob); and union member Jeanette Hawkins.

36. When the UAW Caterpillar workers struck a second time, in June 1994, the union increased their picket pay to three hundred dollars a week and paid their health insurance. When the URW Bridgestone/Firestone workers struck in July 1994, their picket pay was one hundred dollars a week, with no health insurance.

37. Staley worker and spouse survey.

38. *Decatur Herald and Review,* July 26, 1993.

39. *Stand Fast In Liberty,* September 4, 1993.

40. Steven Ashby, "Locked-out Staley Workers Fight Back," *Z Magazine,* January 1994; *Decatur Herald and Review,* June 30, 1993.

41. *Decatur Herald and Review,* July 8, 1993.

42. This section on the local's adopt-a-family program is based on interviews with Barrie Williams and other workers. Williams also shared his adopt-a-family files with the authors, excluding confidential files.

43. *Wall Street Journal,* May 3, 1994.

44. Walter Maus to Chicago Staley Workers Solidarity Committee, letter, June 9, 1994.

45. Judy Maus to Chicago Staley Workers Solidarity Committee, letters, September 27 and October 29, 1995.

46. Authors' estimate based on Local 837's adopt-a-family data.

Chapter 7: Road Warriors and Solidarity Committees

1. According to the local's LM-2 forms filed with the U.S. Department of Labor, through mailings, bucket drops in front of unionized plants, donations received from Road Warrior trips, T-shirt sales, and the efforts of the solidarity committees, the local raised $2.28 million dollars. (This figure does not include additional income from Road Warriors' trips that was used for travel expenses.) An additional $1.25 million was do-

nated through the adopt-a-family program, and many of those donors were reached through the Road Warriors.

2. Quotations without an endnote are drawn from the authors' 2001–3 interviews listed in the appendix.

3. The first issue came out in December 1993, and subsequent issues were published in April, June, August, and December 1994; March/April, May, June, July, August/September, and October 1995; and January 1996.

4. In 2005, however, labor split into two federations, the AFL-CIO (www.aflcio.org) and Change to Win (www.changetowin.org).

5. The national unions instrumental in forming Jobs with Justice were the CWA, AFSCME, SEIU, UAW, USWA, and IAM.

6. *Allied Industrial Worker,* monthly newsletter, September 1993.

7. Martin Fackler, untitled article, February 24, 1994, in authors' files.

8. Plankenhorn, interviews with authors, March 25, 2001; Tom Frank and Dave Mulcahey, "This Is War," *Chicago Reader,* January 20, 1995 (Travis).

9. *Allied Industrial Worker,* August 1993.

10. Frank and Mulcahey, "This Is War."

11. Bill Winter, hand-written response to authors' questions, February 2001.

12. Mary Vecco, "Company May Be Driving Worker to Early Grave," *Labor Paper* (Peoria), May 1993.

13. *Solidarity News,* newsletter, Chicago Staley Workers Solidarity Committee, August 1995.

14. Staley worker and spouse survey conducted by the authors in fall 2001.

15. Jan Griffin, "Locked Out! One Wife's Story of the Staley Struggle," *New Democracy Newsletter,* July–August 1997.

16. "Open letter to members of the Chicago Staley Workers Solidarity Committee," signed by six Chicago trade unionists, April 12, 1994; members of the Minneapolis–St. Paul "Meeting the Challenge Committee" to Dave Watts and the AIW 837 Executive Board, letter, December 1, 1993.

17. Michael Sacco, "A Look at One Local Union's Solidarity with AIW 837," *Solidarity News,* January 1994.

18. Interviews with authors, March 17 (Colburn) and March 23 (Cavanaugh), 2001.

19. *War Zone* (UPIU Local 7837), April 1994.

20. Many local unions were instrumental to the Chicago solidarity committee's success. Teamsters Local 705, with twenty thousand members and led by Jerry Zero, regularly brought Road Warriors to speak to its members and stewards and contributed heavily to the cause. SEIU Local 73, led by Tom Balanoff, heralded the message of the Staley workers through membership and steward meetings, as well as in this local's monthly newsletter, which was sent to its twenty-one thousand members. Through the facilitation of union rep Frank Klein, the ILGWU agreed to let the Chicago SWSC use their mailing address, which helped to credential the committee. UE regional director Carl Rosen worked tirelessly and provided ample resources to the Chicago support group. Seven unions allowed the committee to use their postage meters for regular mailings. ACTWU donated its union hall for the biweekly SWSC meetings. All this

practical support was critical to the operations of the committee since all the funds it raised went directly to the Staley workers.

21. *From the War Zone,* newsletter of the War Zone Education Foundation, May 2000.

22. *Studs Terkel Show,* radio broadcast, October 27, 1993, tape in authors' possession.

23. C. J. Hawking, "Holiday Caravan a Big Success," *Solidarity News,* January 1994.

24. This and remaining quotations in this chapter come from C. J. Hawking, "Solidarity Holiday Caravan," Chicago Staley Workers Solidarity Committee flyer, January 1995.

25. Northwest Indiana alone presented checks for twelve thousand dollars to the Staley workers. Its central labor council had endorsed the caravan and set up a committee that aggressively collected donations throughout the region. Use of the tractor-trailer was made available by Teamsters Local 142, based in Gary.

Chapter 8: Debating the Corporate Campaign

1. "Once, Twice: A. E. Staley Locks Out AIW Local 837," *The Paperworker* (UPIU), July 1993; Kip Voytek, "Staley Workers Locked Out," *Labor Notes,* August 1993.

2. The local sought to target all Tate & Lyle sugar products, which included the brands Domino and GW in the United States, Redpath in Canada, and Bundaberg in Australia, but Domino was the main focus.

3. Quotations without an endnote are drawn from the authors' 2001–3 interviews listed in the appendix.

4. "The Struggle at Staley—A Special Report," *Tate & Lyle Worker News,* undated (summer or fall 1994). This newsletter launched with a May 17, 1994, issue as a result of the inaugural meeting of the Tate & Lyle World Union Council in St. Louis, Missouri, March 26–27, 1994. The council was called together to build "union solidarity against Tate & Lyle's worldwide effort to slash workers' jobs and job conditions." Joe Dwyer headed the group. As discussed in chapter 14, Dwyer joined the workers' delegations at the January 1994 and 1995 Tate & Lyle stockholders' meetings.

5. "Crisis in Decatur," brochure published by AIW 837, 1992.

6. *Decatur Herald and Review,* September 18, 1993.

7. "It's Our Solidarity vs. Theirs: Boycott State Farm," brochure published by AIW 837, 1993.

8. State Farm to customers who wrote supporting the Staley workers, letter, August 1993.

9. From the CCI Web site, www.corporatecampaign.org: "As the veteran labor reporter A. H. Raskin of *The New York Times* wrote: 'Pressure on giant banks and insurance companies and other Wall Street pillars, all aimed at isolating Stevens from the financial community, helped generate a momentum . . . that could not be achieved through the 1976–1980 worldwide boycott of Stevens products or through more conventional uses of union muscle such as strikes and mass picketing." Raskin quoted Ray Rogers: "We took the strength of the company and made that its weakness. . . . We forced the power elite behind J. P. Stevens—its principal leaders and companies with which it had interlocking directorates[—]to put the squeeze on it."

10. "Locked-out Staley Workers Speak Out: Lessons from the War Zone," interviews with Dan Lane, Lorell Patterson, and Art Dhermy, *Socialist Worker,* January 19, 1996.

11. *Decatur Herald and Review,* June 26, 1994.

12. "Brewing Loyalty in Chicago," *Chicago Sun-Times,* August 9, 1994.

13. Videotape of union meeting, August 24, 1993.

14. Mike Sacco, "Unionists Rally in Illinois 'War Zone' against Bosses' Unfair Labor Practices," unpublished article in authors' files.

15. *The Paperworker,* December 1993.

16. Sacco, "Unionists Rally."

17. Jerry Tucker, interview with authors, February 21, 2001; Steven Ashby's notes of conversation with Kip Voytek, November 9, 1993.

18. The United Farm Workers, led by Cesar Chavez, had been able to organize a mass, grassroots "secondary" boycott against other companies—notably Gallo wine, which purchased nonunion-picked grapes, and Safeway supermarkets, which sold Gallo wine and grapes—only because the powerful agribusiness lobby had succeeded in pressuring Congress to exclude farmworkers from the 1935 National Labor Relations Act, and therefore farmworkers were, ironically, not affected by subsequent antiunion amendments to the NLRA such as the 1947 Taft-Hartley Act, which prohibits secondary boycotts.

19. The Allied Industrial Workers international was entirely focused on finding a merger partner when Local 837 produced material calling for a boycott of State Farm. UPIU lawyers, however, closely scrutinized the local's corporate-campaign material and were adamant that the word *boycott* tied to Staley's customers or financial allies not appear on any literature.

20. "Committee Dumps Beer in Protest," *Daily Cardinal* (University of Wisconsin student newspaper), May 4, 1994.

21. "Staley Workers Seek Support Here," *Milwaukee Journal,* March 17, 1994.

22. Miller Brewing Company to "All Miller Customers and Friends," letter, October 12, 1994; UPIU 7837 *War Zone Bulletin,* October 10, 1994.

23. UPIU 7837 *War Zone Bulletin,* October 10, 1994.

Chapter 9: Peacetime Soldiers and Wartime Soldiers

1. Quotations without an endnote are drawn from the authors' 2001–3 interviews listed in the appendix.

2. *Decatur Herald and Review,* September 26, 1993.

3. Ibid., November 30, 1995.

4. Videotape of union meeting, November 14, 1995 (Steve Haseley shouted this from the floor).

5. *Local 837 News,* December 1992 and January 1993. As bargaining committee chair, Shinall frequently wrote a column for the local's newsletter.

6. Red Geurts to all salaried employees, letter, February 19, 1993 (the letter was posted on bulletin boards and distributed to workers in the plant).

7. Eric Jarosinski, "Labor War Zone in Illinois," *The Progressive,* February 1994.

8. *Decatur Herald and Review,* December 3, 1995.

9. Videotape of union meeting, December 10, 1993.

10. Dan Lane, interview with authors, November 20–21, 2001. This is Lane's summary from what other workers told him the Shinall group were saying about him.

11. This and subsequent quotations are drawn from videotape of the January 11, 1994, union meeting.

12. After the December 1993 election, the eight executive board members were: Dave Watts, president; Bob Hull, vice president; Mike Grandon, treasurer; Greg Hill, recording secretary; John Lehew, Gary Lamb, and Steve Haseley, trustees; Terry Hale, sergeant-at-arms; and Bob Willoughby, guide. Five races were contested: vice president, guide, sergeant-at-arms, and two trustee positions. Newcomers were Terry Hale, who defeated Bob Luka for sergeant-at-arms; Bob Willoughby, who defeated Larry Boyles for guide; and Gary Lamb, who defeated several candidates for a trustee position. On the bargaining committee, Lane and Ferris were not up for reelection; Shinall, Strohl, and Larrimore ran unopposed.

13. Videotape of union meeting, January 18, 1994.

Chapter 10: God as Outside Agitator

1. For an analysis of labor's outreach to the religious community and other community organizations, see www.iwj.org, the Web site for Interfaith Worker Justice, a national coalition of religious coalitions advocating for workers' rights; www.jwj.org, the Web site for Jobs with Justice, a national coalition of labor-community-religious coalitions for workers' rights; Dan La Botz, *A Troublemaker's Handbook: How to Fight Back Where You Work and Win!* (Detroit: Labor Notes, 1991), ch. 7; Sonya Huber, "Allying with the Community: Single-Issue Campaigns," in *A Troublemaker's Handbook 2: How to Fight Back Where You Work and Win!* ed. Jane Slaughter, 157–77 (Detroit: Labor Notes, 2005); Steven Hinds, "Allying with the Community: Multi-Issue Coalitions," in *A Troublemaker's Handbook 2,* ed. Slaughter, 178–94; Kim Bobo, Jackie Kendall, and Steve Max, *Organizing for Social Change: Midwest Academy Manual for Activists,* 3d ed. (Santa Ana, California: Seven Locks, 2001), chs. 17 and 19; Jeremy Brecher and Tim Costello, eds., *Building Bridges: The Emerging Coalition of Labor and Community* (New York: Monthly Review Press, 1990); and Dan Clawson, *The Next Upsurge: Labor and the New Social Movements* (Ithaca, N.Y.: ILR Press, 2003).

2. *The Paperworker* (UPIU), January 1995.

3. *Decatur Herald and Review,* July 17, 1993.

4. Ibid., July 27, 1993.

5. C. J. Hawking's notes from clergy meeting, November 1993.

6. *Decatur Herald and Review,* December 15, 1993.

7. Ibid., December 22, 1993.

8. *Conveyor: News and Views of the Decatur Plant,* internal Staley/Tate & Lyle newsletter, December 22, 1993.

9. *Decatur Herald and Review,* January 6, 1994.

10. *The Paperworker,* January 1995.

11. *Springfield Diocesan* newspaper, February 13, 1994.

12. *The Paperworker,* January 1995.

13. After his death in 2001, a Web site in his honor was established at www .frmartinmangan.com.

14. Sermon preached by the Rev. Jim Montgomery on October 7, 2001, from the Mangan memorial Web site, www.frmartinmangan.com.

15. *The Paperworker,* January 1995.

16. C. J. Hawking's notes from clergy meeting, February 1994.

17. *The Paperworker,* January 1995.

18. *U.S. Catholic,* April 1996; *Catholic Times,* May 22, 1994.

19. *U.S. Catholic,* April 1996.

20. Tom Teague, "Candles in Silence," *Illinois Times,* April 9–15, 1995. Also see *Decatur Herald and Review,* September 6, 1994.

21. Staley worker and spouse survey conducted by the authors in fall 2001.

22. Interview with authors, October 25, 2001.

23. Staley worker and spouse survey.

24. *The Paperworker,* January 1995.

25. *Decatur Herald and Review,* March 28, 1994.

26. Ibid.

27. In 1996 Kim Bobo and the Chicago group launched a national organization, the National Interfaith Committee for Worker Justice. In 2005 the group shortened its name to "Interfaith Worker Justice"; it has over sixty affiliates across the United States.

28. Statement by the Commission on Human Rights in the Roman Catholic Archdiocese of St. Louis, March 27, 1995.

29. Springfield religious leaders statement, undated (likely April 1994).

30. *Catholic Times,* May 22, 1994.

31. *Decatur Herald and Review,* May 2, 1994.

32. Ibid., May 5, 1994.

33. Ibid., May 7, 1994.

34. Ibid.

35. *Struggle in the Heartland,* video produced by Labor Vision for UPIU 7837, 1994.

36. Quotations without an endnote are drawn from the authors' 2001–3 interviews listed in the appendix.

37. *Decatur Herald and Review,* June 5, 1994. Previous commitments forced the three to leave before the police worked their way down to arrest them.

38. Ibid., January 1995.

39. Jan Griffin, "Locked Out! One Wife's Story of the Staley Struggle," *New Democracy Newsletter,* July–August 1997.

40. Jane Samuels, "Captive to Capital: Even Church Institutions Can Lose Sight of Human Needs," *Sojourners,* September–October 1998.

41. *Independent,* January 27, 1995; *Guardian,* January 26, 1995; *London Financial Times,* January 27, 1995; *National Catholic Reporter,* February 10, 1995.

42. Mark Singer, "Town on a String," *New Yorker,* October 30, 2000.

43. *National Catholic Reporter,* February 10, 1995.

Chapter 11: The African American Workers

1. For contemporary analyses of labor's response to racism and sexism, see chapters 15 and 16 in Dan La Botz, *A Troublemaker's Handbook: How to Fight Back Where You Work and Win!* (Detroit: Labor Notes, 1991), 151–63, 164–77; "Fighting Discrimination/ Building Unity," in *A Troublemaker's Handbook 2: How to Fight Back Where You Work and Win!* ed. Jane Slaughter, 43–60 (Detroit: Labor Notes, 2005); Dorothy Sue Cobble, ed., *Women and Unions: Forging a Partnership* (Ithaca, N.Y.: ILR Press, 1993); Molly Martin, ed., *Hard-Hatted Women: Life on the Job* (Emeryville, Calif.: Avalon, 1997); Jo-Ann Mort, ed., *Not Your Father's Union Movement: Inside the AFL-CIO* (London: Verso, 1998); Bruce Nelson, *Divided We Stand: American Workers and the Struggle for Black Equality* (Princeton, N.J.: Princeton University Press, 2001); Kim Moody, *An Injury to All: The Decline of American Unionism* (London: Verso, 1988); Dan Clawson, *The Next Upsurge: Labor and the New Social Movements* (Ithaca, N.Y.: ILR Press, 2003); John Hoerr, *We Can't Eat Prestige: The Women Who Organized Harvard* (Philadelphia: Temple University Press, 1997); Gregory Mantsios, ed., *A New Labor Movement for the New Century* (New York: Garland, 1998); Toni Gilpin, Gary Isaac, Daniel Letwin, and Jack McKivigan, *On Strike for Respect: The Yale Strike of 1984–85* (Chicago: Charles H. Kerr, 1988); and Mike Parker and Martha Gruelle, *Democracy Is Power: Rebuilding Unions from the Bottom Up* (Detroit: Labor Notes, 1999).

2. At the nearby Caterpillar and Firestone plants, with 1,850 and 1,270 workers, respectively, the percentages of African American workers were slightly higher.

3. Quotations without an endnote are drawn from the authors' 2001–3 interviews listed in the appendix. The bulk of the quotations are from a March 25, 2001, group interview that included Frankie Travis, Jeanette Hawkins, Al Hawkins, David Conley, John Cook, Dennis Houston, Mike Odeneal, and Eugene Robinson.

4. The first African American woman to work at Staley had been hired as a janitor.

5. Interview, April 14, 1994, published in Calumet Project *Works* newsletter (northwest Indiana), Spring 1994.

6. *People's Weekly World,* April 16, 1994.

7. *Labor Notes,* April 1994.

8. Jeanette Hawkins, letter to the editor, *Decatur Herald and Review,* August 2, 1994. The trial was covered in the *Herald and Review,* September 21, September 24, and November 23, 1994.

9. Interview, Calumet Project *Works* newsletter, 1994.

10. Ibid.

11. Mary Ann Carr, a white woman, served a term as recording secretary in the 1980s.

Chapter 12: Civil Disobedience

1. *Decatur Herald and Review,* December 18, 1993.

2. Danny Wirges to Wayne Glenn, letter, February 23, 1994.

3. Judy Tatham, "Rally Stops Short of Scuffle," *Decatur Herald and Review,* February 23, 1994.

4. Henceforth union strategy sessions were moved to the rectory basement of St. James Church, at the invitation of union supporter Father Martin Mangan. Several years later, during depositions for a civil trial against the Decatur police, the police admitted they had a spy in the union.

5. Quotations without an endnote are drawn from the authors' 2001–3 interviews listed in the appendix.

6. C. J. Hawking, "The Battle of Decatur Escalates," *War Zone* (UPIU Local 7837), April 1994; videotape of union meeting, February 22, 1994.

7. On May 24, after just an hour of deliberations, a jury of six found Scott, Patterson, and Davis guilty of trespassing (*Decatur Herald and Review,* May 25, 1994).

8. James Melvin Washington, ed., *A Testament of Hope: The Essential Writing of Martin Luther King, Jr.* (New York: Harper and Row, 1986), 281.

9. Qtd. in Susan Ferriss and Ricardo Sandoval, *Fight in the Fields: Cesar Chavez and the Farmworkers Movement* (New York: Harcourt, Brace, 1997), 97.

10. Ibid.

11. Peter Rachleff, *Hard-Pressed in the Heartland: The Hormel Strike and the Future of the Labor Movement* (Boston: South End, 1993); Hardy Green, *On Strike at Hormel: The Struggle for a Democratic Labor Movement* (Philadelphia: Temple University Press, 1990); and Dave Hage and Paul Klauda, *No Retreat, No Surrender: Labor's War at Hormel* (New York: William Morrow, 1989).

12. James Green, "Camp Solidarity: The United Mine Workers, the Pittston Strike, and the new 'People's Movement,'" in *Building Bridges: The Emerging Grassroots Coalition of Labor and Community,* ed. Jeremy Brecher and Tim Costello, 15–24 (New York: Monthly Review Press, 1990); "Planting the Seeds of Resurgence: The United Mine Workers Strike Pittston Coal in 1989," in James Green, *Taking History to Heart: The Power of the Past in Building Social Movements,* 227–54 (Boston: University of Massachusetts, 2000); *UMW Journal,* March 1990; and *Labor Notes,* November 1989 and March 1990.

13. *Out of Darkness,* a 1990 documentary film on the 1989–90 Pittston strike directed by Barbara Kopple.

14. Ibid.

15. *Decatur Herald and Review,* July 16, 1993.

16. Videotape of union meeting, June 21, 1994.

17. Videotape of civil disobedience training at the union hall, April 16, 1994.

18. The authors were involved in these discussions. On June 24, 1994, Ashby phoned Burke and Holland and made a written transcript of the calls. Notes in authors' possession.

19. Ibid.

20. Julius Getman, *The Betrayal of Local 14: Paperworkers, Politics, and Permanent Replacements* (Ithaca, N.Y.: Cornell University Press, 1998), 67–68.

21. *Stand Fast in Liberty,* AIW 837 newsletter, September 4, 1993.

22. Videotape of union meeting, June 21, 1994.

23. Audiotape of phone conversation between the authors, May 24, 1994.

24. *War Zone* (UPIU Local 7837), July 1994.

25. Ibid.

26. Dave Watts to the forty-eight arrested in the sit-down, letter, June 9, 1994.

27. Unless otherwise noted, all subsequent quotations in this subsection are from a videotape of the June 21, 1994, union meeting.

28. Although neither of them had sat down to block the west gate on June 4, a few days later the police charged Dave Watts and Ray Rogers with trespassing, mob action, and conspiracy to commit mob action. On May 17 Watts and eight other workers were charged with "residential picketing" for holding a picnic on park district property on April 25, in a park adjacent to A. E. Staley spokesperson Mohan's house.

29. "Rules for June 25th Nonviolent Civil Disobedience," UPIU 7837 flyer.

30. Decatur chief of police James Williams Jr. to Dave Watts, letter, June 23, 1994, evidence submitted during November 2000 trial (plaintiff's exhibit number 2). Copies received from Chicago-based People's Law Office.

31. Transcript of Commander Richard Ryan's June 5, 1996, deposition, pp. 86 and 82. Copies received from People's Law Office.

32. Ibid., 107–9.

33. Ibid. 110–19.

34. Ibid., 88.

35. Ibid., 135.

36. Interview with authors, March 26, 2001; Marc Cooper, "Harley-Riding, Picket-Walking Socialism Haunts Decatur," *The Nation,* April 8, 1996.

37. Videotape from Labor Vision interview, June 25, 1994; *Springfield State Journal-Register,* June 26, 1994.

38. Transcript of Gary Lamb's deposition, June 1996.

39. Richard Ryan deposition, June 5, 1996, p. 149.

40. Gary Lamb deposition, June 1996.

41. Transcript of Dan Rhodes deposition, June 1996.

42. Videotape of Labor Vision interviews.

43. Steven Ashby, "Striking Staley Workers Gassed," *Local 1010 Steelworker,* August 1994.

44. *Struggle in the Heartland,* video produced by Labor Vision for UPIU 7837, July 1994.

45. *St. Louis Post-Dispatch,* June 26, 1994.

46. Videotape (by Mike Griffin) of rally and interviews with participants, June 25, 1994. The interview with Garrett appears in *Struggle in the Heartland.*

47. Videotape of protest, June 25, 1994.

48. *Peoria Labor Tribune,* June 30, 1994; *Struggle in the Heartland.*

49. *Decatur Herald and Review,* June 26, 1994.

50. Interview with authors, June 1994.

51. *Decatur Herald and Review,* July 17, 1994.

52. Illinois State Federation (AFL-CIO) press release, September 24, 1994.

Chapter 13: Strike City, USA

1. For an analysis of the six-year Caterpillar labor conflict see Barry Bearak, "The Strike at Caterpillar," *Los Angeles Times,* May 14–18, 1995; Isaac Cohen, "The Caterpil-

lar Labor Dispute and the UAW, 1991–1998," *Labor Studies Journal* 27, no. 4 (Winter 2003): 77–99; and Stephen Franklin, *Three Strikes: Labor's Heartland Losses and What They Mean for Working Americans* (New York: Guilford, 2001).

2. The UAW did, however, enlist the assistance of two Michigan labor educators, Steve Babson and John Beck, to educate UAW stewards and union officers about the mechanics of work-to-rule at a series of presentations in St. Louis, Missouri, and Peoria, Illinois, in 1992.

3. *Decatur Herald and Review,* December 5, 1995.

4. "Labor Wars Hit Home in Decatur," *Los Angeles Times,* September 5, 1994.

5. *War Zone* (UPIU Local 7837), March–April 1995.

6. Quotations without an endnote are drawn from the authors' 2001–3 interviews listed in the appendix.

7. Tom Frank and Dave Mulcahey, "This Is War," *Chicago Reader,* January 20, 1995; conversation with authors in fall 1993 (McDuffie).

8. It should be noted that the Staley workers were not immune to nationalism. The workers regularly denounced the British company as "Tories," "Lymies," and "foreigners" who came to the United States only to stab the people in the back, as they had done two hundred years before, in the revolutionary era.

9. *War Zone* (UPIU Local 7837), April and August 1994.

10. Ibid., April 1994.

11. After C. J. Hawking returned to Chicago in July 1994, Doug Kandt, fresh from working as a *Labor Notes* intern in Detroit, moved to Decatur to assist the local in its community outreach efforts. Kandt, a talented young writer and organizer, helped the workers publish the *Free Press.*

12. *Decatur Herald and Review,* September 5, 1994, and August 13, 1995.

13. Franklin, *Three Strikes,* 150.

14. Dave Watts, undated handwritten letter to coalition members.

15. Frank and Mulcahey, "This Is War."

16. *AFL-CIO News,* December 12, 1994.

17. David Moberg, "War Zone," *In These Times,* July 24, 1995.

18. During the 1991–92 Cat strike the workers received one hundred dollars a month picket pay, but the UAW International boosted it to three hundred dollars and paid the workers' health insurance (at a cost to the union of about six hundred a month per person) during the 1994–95 strike.

19. *Decatur Herald and Review,* October 16, 1994.

20. *Chicago Tribune,* November 11, 1994.

21. Ibid.; Michael Sacco, "Thousands Take the Streets, Baffle Cops," *IBEW 336 News,* October 1994 (repr., *Decatur Free Press,* October 20, 1994).

22. *The Militant,* November 11, 1994; *Chicago Tribune,* November 11, 1994.

23. *Decatur Herald and Review,* October 16, 1994.

24. William Bole, "Laboring for the Workers," *Our Sunday Visitor,* April 28, 1996.

25. Jan Griffin, "Locked Out! One Wife's Story of the Staley Struggle," *New Democracy Newsletter,* July–August 1997.

26. *Decatur Herald and Review,* August 2, 1993.

27. Ibid., November 21, 1994.

28. Ibid., April 16, 1993.

29. Ibid., July 19, 1994.

30. Ibid., December 4, 1994.

31. *The Gathering Storm*, video produced by Labor Beat, December 1994.

32. Ibid.

33. *Decatur Herald and Review*, October 25, 1994.

34. Ibid., December 1, 1994.

35. Ibid.

36. Rose Feurer, "The Staley Lockout: A View from Below," *Impact: The Rank and File Newsletter* (Youngstown, Ohio), July 1995.

37. *The Gathering Storm*. Congressman Jesse L. Jackson Jr. began service in the U.S. House of Representatives on December 12, 1995. He was elected in a special election in the second congressional district in Illinois after Congressman Mel Reynolds resigned and was sentenced to a prison term for corruption. Jackson became the ninety-first African American elected to Congress.

38. *Decatur Free Press*, December 1994.

39. *People's Weekly World*, February 9, 1995.

40. *Labor Notes*, August 1995.

41. *War Zone* (UPIU Local 7837), August/September 1994; *People's Weekly World*, February 9, 1995. Also see *Decatur Herald and Review*, August 16 and August 23, 1995.

42. *The Gathering Storm*.

43. Ibid.

44. Friends of Labor press release, March 1, 1995.

45. *Our Class of People*, video produced by Labor Beat, 1995.

46. *Decatur Herald and Review*, November 11, 1994.

47. Ibid., April 5, 1995.

48. Larry Dennehy, "Decatur Coalition Elects Unionist to City Council," *The Organizer*, April 24, 1995.

Chapter 14: The Paperworkers

1. *The Paperworker* (UPIU), August 1993.

2. AFL-CIO Executive Council resolution, August 5, 1993.

3. *Allied Industrial Worker*, monthly newsletter, October 1993.

4. Ibid., June and October 1993. One item notably absent from the union's discourse was the fact that the AIW International officers' salaries would be raised to the level of their UPIU counterparts. The business representatives' salaries would increase from roughly $40,000 to $65,000, and the regional directors would be raised from roughly $55,000 to $75,000. Although Serraglio was to retire, his salary was $69,000, while UPIU president Glenn's was $136,500. For AIW staff members, a car and a generous expense account were also provided. Tom Braun, an AIW delegate and former president of his local in Ft. Wayne, Indiana, who opposed the merger, reflected on the impact of the salary increases. "Here's how you do mergers," argued Braun. "You get the AIW [staffer] that makes maybe $20,000 less. . . . You get all of them and part of the agreement is, all

you guys will get to make higher wages . . . , going from $55,000 to $75,000! Now, does that influence anybody? [As a result,] they're going to support the [merger]."

5. AIW Local 847 member Dave Rulo, quoted in *Allied Industrial Worker,* October 1993.

6. *Allied Industrial Worker,* October 1993.

7. Quotations without an endnote are drawn from the authors' 2001–3 interviews listed in the appendix.

8. *Union Democracy Review,* January 1962, January 1965, and November 1979 (this review was published by the Association for Union Democracy).

9. Julius Getman, *The Betrayal of Local 14: Paperworkers, Politics, and Permanent Re-placements* (Ithaca, N.Y.: Cornell University Press, 1998), 163–64. The conflict began in March 1987 when International Paper locked out employees at a paper mill in Mobile, Alabama. Local 14, in Jay, Maine, then struck in June 1987, followed by IP strikers in De Pere, Wisconsin, and Lock Haven, Pennsylvania. Also see Adrienne E. Eaton and Jill Kriesky, "Decentralization of Bargaining Structure: Four Cases from the U.S. Paper Industry," *Relations Industrielles/Industrial Relations* 53, no. 3 (1998): 486–516; and Peter Kellman, *Divided We Fall: The Story of the Paperworkers' Union and the Future of Labor* (Croton-on-Hudson, N.Y.: Apex, 2004).

10. Kellman, *Divided We Fall.*

11. Qtd. in Getman, *Betrayal of Local 14,* 64.

12. Getman, *Betrayal of Local 14,* 44.

13. As a UPUI vice president and regional director, in 1993 Glenn Goss was paid $79,000, three times the pay of the average Staley worker, and had a $14,500 expense account.

14. After the merger Danny Wirges, who had been the AIW regional director, became assistant regional director under Glenn Goss. Goss soon removed Wirges and AIW staff representative Bill Coleman from the bargaining sessions, but Wirges kept abreast of the situation, as he was frequently called by Local 837 Bargaining Committee chairperson Jim Shinall and his supporters.

15. Dave Watts to Bill Taylor, president of the corn council, letter, April 10, 1996; videotape of postdefeat forum in Madison, Wisconsin, sponsored by UPIU Local 1202, January 22, 1996. The corn council, officially the Inter-Union Wet/Dry Corn Milling Council, represented the seventeen local unions and seven international unions in the industry.

16. In 1994 special projects staffers Mark Brooks and Frank Bragg spent many hours assisting the local's campaign against Miller beer. The special projects staff played a vital role in helping Local 7837 get in touch with British union leaders in preparation for the January 1994 and 1995 Tate & Lyle shareholders' meetings in London; Brooks joined the Local 7837 delegation both times. Brooks and *The Paperworker* editor Blinn made a number of trips to Decatur in 1994.

17. There were 1,100 UPIU and 300 AIW local unions.

18. Dave Watts to Wayne Glenn, letter, January 4, 1995.

19. Ibid.

20. *Allied Industrial Worker,* September 1993.

21. Dave Watts to Wayne Glenn, letter, July 25, 1995.

22. See chapter 8 for further discussion of the Domino boycott.

23. Dave Watts to Joy Ann Grune, IUF regional secretary, letter requesting information on Tate & Lyle, February 7, 1992. Grune forwarded the request to Dan Gallin, IUF general secretary, who on March 13, 1992, forwarded the letter to GMB national secretary David Williams. Williams wrote to the Tate & Lyle personnel department and received a reply, dated March 25, 1992, from R. Anderton, divisional director of personnel, Tate & Lyle Sugars.

24. GMB national secretary David Williams to IUF general secretary Dan Gallin, letter, March 18, 1992.

25. David Williams to Dan Gallin, letter, May 4, 1994.

26. Trades Union Congress general secretary John Monks to AFL-CIO president Lane Kirkland, letter, November 4, 1994.

27. Dan Gallin to David Williams, letter (referring to previous conditions put on the Staley workers before the IUF would resume working with them), January 17, 1995.

28. Dave Watts and bargaining committee chair Dike Ferris to Wayne Glenn, letter, November 17, 1994.

29. Wayne Glenn to Dave Watts and Dike Ferris, letter, November 21, 1994.

30. Since the lockout Tucker no longer received even the meager pay of one hundred dollars a day; all he received was reimbursement for his travel and lodging.

31. Dave Watts to Wayne Glenn, letter, January 4, 1995.

32. The UPIU International hired Rogers to conduct a corporate campaign against International Paper in 1983 but then terminated the campaign two weeks later when management expressed a willingness to attempt to repair deteriorating labor relations. In November 1987, five months into a seventeen-month International Paper strike involving 1,200 workers at the Jay, Maine, paper mill and three other locals, UPIU Local 14 pressured Wayne Glenn to rehire Rogers to direct a corporate campaign. Fearing that the local would hire him and work independently of the international if he refused, Glenn overruled objections from many members of the UPIU Executive Board and agreed. As the campaign was getting into full swing, International Paper told Glenn it would negotiate an agreement if Rogers was removed, so in March 1988 Glenn ordered the corporate campaign suspended. The workers decisively rejected an odious contract in April, but the international then fired Rogers. The strike was called off in October. The company had succeeded in permanently replacing the union workers with scabs, and Local 14 was decertified shortly thereafter (Getman, *The Betrayal of Local 14*).

33. Dave Watts to Wayne Glenn, letter, January 4, 1995; Dave Watts, Larry Solomon, and Roger Gates to Wayne Glenn, Owen Bieber, and Ken Coss, letter, January 3, 1995.

Chapter 15: Mission to Bal Harbour

1. Quotations without an endnote are drawn from the authors' 2001–3 interviews listed in the appendix.

2. For an analysis of labor's decline and the debate within the labor movement over how to respond, see Kim Moody, *U.S. Labor in Trouble and Transition: The Failure of*

Reform from Above, the Promise of Revival from Below (New York: Verso, 2007); Bill Fletcher Jr. and Fernando Gapasin, *Solidarity Divided: The Crisis in Organized Labor and a New Path toward Social Justice* (Berkely: University of California Press, 2008); Jane Slaughter, ed., *A Troublemaker's Handbook 2: How to Fight Back Where You Work and Win!* (Detroit: Labor Notes, 2005); Dan Clawson, *The Next Upsurge: Labor and the New Social Movements* (Ithaca, N.Y.: ILR Press, 2003); Gregory Mantsios, ed., *A New Labor Movement for the New Century* (New York: Garland, 1998); Bruce Nissen, ed., *Which Direction for Organized Labor? Essays on Organizing, Outreach, and Internal Transformations* (Detroit: Wayne State University Press, 1999); Ray Tillman and Michael Cummins, eds., *The Transformation of U.S. Unions: Voices, Visions, and Strategies from the Grassroots* (Boulder, Colo.: Lynnee Rienner, 1999); Lowell Turner, Harry C. Katz, and Richard W. Hurt, eds., *Rekindling the Movement: Labor's Quest for Relevance in the 21st Century* (Ithaca, N.Y.: Cornell University Press, 2001); Nelson Lichtenstein, *State of the Union: A Century of American Labor* (Princeton, N.J.: Princeton University Press, 2002); Kim Moody, *Workers in a Lean World: Unions in the International Economy* (London: Verso, 1997); Jo-Ann Mort, ed., *Not Your Father's Union Movement: Inside the AFL-CIO* (London: Verso, 1998); Mike Parker and Martha Gruelle, *Democracy Is Power: Rebuilding Unions from the Bottom Up* (Detroit: Labor Notes, 1999); Rick Fantasia and Kim Voss, *Hard Work: Remaking the American Labor Movement* (Berkeley: University of California Press, 2004); and Vanessa Tait, *Poor Workers' Unions: Rebuilding Labor from Below* (Boston: South End, 2005).

3. Harry Kelber, "The 'Palace Revolution' That Changed the AFL-CIO," Labor Educator pamphlet, 1996.

4. UAW president Douglas Fraser's 1978 statement upon resigning from the President Carter's Labor-Management Group, cited in Kim Moody, *An Injury to All: The Decline of American Unionism* (New York: Verso, 1988), 147.

5. Ibid.

6. *Washington Post*, May 23, 1995.

7. Dave Watts to Wayne Glenn, copied to UPIU International, AFL-CIO, and Local 7837 officers, letter, October 18, 1995.

8. CWA vice president Jan Pierce, Teamsters vice presidents Diana Kilmury and Dennis Skelton, and UMWA vice president Cecil Roberts spoke at the June 25, 1994, rally. Pierce was a lone voice on the CWA Executive Board, however, and the Teamsters under Ron Carey and the Mineworkers under Richard Trumka were two of the few national unions that took solidarity to heart.

9. "Decatur Workers Send Wake-Up Call to AFL-CIO Leaders," *Solidarity Report*, newsletter of the Chicago Staley Workers Solidarity Committee, March 1995.

10. Dave Watts, Larry Solomon, and Roger Gates to presidents of the UPIU, UAW, and URW, letter, February 14, 1995.

11. Owen Bieber to Watts, Solomon, and Gates, letter, February 16 (in response to faxed letter from the three local union presidents to UPIU president Wayne Glenn, UAW president Owen Bieber, and URW president Ken Coss, February 14, 1995); "Mr. Watts Goes to Bal Harbour," *McClure's Labor News*, April 1995.

12. Glenn to Solomon, Watts, and Gates, faxed letter, February 14, 1995.

13. UPIU 7837 *News from the War Zone,* January 1996.

14. Hy Clymer, "War Zone Strikers Take Case to AFL-CIO," *People's Weekly World,* February 1995.

15. "Mr. Watts Goes to Bal Harbour."

16. Interviews with authors, February 1995 and July 10, 2002, quoted in "Decatur Workers Send Wake-Up Call."

17. "Mr. Watts Goes to Bal Harbour."

18. Louis Uchitelle, "Labor Chiefs Get Glimpse of Casualties," *New York Times,* February 23, 1995.

19. "Decatur Strikers Push AFL-CIO Top Brass for More Action" and "Labor Chiefs Get Glimpse of Casualties," *Decatur Herald and Review,* February 21, 1995.

20. *Our Class of People,* video produced by Labor Beat, July 1995.

21. *Chicago Tribune,* February 21, 1995.

22. *Our Class of People.*

23. Other labor leaders followed: CWA president Morton Bahr came to Decatur on April 29, and AFT president Al Shanker came on May 23. On June 25, 1995, a number of leaders came for the march and rally commemorating the second anniversary of the lockout, including presidents of the Retail, Wholesale, and Department Store Union–United Food and Commercial Workers (RWDSU); Glass, Molders, Pottery, Plastics and Allied Workers (GMPPAW); OCAW; UPIU; UMWA; URW; and AFSCME.

24. *New York Times,* February 26, 1995. Opposing Kirkland were the presidents of the United Steel Workers of America; Service Employees International Union; American Federation of State, Council, and Municipal Employees; the International Association of Machinists; the International Brotherhood of Teamsters; the United Mine Workers; Oil, Chemical and Atomic Workers; Communication Workers of America; and the United Auto Workers.

25. Kelber, "The 'Palace Revolution.'"

26. *Daily Labor Report,* March 31, 1995.

27. *U.S. News & World Report,* June 12, 1995; UFCW spokesperson Greg Denier quoted in *Chicago Tribune,* May 18, 1995.

28. Audiotape of Kirkland speech at AFL-CIO meeting in Boston, June 1995.

29. Mike Griffin, speech to the Independent Progressive Politics Network conference in Decatur, Illinois, May 3, 1997.

30. *New York Times,* June 13, 1995.

Chapter 16: Still in the Fight

1. Interview with authors, July 11, 2001; op-ed piece, *Decatur Herald and Review,* November 30, 1995.

2. After the December 1994 election, the activists held five of the nine executive board seats: Dave Watts, president; Dike Ferris, vice president; Ron VanScyoc, recording secretary; and Gary Lamb and Bob Scheibly, trustees. In addition, all five members of the bargaining committee were activists. After Denton Larrimore and Jim Shinall resigned in the late summer of 1994, Bill Stroll felt he could resign without giving control to the

conservatives. The 1995 bargaining committee comprised Dan Lane, Jeanette Hawkins, Art Dhermy, Tom Force, and Ron VanScyoc.

3. Earl Silbar, "War Zone," *Crossroads,* May 1995.

4. All quotations from June 12 strategy meeting are drawn from Steven Ashby's notes.

5. Dave Watts to Staley solidarity committees, letter, June 15, 1995.

6. "A Call to the Nation's Labor Activists to Attend an AFL-CIO Pre-Election Forum," UPIU 7837 flyer, May 1995.

7. Wayne Glenn to Dave Watts, faxed letter, May 25, 1995.

8. Mary Vecco, who had written on the Staley struggle a number of times for the *Peoria Labor Paper,* helped build the conference and the July 25 rally in the summer of 1995. Vecco followed Hawking and Kandt to become the third non-Decaturite welcomed as an organizer at the Kandy Lane office. Following Vecco in 1995 as Kandy Lane organizers would be Laura Kurre and Tom Johnson.

9. *Decatur Herald and Review,* June 25, 1995. The conference discussed reforms that would strengthen and democratize the AFL-CIO, and numerous resolutions were passed with the intention of raising them at the federation's October 1995 convention. Staley and Cat workers introduced a discussion on the necessity and difficulties of stopping production during a strike or lockout. A unanimous resolution called on the AFL-CIO to "call on all its affiliates and international allies to mobilize mass pickets" at the sites of Staley, Caterpillar, and Bridgestone/Firestone and to "coordinate with all unions foreign and domestic to stop production, transportation, installation and use of struck goods." The conference discussed labor's failure to achieve progressive legislation despite decades of monumental support to the Democratic party and passed a resolution in support of the Labor party's founding convention set for May 1996. "The formation of a democratically based and run Labor Party is the only way for working people to secure their rights and gains," declared the resolution. Attendees heard from the three local unions about how they had enthusiastically participated in labor-management programs only to be betrayed as the companies used the information gained from the workers to train scabs in order to break the three unions. The AFL-CIO, read the resolution resulting from that discussion, must "reject and withdraw from all 'labor-management cooperation' schemes, which are all aimed at undermining the collective bargaining process."

10. *Madison Capital Times,* June 26, 1995.

11. After Lane Kirkland announced that that he would resign (see chapter 15), Thomas Donahue—who had stated in May that he, too, intended to retire—announced he would run for the AFL-CIO presidency. Donahue won by a vote of twenty-two to eleven at the August AFL-CIO Executive Council meeting.

12. Unless otherwise noted, all quotations from June 25 rally speeches are drawn from Steven Ashby's notes or the *Decatur Herald and Review,* June 26, 1995.

13. Joey VanScyoc, Mary Ferriell, and Bailey Elliott's speeches, copies in authors' possession.

14. *The Organizer,* July–August 1995.

15. *Our Class of People,* video produced by Labor Beat, July 1995.

16. Wayne Glenn to Dave Watts, letter, September 29, 1995.

17. Both authors were on trial, and C. J. Hawking was the Decatur Fifty coordinator, so this section is largely drawn from the authors' firsthand knowledge. All quotations in this section, unless otherwise cited, are from "First Trial of Decatur 50 Ends in Victory!!" a two-page narrative of the trial written by C. J. Hawking and mailed to the defendants, the scores of people who contributed to the legal defense fund (more than seven thousand dollars was raised), and the Staley workers solidarity committees. Also see "Staley Demonstrators' Trial Begins," *Decatur Herald and Review*, June 27, 1995; "Union Supporters Take Argument to Jury," *Herald and Review*, June 28, 1995; and "Trespassers Claim Victory in Verdicts," *Herald and Review*, June 29, 1995.

18. Mona Williams's typed statement prepared for the Decatur Fifty trial.

19. *Unity*, Local 7837 internal newsletter, May 23, 1995 (it began publication in spring 1995).

20. *Decatur Herald and Review*, July 10, 1995.

21. *Labor Notes*, August 1995.

22. As a result of retirements and resignations, the local had dropped from 762 workers at the time of the June 1994 lockout to around 600 by 1995.

23. *Decatur Tribune*, July 12, 1995.

24. *Labor Notes*, August 1995.

Chapter 17: In the Fast Lane

1. UPIU press release, April 12, 1995.

2. Mark Brooks to Rose Feurer and Dave Rathke, coordinators of the St. Louis Staley Workers Solidarity Committee, letter, April 4, 1995.

3. Rose Feurer to Dan Lane, letter, April 20, 1995.

4. Henry Bayer to PepsiCo CEO Wayne Callaway, letter, July 18, 1995.

5. In 1997 Pepsi spun off the three-fast food chains, plus A&W and Long John Silver's, into the Yum! corporation.

6. Mark Brooks to Staley solidarity committees, letter, February 27, 1995. Emphasis in original. This language, with slight variations, was repeated in the periodic letters from Brooks to the solidarity committees.

7. Quotations without an endnote are drawn from the authors' 2001–3 interviews listed in the appendix.

8. Thomas Geoghegan, *Which Side Are You On? Trying to Be for Labor When It's Flat on Its Back* (New York: Farrar, Straus and Giroux, 1991), 33–34.

9. Lynn Agee to Steven Ashby, letter, August 28, 1995; Steven Ashby, writing for the Chicago SWSC, to Lynn Agee, letter, October 12, 1995.

10. Steven Ashby, writing for the Chicago SWSC, to Dave Watts, faxed letter, August 28, 1995.

11. Mark Brooks to Dave Watts, letter (marked "legal and confidential"), October 11, 1995; Dave Watts to Steven Ashby and the Chicago SWSC, letter, October 20, 1995.

12. "'Corporate Crime' Fighter Not Chicken to Aid Local Labor," *Decatur Herald and Review*, August 9, 1995.

13. Unless otherwise cited, quotations on the fast are drawn from Dan Lane, interview

with authors, November 20–21, 2001; Lane, interview in the *Impact* labor newsletter, November 1995; and C. J. Hawking's recollections and notes from her 1995 phone calls to Lane and her four trips to Decatur during the two-month fast.

14. *Chicago Tribune,* September 26, 1995.

15. *Union Labor News* (Madison, Wisc.), October 1995.

16. *War Zone* (UPIU Local 7837), August–September 1995.

17. *Decatur Herald and Review,* September 30, 1995.

18. *Union Labor News,* October 1995.

19. *War Zone* (UPIU Local 7837), August–September 1995.

20. *Decatur Herald and Review,* September 3, 1995.

21. "Fast for Justice Day 36," daily bulletin.

22. "Fast for Justice Day 44," daily bulletin.

23. UPIU 7837 *War Zone Support Group Newsletter,* October 26, 1995.

24. *Decatur Herald and Review,* September 30, 1995.

25. Ibid., October 28, 1995.

26. Laura McClure, "AFL-CIO Changes," *Z Magazine,* January 1996.

27. David Bacon, "Will the AFL-CIO's New Leaders Change Its Old Cold War Policies?" October 29, 1995 (available at his Web site, www.dbacon.igc.org).

28. Edited videotape of the 1995 AFL-CIO convention.

29. *Decatur Herald and Review,* November 2, 1995; "Fast for Justice Day 63," daily bulletin.

30. C. J. Hawking to Steven Ashby, fax, November 3, 1995.

31. *Decatur Herald and Review,* November 5, 1995.

32. John Sweeney to Dan Lane, letter, November 3, 1995; UPIU 7837 press release, November 4, 1995.

33. UPIU 7837 press release, November 4, 1995.

Chapter 18: Showdown

1. Wayne Glenn to Henderson, letter, September 6, 1995 (in response to Henderson's August 24 letter); Dave Watts to Glenn, letter, September 12, 1995; Wayne Glenn to Watts, letter, September 19, 1995.

2. Dave Watts shared some of his files, including the letter, with the authors.

3. As remembered by Royal Plankenhorn, interview with authors, March 25, 2001.

4. Mike Dulaney to members of the Chicago Staley Workers Solidarity Committee who had pooled their donations to adopt the Dulaney family, letter, November 27, 1995.

5. Quotations without an endnote are drawn from the authors' 2001–3 interviews listed in the appendix.

6. Videotape of forum in Madison, Wisconsin, on the lessons of the Staley fight, sponsored by UPIU Local 1202, January 22, 1996.

7. Bill Winter, handwritten notes, January 11, 1996.

8. Dave Watts to Wayne Glenn, faxed letter, September 29, 1995; Wayne Glenn to Watts, letter (response), September 29, 1995.

9. Dave Watts to Glenn, letter, October 18, 1995.

10. Videotape of UPIU 7837 union meeting, November 14, 1995.

11. *Decatur Herald and Review,* January 21, 1996; interview with authors, March 12, 2001.

12. *War Zone* (UPIU Local 7837), January 1996.

13. Videotape of UPIU 7837 union meeting, December 5, 2001.

14. Wayne Glenn, "Understanding the Lessons of the Staley Lockout," *AIL [American Income Life] Labor Agenda,* special supplement to the *AIL Labor Letter.* (American Income Life provides insurance exclusively for union members).

15. *Decatur Herald and Review,* October 11, 1995.

16. Videotape of UPIU 7837 union meeting, November 14, 1995.

17. Walt Maus to Steven Ashby and C. J. Hawking, letter, December 4, 1995.

18. *Decatur Herald and Review,* December 3, 1995.

19. In addition to Shinall (president), conservatives Steve Haseley and John Lehew, both former members of the executive board, were elected to the board as trustees. Gary Lamb (vice president), Ron VanScyoc (secretary), Bob Scheibly, Dave Duncan, and Stoy Bliss remained on the board. Shinall allies Terry Hale, Monte Henson, and Mike Barber won election to the bargaining committee.

20. In a March 3, 1994, letter from Red Geurts to UPIU assistant regional director Danny Wirges and bargaining committee chair Dike Ferris, the company declared that it would reinstate those who were laid off in August 1993 "to active status."

21. Wayne Glenn to Watts, letter, December 14, 1995.

22. Ibid.; Wayne Glenn to all UPIU officers, letter, January 17, 1996.

23. UPIU press release, December 22, 1995 (Goss); interview with authors, June 28, 2001 (Ferris).

24. Gordon Brehm had been fired by the AIW in 1976 for misuse of union funds and then went to work for the UPIU when his friend Wayne Glenn hired him. Brehm's 1992 salary as Wayne Glenn's assistant was $72,000 a year, plus expenses.

25. *Paperworkers for Reform Newsletter,* vol. 1, no. 1, undated (around April 1996).

26. Gordon Brehm to Mike Griffin, letter, December 18, 1995. In the letter Brehm reaffirmed that he viewed the severance package as "generous" and that in his opinion "this would be the last chance for the members to accept a contract in the foreseeable future."

27. *Decatur Herald and Review,* December 14, 1995.

28. Videotape of UPIU 7837 union meeting, December 21, 1995. Watts read from a July 25, 1991, letter from UPIU president Wayne Glenn to all UPIU local unions.

29. *Decatur Herald and Review,* December 21, 1995.

30. Glenn Goss, "Open Letter to Supporters of Locked-out Staley Workers," December 29, 1995.

31. Interview with authors, January 8, 1996.

32. *Decatur Herald and Review,* December 23, 1995; press release issued by UPIU 7837 executive board members Gary Lamb, Ron VanScyoc, Bob Scheibly, Dave Duncan, and Stoy Bliss, January 22, 1996.

33. Videotape of union meeting, December 27, 1995.

34. A number of the union's activists were involved in discussions on what should go in the last *War Zone,* but it was written primarily by Jerry Tucker and Tom Johnson, a mineworker who moved to Decatur to volunteer at the Kandy Lane office the last few months of the struggle.

35. After the Kandy Lane office sat vacant for a few months, its owner leased the space to a gun shop.

36. *Industrial Worker,* March 1996.

Chapter 19: Aftermath

1. Quotations without an endnote are drawn from the authors' 2001–3 interviews listed in the appendix.

2. Steven Ashby's handwritten notes from retreat.

3. *Decatur Herald and Review,* January 19, 1996.

4. Madison, Wisconsin, Central Labor Council president Jim Cavanaugh, who had aggressively built solidarity for the Staley workers throughout the lockout, was furious. Cavanaugh sympathized with their frustrations—"Sweeney promised that he was going to appoint a task force to work on the Staley struggle and that never materialized"— but he was not pleased with their protest. "When I talked to Dave Watts a week later," related Cavanaugh, "I told him, 'What were you trying to do? What were you trying to accomplish? . . . You kind of crashed our party, and when we did solidarity activities for the Staley Workers, we did whatever the program was'" (interview with authors, March 23, 2001).

5. Robert Weissman, "A Bitter Defeat at A. E. Staley," *The Multinational Monitor,* January–February 1996.

6. *Decatur Herald and Review,* November 2, 2000.

7. Peter Miller, "Jury Finds in Favor of Decatur Police, against Staley Protesters," available through the Chicago Independent Media Center at its Web site, www.chicago indymedia.org.

8. Ibid.

9. Ibid.

10. The two Eighth Day nuns, along with other peace activists, had been trying for two years to meet with Senator Fitzgerald to protest the U.S.-run School of Americas, renamed the Western Hemispheric Institute for Security Cooperation, because it trained Latin American military officers in torture techniques. When they again couldn't get a meeting, the activists occupied the senator's office in a sit-down and were subsequently arrested.

11. Kathleen Desautels to C. J. Hawking, e-mail, January 23, 2001.

12. Gary Lamb, interview with authors, July 10, 2002.

13. The contract ended pattern bargaining in the earthmoving equipment industry; no longer would workers at Deere and Caterpillar have virtually identical contracts. New hires' pay would start at 70 percent of the union wage. Management won a six-year contract giving it the right to expand hiring of low-wage temporary workers with no benefits, to introduce flexible schedules, to increase downsizing, and to make lump-sum

payments in place of wage increases for five of the six years. Adding insult to injury, four thousand scabs continue working in the plants.

14. Kate Bronfenbrenner and Tom Juravich, "The Evolution of Strategic and Coordinated Bargaining Campaigns in the 1990s: The Steelworkers' Experience," 2001, available at http://digitalcommons.ilr.cornell.edu/cgi/viewcontent.cgi?article=1016&context= articles; and Bruce M. Meyer, *The Once and Future Union: The Rise and Fall of the United Rubber Workers, 1935–1995* (Akron, Ohio: University of Akron Press, 2002).

15. See, in addition to widespread news coverage, Alan B. Krueger and Alexandre Mas, "Strikes, Scabs and Tread Separations: Labor Strife and the Production of Defective Bridgestone/Firestone Tires," available at http://www.uswa1155.org/archive/downloads/ Firestone%20Scab%20Tires.pdf; and Stephen Franklin, *Three Strikes: Labor's Heartland Losses and What They Mean for Working Americans* (New York: Guilford, 2001).

16. Staley worker and spouse survey conducted by the authors in fall 2001.

Chapter 20: A Winnable Fight

1. *War Zone* (UPIU Local 7837), December 1995.

2. Quotations without an endnote are drawn from the authors' 2001–3 interviews listed in the appendix.

3. Tom Frank and Dave Mulcahey, "This Is War," *Chicago Reader*, January 20, 1995.

4. As reported earlier in this book, in the early 1990s there were about 600 central labor councils. After some of them consolidated, the AFL-CIO's Web site reported 525 CLCs in 2008.

5. Barry Hirsch and David Macpherson, *Union Membership and Earnings Data Book: Compilations from the Current Population Survey* (Washington, D.C.: Bureau of National Affairs Books, 2002), data available at http://www.bna.com/bnaplus/labor/laborrpts .html. Hirsch and Macpherson provide the following figures:

Union members

Illinois:	1,042,000
Indiana:	443,000
Iowa:	152,000
Kentucky:	195,000
Michigan:	947,000
Missouri:	342,000
Wisconsin:	429,000

6. Workers interested in building power on the job should consider these excellent resources: the monthly magazine *Labor Notes*; Dan La Botz, *A Troublemakers' Handbook: How to Fight Back Where You Work and Win!* (Detroit: Labor Notes, 1991); Jane Slaughter, ed., *A Troublemaker's Handbook 2: How to Fight Back Where You Work and Win!* (Detroit: Labor Notes, 2005); *Power at Work* and *Unhappy Holidays*, two internal organizing videos produced by AFSCME; and *Power at Work* and *Turn It Around*, two internal organizing videos produced by the Teamsters.

7. "Locked-out Staley Workers Speak Out: Lessons from the War Zone," interviews with Dan Lane, Lorell Patterson, and Art Dhermy, *Socialist Worker*, January 19, 1996.

8. Ibid.

9. *Out of Darkness,* documentary film on the 1989–90 Pittston strike, directed by Barbara Kopple, 1990. The film is available through the UMWA Web site.

10. In 1999 the UPIU merged with the Oil, Chemical and Atomic Workers to form PACE, the Paperworkers, Allied industrial, Chemical and Energy Workers union. In 2005 PACE merged with the United Steel Workers of America to form the United Steel, Paper and Forestry, Rubber, Manufacturing, Energy, Allied-Industrial and Service Workers International Union, with the acronym USW.

11. Videotape of postdefeat forum in Madison, Wisconsin, January 22, 1996.

12. Rand Wilson and Matt Witt, "The Teamsters' UPS Strike of 1997: Building a New Labor Movement," *Labor Studies Journal* 24, no. 1 (Spring 1999): 58–72, gives an outstanding and detailed account of one of the best contract campaigns and well-run strikes in recent labor history.

13. Videotape of press conference at UPIU 7837 union hall, March 1995.

14. Videotape of forum in Madison, Wisconsin, on the lessons of the Staley fight, sponsored by UPIU Local 1202, January 22, 1996.

15. Robert Weissman, "A Bitter Defeat at A. E. Staley," *The Multinational Monitor,* January–February 1996; Marc Cooper, "Harley-Riding, Picket-Walking Socialism Haunts Decatur," *The Nation,* April 8, 1996.

16. David Moberg, "All Quiet on the Midwestern Front," *In These Times,* January 22, 1995.

17. *Industrial Worker,* March 1996.

18. James L. Tyson, "AFL-CIO Tries to Turn the Tide in Labor Dispute," *Christian Science Monitor,* November 29, 1995.

19. Mark Brooks to Dave Watts, faxed letter titled "A. E. Staley–AFL-CIO Task Force," November 14, 1995. In fall 2006 Trumka met with Pepsi officials in an effort "to get them to come to their senses." Trumka told Pepsi that by refusing to switch to another supplier, the company was "condoning, advocating, and supporting everything Staley was doing." Trumka told the executives, "If that's the reputation the Pepsi company wants to have, then you're about to get it." Under Trumka's direction, the AFL-CIO's Staley task force discussed new ideas for escalating the campaign, such as a plan to mail thousands of empty Coke bottles to Pepsi with notes attached reading, "This could have been a Pepsi. Dump Staley!" (Trumka, interview with authors, May 20, 2003; Mark Brooks to Wayne Glenn, letter reporting on a conversation Brooks had with Ken Zinn, a United Mine Workers of America staffer whom Trumka assigned to do work on Pepsi, December 5, 1995). In early November Sweeney told Joe Uehlein that he should coordinate the AFL-CIO's solidarity work for the Staley workers, but in late November jobs were reshuffled, and Ken Zinn was assigned the position.

20. Weissman, "Bitter Defeat."

21. Videotape of forum in Madison, Wisconsin, January 22, 1996.

22. Jeremy Brecher, *Strike!* rev. ed. (Cambridge, Mass.: South End, 1997), 357.

23. Joe Uehlein to authors, e-mail, October 1, 2001.

24. Weissman, "Bitter Defeat"; Cooper, "Harley-Riding, Picket-Walking Socialism."

25. *War Zone* (UPIU Local 7837), January 1996.

26. Mark Gruenberg, "Labor's Role in the Election," www.politicalaffairs.net, Nov. 8–13, 2004.

27. Jonathan Tasini, "Labor's Election Ground War—and How the Media Is Missing It," Aug. 25, 2008, available at http://www.workinglife.org/blogs/view_post.php?&post_id=1685; Steven Greenhouse, "Labor Group Gears up for Election," *New York Times,* May 13, 2008. Labor's campaign expenditures are listed at www.opensecrets.org.

28. Moberg, "All Quiet."

29. Ruth Milkman and Kim Voss, "New Unity for Labor?" *Labor* 2, no. 1 (Spring 2005): 15–26.

30. Walter Maus to Chicago Staley Workers Solidarity Committee, letter, January 1996.

31. The AFL-CIO Web site is www.aflcio.org; the Change to Win Web site is www.changetowin.org. Documents and articles on the debate and split can be found on the *Labor Notes* Web site at www.labornotes.org. Also see Milkman and Voss, "New Unity for Labor?"; Richard Hurd, "The Failure of Organizing, the New Unity Partnership, and the Future of the Labor Movement," *WorkingUSA,* September 2004; Jonathan Tasini, "After the Big Rift: Questions the Labor Movement Must Now Confront," *New Labor Forum* (Fall 2005): 9–16; "Turmoil in the AFL-CIO: A Dollars & Sense Roundtable," *Dollars and Sense,* September–October 1995; "Symposium: Split to Win? Assessing the State of the Labor Movement," *Dissent,* Winter 2006.

32. Steven Ashby, "Staley Lockout Ends in Defeat," *Labor Notes,* February 1996.

Glossary

AFL-CIO—A Washington, D.C.–based federation of fifty-three national unions with 8.5 million members. Formed by a 1955 merger of the American Federation of Labor, founded in 1886, and the Congress of Industrial Organizations, founded in 1935.

Allied Industrial Workers (AIW)—The Staley workers' national union, headquartered in Milwaukee at the time of the lockout. The 48,000-member AIW merged into the 230,000-member UPIU on January 1, 1994, changing the Staley workers' union from AIW Local 837 to UPIU Local 7837.

Arbitration—When repeated attempts to resolve a grievance between management and the union fail, the union can request a hearing from a professional, neutral third party (usually a member of the American Arbitration Association) who issues a binding decision.

Bargaining committee—Union officers elected to negotiate a contract with the company.

Boycott—The refusal to purchase a product, with the goal of pressuring a company to treat their workers fairly.

Business unionism—A narrowly focused, top-down philosophy of unionism in which union officers and staff run the union like a business, negotiating and administering the contract with limited membership involvement.

Central labor council—A regional body that unites local unions in a geographic area. In some cases, as in Decatur, it is called a "trades and labor council."

Change to Win—The new labor federation created in 2005 when seven unions with 6 million members split from the AFL-CIO.

Collective bargaining—The negotiation of a contract between the union and management. Also known as "contract negotiations."

Concessions—Changes in the contract that reduce workers pay or benefits or worsen working conditions.

Contract—A legal document, to which both the union and management agree, that outlines wages, benefits, grievance procedure, and rules about employment and working conditions. A contract is usually in effect for three to five years. Also called a "collective bargaining agreement."

Contracting out—The practice of sending work previously done by union members to another, usually non-union, shop. Such work may also be done inside the workplace by employees of a contractor. Also known as "outsourcing" and "sub-contracting."

Corporate campaign—A union mobilization to tarnish a corporation's image and pressure management for a fair contract. Also known as "strategic campaigns" or "comprehensive campaigns."

Dues—A monthly payment, generally two to three hours pay per month, that workers make to their local unions to cover union operating expenses for, among other things, staff, training, offices, bargaining costs, with a portion sent to the international and regional bodies.

Dues check-off—An automated process in which the company agrees to deduct each worker's union dues from the worker's paycheck and transfer it to the union.

Executive board—Elected officers of the union.

Fair Labor Standards Act—A 1938 law that banned child labor and established a minimum wage and overtime pay.

Grievance—A worker's complaint about an unsafe working condition or a violation of the contract or the law. After a written grievance, a worker and his or her steward have a hearing with the supervisor. If unresolved, the next steps involve higher-level union and management officials and possibly arbitration.

Impasse—A state of contract negotiations that is reached when the union is unwilling to accept concessions, often resulting in management's imposing its contract.

In-plant campaign—The union's mobilization of members to gain a fair contract, involving tactics such as collectively confronting management, wearing union buttons and T-shirts, and staging off-hours demonstrations. A high-level campaign involves working to rule. Also called a "contract campaign."

International union—The national governing body to which local unions affiliate. The "international" label is a misnomer, for only a small number of U.S. unions represent Canadian and Puerto Rican workers, and none represents other countries' workers.

Kandy Lane—The Staley workers' Campaign for Justice office, named for its street address.

Labor-management cooperation—The practice whereby the union agrees to work closely with management to increase productivity and give the company greater flexibility in work rules, in the name of combating competition.

Labor movement—Organized labor and supporters involved in the struggle for workers' rights, including students and community and religious activists.

Local union—An association of workers that collectively represents a workforce in negotiating a contract and handling workers' grievances.

Lockout—Occurs when a contract expires without agreement and management escorts its union workforce out of the workplace and locks the gate to prevent employees from working.

National Labor Relations Act—Bedrock labor legislation passed in 1935 that protected workers from firings and harassment when organizing a union and mandated that companies bargain in good faith. These gains were scaled down by the 1947 Taft-Hartley and 1959 Landrum-Griffin Acts. Also known as the Wagner Act.

National Labor Relations Board—Created by the National Labor Relations Act to monitor union certification elections and conduct hearings on legal violations known as unfair labor practices.

Occupational Safety and Health Administration (OSHA)—U.S. government body that administers the 1970 Occupational Safety and Health Act, a federal law that set minimum safety and health regulations in the workplace.

Organized labor—All unionized workers in America, including those in the AFL-CIO and Change to Win union federations and unaffiliated unions.

Pattern bargaining—A method of contract negotiations in which the international union settles with one company, after which it approaches other corporations in the same industry and secures a nearly identical contract. Wages and benefits are thus taken out of competition.

Permanent replacement—The legal prerogative given to a company to declare that unionists engaged in an economic strike have been fired or permanently replaced by scabs after one year.

Rank-and-file—The members of the union, excluding elected officers and paid staff.

Road Warriors—The Staley workers' term for rank-and-file workers who traveled the country garnering support and building solidarity committees.

Rotating shifts—A system in which workers alternate between working day and night shifts that destroys family life.

Scab—A person who crosses a picket line and takes a union member's job during a strike or lockout.

Secondary boycott—An illegal action in which a union calls for supporters to boycott a business associated with the company with which they are engaged in struggle.

Seniority—The length of time an employee has worked at a company, used in determining promotions, layoffs, schedules, and vacations.

Solidarity—The labor movement principle that workers must aid one another, embodied in labor's motto that an "injury to one is an injury to all."

Steward—A rank-and-file worker elected or appointed to voluntarily represent his or her department in grievances. Most unions elect a chief steward to assist departmental stewards on difficult grievances and arbitrations.

Strike—A work stoppage initiated by workers to pressure the company to negotiate a fair contract. In an unfair labor practice strike, strikers cannot legally be permanently replaced; in an economic strike, they can.

Taft-Hartley Act—A 1947 law that severely restricted the labor gains made in the 1935 National Labor Relations Act.

Tax abatement—A substantial reduction in city, county, and state property taxes given to corporations, often derided as corporate welfare.

Unfair labor practice—Management's or the union's violation of labor law as determined by the National Labor Relations Board.

Union representative—A staff member from the international or local union who assists with contract negotiations, grievances, and arbitrations. Also called a "business agent," "business representative," "international representative," or "service representative."

United Auto Workers (UAW)—Formed in 1935 and based in Detroit, the UAW organized the auto industry and was a key union in the rise of the Congress of Industrial Organizations.

United Paperworkers International Union (UPIU)—Founded in 1884, after a number of mergers the union took the name UPIU in 1972. Based in Nashville, Tennessee, the 230,000-member UPIU took in the 48,000-member AIW on January 1, 1994, and then merged with the United Steel Workers in 2005.

United Rubber Workers (URW)—Formed in 1935 and based in Akron, Ohio, the URW organized the tire industry and was a key union in the rise of the Congress of Industrial Organizations. The URW merged with the United Steel Workers in 1995.

Wagner Act—See *National Labor Relations Act.*

Weingarten rights—The legal right for a worker to have union representation in discussions with supervisors when the worker feels the meeting might lead to disciplinary action.

Workers' compensation—Laws passed by states that give workers a monthly payment for injuries suffered on the job but ban workers from suing the company for compensation, even in the event of a death.

Work-to-rule—An in-plant strategy in which workers slow production by doing only what they are ordered to do and by strictly following company work rules.

Index

Note: The Staley workers' union is represented by two different names because of its January 1994 merger with another union. AIW (Allied Industrial Workers) Local 837 refers to the Staley workers' union before the merger, and UPIU (United Paperworkers International Union) Local 7837 refers to the Staley workers' union after January 1994.

Goss, Glenn, 120, 212, 215, 216–17, 264–65
Grainmillers Local 103, 42, 83
Grandon, Mike, 70, 121, 125
Graphic Communications International Union (GCIU), 234
Green, Eugene, 139–41
Grider, Shari, 84
Griffin, Jan, 68, 87, 103, 148, 202
Griffin, Mike: on AFL-CIO leadership, 235; on civil disobedience, 182; on creative resistance and his firing, 68; FBI harassment, 202–3; on first conservative faction vote victory, 240; on Gus Staley, 13; on June 4, 1994, demonstration, 181; on June 25, 1995, rally, 242–43; on labor movement history, 290–91; on PepsiCo corporate campaign, 296–97; on picket shelters battle, 205; Road Warrior, 96, 98; on Rogers firing, 224; on rotating 12–hour shift problems, 64; on Shinall, 263; solidarity committee leadership role, 107; on Spiegel, 108–9; on Staley management policies of 1970s and 1980s, 16; on Staley/Tate & Lyle management proposal of 1992, 41; on Staley workers and in-plant strategy, 49; on union solidarity, 200; on union work during struggle with Staley/Tate & Lyle, 289; on worker grievance hearings, 53; on work-to rule-campaign, 45

Halas, George, 8–9
Hale, Terry, 125
"Hands Across Decatur" rally, 72–73, 74, 79, 197
Hanna, Bill, 273
Hanna, Nancy, 72, 88, 157, 170
Hard-pressed in the Heartland: The Hormel Strike and the Future of the Labor Movement (Rachleff), 109
Harjes, George, 144, 147
Harmon, Bob, 236
Harmony Construction Company, 25
Haseley, Steve, 125, 281
Hawking, C. J.: biographical information, 162; Black Community Awareness Committee role, 162, 165; Caterpillar, 243; civil disobedience education and tactics role, 147, 175, 179, 184; Decatur Fifty role, 243, 335n17; demonstration planning and organization roles, 179, 184; Holiday Solidarity Caravan, 110; Lane hunger strike support, 260; religious community outreach, 138–41, 149
Hawkins, Al, 76, 89, 154, 155
Hawkins, Jeanette: biographical informa-

tion, 152; on Black Community Awareness Committee, 163; election to bargaining committee, 168; on emotional toll of lockout, 86; on lockout beginning, 76; on Martin Luther King Day parade, 165; on picnic arrests, 166; racial discrimination at Staley/Tate & Lyle, 152, 153; Road Warrior, 101, 167; on rotating shifts and seniority, 65; on safety stand-down, 71; on scabs, 80, 86; on seniority issues under Staley/Tate & Lyle management, 65; on sexual harassment at Staley/Tate & Lyle, 156, 159; on skill blocks, 159; on 12–hour rotating shifts, 161; union leadership, 168; on Women's Support Group, 87–88; on workers rights' struggle impact on civil rights in Decatur, 286–87; work-to-rule campaign, 56–57, 160
Hawthorne, Paula, 90
Hays, Dave, 64, 100–101, 253
Hemrich, Ed, 200
Henderson, Dewey ("Monty"), 261
high-fructose corn syrup, 14
Hill, Greg, 121, 125
Hill, Norman, 166
Hinds, Steve, 106, 122
Holland, Michael, 177
Honor Roll of Solidarity, 233–34
horizontal unionism, 197–98
Hormel strike of 1985–86, 174
Houston, Dennis, 155
Howley, Terry, 211
Hughes, Jean, 146, 147, 176
Hull, Bob: demonstration planning role, 184–85; family support leadership role, 91; on Lane replacement of Shinall as bargaining committee chair, 132; picket line organization, 77; on Shinall and conservative faction of UPIU Local 7837, 268; on Staley/Tate & Lyle toxic dumping policies, 208; on Tate & Lyle acquisition of Staley, 23
Hull, Susan, 85, 273, 278
hunger strike, 253–60. *See also* Lane, Dan

Illinois Department of Employment Security, 78
The Informant (movie), 21
The Informant: A True Story (Eichenwald), 21
International Association of Machinists (IAM), 234
International Brotherhood of Electrical Workers (IBEW), 60, 78, 107, 219
International Brotherhood of Teamsters (IBT), 123, 186, 200, 296

STEVEN K. ASHBY is an associate clinical professor in the School of Labor and Employment Relations, University of Illinois at Urbana-Champaign, and is the coordinator of online programs in Global Labor Studies.

C. J. HAWKING, a United Methodist pastor and visiting lecturer in labor and social movements, was a national consultant with Interfaith Worker Justice and is the executive director of its affiliate Arise Chicago.

Wobblies on the Waterfront: Interracial Unionism in Progressive-Era Philadelphia
  Peter Cole
Red Chicago: American Communism at Its Grassroots, 1928–35   *Randi Storch*
Labor's Cold War: Local Politics in a Global Context   *Edited by Shelton Stromquist*
Bessie Abromowitz Hillman and the Making of the Amalgamated Clothing Workers
  of America   *Karen Pastorello*
The Great Strikes of 1877   *Edited by David O. Stowell*
Union-Free America: Workers and Antiunion Culture   *Lawrence Richards*
Race against Liberalism: Black Workers and the UAW in Detroit
  David M. Lewis-Colman
Teachers and Reform: Chicago Public Education, 1929–70   *John F. Lyons*
Upheaval in the Quiet Zone: 1199/SEIU and the Politics of Healthcare Unionism
  Leon Fink and Brian Greenberg
Shadow of the Racketeer: Scandal in Organized Labor   *David Witwer*
Sweet Tyranny: Migrant Labor, Industrial Agriculture, and Imperial Politics
  Kathleen Mapes
Staley: The Fight for a New American Labor Movement   *Steven K. Ashby and
  C. J. Hawking*

The University of Illinois Press
is a founding member of the
Association of American University Presses.

Composed in 10.5/13 Adobe Minion Pro
with Meta display
by Jim Proefrock
at the University of Illinois Press
Manufactured by Cushing-Malloy, Inc.

University of Illinois Press
1325 South Oak Street
Champaign, IL 61820-6903
www.press.uillinois.edu